CONTENTS

THE GALLIC WARS

THE CIVIL WARS

WAR
COMMENTARIES
OF
CAESAR

Translated by

REX WARNER

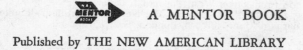
A MENTOR BOOK

Published by THE NEW AMERICAN LIBRARY

Library of Congress Catalog Card No. 60-9463

MENTOR TRADEMARK REG. U.S. PAT. OFF. AND FOREIGN COUNTRIES
REGISTERED TRADEMARK—MARCA REGISTRADA
HECHO EN CHICAGO, U.S.A.

MENTOR BOOKS are published *in the United States* by
The New American Library of World Literature, Inc.,
501 Madison Avenue, New York, New York 10022,
in Canada by The New American Library of Canada Limited,
156 Front Street West, Toronto 1, Ontario,
in the United Kingdom by The New English Library Limited,
Barnard's Inn, Holborn, London, E.C. 1, England

PRINTED IN THE UNITED STATES OF AMERICA

THE GALLIC WARS

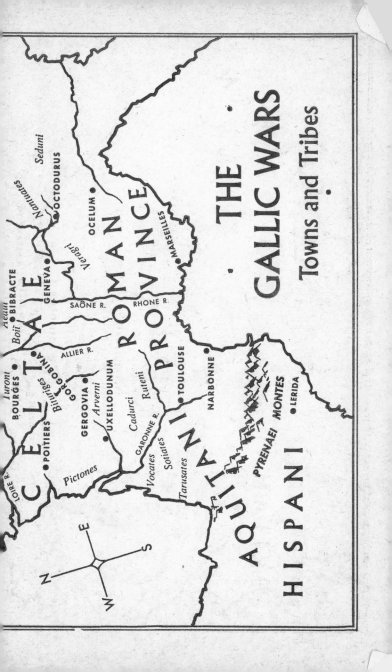

THE GALLIC WARS

Towns and Tribes

ROMAN PROVINCE

CELTAE

AQUITANI

HISPANI

PYRENAEI MONTES

Seduni

Nantuates

• OCTODURUS

• OCELUM

Veragri

• MARSEILLES

• GENEVA

BIBRACTE •

Aedui

Boii

• SAÔNE R.

RHONE R.

ALLIER R.

Iuroni

BOURGES •

Bituriges

GORGOBINA •

• POITIERS

GERGOVIA •

Arverni

• UXELLODUNUM

Cadurci

Ruteni

• TOULOUSE

NARBONNE •

GARONNE R.

Vocates

Sotiates

Tarusates

LOIRE R.

Pictones

• NARBONNE

• LERIDA

1   DESCRIPTION OF GAUL. FIRST OPERATIONS AGAINST THE HELVETII.

The country of Gaul consists of three separate parts, one of which is inhabited by the Belgae, one by the Aquitani, and one by the people whom we call "Gauls" but who are known in their own language as "Celts." These three peoples differ from one another in language, customs, and laws. The river Garonne forms the frontier between the Gauls and the Aquitani, the rivers Seine and Marne between the Gauls and the Belgae. The toughest soldiers come from the Belgae. This is because they are farthest away from the culture and civilized way of life of the Roman Province; merchants, bringing the influences which tend to make people effeminate, hardly ever go into those parts; and they are also nearest to the Germans across the Rhine and are continually waging war with them. For the same reason the Helvetii are the bravest tribe among the Gauls; they too are in almost daily contact with the Germans, either fighting to keep them out of Gaul or launching attacks on them in their own territory.

That part of the country which, as I have said, is occupied by the Gauls starts from the Rhone and is bounded by the Garonne, the ocean, and the country of the Belgae; on the side where the Sequani and Helvetii live it extends up to the Rhine; it may be said to face north.

The country of the Belgae, beginning at the Gallic frontier, extends as far as the lower Rhine and faces northeast.

Aquitania starts at the Garonne and extends up to the Pyrenees and the ocean west of Spain; it faces northwest.

Among the Helvetii at this time much the richest and most distinguished man was a certain Orgetorix. This man aimed at making himself king over his tribe and, during the consulship of Marcus Messalla and Marcus Piso, organized a conspiracy among the nobility and persuaded the people to migrate from their territory in full force; it would be perfectly easy, he said, since they were the bravest of the Gauls, for them to conquer the whole country. His arguments were all the more persuasive because the Helvetii were in fact shut in on every side by natural geographical boundaries. On one frontier there was the broad and deep stream of the Rhine, separating them from Germany; on another the high range of the Jura Mountains separated them from the Sequani; while between them and the Roman Province, on their third frontier, lay the Lake of Geneva and the Rhone. In these conditions their range of movement was restricted and it was not easy for them to fight campaigns against their neighbors. This they greatly resented, since they were naturally fond of war. And they considered that their territory (measuring 227 by 170 miles) was too small for a people like themselves, so populous and with so lofty a military reputation.

These considerations and the great influence of Orgetorix made the Helvetii decide to prepare all the necessary arrangements for a mass migration. They were to buy up all the wagons and pack animals that they could, sow as much grain as possible so as to have adequate supplies on the march, and make treaties of friendship with neighboring states. Reckoning that they would need two years for effecting all this, they passed a law binding them to set out in the third year.

Orgetorix was appointed to deal with these preparations, and he set out in person on a conciliatory mission to the neighboring states. While on this mission, he urged the Sequanian Casticus (whose father, Catamantaloedes, had for many years been king of the Sequani and had been given by the senate the title of "Friend of the Roman People") to usurp the royal power which his father had previously held. He also encouraged Dumnorix, the Aeduan (brother of Diviciacus, who, with the support of the great mass of the people, held the chieftainship at this time), to make a similar attempt at seizing royal power, and gave him his own daughter in marriage. He assured both that there would be no difficulty in what he was suggesting. He himself, he said, would soon seize supreme power in his own state. There was no doubt that the Helvetii were the most powerful people in Gaul, and he promised them that he would use his own army and his own resources to make them safe in their kingdoms. These arguments of Orgetorix proved effective. Promises were exchanged and confirmed by oath, and it was confidently expected that once they had seized the kingship of these three powerful and valiant nations, they would make themselves masters of the whole of Gaul.

The conspiracy, however, was reported to the Helvetii by an informer, and Orgetorix was told that according to tribal custom, he must stand his trial in chains. If found guilty, the legal penalty was death by burning. On the day fixed for the trial Orgetorix brought with him to the place of judgment all ten thousand of his retainers together with a great many other tribesmen who owed him money or were bound to him in some way or other. With their aid he avoided the necessity of having to stand trial. The people as a whole, however, were angry at this evasion of justice. They determined to assert their rights by force of arms, and the magistrates were already mobilizing large bodies of men from various parts of the country when Orgetorix was found dead. It was strongly suspected among the Helvetii that he had taken his own life.

The death of Orgetorix, however, made no difference to the determination of the Helvetii to carry out their plans for the migration. When finally they considered that all their preparations were complete, they set fire to their fortified towns (there were twelve of these), four hundred villages, and all private dwelling houses; they burned all their grain except that which they planned to carry with them, so that, with nothing left at home to encourage them to return, they might be all the readier to face the perils that lay ahead. Each man was ordered to take with him three months' supply of flour. They persuaded their neighbors, the Rauraci, Tulingi, and Latobrigi, who were to join them in the migration, to follow their own example and burn their towns and villages; and they also took with them as allies the Boii, who had previously lived on the other side of the Rhine but had crossed over into Austria, where they had attacked the town of Noreia.

There were but two possible routes by which the Helvetii could leave their country. One was through the territory of the Sequani. It was a difficult route, with the Jura Mountains on one side and the Rhone on the other, so narrow that wagons could scarcely move along it in single file, and the high mountains that overhung the road would enable a mere handful of men to block the pass. The other route was through the Roman Province. It was much easier and more convenient, since the Rhone, which flows between the territory of the Helvetii and that of the recently subdued Allobroges, can be forded at various points. There is also a bridge at the Allobrogian frontier town of Geneva which connects that country with the Helvetii. The Allobroges were considered to be still disaffected toward Rome, and the Helvetii felt confident that, either by persuasion or by force, they could secure a free passage through the country. So, when everything was ready for departure, they fixed a date on which they were all to assemble on the banks of the Rhone. This date was the 28th of March, in the consulship of Lucius Piso and Aulus Gabinius.

On receiving the news that the Helvetii intended to try to march through our Province, I left Rome at once for Transalpine Gaul and, traveling as fast as possible, reached the neighborhood of Geneva. In the whole of Transalpine Gaul there was but one legion. I gave orders for the mobilization of as many more troops as possible and had the bridge over the Rhone destroyed. When they heard of my arrival, the Helvetii sent a deputation of their chief men to me. The deputation was led by Nammeius and Verucloetius and was instructed to say that their intentions in marching through the Province were entirely peaceable; there simply existed no alternative route; and they asked me to allow them to do so without raising any objections. I remembered, however, that it was these Helvetii who had defeated and killed the consul Lucius Cassius and sent his army under the yoke. It did not seem to me that any concessions ought to be made to such people; they were no friends of ours, and I did not believe that, if they got the chance of marching through the Province, they would refrain from acts of robbery and violence. However, it was necessary to gain time for the mobilization of the troops which I had ordered to be raised. I therefore told the deputation that I should have to consider the matter at my leisure; they were to return, if they wished to raise the question again, on the 13th of April.

Meanwhile I used the legion which I had with me and the fresh troops which had been enlisted in the Province to construct a wall sixteen feet in height and a trench along the whole distance of eighteen miles between the Lake of Geneva, where it flows into the Rhone, and the Jura Mountains on the frontier between the Helvetii and Sequani. When this fortification was finished, I posted garrisons at various strong points along the line so as to make it easier to repulse the Helvetii if they should try to force their way through.

The Helvetian deputation visited me again on the day I had fixed. I told them that I must act in accordance with the precedents and traditions of the Roman people and was therefore unable to allow anyone to march through the Province; I made it clear that if they attempted to use force I would resist them.

The Helvetii had failed to get what they wanted. They now

made a number of attempts, sometimes by day but more often by night, at breaking through our line. Sometimes they tried to get across by means of boats and rafts lashed together to form a bridge; sometimes they forded the river at its shallowest points. However, they were faced by strong fortifications and by troops who concentrated quickly at the points of danger and poured a heavy fire on their attackers. In the end they abandoned these attempts.

The only road left to them was the one through the country of the Sequani and this was too narrow to be practicable unless the Sequani themselves were willing to let them use it. Acting on their own initiative, the Helvetii failed to secure the necessary permission, and therefore they sent a deputation to Dumnorix the Aeduan, asking him to use his good offices with the Sequani so as to get this permission for them. Dumnorix was a man who carried much weight among the Sequani; he was personally well liked and had spent money on increasing his popularity; he was also friendly toward the Helvetii, for his wife, the daughter of Orgetorix, had come from their country. He was extremely ambitious to make himself king, was implicated in revolutionary activities, and wished to have as many states as possible bound to him by ties of gratitude. He was therefore very willing to take on this commission and arranged matters so that the Sequani promised to allow the Helvetii to march through their country. He organized an exchange of hostages to guarantee that the Sequani would allow the Helvetii freedom of passage and the Helvetii would do no damage and resort to no violence while on the march.

I now received information that the Helvetii proposed to march through the territory of the Sequani and the Aedui into the country of the Santones. This is quite near the frontiers of Toulouse, a state in the Roman Province, and I recognized that the Province itself would be in great danger if this were to happen. It would mean having a warlike tribe, hostile to Rome, on a frontier which had no geographical defenses and which led to areas that were particularly rich in grain. I therefore left my deputy commander, Titus Labienus, in charge of the fortifications at Geneva and went myself to Italy with as much speed as possible. There I raised two new legions, withdrew three others from their winter quarters near Aquileia, and with these five marched back to Transalpine Gaul by the shortest route, which was over the Alps. While we were crossing the Alps the Ceutrones, Graioceli, and Caturiges occupied various heights and attempted to prevent the army from getting through. We fought several engagements with them before driving them off. Seven days after leaving Ocelum, which was our last stop in Cisalpine Gaul, we reached the territory of the Vocontii in the Transalpine Province. From here we marched into the country of the Allobroges and then on to the country of the Segusiavi, who are the first tribe outside the Province on the other side of the Rhone.

By this time the Helvetii had marched with all their forces through the narrow passes of the country of the Sequani and had reached and begun to pillage the country of the Aedui. Unable to defend themselves or preserve their property, the Aedui sent a deputation to me to ask for help. They claimed that their tribe had always been loyal to Rome and that it was therefore not right for my army to be standing by inactive while their country was being laid waste, their children carried off into slavery, and their towns pillaged. At the same time the Ambarri, who are both kinsmen and allies of the Aedui, informed me that their fields had been laid waste and that they were having the greatest difficulty in keeping their towns safe from enemy attack. Finally the Allobroges, who had once owned property and inhabited villages across the Rhone, came to me for refuge and told me that they now had nothing left except the bare ground on which their possessions had stood. All this convinced me that I ought to take action at once and not remain inactive while the Helvetii went on to the country of the Santones, destroying all the possessions of our allies on their way.

There is a river called the Saône which flows through the country of the Aedui and Sequani into the Rhone. The stream is so extraordinarily slow that when one looks at it it is impossible to say in which direction it flows. The Helvetii were in the act of crossing this river by means of a bridge of boats and rafts, and my patrols came in with the information that three-quarters of them had already crossed the river, but about one-quarter was still on the near bank. I set out from camp soon after midnight with three legions and came up with that division of the enemy which had not yet crossed the river. They were hampered by their baggage and our attack took them by surprise. We killed great numbers of them, and the rest took to flight and hid in the forests nearby. This particular division, or clan, one of the four into which the people of the Helvetii are divided, was known as the Tigurini. It was these same Tigurini who, about fifty years previously, had marched out of their country alone, killed and defeated the consul Lucius Cassius, and sent his army under the yoke. So, whether by chance or by divine providence, that section of the Helvetii which had inflicted such a terrible disgrace on Roman arms was the first of them all to pay the penalty. In this action I had personal as well as patriotic reasons for rejoicing in the revenge which we took, since in the battle with Cassius, the Tigurini had also killed his second in command, Lucius Piso, the grandfather of that Lucius Piso who was now my father-in-law.

After the battle I had a bridge built over the Saône and brought the army across so as to be able to pursue the remainder of the Helvetian forces. My sudden appearance had a disturbing effect upon the enemy when they observed that the business of crossing the river, which had caused them much trouble and over which they had taken twenty days, had been done by us in the space of a single day. They sent a deputation to me which was led by Divico, who had commanded the Helvetian forces in the campaign against Cassius. The representations he made were as follows. If Rome would make peace with the Helvetii, then the Helvetii would go and settle wherever I decided that I would like them to be. If, on the other hand, I proposed to continue to treat them as enemies, I would do well to remember the traditional bravery of the Helvetii and how Rome had suffered on a previous occasion. It was true that I had made a surprise attack on one of their clans at a time when the rest of them, who had crossed the river, were not able to come to the help of their comrades; but it would be unwise for me, on the basis of this incident, to overrate my own strength or despise theirs. The Helvetii had learned from their fathers and their ancestors to fight with courage rather than with guile or recourse to stratagems. I was therefore advised to think again and to avoid acting in such a way that this place where we parleyed might become famous in history for a disaster to the Roman people and the destruction of one of her armies.

I replied as follows: "As a result of what you have said, my mind is more firmly made up than ever. I remember well the events to which you refer, and I bitterly resent the misfortune which we then suffered, because we had done nothing to deserve it. If we had known that we had injured you in any way, it would not have been difficult for us to have taken the necessary precautions. As it was, we were deceived: we were not aware that we had done anything to give us cause for alarm, and it is not our way to feel alarm without good reason. But even if I were prepared to overlook these old insults, how could I forget the injuries which you have inflicted on us just recently? You attempted, after having been refused permission by me, to force your way through our Province; you have robbed and made war against the Aedui, the Ambarri, and the Allobroges. You may be insolent enough to boast of your victory and to preen yourselves for having escaped so long the punishment due you; yet these facts point

to one and the same conclusion. When the gods wish to punish
wicked men for their crimes, they often allow them for a time
a more than usual prosperity and an even longer impunity,
simply so that they will suffer all the more bitterly when
their fortunes eventually are reversed. Nevertheless, I am still
willing to make peace on the following conditions: you must
give me hostages as a security that you will do what you promise; and you must pay reparations for the damage you have
done to the Aedui, the Allobroges, and their allies."

Divico replied that the Helvetii throughout their long history had always been accustomed to take, never to give, hostages; and this, he added, the Romans knew well enough.
With these words he went away.

2
END OF THE CAMPAIGN
AGAINST THE HELVETII.

Next day the Helvetii moved camp, as did I. Our whole
cavalry force, consisting of about four thousand men raised
from all parts of the Province, from the Aedui, and from
their allies, was sent on ahead to observe the enemy's line of
march. They followed up the enemy rear guard rather too
eagerly, and joining battle with the Helvetian cavalry on
ground that was unfavorable, suffered a few casualties. The
Helvetii were much elated by this engagement, having routed
so many of our cavalry with a mere five hundred of their
own; their morale improved and their rear guard would often
halt and challenge us to make another attack. However, I
kept my men back from fighting. We had enough to do for
the moment in preventing the enemy from foraging and loot-
ing and generally devastating the countryside. So for about
a fortnight the two armies moved on, the enemy's rear guard
and our vanguard always within five or six miles of each
other.

Meanwhile I was constantly urging the Aedui to send the
grain which their government had promised me. Gaul, as
already stated, is a northern country and because of the
cold the grain in the fields was still not ripe, nor was there
even an adequate supply of food for the animals. Moreover, I
was no longer able to rely as before on the supplies of grain
which were brought up the Saône in boats, because the
Helvetii had moved away from the river and I did not want
to lose contact with them. Day after day the Aedui kept putting things off, saying that the grain was being collected, it

was actually on its way, it would arrive at any moment, and so forth. I realized that these postponements were going on indefinitely and we were not far from the day on which the troops should be issued their rations; so I summoned a meeting of the Aeduan chiefs, of whom there were a great many in our camp. Among them were Diviciacus and Liscus, the latter of whom held the highest office in his state, being *Vergobret,* as the Aeduans call him. The *Vergobret* is an annually elected magistrate, with powers of life and death over his countrymen. I spoke severely to the Aeduan chiefs, accusing them of being no help to me at all at this critical moment, when grain could neither be bought nor harvested and when the enemy were so close to us. I pointed out that it was largely because of their entreaties that I had undertaken this campaign in the first place—a fact which made their betrayal of me even harder to tolerate.

This speech of mine had its effect on Liscus, who now at last revealed some information which up to then he had kept secret. According to him there were among the Aedui certain individuals who had great influence with the people and indeed were in their private capacity more powerful than the magistrates themselves. These men had been engaging in a criminal and seditious agitation designed to intimidate the people and prevent them from collecting the amount of grain due. Their general theme was that if the Aedui themselves could no longer hold supreme power in Gaul, it was better to have other Gauls rather than Romans as their overlords; for they were convinced that if the Romans conquered the Helvetii, their next step would be to deprive both the Aedui and the other Gallic tribes of their liberty. It was these same people, Liscus said, who were in the habit of informing the enemy of our plans and of everything that went on in our camp. He himself could do nothing to control them; indeed, he fully realized that in giving me this information, as he felt obliged to do, he had put himself into considerable danger, and this was why he had kept silent for as long as he could.

I felt pretty certain that the person to whom Liscus was referring was Dumnorix, the brother of Diviciacus, but because I did not want the affair to become the subject of general discussion, I quickly dismissed the meeting, asking Liscus to stay behind. When he was by himself I put some more questions to him about what he had said at the meeting, and now he spoke with less restraint and more confidence. By secretly questioning various other people, I checked his information and found it to be correct. Dumnorix was the man responsible.

Daring and unscrupulous, exceedingly popular with the masses because of his generosity, Dumnorix was aiming at a revolution. It appeared that for several years he had contracted to collect the customs and all the rest of the Aeduan taxes. He had paid very little for this contract, simply because nobody dared bid against him. In this way he had become even richer than before and had amassed large sums to be used for bribery. He went about with a large bodyguard of cavalry which he maintained at his own expense. He was a man of authority not only in his own country but in neighboring states; and to strengthen this influence of his abroad he had arranged for his mother to marry one of the most distinguished nobles among the Bituriges, had himself taken a wife from the Helvetii, and had married his half-sister and other female relatives to men from various other states. Because of his marriage he was strongly on the side of the Helvetii; and he had reasons of his own for hating both the Romans in general and me personally, because one of the results of our arrival in the country had been the diminution of his power and the restoration of his brother Diviciacus to the position of honor and authority which he had held previously. He was convinced that if we were defeated, the Helvetii would help him to become king; whereas if the country came under Roman control, he saw no prospects either of gaining the kingship or of keeping the influence which he had already. In the course of my inquiries I also discovered that it was Dumnorix and his cavalry who were responsible for starting the flight of our whole cavalry force when it had suffered the defeat a few days previously. Dumnorix was the commander of the cavalry contingent that had been sent me by the Aedui, and when his men had started to run away, their panic had spread to all the rest.

All this gave me good reason to distrust him, and the evidence was confirmed by other indisputable facts. It was Dumnorix who had arranged for the Helvetii to go through the country of the Sequani and who had seen that hostages were exchanged; he had, moreover, done all this without any orders either from me or from his own government—indeed, neither I nor they had known anything about it—and now he was being accused by the chief magistrate of the Aedui. It seemed to me, therefore, that I should be perfectly justified either in punishing him myself or in instructing his own government to do so.

There was one objection, however, to following either of these courses. I had come to know Diviciacus, the brother of Dumnorix, well. He was entirely on our side, very devoted to me personally, and altogether a man who was quite remarkable for his loyalty, his fair-mindedness, and his good sense. I was afraid of hurting his feelings if I punished Dumnorix. Therefore, before taking any further steps, I summoned him to my quarters. Here I asked the regular interpreters to withdraw and spoke with Diviciacus through the medium of Gaius Valerius Procillus, a leading man in the Province and a great friend of mine in whom I had the most complete confidence. I reminded Diviciacus of what he had himself heard said about Dumnorix in the council of chiefs, and I went on to tell him of the additional information I had received about his brother from various individuals. I then most solemnly begged him not to take offense but to approve of my suggestion that I should either try the case myself and decide upon the penalty or else instruct the Aeduan government to do so.

Diviciacus threw his arms around me and burst into tears. He began to beg me not to be too severe with his brother. "I know well," he said, "that what you have told me is true, and no one is more sorry about it than I am. There was a time when, both at home and abroad, I had very great power and Dumnorix, because of his youth, very little. It was through me that he grew great. Now he is using the strength and resources which I gave him not only to weaken me, but practically to destroy me. Nevertheless I feel for him as a brother ought to feel and I must also consider the question of public opinion. I myself am known to be a friend of yours. If you take severe measures against my brother, everyone will believe that I also was in favor of them, and the result will be that I shall become hated all over Gaul."

He was continuing to speak, still weeping and still begging me to relent, but I took him by the hand and told him reassuringly that he need say no more, making him see that I had such good will for him that I was prepared, for his sake, to do as he asked and to forgive both the injury done to Rome and the grievance which I felt personally. I then had Dumnorix brought in, and in the presence of his brother told him the reasons I had for being dissatisfied with his conduct; I informed him of the results of my inquiries and of the complaints made against him by his fellow countrymen; I advised him to be careful not to give cause for suspicion in the future and told him that it was only because of his brother Diviciacus that he was being forgiven for the past. After this I had agents constantly on the watch so that I could know what Dumnorix was doing and with whom he was in communication.

On the same day my patrols informed me that the enemy had halted at the foot of a hill eight miles from our camp. A party was sent to reconnoiter the hill and find out what the ascent was like on the further side. They reported that it was easy. So, after discussing my plans with Labienus, my second in command, I instructed him to set out soon after midnight with two legions and climb to the top of the hill; he was to be guided by the men who had just reconnoitered the ground. An hour or so later I set out myself and marched toward the enemy by the same route as that which they had taken themselves. I sent the whole cavalry force ahead; in front of them were patrols under the command of Publius Considius, who was supposed to be a first-class soldier and had seen service under Lucius Sulla and, later, under Marcus Crassus.

By dawn Labienus had occupied the summit of the hill and I was not more than a mile and a half from the enemy's camp. As we discovered later from prisoners, the enemy had no idea that we were anywhere near. At this point Considius came galloping up to me and told me that the hill which I had wanted Labienus to occupy was in fact occupied by the enemy: he had recognized them, he said, by their Gallic armor and the crests on their helmets. I withdrew my troops to the nearest high ground and formed them up in line of battle. In order that the enemy should be attacked simultaneously on both sides, I had instructed Labienus not to attack until he could see my troops near the enemy's camp. So, after seizing the hill, he waited for us to appear and made no move himself. It was already late in the day when my patrols put me in possession of the real facts—that the hill had all the time been in our hands, that the Helvetii had by now moved on, and that Considius had evidently lost his nerve and said that he had seen what was simply not visible. So for the rest of the day we followed the enemy with the usual interval between the armies and pitched camp three miles away from their camp.

In two days' time the troops were due to receive their rations. We were now not more than sixteen miles from Bibracte, which is much the largest and best supplied of the Aeduan strongholds, and it seemed to me that something must be done to secure our grain supply. So on the next day I stopped following the Helvetii and marched in the direction of Bibracte. This change of plan was reported to the enemy by some deserters from the Gallic cavalry commanded by Lucius Aemilius. The Helvetii may have believed that we were marching away because we were frightened; and our failure to attack on the previous day, after we had occupied the high ground, would support such a view. Or they may have thought that they could cut us off from our grain supply. Whatever the reason, they too changed their plans and altered the

direction of their march. They began to follow us and to harass
our rear guard.

Seeing what was happening, I withdrew my forces to the
nearest hill and sent forward the cavalry to hold up the
enemy's attack. In the meantime I formed up the four veteran
legions in three lines halfway up the hill; behind them, on the
summit, were posted the two legions that had recently been
enlisted in Italy and all the auxiliary troops; so the whole
hillside was covered with men. Meanwhile, I ordered the
packs to be collected in one place which was to be entrenched
by the troops in line on the higher ground. The Helvetii, with
all their wagons, came after us. They deposited all their heavy
baggage in one place, and then, fighting in very close order,
drove back our cavalry and came on in a dense mass up to
our front line.

I first of all had my own horse taken out of the way and
then the horses of other officers. I wanted the danger to be
the same for everyone and for no one to have any hope of
escape by flight. Then I spoke a few words of encouragement
to the men before joining battle.

Hurling their javelins from above, our men easily broke
up the enemy's mass formation and, having achieved this,
drew their swords and charged. In the fighting the Gauls were
seriously hampered because several of their overlapping shields
were often pierced by a single javelin; the iron head would
bend and they could neither get it out nor fight properly with
their left arms. Many of them, after a number of vain efforts
at disentangling themselves, preferred to drop their shields
and fight with no protection for their bodies. In the end the
wounds and the toil of battle were too much for them and
they began to retire to a hill about a mile away. This hill
they occupied, and our men pressed on after them. However,
we were now attacked by the Boii and Tulingi, who, some
fifteen thousand strong, had been the rear guard in the
enemy's column of march. They now launched an attack
on our exposed right flank and swept around behind us. The
Helvetii who had retired to the hill saw them go into action
and themselves began to press forward again in a counterattack.

We formed a double front; the rear line faced about to
meet the new attack while the first and second lines went
on fighting against those whom they had already defeated
and driven back. This fighting in two directions went on for
a long time and was bitterly contested. Finally, when they
could stand up to us no longer, one division of the enemy retired, as they had begun to do originally, toward the higher

ground and the others fell back on the stockade sheltering their wagons and baggage train. In the whole of this battle, which had lasted from midday until the evening, not a single man was seen to turn and run. Around the stockade, fighting went on far into the night. The enemy had drawn up their wagons so as to form a kind of rampart and from this hurled down their weapons on our men as we came up, while others from underneath the wagons and between the wheels shot their native darts and javelins at us with damaging effect. It was a long fight, but in the end we gained possession of the baggage and the camp, and took as prisoners the daughter of Orgetorix and one of his sons. About 130,000 of the enemy survived the battle. They marched all that night without stopping for a moment's rest and three days later reached the country of the Lingones. We had been unable to follow them, since we spent three days in looking after the wounded and burying the dead. But I sent messengers with letters to the Lingones, warning them not to give the Helvetii food or help of any kind and threatening, if they did so, to treat them also as enemies. Then, after the three days were up, I continued the pursuit, taking the whole army with me.

The Helvetii had now no supplies of any kind and could therefore do nothing except send a deputation to discuss terms of surrender. Their representatives met me on the road. Flinging themselves on the ground before me in the attitude of suppliants and with tears streaming from their eyes, they begged for peace. I told them that their army was to remain where it was until I arrived, and this order was obeyed. When I reached them I demanded the surrender of hostages, arms, and those slaves of ours who had deserted to them. While the men were being rounded up and the arms collected, night fell and about six thousand men of the clan called Verbigene took advantage of the darkness to slip out of the Helvetian camp and make for the Rhine and the country of the Germans. They may have been in a panic, imagining that once their arms had been given up, they were going to be put to death; or they may have hoped to get away safely, thinking that in such a vast number of prisoners their own escape might not be discovered at once or might not be noticed at all. However, as soon as I found out what had happened, I sent out orders to the native tribes through whose territory the escaped prisoners had passed and demanded that they should round them up and bring them back to me, unless they wanted me to regard them as accomplices in the escape. My orders were carried out and the men were treated as enemies are treated.

As to all the rest, I accepted their surrender once they had produced the hostages and given up their arms and the run-away slaves. I ordered the Helvetii, the Tulingi, and the Latobrigi to go back to the lands which they had occupied before the migration started. Because they had lost all the produce of their land and had no means of subsistence, I instructed the Allobroges to supply them with grain. The Helvetii themselves were to rebuild the towns and villages which they had burned. My chief reason for taking these measures was that I did not want that part of the country from which the Helvetii had come to remain uninhabited. It was rich country, and I feared that the Germans from across the Rhine might move from their own land into the land of the Helvetii and thus become neighbors of the Allobroges and of Roman Gaul.

As for the Boii, who were known for their outstanding fighting qualities, the Aedui asked to be allowed to settle them in their own country. I granted their request. The Aedui gave them land and later made them full citizens with the same rights and privileges that they enjoyed themselves.

I was shown some documents written in Greek script which had been found in the Helvetian camp; they turned out to be a complete list of the names of all those who had taken part in the migration and were able to bear arms. There were also separate lists of the children, old men, and women. The grand total came to 368,000, and was made up of 263,000 Helvetii, 36,000 Tulingi, 14,000 Latobrigi, 23,000 Rauraci, and 32,000 Boii. There were 92,000 men capable of bearing arms. On my orders, a census was taken of those who returned to their homes and the number was found to be 110,000.

At the conclusion of the campaign against the Helvetii, the leading men from nearly every state in Gaul came to me to offer their congratulations. They were fully aware, they said, that in this campaign I had been avenging wrongs done in the past by the Helvetii to Rome; nevertheless, Gaul had benefited just as much as Rome by the result, since the Helvetii, when things were going perfectly well with them, had left their own country with the express purpose of making war on the whole of Gaul and bringing it into subjection to them; their plan was to select out of the whole great country some particularly fertile and convenient area for themselves to occupy and to make the rest of the states pay tribute to them.

The deputies then asked to be allowed to summon under my sponsorship a council of the whole of Gaul on a date to be decided. They said that they had certain requests which they

would like to submit to me once general agreement had been
reached. I gave them permission to do this, and they fixed
a day for the meeting of the council. Each of them took an
oath not to divulge its proceedings unless authorized to do so
by general consent of all members.

3 ARIOVISTUS. PRELIMINARY MOVES.

When this council had been held, the same tribal chiefs as
before came back to me and asked to be allowed to meet me
secretly for private discussions on a question which affected
their personal safety and the good of the whole country. I
granted their request, and at the interview they prostrated
themselves before me and spoke with tears streaming. Anxious
as they were, they said, to gain their requests, it was just as
important for them that what they said should go no further;
if it did, they would be likely to suffer for it most cruelly.
Then Diviciacus, the Aeduan, who acted as their spokesman,
gave the following account of the situation: In Gaul, he said,
there were two large factions, one led by the Aedui and one
by the Arverni. For many years these two had struggled
bitterly between themselves for supremacy, until in the end
the Arverni and Sequani had hired German mercenaries to
help them. Originally about fifteen thousand Germans had
crossed the Rhine, but soon these fierce and violent savages
took a liking for the good land and the high standard of living
to be found in Gaul, and many more crossed over. There
were now about 120,000 of them in the country. The Aedui
and their dependent states had fought in battle with the Germans over and over again; but they had been defeated with
disastrous results, losing all their nobles, the whole of their
national council, and their cavalry. After these disastrous
battles the Aedui, who because of their own courage and
the friendship and kindness of the Roman people had once
been the most powerful state in Gaul, were now forced to
hand over to the Sequani their most prominent men as
hostages; they had been compelled to bind themselves by oath
not to ask for the return of the hostages, not to seek help
from Rome, and to submit permanently to the power and
authority of the Sequani.

"I myself," said Diviciacus, "am the only man among the
Aedui who could not be induced to take the oath or to give
up my children as hostages. It was because of this that I

fled from my own country and came to Rome to ask the senate for help, being the one man not bound by oath or by the knowledge that his children were in enemy hands."

However, he continued, things had turned out even worse for the victorious Sequani than for the conquered Aedui. First, Ariovistus, the king of the Germans, had settled in their country and seized a third of their land, which was the best in the whole of Gaul; and now he was ordering them to evacuate another third. The reason for this was that several months earlier he had been joined by twenty-four thousand of the Harudes and he wanted to find land for them to occupy. Thus in a few years it seemed likely that all Gauls would be driven from their country and the whole German nation would cross the Rhine; for there was no comparison between the land in Gaul and the land in Germany, or between the Gallic and German way of life. And ever since Ariovistus had defeated the armies of the Gauls at the battle of Magetobriga, he had behaved like an arrogant and cruel tyrant. He demanded as hostages the children of all the Gallic nobles, and would inflict every sort of torture upon them if everything were not done precisely according to his will and pleasure. The man was a savage, incapable of controlling his passions or ambitions; it was impossible to put up with his tyranny any longer. And, as Diviciacus said, unless some help were forthcoming from me and from the Roman people, all the Gauls would have to act as the Helvetii had done. They would have to migrate and find some other part of the earth, far away from the Germans, to live in; and they would have to take any risks necessary in order to do so.

"If," he concluded, "Ariovistus ever hears a report of what I have said, I am quite sure that he will take the most dreadful revenge on all the hostages who are in his power. But you, Caesar, have the power to stop him. Your own prestige and that of your army, the victory you have just won, the very name of Rome could have the effect of preventing still more Germans from crossing the Rhine and of saving the whole of Gaul from the outrages of Ariovistus."

When Diviciacus had finished speaking, all those present began, with tears in their eyes, to beg me to help them. I noticed, however, that the representatives of the Sequani were an exception; instead of acting like the rest, they kept their eyes downcast. I was surprised at this and asked them why they were behaving in this way, but they preserved the same sullen silence as before. I repeated my question several times but still could not get a word out of them. In the end Diviciacus the Aeduan spoke again.

"The Sequani," he said, "are in an even worse and more

miserable state than the rest of us. They alone dare not complain or ask for help even in secret, since, though Ariovistus is far away, they fear his cruelty just as if he were present. The rest of us can at least find safety in flight; but the Sequani, who have admitted Ariovistus to their own country and whose towns are all in his power, are exposed to every kind of torture that he may devise."

After receiving this information, I made a short speech in which I attempted to give the Gauls some encouragement. I promised them that I would look into the matter myself and told them that I felt fairly confident that Ariovistus, in consideration of the authority which I held and the kindness which I had shown him in the past, would stop behaving as he had done. After making this speech, I pronounced the meeting at an end.

Now in addition to what I had heard, there were many other reasons also which made me think that I must look into this matter and attempt to deal with it. First of all was the fact that the Aedui had often been given by the senate the title of "Friends and Brethren"; yet now I saw that they were merely slaves under German authority and I knew that Aeduan hostages were in the hands of Ariovistus and of the Sequani. When I considered the greatness of our empire, I thought this a terrible disgrace both to myself and to Rome. I saw too that the Germans were gradually getting used to the idea of crossing the Rhine, and I realized that it would be very dangerous for us to have great numbers of them coming into Gaul. One could not imagine that these wild savages would be content with the conquest of the whole of Gaul; instead they would, as the Cimbri and Teutons did in the past, break out into our Province and go on from there into Italy. As it was, only the Rhone stood between the land of the Sequani and the Roman Province. To me this seemed to be a critical situation which must be faced at once. Moreover, Ariovistus had given himself such airs and had adopted an attitude of such arrogance that I considered him quite intolerable.

I therefore decided to send envoys asking him to name some place halfway between us where we could meet for a conference, since I wished to discuss with him matters of state which were of the utmost importance to both of us. Ariovistus' reply was as follows: "If I wanted anything from Caesar I would go to him; if Caesar wants anything from me, then he ought to come to me. Also I would not venture to go without an army into the part of Gaul that is occupied by the Romans, and the raising of an army would mean much trouble and much expense. In any case I cannot understand what sort of business

Caesar, or the Roman people for that matter, can have with my part of Gaul—mine by right of conquest."

When I received this reply I sent another deputation to him with the following message:

You are under considerable obligations both to me personally and to the Roman people. You will recall that it was during my consulship that you received from the senate the title "King and Friend." I observe that you show gratitude for this by making difficulties about an invitation to a conference and pretending that matters that concern both of us are of no interest to you.

I must therefore make the following requests: First, that you bring no more forces of Germans across the Rhine. Secondly, that you give back the Aeduan hostages which you now hold, and authorize the Sequani to give back the hostages held by them. Thirdly, that you undertake to do no harm to the Aedui and to enter into no hostilities either with them or with their allies.

If you accept these terms, you can be sure that you will never lose the friendship and good will both of myself and of the Roman people. If you reject them, then I shall have to act in accordance with the decree of the senate, passed in the consulship of Marcus Messalla and Marcus Piso, which requires the governor of the Province of Gaul to protect, consistently with the interests of the republic, both the Aedui and other allies of Rome. I should not, in other words, be able to overlook the wrong which you have done to the Aedui.

Ariovistus replied as follows:

In war it is a recognized thing that the conqueror can dictate his own terms to the conquered. Certainly Rome has always governed her own subjects in her own way without waiting to be told what to do by someone else. And, just as I am giving Rome no instructions about how to exercise her proper rights, so Rome should refrain from interfering with me in the exercise of mine.

As for the Aedui, they took the risk of going to war with me and were defeated in battle. They now pay tribute to me. And your arrival has done me considerable harm, since it has resulted in a loss of revenue to me from this source. I shall not give back their hostages to the Aedui; but I will not make war without good reason on them or on their allies, so long as they abide by their agreement and pay their taxes every year. If they fail to do so, they will find that their title "Brethren of the Roman People" will not be of the slightest use to them.

You threaten me with "not overlooking the wrongs done to the Aedui." Let me tell you that so far no one has made war

on me without being destroyed. You may attack whenever you
like. You will then discover what can be done by the valor
of German soldiers who have never been conquered in war, who
are perfectly trained in arms, and who for fourteen years have
never sheltered beneath a roof.

Just at the time I received this message, deputations arrived
from the Aedui and the Treveri. The Aedui came to complain
that their country was being devastated by the Harudes, who
had recently been brought across the Rhine into Gaul, and
said too that, even after giving up still more hostages, they
had been unable to buy peace from Ariovistus. The Treveri reported that a hundred clans of the Suebi, led by the brothers
Nasua and Cimberius, were encamped on the far bank of the
Rhine and were trying to get across.

This news was extremely disturbing and made it clear to me
that I must act fast, since, if this new band of Suebi joined
up with the existing forces of Ariovistus, it would not be so
easy to stand up to them. I therefore made arrangements for
the grain supply as quickly as possible and set out, marching
by forced marches, in the direction of Ariovistus.

We had been on the road for three days when I was informed
that Ariovistus with his whole force was moving against
Besançon, which is the largest town of the Sequani, and that
he had already advanced a three days' march from his own
frontier. It seemed to me that I must do everything possible to
prevent him from occupying the place. Besançon was an
arsenal, filled with military matériel of all kinds; and it had
such strong natural defenses that whoever held it would be in
an excellent position for prolonging a campaign. It is almost
completely surrounded by the river Doubs, which winds
around it in a circle that might have been made by compasses;
the gap in this circle is not of more than sixteen hundred feet
and is closed by a high hill which on each side slopes right
down to the banks of the river. There are fortifications all
around the hill connecting it with the town and making the hill
itself into a kind of citadel. Marching both by day and by
night I hurried on to this place, occupied it, and posted a garrison there.

We then halted for a few days in the area, while grain and
other supplies were brought in. During this time our troops
began to ask questions about the Germans from the Gauls and
the traders who were in the neighborhood. They were told that
these Germans were people of prodigious size, incredibly fine
soldiers, and extraordinarily well trained. The Gauls, so they
said, had had frequent experience of them in battle and found
that it was impossible even to stand up to the fierce, keen look

in their eyes. The result of these conversations was that the whole army fell into such a state of panic that almost everyone seemed to become more or less insane. The trouble started with those temporary officers and officials who had come out from Rome in order to cultivate my friendship and who were rather lacking in military experience. Many of these people now began asking me for leave, each finding some excellent reason why it was necessary for him to go. Others had rather more self-respect and, not wanting to look as though they were cowards, stayed behind. All the same they could not control the expressions on their faces and sometimes even burst into tears. They hid themselves away in their tents, where they spent the time bewailing their fate or else commiserating with their friends about the terrible danger in which they all stood. All over the camp people were making their wills and getting them signed. The panic and the general conversation of these people gradually began to have a disturbing effect even on others with considerable experience in the army—soldiers, centurions, and cavalry commanders. Some of these, who did not want to appear as frightened as they were, declared that they were not at all afraid of the enemy; it was rather the narrow routes and the great forests between us and Ariovistus which gave cause for anxiety, or else the question of the grain supply and the possibility of a failure in its delivery. Some actually told me that when I gave the order to strike camp and advance, the soldiers would not obey orders and would be too frightened to move.

When I saw how things were I summoned a meeting of officers and ordered centurions of all grades to be present. I began by reprimanding them severely for imagining that it was any business of theirs to discuss or even to think about where they were being led or for what reasons.

"Ariovistus," I said, "showed himself during the period of my consulship remarkably anxious to be on good terms with Rome. What reason now has anyone for supposing that he will be so foolhardy as to evade his obligations? Personally I feel sure that when Ariovistus realizes what I am asking from him and sees how fair my proposals are, he will not reject the offer of my good will and that of the Roman people. If, on the other hand, he were to go off his head and be insane enough to make war, what, may I ask you, have you got to be frightened about? What makes you downhearted? Is it your own lack of courage or is it my incapacity as a general?

"We had experience with this enemy in our fathers' time when the Cimbri and Teutons were defeated by Gaius Marius and it was generally agreed that the army deserved as much credit as the general for the victory. We recently met the same enemy again in Italy during the revolt of the slaves, and on that occasion they had the advantage of the discipline and training which they had learned from us. This slave revolt, incidentally, is a good example of what courage and resolution can do. For a long time, while these slaves were unarmed, our men had been needlessly frightened of them; but in the end, though they had won victories and furnished themselves with arms, we defeated them. Finally, these Germans are the same people whom the Helvetii have often fought and very often defeated both in Germany and in their own country; yet the Helvetii could not stand up to our army.

"Some of you seem to have been disturbed by the defeat and rout of the Gauls; yet, if you look into the matter, you will find that the facts were these: the Gauls had become exhausted by the length of a campaign during which Ariovistus for month after month had kept to the shelter of his camp or of the marshes without giving them a chance of engaging him; it was only when they had given up all hope of meeting him in battle and had allowed their forces to become dispersed that he suddenly made an attack on them and won a victory that was the result of intelligent generalship rather than of superior prowess. Against inexperienced native troops there was certainly room for generalship of this sort, but not even Ariovistus himself can imagine that our armies can be taken in by such tactics.

"As for those of you who are hiding your own cowardice behind a pretended anxiety about the grain supply or about the narrow passes on the route, let me tell you that you are acting in an extraordinarily arrogant way. Your view seems to be either that I am incapable of doing my duty or else that I have to be instructed in how to do so by you. In fact, these matters are my own concern. Grain is being brought in by the Sequani, the Leuci, and the Lingones; the crops in the fields are already ripe. As for the route before us, you will soon be able to see what it is like for yourselves.

"I have been told that the soldiers will refuse to obey orders to advance. Such a statement leaves me completely unmoved. I know that in all cases where an army has failed to obey its general, this has happened because of some misfortune brought on by the general's incompetence or else because some crime of the general's has been discovered and he has been convicted of avarice. In my own case you can look at my whole life for evidence of my integrity and you can recall the Helvetian campaign for evidence of my fortune in war.

"I shall therefore now take a step which previously I had intended to postpone for a few days. We shall strike camp between three and six A.M. tomorrow. In this way I shall soon find out which are the stronger motives with you—a sense of duty and honor, or sheer panic. And even if no one else will follow me, I shall still go forward with only the Tenth Legion. I have no doubts of the loyalty of that legion and I shall have it as my bodyguard." (I had always shown a particular affection toward the Tenth and had complete confidence in the courage of its men.)

My speech had a remarkable effect. There was a complete change of heart and now everyone was eager to go into action at once. First of all, the soldiers of the Tenth asked their officers to convey to me their gratitude for the high opinion I held of them and to assure me that they were ready for battle whenever I wanted. Then the other legions, through their officers and senior centurions, sent messages to me in order to excuse or explain their conduct. They had never, they said, felt any doubt or fear, and they fully realized that the strategy of the campaign was the general's business and had nothing to do with them. I accepted these explanations.

The route had been explored by Diviciacus, whom I trusted more than any other Gaul, and he had found that by making a detour of more than fifty miles it was possible to march through open country. We started at about three A.M., as I said we would do, and, after marching continuously for six days, were informed by our scouts that Ariovistus and his army were about twenty-two miles away from us.

4 THE DEFEAT OF
ARIOVISTUS.

When Ariovistus heard of our arrival, he sent a deputation to say that he was now quite ready to accept my previous proposal for a conference, since I had come nearer to him and he felt that it was safe for him to comply with my request. I did not reject his offer. Indeed I thought that he was now coming to his senses in voluntarily suggesting to do what he had refused when asked; and I was full of hope that, in return for all the kindness he had received from me and from the Roman people, he would adopt a less obstinate attitude when he understood what I wanted from him.

It was arranged that the conference should be held five days later. Meanwhile messengers frequently passed between us. Ariovistus stipulated that I should not bring any infantry with me to the conference; he was afraid, he said, that I would surround him by some trick or other and proposed that each of us should come attended only by a mounted escort; otherwise he would not come at all. On my side, I had no wish for the conference to be broken off simply because of some such excuse; at the same time I did not want to entrust my personal safety to a body of Gallic cavalry. I decided that the best thing to do was to take horses from the Gallic troopers and give them as mounts to soldiers of the Tenth Legion, whom I could trust absolutely; so, if there were any need of action, I should have as devoted a bodyguard as I could wish for. While this order was being carried out, one of the legionaries remarked rather wittily, "Caesar's doing better than he said. He promised that the Tenth would be his bodyguard, and now he's knighting us!"

The place where we had arranged to meet was a fairly large mound of earth in the middle of a great plain and about half-way between our two camps. When we reached the place I halted my mounted legionaries about two hundred yards away and Ariovistus halted his own cavalry escort at the same distance. Ariovistus demanded that our conference should be held on horseback and that each of us should bring with him ten horsemen.

When we met together I began my speech by reminding him of the kindnesses he had received from me and from the senate. He had been given by the senate the titles "King" and "Friend"; and he had also received a number of magnificent presents—a very rare privilege indeed, as I pointed out to him, and one usually reserved only for those who had done great personal service to Rome. Yet he, without any proper right even to be received by the senate and with no real reason for making any petition, had been rewarded as I had mentioned. He owed these rewards entirely to my generosity and that of the senate. I then explained to him that the alliance between us and the Aedui was of long standing and was based on principles of justice. I told him of the many senatorial decrees which had been passed to do honor to the Aedui, and informed him that, even before they had asked for our friendship, they had always been the chief state in Gaul.

"It is the way of Romans," I said, "to want our friends and allies, rather than lose what belongs to them, to be constantly growing in influence, importance, and prestige. Certainly we cannot tolerate a state of affairs where they are stripped of what they already possessed at the time they became our friends."

In conclusion I repeated the demands that I had sent to him before by messengers: he was not to make war on the Aedui or on their allies; he was to give back the hostages;

and, though it might be impossible to send back home any of the Germans he had with him, he must at least undertake not to allow any more of them to cross the Rhine.

Ariovistus in reply said very little about these demands of mine and a great deal about himself and his superior abilities. It was not, he said, on his own initiative that he had crossed the Rhine; he had come in answer to a summons from the Gauls themselves, who had invited him into their country; and it was only because he had reckoned on securing great rewards that he had left his own home and his own people. The lands which he now occupied had been granted to him by the Gauls themselves, who had also freely given him the hostages which he held. As for the tribute which he took, that came to him by the natural law of war which allows the conqueror to impose his terms on the conquered. Moreover, in his war with the Gauls it was the Gauls, not he, who were the aggressors. All the states in the country had combined and brought up their forces against him. In one battle he had overpowered and defeated them. If they wanted to try the same experiment again, he was prepared to fight it out; but if they wanted to enjoy peace, they had no right to refuse to pay the tribute which up to now they had paid willingly enough.

He considered that the friendship of the Roman people ought to be not only an honor but also of some use to him; and it was in this belief that he had sought it. Certainly it ought not to do him harm; and if because of Rome he was to receive less tribute than before or have to give up people who had surrendered to him, then he would reject Roman friendship as energetically as he had once asked for it. As for the great numbers of Germans whom he was bringing across the Rhine, this was not a move aimed against Gaul but was purely a measure of self-defense, as could be proved by the fact that he had only come to Gaul because he had been invited and that in war he had resisted attacks but never initiated them.

He then claimed that he had come to Gaul before the Romans. Up to this time, he said, no Roman army had advanced beyond the frontiers of the Roman Province of Gaul. What then did I mean by coming into country which belonged to him? This part of Gaul was his province, just as the other part was ours. If he were to invade our territory, we should rightly object; and just in the same way we had no right whatever to interfere with him in an area which was under his control.

As for what I had said about the Aedui being called "Brethren" by the Romans, he was not such an uncivilized barbarian as to be ignorant of the fact that the Aedui had given Rome no help in her recent war with the Allobroges, and had received none from us in their own quarrels with himself and with the Sequani. He was bound, therefore, to suspect that all I said about "friendship" was a mere ruse and that my real reason for having an army in Gaul was so as to use it in order to destroy him.

"And," he concluded, "unless you take yourself and your army away from this part of the country I shall treat you not as 'Friend,' but as an enemy to be hunted down. There are many members of the nobility and many leading politicians in Rome who would be extremely glad to hear that you had been killed by me. This is a fact I know for certain, because they have sent their own agents to tell me that I can count on their gratitude and friendship if I get rid of you. If, however, you go away and leave me in undisputed possession of Gaul, I will reward you handsomely, and if you want any wars fought I will see that they are all won for you without your having to take any risks or undergo any hardships."

I then spoke to him at some length, explaining that it was impossible for me to go back on what I had undertaken to do. It was against my principles and against the principles of the Roman people to desert allies who had proved their loyalty. I could not agree that Gaul belonged to him more than it did to us. I pointed out that the Arverni and the Ruteni had been defeated in war by Quintus Fabius Maximus and had then been pardoned by the Roman people, who had neither formed them into a province nor imposed a tribute on them. If the question of sovereignty in Gaul was to be judged by the standard of "who was there first," then our claims were the most just; and if the judgment of the senate were to be upheld, then the country ought to be independent, since the senate had decided that although Gaul had been conquered, it should continue to be governed by its own laws.

While the interview was proceeding along these lines, I was informed that Ariovistus' cavalry were drawing nearer to the mound, riding up quite close to our men, and hurling stones and javelins at them. I broke the conversation off and went back to my men. I instructed them not to throw a single javelin back in reply; for, though I could see that absolutely no risk was involved in a fight between picked legionaries and this German cavalry, I still did not want to take any action which would result in its being said, after the enemy had been defeated, that I had broken my word and lured them into an ambush during a conference. But when the rank and file of our army got to know how arrogantly Ariovistus had behaved at the conference, how he had told us to clear out of Gaul, how his cavalry had attacked ours and so put an end to the

discussions, the men were much keener than before and still
more eager for battle.

Next day Ariovistus sent envoys to me to say that he would
like to reopen the negotiations that had been interrupted. He
asked me to name a day for meeting again or, if I preferred,
to send him one of my senior officers. Personally I could
see no good reason for holding another conference, especially
as on the previous day Ariovistus had been incapable of stopping his men from hurling javelins at us. And I thought it
would be too risky to send him one of my staff officers; it
would be like throwing him to a lot of savages. The best plan
seemed to be to send Gaius Valerius Procillus, son of Gaius
Valerius Caburus, who had been given Roman citizenship by
Gaius Valerius Flaccus. He was a highly educated young man
and a fine soldier. He was thoroughly reliable and knew the
Gallic language which, from long practice, Ariovistus too
could speak fluently. Moreover, in his case the Germans could
have no motive for doing him any harm. I sent with him
Marcus Mettius, who had at one time been entertained by
Ariovistus. Their instructions were to find out what Ariovistus
had to say and report back to me. But as soon as Ariovistus saw
them in his camp and approaching him, he shouted out in
front of his whole army: "What are you here for? Spying, I
suppose," and, refusing to allow them to speak, he had them
thrown into chains.

On the same day he moved forward and camped on the
lower slopes of a hill about six miles away from us. Then, on
the following day, he led his forces right past our position and
camped two miles beyond us. The object of this maneuver was
to cut us off from the grain and other supplies that were being
brought up from the country of the Sequani and the Aedui.
For five days running I led my own troops out of camp and
kept them formed up in line of battle, giving Ariovistus every
opportunity to fight a general engagement if he wished to do
so. During all this time Ariovistus kept his main forces confined to their camp, though engagements between the cavalry
took place daily. As regards cavalry fighting the Germans were
specially trained in methods of their own. They had six
thousand cavalrymen, who went into battle accompanied by an
equal number of foot soldiers. The latter, particularly good
runners and remarkable for their courage, had been chosen
out of the whole army, each cavalryman picking his own
infantryman to look after him. When the cavalry were in
difficulty, they fell back on this body of infantry and the
infantry would quickly concentrate. The foot soldiers would
rally round any horseman who was wounded and had fallen
from his mount. Long training had made them so fast on

their feet that in a prolonged advance or a quick retreat they could keep pace by running alongside the horses and clinging to their manes.

When I saw that Ariovistus was staying in his camp, I had to make a move to prevent myself from being cut off any longer from supplies. I selected a good place for a camp about six hundred yards from the German position and marched there with the army drawn up in three lines. The first and second lines were ordered to stand by under arms, while the third line built the fortifications for the camp. The place was, as already stated, only six hundred yards away from Ariovistus, and he sent out against us about sixteen thousand light troops and all his cavalry with the idea of frightening our soldiers and stopping their work. However, I kept to my original plan and instructed the first two lines to keep off the enemy and the third to complete the fortification. When the work was finished, I left two legions there and some of the auxiliary troops, taking back with me the other four legions into the larger camp.

Next day, as usual, I led out my troops, this time from both camps, advanced a little beyond the larger camp, formed up in order of battle, and gave the enemy an opportunity to engage. About midday, realizing that even now they were not going to make a move, I led the army back to camp. Then at last Ariovistus did send out some sections of his army to attack the smaller camp. Hard fighting on both sides went on until the evening. At sunset, after there had been a number of casualties on both sides, Ariovistus withdrew his men to their camp. By questioning prisoners, I discovered why Ariovistus declined to fight a pitched battle. Apparently it was a German custom for the matrons to declare by means of lots and other methods of divination whether or not it would be a good thing to engage in battle; on this occasion their verdict was that fate was against a German victory if they fought before the new moon.

Next day I left what I considered to be adequate garrisons in both camps and stationed all the auxiliaries in front of the smaller camp in sight of the enemy. I hoped that their appearance would make some impression on the enemy, since the actual numbers of the legionary troops were not very great compared with the numbers opposed to them. Then, with the army drawn up for battle in three lines, I advanced right up to the enemy's camp. Now at last the Germans were forced to action. Their troops were led out of camp and drawn up by tribes at regular intervals from each other—Harudes, Marcomani, Triboces, Vangiones, Nemetes, Sedusii, Suebi. In the rear of their line, so that there should be no hope of running away, they made a barrier out of their carts and wagons, and here they placed their women, who stood there with hands outstretched and tears streaming from their eyes, imploring the men, as they marched out to battle, not to deliver them into Roman slavery.

I placed each of my five senior officers in command of a legion and entrusted the remaining legion to my quaestor, so that each man might know that he was displaying his courage under the eyes of a high-ranking officer. I then began the action by leading our right wing into battle, since I had noticed that the enemy's left was the least steady part of his line.

When the signal was given, our men rushed forward so fiercely and the enemy came on so swiftly and furiously that there was no time for hurling our javelins. They were thrown aside, and the fighting was with swords at close quarters. The Germans quickly adopted their usual close formation to defend themselves from the sword thrusts, but many of our men were brave enough to leap right on top of the wall of shields, tear the shields from the hands that held them, and stab down at the enemy from above. The German left was pushed back and routed, but their right, by sheer weight of numbers, pressed us hard. Young Publius Crassus, in command of the cavalry, saw what was happening and being in a more maneuverable position than the officers engaged in the fighting, he ordered the third line forward to the relief of our troops who were in difficulty. The result was that the battle again swung our way and the whole enemy army turned and ran. They fled without stopping until they came to the Rhine, about fifteen miles away. A very few, who thought their strength equal to the task, tried to swim across, or managed to find boats and so escaped. Among these was Ariovistus, who found a small craft moored to the bank and got away safely in it. All the rest were overtaken and killed by our cavalry. Ariovistus had two wives, both of whom were killed in the general rout. One of these was of Suebian nationality, and he had brought her with him from home; the other was the sister of King Voccio of Noricum, who had sent her to Gaul to be married. Of Ariovistus' two daughters one was killed and one taken prisoner.

Having joined in the pursuit with the cavalry, I came upon Gaius Valerius Procillus, who was being dragged off by his guards in the general rout, closely fettered with three chains. This meeting gave me as much pleasure as the victory itself. It was good to see this man, one of the best in the whole Province and a great friend of mine whose hospitality I had enjoyed, rescued from the enemy and restored to me; and it was good to think that, by preserving him safe and sound,

Providence had done nothing to mar our feelings of joy and triumph. Procillus told me that the Germans had three times consulted the lots in his presence as to whether he should be burned alive then and there or reserved for another occasion. It was only thanks to the way the lots turned out that he was saved. Marcus Mettius was also discovered and brought back to me.

When the news of the battle reached the other side of the Rhine, the Suebi, who had advanced as far as the banks of the river, began to go home again. The tribes living in the Rhineland, seeing how frightened they were, turned on them and killed great numbers of them.

So during one summer two great wars had been fought and won. I now led the army back into winter quarters among the Sequani, rather earlier than the weather required. Leaving Labienus in command, I set off myself for Cisalpine Gaul to hold the assizes.

❧ BOOK TWO: 57 B.C. ❧

1 CONSPIRACY OF THE BELGAE.

For the winter I was, as already stated, in Cisalpine Gaul, and during this time I constantly heard rumors, which were confirmed by dispatches from Labienus, that the Belgae (who, as I have explained, occupy a third of the whole area of Gaul) were conspiring against Rome and exchanging hostages. It appeared that the reasons for the conspiracy were: First, they were afraid that our army would invade their country, once the Celtic part of Gaul was subdued. Second, they were being urged to take action by certain elements among the Gauls; some of these, who had resented the continued presence of the Germans in Gaul, were equally averse to a Roman army permanently in their country and establishing itself there for the winter; others were looking for a new form of government simply because they were naturally fickle and always wanted a change. Another element in the situation was the fact that in Gaul it was a common occurrence for a powerful chieftain who could hire mercenaries to make himself king in his own state, and such people realized that it would not be so easy to do this if Rome was in control of the country.

I was disturbed by the news I received and by the dispatches from Labienus. So I raised two new legions in Cisalpine Gaul and, at the beginning of the summer, sent them into Gaul beyond the Alps under the command of the general Quintus Pedius. As soon as supplies of fodder began to appear, I rejoined the army myself and instructed the Senones and other Gallic tribes on the Belgian frontier to find out what the Belgae were up to and to inform me of the result of their inquiries. The reports I received from them all agreed that troops were being raised and concentrated in one area. It seemed clear to me that we ought to move against them at once, and so as soon as I had arranged for the grain supply, I struck camp and reached the Belgian frontier in about a fortnight.

My arrival was unexpected, since we had come more quickly than had been thought possible. The Remi, who are the first Belgic tribe across the frontier from Gaul, sent a deputation to me consisting of the two leading men of their nation, Iccius and Andecumborius. They were instructed to say that the Remi wished to place themselves and their possessions under the power and protection of Rome; that they had not joined the other Belgae in the conspiracy against Rome, that they were prepared to give hostages, to obey my orders, to place their towns at my disposal, and to supply me with grain or anything else I wanted. They informed me that all the rest of the Belgae were under arms and had been joined by the German tribes on this side of the Rhine; and that there was such general enthusiasm among all these tribes that the Remi themselves had not been able to dissuade the Suessiones from joining the conspiracy, although these Suessiones were close kinsmen of theirs, observing the same laws and customs and sharing the same government and central authority.

I inquired what states were under arms, how large their numbers, and how strong in a military sense. I received the following information in reply. Most of the Belgae were of German origin. They had crossed the Rhine a long time ago and, because of the fertility of the soil, had settled in the areas which they now occupied, after having driven out the original Gallic inhabitants. When, in the last generation, the whole of Gaul was overrun by the Cimbri and Teutons, the Belgae were the only people who had succeeded in keeping them out of their country; and because of this known and remembered achievement of theirs, they had a particular pride and confidence in their military importance. As to their numbers, the Remi claimed to have exact information; related as they were by kinship and intermarriage, they discovered what had been said at the general council of the Belgians and how large an army each tribe had undertaken to raise for the war. The most powerful of these tribes, in courage, population, and general prestige, were the Bellovaci; they could put one hundred thousand men into the field and out of this number had promised sixty thousand picked troops, claiming at the same time the right to be in supreme command of operations. Then there were the Suessiones, who lived next to the Remi in a country that was not only large but extremely fertile. Within living memory they had had a king, Diviciacus by name, who had been the most powerful ruler in the whole of Gaul, with authority over wide areas in these parts and even over some of Britain.

Their present king was called Galba, and it was he who, because of his reputation for integrity and good sense, had been appointed by general consent to the supreme command. He had twelve towns and had promised to bring an army of fifty thousand men. The same number had been promised by the Nervii, who lived in the most remote parts of the country and were considered by the Belgae themselves to be the finest warriors of all. Fifteen thousand men had been promised by the Atrebates, ten thousand by the Ambiani, twenty-five thousand by the Morini, seven thousand by the Menapii, ten thousand by the Caleti, ten thousand by the Veliocasses and Viromandui, nineteen thousand by the Aduatuci. In addition it was thought that the so-called German tribes (the Condrusi, the Eburones, the Caeroesi, and the Paemani) had promised to supply forty thousand men.

I spoke politely and in an encouraging way to the Remi and then gave orders that the whole of their council was to meet at my headquarters and that the children of their leading men should be brought to me as hostages. All my instructions were carried out punctually and efficiently. I then made a strong personal appeal to Diviciacus the Aeduan, pointing out to him how very important it was for the interests of Rome and indeed for the safety of us both to make the enemy disperse their forces so that we should not have to fight such an enormous army all at once. We could achieve our aim, I told him, if the Aedui would invade the country of the Bellovaci and start devastating their land, and I sent Diviciacus back to his own people with these instructions.

I heard next that the whole army of the Belgae had been joined and was marching against me. When my patrols and also the Remi informed me that the enemy were not far away, I quickly crossed the river Aisne, which is almost on the frontier of the Remi, and fortified a camp on the other side. In this way I had one side of the camp protected by the banks of the river, which also protected my rear from enemy attack and made it possible for supplies to be brought up safely from the Remi and the other states. There was a bridge over the river, and I posted a guard on it, leaving on the other bank a senior officer, Quintus Titurius Sabinus, with six cohorts. Sabinus was ordered to build a camp there with a rampart twelve feet high and a ditch eighteen feet broad.

Eight miles from this camp was a town of the Remi called Bibrax. The advancing army of the Belgae made a vigorous attempt to storm this place. In fact, on that day the defenders

had the greatest difficulty in holding out. Both the Gauls and
the Belgae use the same methods in attacking a fortified
place. The whole circuit of the defenses is surrounded by
a mass of men; stones are hurled from every direction until
the defenders are driven from the walls; and then the attackers lock their shields over their heads, forming a "tortoise," move up to the gates, and try to undermine the wall.
It was a method which could be employed easily on this occasion. The attacking army was so enormous and the stones and
missiles rained down in such numbers that it was quite impossible to stand one's ground on the wall. The attack had
to be broken off at nightfall, and then Iccius—a particularly
distinguished and influential nobleman of the Remi who
was in charge of the defense and had been one of the envoys
who had come to me to ask for peace—sent me a message to
say that unless he received help he could hold out no longer.

About midnight I sent out detachments of Numidian and
Cretan archers and Balearic slingers to relieve the defenders
of Bibrax. They were guided on their way by the messengers
who had come from Iccius.

The reinforcements not only gave the Remi fresh courage for
defense but emboldened them to fight back aggressively. The
result was that the enemy gave up hope of capturing the place.
They halted near the town for a short while, laid waste the
lands of the Remi, set fire to all the villages and isolated buildings within reach, and then marched on in full force toward
our camp. They made their own camp less than two miles away
from us. As could be seen from the smoke and flame of their
watch fires, it extended over more than eight miles.

Bearing in mind the huge numbers of the enemy and their
great reputation as soldiers, I decided to avoid battle for the
time being, though every day cavalry engagements took place
in which I was able to test the enemy's fighting qualities and
also to see how our own troops stood up to them. It soon
became clear that we were just as good as they. The ground
in front of our camp was perfectly adapted for drawing up
an army in line of battle. The hill on which the camp was
situated rose slightly above the level ground and was just
about wide enough to give room for an army in battle formation; at each end there was a steep descent and in front it
sloped down gently into the plain. Now at each end of the hill
I had a trench dug about six hundred yards long and at right
angles to the front. At the ends of the trenches I placed redoubts and artillery to prevent the enemy from using their
great superiority in numbers to sweep round our flanks
when battle was joined. When this was done, I left behind
in camp the two legions that had recently been recruited, to

be used as reserves if necessary, and drew up the other six legions in front of the camp in line of battle. The enemy also had marched out from their camp and formed up in battle order.

Between the two armies there was a small marsh. The enemy waited in the hope that we would be the first to cross it, and we on our side stood ready to charge down on them and catch them at a disadvantage if they took the risk first. Meanwhile a cavalry action was fought in the space between the two lines of infantry. In the cavalry fighting we had rather the better of things, and when it became clear that neither army was going to take the initiative in crossing the marsh, I withdrew our troops to camp.

The enemy immediately left their lines and hurried toward the river Aisne, which, as I have already mentioned, was behind our camp. They discovered fords and attempted to get part of their army across, their plan being to capture, if possible, the fort commanded by Sabinus and to destroy the bridge; or, if this proved impossible, to lay waste the country of the Remi, which was of great importance to us as a base for the campaign, and to cut us off from our supplies.

I was informed of this situation by Sabinus. Taking with me all the cavalry, the light-armed Numidians, slingers, and archers, I crossed the bridge and marched against the enemy. Soon very fierce fighting took place, as our men bore down on the enemy while they were engaged in crossing the river and thus impeded in their movement. Great numbers of the enemy were killed there, and others who, showing the most remarkable courage, attempted to get across on the bodies of the dead were driven off by the sheer weight of our missiles. Our cavalry surrounded and wiped out those who had succeeded in crossing the river at the beginning of the action.

The enemy now had to admit failure both as regards their plan of capturing Bibrax and their hopes of crossing the Aisne. They saw too that we were not coming down to fight a battle on unfavorable ground. Moreover, their own supplies of grain were beginning to run short. At a council of war, they decided the best thing to do was for everyone to return home, and then to come together again in force for the defense of whatever part of their country was first invaded by the Romans; in this way, instead of fighting outside their frontiers, they would be fighting on their own ground and have food supplies to fall back upon. An additional reason for this decision was the news that Diviciacus and an Aeduan army were approaching the country of the Bellovaci. This meant that the Bellovaci could not be induced to stay any longer without going to the help of their own people.

Having reached this decision, they left their camp about an hour before midnight. There was much shouting and confusion, no regular marching order and no discipline, as each individual tried to push his way forward in his hurry to get home. It was therefore more a headlong flight than an orderly breaking of camp. I was immediately informed by my scouts of what was happening, but since I did not yet know their reasons for departure, I was afraid of an ambush and kept both the infantry and cavalry in camp. At dawn, when the information received was confirmed by our patrols, I sent out the whole force of cavalry with orders to delay the enemy rear guard. This force was commanded by Quintus Pedius and Lucius Aurunculeius Cotta. Titus Labienus was ordered to follow in support with three legions. The cavalry attacked the rear guard and kept up the pursuit for many miles, killing vast numbers as they fled. For, while the men at the extreme rear of the enemy column stood firm and made a brave resistance to our troops when they bore down on them, those in front imagined that they were out of danger. They saw no actual need to preserve any order and had no officers to control them; so, when they heard the shouting, they broke ranks and tried to escape each on his own. In this way our troops, without any risk, were able to go on killing them as long as daylight lasted. They did not stop until sunset and then, according to orders, retired to camp.

Next day, before the enemy could recover from this panic-stricken rout, I led our army into the country of the Suessiones, who are neighbors of the Remi. A long march brought us to the fortified town of Noviodunum and, since I had heard it was virtually undefended, I made an attempt to storm it as soon as we arrived. However, although the defenders were few, it was surrounded by a very wide ditch and a high wall, and we were unable to take the place by storm. We therefore fortified a camp and began to move up mantlets and to get ready all the other siege equipment necessary. Meanwhile the whole army of the Suessiones who had returned from the flight got into the town during the following night. We quickly brought the mantlets up to the walls, began to fill in the ditch, and erected siege towers. Such things had never been seen or heard of in Gaul before, and alarmed by the size of our works and by the speed with which we were operating, the enemy sent a deputation to ask for terms of surrender. The Remi begged me to spare them and I granted their request. The surrender of the Suessiones was accepted after they had given up to me as hostages some of their leading men, including the two sons of King Galba himself, and had handed over all arms in the place.

I then led the army into the country of the Bellovaci, who had retired with all their belongings into the fortified town of Bratuspantium. When we were about five miles away from this place, all the elders of the tribe came out of the town and, stretching out their hands to me, cried out that they wished to come under my protection and authority and had no intention of bearing arms against Rome. So, in the same way, when we had marched up to the town and were beginning to pitch camp, the women and children stood on the walls with hands outstretched in their suppliant way, begging us for peace. Their entreaties were supported by Diviciacus, who after the breakup of the Belgic army had disbanded his Aeduan forces and returned to my headquarters. He said that the Bellovaci had always enjoyed the friendship and protection of the Aedui. They had been incited to break off relations with the Aedui and take up arms against Rome by their chiefs, who claimed that I had reduced the Aedui to slavery and was inflicting every kind of insult and indignity upon them. The ringleaders had now realized what a disaster they had brought upon their country and fled to Britain.

"Not only the Bellovaci," Diviciacus concluded, "but the Aedui also in their behalf beg you, Caesar, to treat them with that mercy and forbearance for which you are well known. If you do so you will greatly increase the prestige of the Aedui among all the Belgae, on whose aid and resources we rely whenever we get involved in a war."

I replied that I would show my respect for Diviciacus and the Aedui by receiving the Bellovaci into my protection and by sparing their lives. But since this tribe had such great influence among the Belgae and was the most populous of them all, I demanded the surrender of six hundred hostages. When these hostages had been handed over and all arms in the town had been collected, we moved on from there into the country of the Ambiani, who immediately surrendered unconditionally.

2 CAMPAIGN AGAINST
THE NERVII.

Beyond the frontiers of the Ambiani live the Nervii. I inquired what sort of people they were and how they lived, and received the following information. No traders ever came into their country because they did not allow wine to be imported or any other luxury, in the belief that indulgences of this sort make men feeble-spirited and lacking in courage. A fierce people and extremely courageous, they were very bitter in their denunciations of the other Belgae for having forgotten the traditional courage of their race and given in to Rome. As to themselves, they had declared that they would never send envoys to us and never accept any kind of peace.

We marched for three days through Nervian territory and then found out from some prisoners that the river Sambre was only ten miles away from our camp and that on the farther bank of this river the entire army of the Nervii had taken up its position and was awaiting our arrival. We were told that they had with them the Atrebates and the Viromandui, neighboring tribes whom they had persuaded to share the fortunes of war with them; that they were waiting for further contingents, already on the march, from the Aduatuci; and that they had brought together their women and all who were considered too young or too old to fight into a place surrounded by marshes and inaccessible to an army.

On receiving this information, I sent forward a reconnaissance party with some centurions to choose a good place for a camp. Following us or marching with us were a good number of surrendered Belgae and other Gauls. It was later discovered from prisoners that some of these, who had observed our usual order of march during this time, had gone to the Nervii by night and told them that between each legion and the next there was always a long column of baggage. It would be perfectly easy, they suggested, to attack the first legion as soon as it reached camp, while the men were still burdened with their packs and the other legions some way off; and once it was driven back and its baggage train plundered, the rest would scarcely venture to make a stand.

The informers' plan was favored by a traditional tactic of the Nervii. They were practically without cavalry; indeed, even to this day they give no attention to this arm and rely entirely on their infantry. However, they had their own way of stopping the attacks of enemy cavalry who attempted to raid their territory. They cut off the tops of saplings and bend them over, letting the side branches grow as much as possible and twining brambles and thorns in and out so as to make hedges almost like walls and capable of being used as defense works. Far from being able to penetrate these hedges, one could not even see through them. This type of obstacle would hinder our columns on the march, and therefore the Nervii thought that the proposed plan ought to be tried.

The main features of the place chosen by us for a camp were as follows. The site was a hill which sloped down evenly from its top to the river Sambre, already mentioned. On the other side of the river and opposite this hill there was another hill with the same sort of slope. Its lower slopes were open for about three hundred yards, but the upper part was so thickly wooded that one could not see into it. Here, among the trees, the main enemy army lay hidden. On the open ground by the river a few cavalry pickets could be seen. The river was about three feet deep.

I had sent the cavalry on ahead and was following with the rest of my forces; but the column was marching in a different order from that described by the deserters to the Nervii. Since we were now drawing near the enemy, I adopted my usual procedure, which was to lead the way with six legions in light marching order; behind these I had placed all the baggage of the army; and bringing up the rear of the column came the two recently recruited legions, whose duty it was to guard the baggage.

Our cavalry, with detachments of slingers and archers, crossed the river and engaged the enemy cavalry in battle. The enemy kept falling back on their own main body in the woods and then darting out again to make another charge on our men, who did not venture to pursue them beyond the open ground. Meanwhile the six legions that had arrived first had marked out the ground for the camp and begun to dig the fortifications. The infantry of the Nervii, full of confidence, were all this time drawn up in battle order under cover of the woods. They had agreed to make their attack the moment that our baggage train appeared. Now, as it came into sight, they suddenly rushed out of the woods in full force and charged down on our cavalry, whom they brushed aside and routed with the utmost ease. They then swept on down to the river, moving at such an incredible speed that to us it looked as though they were at the edge of the woods, in the river, and on top of us all in the same moment. With the same extraordinary speed they swarmed up the opposite hill toward our camp and fell upon the men who were engaged in fortifying it.

I had everything to do at once—hoist the flag (which was the signal for a call to arms), sound the trumpet for action, call the men back from their work on the entrenchments, bring in the others who had gone farther afield to get material for the rampart, form the troops up in battle order, address them, give the signal for attack. As the enemy were practically upon us, there was simply not time for doing most of these things, but in this very awkward situation we were helped by two factors. First, the training and experience of the troops themselves, who from their knowledge of previous battles were able to dispense with orders and judge on their own what should be done; and second, the order which I had issued to commanders of legions, instructing each of them to stay with his own unit while it was at work and not leave until the fortifications were finished. Thus the legionary commanders, seeing the enemy so close and advancing so fast, did what they thought best on their own initiative, without waiting for orders from me.

As it was, I only gave the orders that were most essential and then ran down to address the troops where I could first find them. Happening upon the Tenth Legion, I spoke only a very few words to the men, telling them to remember their reputation for courage, to keep their spirits up, and to stand firmly against the enemy's charge. Then, as the enemy were only a javelin throw away, I gave the signal for battle. I set out from there intending to address the troops at the other end of the line, but found that they were already in action. So short a time had they had to get ready, and so eager for battle had the enemy shown themselves, that our men, far from being able to put on badges and decorations, had not even had the time to don their helmets or take the covers from their shields.

As they came up from their work on the entrenchments, each man fell in at the point where he happened to reach the line and under the first standards that he saw, so as not to waste time in looking for his own unit. The position of our line was determined by the nature of the ground, the slope of the hill, and the needs of the moment, rather than by military theory. In fact, the legions did not stand in one line but had to face in different directions to meet different attacks. Visibility was impeded by the thick hedges already described; it was impossible to decide precisely where our reserves should be stationed or in what sector they would be needed; one man, in fact, could not conceivably give all the orders required. In conditions so entirely unpredictable, it was natural that fortune swung now this way and now that.

On our left were the Ninth and Tenth Legions, and facing them were the Atrebates. After hurling their javelins and inflicting a number of casualties on the enemy, who were already breathless and exhausted from running, our men quickly drove them downhill into the river and followed hard behind, killing great numbers of them with their swords while they were struggling across the stream. Our legionaries then without any hesitation crossed the river themselves and advanced up the hill until the enemy again turned and made a stand. We engaged them again and once more drove them back in flight.

On another sector too, facing in a rather different direction, two more of our legions, the Eleventh and Eighth, had joined battle with the Viromandui and driven them down from the higher ground to the riverbank, where the fighting continued.

The result of all this was that, although the Twelfth and Seventh Legions were drawn up quite close to each other on our right, our camp was entirely exposed on the left and in front. It was here that the whole army of the Nervii, under their supreme commander, Boduognatus, surged forward in one solid mass. Some of them began to envelop the legions on their exposed flank; others made for the top of the hill where the camp was situated.

As already mentioned, our cavalry and the light infantry with it had been routed in the first enemy attack. They were now retiring to camp when they found themselves confronted by another enemy force and made off in flight again, this time in a different direction. The settlers who, watching from the rear gate of the camp at the top of the hill had seen our men pushing the enemy across the river, had gone out themselves to pick up plunder. Now, when they looked back and saw the enemy actually in our camp, they fled headlong. At the same time a tremendous noise of shouting arose from those who were bringing up the baggage. In a state of utter panic they began to run away in all directions. All this had a most disturbing effect on the cavalry detachments of the Treveri (a tribe with a unique reputation for courage among the Gauls), who had been sent by their government to serve as auxiliaries in my army. Now, seeing the enemy swarming into our camp, our legions only just holding out and practically surrounded, the sutlers, cavalry, slingers, and Numidians scattered and, fleeing in different directions, came to the conclusion that our position was quite hopeless and hurried back home. There they reported to their government that the Romans had suffered a great defeat and had lost both their camp and baggage train to the enemy.

After speaking to the men of the Tenth Legion, I had set out for our right wing, where I found that our troops were in grave difficulties. The men of the Twelfth Legion had got their standards all bunched together and were huddled so close that they were getting in each other's way. In the fourth cohort every single centurion had been killed; so had the standard-bearer, and the standard had been lost. And in the other cohorts nearly all the centurions had been either wounded or killed. Among these was the senior centurion, Publius Sextius Baculus, a very fine soldier indeed, who had been wounded so often and so badly that he could no longer stand up. The men were clearly losing heart, and there were some in the rear rank who had given up all idea of fighting and thought only of getting out of range.

Meanwhile the enemy in front kept on pouring up the hill and were at the same time pressing us hard on both flanks. It was, as I could see, an extremely critical state of affairs, and I had no reserves available. Having no shield with me, I snatched one out of the hands of a soldier in the rear rank and went forward to the front line. Here I called out to all the centurions by name and shouted encouragement to the rest, ordering them to advance and to open out their ranks so that they would have space to use their swords properly. My arrival put heart into the men and gave them fresh confidence. Each of them, under the eyes of the commander-in-chief, wanted to do his best at whatever risk to himself. And so we managed to slow down the enemy's attack somewhat.

Seeing that the Seventh Legion, which stood close to the Twelfth, was also in difficulty, I ordered the commanding officers to close the gap between the two units and then wheel around so as to form a square. In this way we should be able to resist the enemy from whatever direction they attacked. This maneuver was carried out with the result that our men were now able to give each other support and no longer were in fear of an attack from the rear. They began to stand up with greater confidence to the enemy's attacks and to fight better. Meanwhile the two legions who had been marching at the very rear of the column to guard the baggage had received news of the fighting. They had quickened their pace and could now be seen by the enemy coming over the top of the hill; and Titus Labienus, who had captured the enemy's camp and from its high ground could see what was happening in our own camp, sent back the Tenth Legion to relieve us. The men of the Tenth, seeing the cavalry and the sutlers in full flight, realized how serious the position was and understood the danger threatening the camp, the other legions, and their commander-in-chief. They therefore came up to join us as fast as they possibly could.

Their arrival changed everything. Even the wounded who had fallen to the ground struggled to their feet and began to fight again, supporting themselves on their shields. Then the sutlers, seeing the enemy's loss of nerve, ran to meet them face to face, though the enemy were armed and they were not. The cavalry too were anxious now to show a daring that would wipe out the disgrace of their flight and fought wherever they could, trying to outdo the soldiers of the legions.

The enemy's position was now entirely hopeless, yet they showed quite extraordinary courage. When their front ranks had fallen, those behind stepped forward onto the bodies of the dead and fought from on top of them. When these men also were cut down and the corpses piled up in heaps, the survivors still stood as it were upon a mound, hurling their weapons down at us or catching our javelins and throwing them back again. Indeed one must say that these were people of absolutely outstanding courage. Their daring had carried them across a very broad river, up the steep banks on the other side, and then forward against a strong defensive position. Certainly their spirit must have been great to make light of such difficulties as these.

So ended this battle, by which the name and the nation of the Nervii were virtually wiped out. When its result was known, the old men of the tribe, who as already mentioned had been sent away with the women and children into the marshes and tidal creeks, realized how total was our victory and how defenseless they were in their defeat. With the consent of all the survivors, they sent a deputation to me to offer to surrender. In describing the disaster which had come upon their people, they told me that out of their council of six hundred only three men were still alive and that their military force of sixty thousand had been reduced to barely five hundred. I was anxious to let them see that I was ready to show mercy to them in their distressed and humble state, and so I was most careful to provide for their safety. I told them to keep their lands and their towns, and I ordered the tribes on their frontiers to refrain from doing any damage or injury to them and to see that their dependents also kept their hands off the Nervii.

3 DEFEAT OF
   THE ADUATUCI.

I have already mentioned that the Aduatuci were coming in full force to help the Nervii. Now, on hearing the news of the battle, they marched straight back to their own country. They abandoned all their other towns and strongholds and brought all their property into one town which had remarkably strong natural defenses. It was surrounded by precipices except at one point where it could be approached by a gradual slope. This approach was only two hundred feet wide, and they had fortified it with a double wall of very great height on top of which they were now collecting heavy stones and great beams sharpened to a point.

These Aduatuci were descendants of the Cimbri and Teutons. At the time of their invasion of our province and Italy, they had left the cattle and goods that they could not drive or carry with them on the west bank of the Rhine under the guard of six thousand of their own people. After the destruction of the rest of the Cimbri and Teutons, these six thousand fought for many years with their neighbors, sometimes invading their territory and sometimes defending their own, until in the end peace was made by general agreement and they chose this area as a permanent home.

When our army reached their territory, they at first made a number of sorties from the town and fought a number of minor engagements with our troops. Afterwards, when we had surrounded them with an earthwork twelve feet high and five miles in circumference, with redoubts at frequent intervals, they stayed inside their own fortifications. We brought up our mantlets and began to build a ramp, and soon the enemy could see us erecting a siege tower at a considerable distance from their lines. This sight at first caused them a good deal of amusement. They would stand on their wall and shout insults at us. What on earth, they asked, were we doing, setting up such a huge machine so far away? As a rule, the Gauls look down on us for being so small of stature compared with their own larger selves; and so now they inquired how little creatures like us, with our weak hands and feeble physiques, could possibly imagine that we were going to lift up so massive a tower and place it on top of their wall. However, when they saw the tower actually moving and drawing near to the fortifications, they were completely unnerved. It was something which they had neither seen nor expected to see, and they sent a deputation to me to ask for peace.

"It seems to us," they said, "that you Romans must have divine help in your warfare, since you can move up engines of such a size so quickly. We therefore place ourselves and all that we have at the disposal of Rome. One thing only we pray. If you, Caesar, will act toward us with that mercy and forbearance of which we have been told by others and will grant us our lives, then we beg you not to take away our arms. Nearly all our neighbors are hostile to us and jealous of our courage in war. If we hand over our arms we cannot defend ourselves from them, and we would rather, in such a case, suffer any fate at the hands of Rome than be tortured to death by people whom we have grown accustomed to consider as our inferiors."

I replied that if they surrendered before a battering-ram had touched their walls, I would spare their lives, but that I was showing them mercy rather because it was my nature to be merciful than because they deserved such treatment. I told them that I could not accept their surrender unless their arms were handed over; but I would do for them what I had done for the Nervii and forbid their neighbors to do any harm to them once they had submitted to Rome.

After reporting back to their people, they returned and promised to carry out my instructions. Great quantities of arms were thrown down from the wall into the trench in front of the town—so many, indeed, that the piled-up weapons nearly reached the top of the wall and the level of our ramp. Nevertheless, as we found out afterwards, about a third of their arms had been kept back and hidden in the town. They then opened their gates and enjoyed peace for that day.

In the evening I ordered the gates to be closed and our troops to leave the town, because I did not wish the towns-people to suffer any ill treatment from our soldiers during the night. However, as we discovered later, the townspeople had already made their own plans. They assumed that after the surrender our men would withdraw from their advanced posi-tions or, at any rate, would keep a slacker watch than usual. Some of them were equipped with the arms which they had kept hidden; others made themselves shields out of bark or plaited osiers which they hastily (as everything had to be done in a hurry) covered with skins. Then, soon after mid-night, they suddenly sallied out of the town in full force and attacked our fortifications at the point which they con-sidered easiest to scale. I had already given the necessary instructions for dealing with such an attack. The alarm was quickly given by means of flares, and detachments from the nearest redoubts came running up to the point of danger. The enemy fought fiercely, as was to be expected considering that they were brave men and fighting desperately for their lives. The ground was against them, and we were able to hurl down weapons from our rampart and towers, so that courage was the only thing that could give them any hope of survival. About four thousand of them were killed and the rest forced back into the town. Next day we met with no opposition. The gates were smashed open and the soldiers let in. I sold the whole population of the place by auction in one lot. The purchasers reported that the total number of persons sold came to fifty-three thousand.

About this time I heard from Publius Crassus, whom I had sent with one legion to deal with the tribes on the Atlantic coast—the Veneti, Venelli, Osismi, Curiosolites, Esubii, Aulerci, and Redones. Crassus now reported that all these states had made submission to the power of Rome.

These operations had brought peace to the whole of Gaul.

The accounts of the campaign which reached the natives made such an impression on them that deputations were sent to me from the tribes on the other side of the Rhine, promising to give hostages and to obey whatever orders I might give. As I was anxious to reach Italy and Illyricum as soon as possible, I told these deputations to come back at the beginning of the following summer. The legions were withdrawn to winter quarters among the Carnutes, the Andes, the Turones, and other states near the scenes of our recent operations. I then set out for Italy myself. When my dispatches were received in Rome, a fifteen-day public thanksgiving was decreed. This honor had never previously been given to anyone.

❧ BOOK THREE: 56 B.C. ❧

1 GALBA'S CAMPAIGN IN THE ALPS.

Just before starting for Italy I sent Servius Galba with the Twelfth Legion and a detachment of cavalry into the country of the Nantuates, Veragri, and Seduni, an area which extends from the frontier of the Allobroges, the Lake of Geneva, and the Rhone to the high Alps. The reason for the expedition was that I wanted to open up the route through the Alps which had normally been used by traders but which entailed considerable risks and the payment of heavy tolls. I gave Galba leave to quarter his legion in this district for the winter, if he thought it necessary.

After fighting several successful actions and capturing a number of the enemy's strongholds, Galba received deputations from the whole area, took hostages, and made peace with the tribes. He decided to station two cohorts in the country of the Nantuates and to spend the winter himself with the remaining cohorts of the legion in a village of the Veragri called Octodurus, which lies in a valley with very little level ground around it and is completely shut in by very high mountains. Since a river ran through the middle of the village, Galba gave one half of the village to the Gauls and made them evacuate the other half for the use of his cohorts. This part he fortified with a rampart and a trench.

A few days went by and orders had been given for grain to be brought in, when Galba suddenly received information from his patrols that during the night every single person had moved out of the Gallic part of the village and that the mountains which overhung the valley were occupied by an enormous host of Seduni and Veragri.

There were several reasons why the Gauls had come to this sudden decision to reopen hostilities and attempt to destroy our army. In the first place, they were contemptuous of the numbers of Galba's force. The legion had never been at full strength, and now two cohorts had been withdrawn from it and a number of individual soldiers had been sent off to bring in supplies. Secondly, they considered that we were in a bad position; they would be charging downhill into the valley, hurling their weapons at us from above, and it seemed unlikely that we would be able to stand up even to their first attack. They also resented having their children torn away from them and called "hostages," and they were convinced that the Romans were now attempting to seize the summits of the Alps not simply to secure our trade routes, but to hold forever; that we intended, in fact, to add this part of the world to our neighboring province.

When Galba received this news, his winter camp was still under construction; the fortifications were not fully completed, and no adequate arrangements had been made for the supply of grain and other necessities. This was because after the surrender and the handing over of hostages he had assumed that he had no reason to fear any further hostilities. He now called a council of war and asked those present for their opinions. The danger which had arisen so suddenly and unexpectedly was certainly serious; already nearly all the neighboring heights were packed, as could be seen, with hordes of armed men; the roads were blocked, so that it was impossible for reinforcements to arrive or for supplies to be brought in. Some members of the council therefore considered the situation almost hopeless and were in favor of abandoning the baggage, breaking through the enemy lines, and making for safety by the same road as that by which they had come. However, the majority decided to adopt this plan only as the last resort and meanwhile to await developments and defend the camp. Almost immediately—indeed so soon that they scarcely had time to make the dispositions of troops and other arrangements decided upon—the enemy gave the signal for attack, charged down from all sides, and began to hurl stones and spears at the rampart. At first, while our men were still fresh, they fought back well. Every missile that they hurled down from the rampart found its mark, and if any part of the camp was short of defenders and seemed to be in danger they ran to the threatened spot and brought relief to it. However, they were at a disadvantage compared with the enemy, who when they tired could drop out of the battle and be replaced by fresh troops. We, on the other hand, were too few in numbers to be able to do anything of the kind. Not only was it impossible for a man to drop out of the battle when he was tired; even the wounded had to stand fast and not move from their posts.

The fighting went on continuously for six hours. Our men's strength was failing and their weapons had been nearly all used up. The enemy pressed on more eagerly than ever and, as our men weakened, began to break down the rampart and fill in the trench. The situation was one of the very greatest danger. The senior centurion, Publius Sextius Baculus (whom I mentioned as having been disabled by a number of wounds in the battle with the Nervii), and Gaius Volusenus, a very able officer and a very brave man, hurriedly went to Galba and told him that the only hope of getting away safely was to try their last resource and break through the enemy's lines. So the centurions were called together and the men were quickly given their instructions. They were to pause from fighting for a while, merely defending themselves from the weapons thrown at them. After this rest, the signal would be given and they were to charge out of the camp. Only their courage could save them.

The troops did as they were told. They charged suddenly from each of the four gates of the camp, giving the enemy no chance to realize what was happening or to rally against the attack. Fortune swung round completely. Those who had come in hope of capturing the camp now found they were being assaulted from every side. Of the more than thirty thousand natives known to be in the attack on our camp, over a third were killed; the rest fled in panic and were not allowed to stop running even when they had reached the higher ground. When the entire enemy force was routed, our men stripped the dead bodies of their arms and retired to the fortifications.

After this battle Galba did not dare to take any more chances. He realized that he had involved himself in hazards that were very different from what he had expected when he came into these parts to spend the winter, and he was worried too about the shortage of grain and other supplies. On the next day he set fire to every building in the village and then set out on his return march to the Roman Province. No enemy forces attempted to stop him or to delay his march, and he brought the legion back safely into the country of the Nantuates and from there went on to the country of the Allobroges, where he spent the winter.

2 REVOLT OF THE COASTAL TRIBES.

After these actions I had every reason to believe that Gaul was in a state of peace. The Belgae had been defeated, the Germans driven back over the Rhine, and the Seduni conquered in the Alps. I had therefore set out for Illyria at the beginning of the winter, since I wanted to visit the tribes in that area too and to make myself acquainted with the country. Suddenly, however, war broke out again in Gaul. The reasons for the renewal of hostilities were as follows.

Young Publius Crassus with the Seventh Legion had been in the winter quarters that were nearest the Atlantic, in the territory of the Andes. As there was a shortage of grain in these parts, he had sent out officers of various ranks to the neighboring states to secure supplies. Among others, Titus Terrasidius was sent to the Esubii, Marcus Trebius Gallus to the Curiosolites, Quintus Velanius and Titus Silius to the Veneti.

These Veneti are much the most powerful people in all this part of the coast. They have the biggest fleet in the area and are in the habit of sailing to and from Britain. In the theory and practice of navigation they are superior to all the other tribes. They live on a stretch of open sea which is particularly rough, and as they themselves control the few harbors that exist, they are able to impose taxes on almost all vessels that normally sail in these waters.

It was the Veneti who first took action against us by detaining Silius and Velanius. They hoped in this way to get back their own people whom they had given to Crassus as hostages. It is characteristic of the Gauls to be always taking sudden impulsive decisions, and now the neighbors of the Veneti, influenced by their example and acting for the same reasons, detained Trebius and Terrasidius. Quickly sending messengers from chief to chief, all bound themselves by oath not to act except on mutual agreement and to stand together to meet whatever fortune might bring. They also urged the other tribes in the area to preserve the liberty which they had inherited from their fathers rather than submit to Roman slavery. Soon every tribe along the coast had been won over, and they sent a joint deputation to Publius Crassus telling him to give them back their hostages if he wanted to see his own officers again.

I myself was a long way away from the scene of action when I received the news of these events from Crassus. For the time being I ordered warships to be built in the river Loire, which flows into the Atlantic, crews to be raised in the Province, and steersmen and sailors to be assembled. These orders were quickly carried out, and as soon as the season allowed, I set out myself to join the army. The Veneti and the other states allied with them heard of my arrival. At the same time they began to realize the gravity of the crime which they had committed. The title of envoy has always among all nations been a guarantee of safety; yet they had detained our envoys and thrown them into prison. So now they began to prepare for war on a scale proportionate to the danger with which they were faced. They gave particular attention toward fashioning every kind of provision for their fleet, all the more hopefully because they relied very much on the strength of their position geographically. They knew that on land the roads were intersected by tidal estuaries and that on sea our navigation would be handicapped by our ignorance of local conditions and by the scarcity of harbors. They felt sure too that the mere shortage of grain would prevent our army from staying in their country for long. And even if things turned out quite differently from what they expected, they still had their very formidable sea power, whereas we had no ships available and no knowledge of the shoals, harbors, and islands in the area where fighting would have to take place. They could see too that to carry out naval operations in the vast open spaces of the Atlantic was a very different thing from sailing in a landlocked sea like the Mediterranean.

So, having resolved on their course of action, they fortified their towns, brought into them all the grain from the fields, and assembled as many ships as they could in Venetia, where it was generally believed that I would open hostilities. As allies in this campaign they secured the services of the following tribes: the Osismi, the Lexovii, the Namnetes, the Ambiliati, the Morini, the Diablintes, and the Menapii. They also sent for extra help from Britain, which lies opposite their part of the coast.

In this campaign the difficulties described above were real ones; nevertheless I had many good reasons for undertaking it. High-ranking Romans had been disgracefully deprived of their liberty; war had broken out again after surrender; a revolt had followed the handing over of hostages. There was also the number of states involved in the conspiracy, and in particular there was the danger that, if this part of the country were not dealt with, the other nations too might think that they were at liberty to act in the same way. I was also aware that the average Gaul tends always to be a revolutionary, ready at the slightest provocation to go to war, and I knew that all men naturally love freedom and hate slavery. I therefore thought it advisable to divide my army so that it could cover a larger area before more states could join in the movement against us.

I sent Titus Labienus with a force of cavalry into the country of the Treveri, who live in the Rhineland. He was instructed to keep in contact with the Remi and the other Belgic tribes and to see that they stayed loyal. It was reported that a force of Germans had been called in as auxiliaries by some of the Belgae, and Labienus was ordered to resist them if they built boats and attempted to force a passage of the Rhine. Publius Crassus, with twelve cohorts of regular legionaries and a large cavalry force, was instructed to set out for Aquitania in order to prevent reinforcements being sent from there into Celtic Gaul and an alliance being formed between these two important parts of the country. Quintus Titurius Sabinus was sent with three legions into the country of the Venelli, the Curiosolites, and the Lexovii so as to keep that section of the rebels isolated from the rest. Young Decimus Brutus was given command of our fleet and of the ships which I had already ordered the Pictones, the Santones, and other subjugated tribes to produce. His instructions were to start as soon as possible for the country of the Veneti. I myself marched there with our land forces.

Most of the towns of the Veneti were built at the far ends of long spits or promontories. It was therefore impossible to approach them on foot when the tide rushed in from the sea, as it did regularly every twelve hours; and it was equally difficult to get near such places by way of the sea, because of the danger of our ships running upon shoals at low tide. In both instances, therefore, it was very hard to make a direct assault on these strongholds. In some cases we built huge siege works, great breakwaters as high as their own town walls, to hold back the sea, and in this way succeeded in overpowering them. But they had very great naval resources, and when they began to realize that their position was hopeless, they would bring up numbers of ships, load them with their possessions, and retire to the next fortified town, where they would once again defend themselves with the same advantages of position as before. For most of the summer they were able to pursue these tactics quite easily, since our own ships were held back by bad weather and by the very great difficulties involved in the navigation of this vast open sea, with its strong tides and an almost complete absence of harbors.

The Gauls' own ships were better adapted to the conditions. They were built and rigged as follows: Their bottoms were considerably flatter than those of our ships, so that they were better able to sail over shoals or in the shallow water of ebb tides. Both their prows and sterns were very high and well able to stand up to high seas and great storms. The hulls were made entirely of oak so that they could endure any shock or hard treatment. The cross-timbers consisted of beams a foot thick and were fastened with iron bolts as thick as a man's thumb. The anchors were secured by iron chains instead of ropes. For their sails they used raw hides or thin leather, either because they had no flax or did not know how to use it, or—more probably—because they thought that ordinary sails would not stand the force of great Atlantic storms and squalls or be strong enough for the handling of ships of such great burden. In any encounter between these ships and ours, our one advantage was in speed and in the fact that our ships were propelled by oars; in all other respects their ships were much better adapted to sailing in stormy weather and to the general conditions of that coast. They were so strongly built that we could do them no damage with our rams, and they towered up so high that they were almost out of range of our javelins and, for the same reason, were hard to lay hold of with grappling irons. Then too when a storm arose and they ran before it, they weathered it better than we could and they were able to heave to in shallow water more safely, with no fear of reefs or rocks if left aground by the tide; whereas our ships were in very real danger in all these circumstances.

After I had captured several of their strongholds, I realized that our efforts were simply being wasted. The capture of the towns did not prevent the enemy from escaping, nor was I able in this way to do them any real damage. I therefore decided that I must wait for the arrival of our fleet. As soon as it came into sight, about 220 ships of the enemy, all perfectly equipped and ready for action, sailed out of harbor and took station opposite us. Neither Brutus, who was in command of our fleet, nor the officers and centurions in charge of individual ships, had any very clear idea of what to do or what tactics to adopt. They knew that they could do the enemy no harm by ramming; and even when turrets had been constructed on our ships they were still not as high as the lofty sterns of the native ships, with the result that our javelins, thrown from below, would necessarily be thrown

badly, while those of the Gauls would have an additional
force on impact.

There was one extremely useful piece of apparatus, however,
which our men had got ready beforehand.

Sharp-pointed hooks were fixed into the ends of long poles
—rather like grappling hooks in appearance—and with these
they hooked the halyards which fastened the yards to the
masts. The halyards were first pulled taut and then snapped
when our people rowed their ships hard ahead. Once the
halyards were cut, the yardarms naturally collapsed, and
as the Gallic fleet relied entirely on its sails and rigging, the
result was that the ships lost all power of maneuver. All that
was left was a contest that had to be determined by sheer
fighting ability, and in this our soldiers were easily the superior,
especially as this battle was fought under my own eyes and
those of the whole army, so that every particularly gallant
piece of fighting was bound to be noticed. Our troops occupied
the cliffs and the high ground from which one could get a
good view of the sea.

Once the yardarms of an enemy ship had collapsed, as described, two or three of our ships would come alongside
and our soldiers would vie with one another in storming
their way aboard. After several ships had been taken in this
way, the natives realized what was happening, and as they
could think of no answer to these tactics of ours, tried to
escape by running away. All their ships were already headed
down wind when suddenly there fell such an absolutely dead
calm that they were entirely immobilized. Nothing could
have suited us better, for now we were able to finish the job.
We pursued and boarded their ships one by one, with the
result that only a very few out of their whole fleet managed,
when night came on, to get to shore. The battle had lasted
from ten A.M. until sunset.

The war against the Veneti and the peoples of the coast
was brought to a successful conclusion by this victory. All
their men of military age and indeed all the older men of any
distinction or known ability had been brought together for
the battle, and every available ship too had been concentrated
for this occasion. Thus after their great losses, the survivors
had nothing on which to fall back and no means of defending
their strongholds. They therefore surrendered to me unconditionally. I decided that they should be treated severely, so that
in future the natives should be taught to respect more carefully the laws respecting the rights of envoys. So I had the
whole of their national council put to death and sold the rest as
slaves.

While these operations were going on in the country of the

Veneti, Quintus Titurius Sabinus with the troops which I had given him arrived in the country of the Venelli. The chief of the Venelli, Viridovix, was in supreme command of all the revolted states in that area and had brought together a considerable army. Also in the last few days the Aulerci, Eburovices, and Lexovii had put to death their councilors because they had refused to sanction going to war and had closed their gates against us and joined Viridovix. Then too from all over Gaul a great host of desperadoes and bandits had come together, regarding the prospect of plunder and the delight of fighting as more attractive than their normal work on the land. Sabinus kept inside his camp, which was ideally situated, while Viridovix, who had made his own camp opposite him at a distance of about two miles, every day led out his forces and gave Sabinus an opportunity to fight a pitched battle. Sabinus soon became despised by the enemy and had to undergo a certain amount of criticism even from his own troops; indeed he gave such an impression of being frightened that in the end the Gauls ventured to come right up to our rampart. His reason for behaving as he did was that in his view a subordinate commander ought not to fight an engagement with such an enormous host of the enemy, especially in the absence of his commander-in-chief, unless he has the advantage of position or something happens which gives him an exceptionally good chance of success.

After he had thus established a reputation for cowardice, he selected one of the Gauls serving as auxiliaries, a cunning man who seemed the right person for the job in hand, and with the promise of a large reward, instructed him to go over to the enemy. As soon as he reached the enemy lines, the Gaul pretended he was a deserter, made much of the state of terror in which the Romans found themselves, informed them that Caesar himself was hard pressed by the Veneti, and said that Sabinus was to go to his aid and would be leading the army secretly out of camp on the very next night.

On hearing this, they all clamored for an attack on our camp; this, they said, was a chance of winning a complete victory and it ought not to be lost. In adopting this plan, the Gauls were influenced by many considerations—the hesitation shown by Sabinus in the past few days; the assurances of the deserter; the shortage of food (since they had given inadequate attention to supply); the hopes inspired by the Veneti; and the general willingness of men to believe what they want to believe. All this was enough to make the Gauls so enthusiastic that they would not let Viridovix and the other chiefs leave the council until they had agreed to their arming and marching on our camp at once. When their leaders gave their consent, they were as happy as though they had already won the victory. With bundles of faggots and brushwood for filling up our trench, they all set out against our camp.

The camp was on high ground at the top of a gentle slope about a mile long. Up this slope the enemy ran as fast as they could, so as to give the Romans the least time possible for arming and manning the defenses. By the time they arrived they were out of breath. Sabinus addressed his men and gave them the signal they longed for, ordering a sudden sortie to be made from two of the gates against an enemy still hampered by their bundles. Thanks to our favorable position, to the weariness and inexperience of the enemy, and to the courage of our soldiers, trained as they were in earlier battles, the enemy could not stand up even to the first shock of our attack. They immediately turned and fled. Our men, still quite fresh, followed them up and, hampered and exhausted as the enemy were, killed great numbers of them. Our cavalry rounded up the rest, leaving only a very few who managed to get away.

It so happened that Sabinus heard of our naval victory and I heard of this victory of his at the same time. All the states in the area immediately surrendered to him, for while the Gallic temperament is quick and eager to start a war, they lack the strength of character and resolution necessary for enduring disasters.

3   OPERATIONS IN AQUITANIA
AND ON THE CHANNEL COAST.

About the same time Publius Crassus arrived in Aquitania. As I have already said, Aquitania, both in its geographical extent and in the numbers of its inhabitants, must be considered a third of the whole country of Gaul. Crassus knew well enough that he must proceed with great caution, since he had to fight in a country where a few years previously one of our generals, Lucius Valerius Praeconinus, had been defeated and killed, and from which the proconsul Lucius Mallius had had to retire after losing all his heavy equipment. Crassus therefore made arrangements to assure his grain supply, raised a force of cavalry and of auxiliaries, and then called up individually a number of men with good military records from Toulouse and Narbonne, towns in our Province near the scene of his future operations. He then led his army into the country of the Sotiates.

When this tribe heard of his approach, they got together a large army and a great force of cavalry, in which they were particularly strong, and attacked our column on the march. First their cavalry engaged ours; then, when their horsemen had been driven back and ours were in pursuit, their infantry, which had lain hidden in ambush in a valley, suddenly came into view and renewed the battle, falling on our men while they were scattered and in disorder.

The fighting was fierce and lasted for some time. The Sotiates had the confidence derived from previous victories and believed that the fate of Aquitania depended on them and their courage alone; and our troops were eager to show what they could do under a young general, without their commander-in-chief and without the help of the other legions. In the end, after suffering heavy casualties, the enemy turned and fled. Great numbers of them were killed, and Crassus then marched directly against their main stronghold and began to attack it. Finding that the defenders were prepared to put up a stout resistance, he brought up his mantlets and siege towers. The enemy first attempted a sortie against these works and then succeeded in tunneling up to our rampart and mantlets. The Aquitani are exceedingly good at making tunnels, for in many parts of their country there are copper mines and quarries. However, they found our troops too efficient for them and, realizing that their efforts were coming to nothing, sent a deputation to Crassus and asked him to accept their surrender.

Crassus did so and they handed over their arms to him as ordered. But while our men's attention was fully occupied with all this, Adiatunnus, the enemy commander-in-chief, attempted to break out from another part of the town with six hundred companions all bound to him by an oath of loyalty. The native word for such people is *soldurii*, and they have the following rule of life: They share all the good things of life with the friend to whom they have attached themselves and if this friend meets a violent death they must either die with him or commit suicide. There is no case on record of one who has refused to die after the death of the comrade to whom he has sworn the oath of friendship.

Now a shout was raised from our fortifications opposite the part of the town from which the sortie was being attempted. Our men armed themselves and, after some fierce fighting, Adiatunnus was driven back again. In spite of this, he succeeded in inducing Crassus to accept his surrender on the same terms as the others.

When the arms and hostages had been handed over, Crassus set out for the country of the Vocates and Tarusates. By this time the natives had heard of how a town with strong fortifications and excellent natural defenses had been captured within a day or two of his arrival, and they were thoroughly alarmed. They began to send envoys to all the states in the neighborhood, to form alliances, exchange hostages, and mobilize their forces. They even sent emissaries to the tribes of northern Spain on the Aquitanian frontier, requesting troops and leaders. These Spanish reinforcements enabled them to take the field with an army formidable both in size and in prestige. Their commanders were men who had served under Quintus Sertorius in all his campaigns and were considered to be brilliant and experienced officers. They now began to wage war on Roman lines—carefully choosing their positions, fortifying their camps, and attempting to cut us off from our supplies. Crassus saw what they were doing. He was aware that while his own troops were too few in number for him to be able to disperse them without danger, the enemy could range all over the country, block the roads, and still have enough men left to garrison their camp. As a result of this, grain and other supplies would become, he knew, more and more difficult to obtain, while the enemy's numbers increased every day. He therefore came to the conclusion that he should fight a pitched battle without any further delay. After putting this plan before a council of war and finding that all those present agreed with him, he decided to fight on the following day.

At dawn he led out his whole army and drew it up in two lines, with the auxiliaries in the center. He then waited to see what action the enemy proposed to take. In view of their numbers, their long and proud military record, and the small size of our army, they felt they could safely engage us in battle, but thought it would be better still to win a victory without bloodshed by blocking the roads and cutting us off from supplies. They also planned, if we started to withdraw owing to a shortage of food, to attack us on the march, when our men would be hampered by their baggage and have less spirit for a fight. These plans were approved by the enemy leaders, and therefore they kept themselves inside their camp when our forces were led out.

Crassus saw how matters stood. By showing hesitation, the enemy had given the impression that they were afraid and had made the Romans more eager than ever to fight; our men could be heard saying on all sides that the camp ought to be attacked at once. And so, after addressing the men, Crassus advanced to the assault and the whole army followed enthusiastically.

When they reached the camp, some began to fill up the trenches and others kept up a heavy fire of missiles in an attempt to drive the defenders off the ramparts and the lines of fortification. Crassus had not much confidence in the fighting qualities of his auxiliaries, but by handing up stones and javelins and carrying turf for building a ramp, they succeeded in looking like combat troops. Meanwhile the enemy fought back with courage and resolution, hurling their weapons down on us from above with considerable effect. However, some of our cavalry who had ridden around the camp reported that the far side was not as well defended and was easier to approach. Crassus told his cavalry commanders to stimulate their men by promising them large rewards and then informed them what he wanted done. In accordance with his instructions, they took the cohorts that had been left to guard our camp and were therefore still fresh and led them on a long detour so that they could not be seen from the enemy's camp. While everyone's attention was concentrated on the fighting, they quickly reached the above-mentioned section of the defenses, tore down the fortifications, and gained a firm foothold in the camp before the enemy could clearly see them or understand what was happening.

As the noise of shouting rose from this sector, our men at the other side of the town seemed to gain fresh strength and, as usually happens when victory appears to be in sight, began to press on still more fiercely to the attack. With our troops on all sides, the enemy gave up hope, jumped from the ramparts, and tried to run to safety. Our cavalry pursued them over a perfectly flat plain; of the fifty thousand troops from Aquitania and the Cantabrian country who were known to have formed this army, scarcely one quarter were left alive when, late in the night, our cavalry returned to camp.

As the news of this battle spread, most of the states in Aquitania surrendered to Crassus and sent hostages of their own accord. Among these states were the Tarbelli, Bigerriones, Ptianii, Vocates, Tarusates, Elusates, Gates, Ausci, Garumni, Sibuzates, and Cocosates. A few of the more remote tribes, relying on the approach of winter to save them, failed to make submission.

At about the same time, although the summer was nearly over, I led my army against the Morini and Messapii. While all the rest of Gaul was subdued, these tribes still remained under arms and had never sent ambassadors to ask for peace. I imagined that the campaign against them would be a short

one. However, they at once employed tactics that were quite
different from those of the other Gauls. They had seen how
the strongest tribes had been utterly defeated by us in the
open field, and so they withdrew with all their possessions
into an area of their country which consisted of nothing but
forests and marshes. I reached the outskirts of these forests
and, having seen no sign of the enemy so far, began to build
a camp. But when our men were busy on this work and dispersed in different directions, the enemy made a sudden
attack on us, rushing out of the woods on all sides. Our men
quickly took up arms and drove them back into the woods
again, killing quite a number. But we also suffered a few
losses through pressing the pursuit too far over this very
difficult country.

The succeeding days were spent in cutting down the forests.
To prevent any flank attack on our men when they were unarmed and unprepared for fighting, we used the timber that
had been cut as a barrier against the enemy, stacking it up
like a rampart on each side of us. Work was done at incredible
speed and in a few days a huge area had been cleared. The
enemy were going farther and farther into the woods, but
we had already caught up with their cattle and the rear of
their baggage column when the weather turned so bad that
we were forced to put an end to operations. Rain fell without
cease, and it was impossible to keep the troops any longer
under canvas. We devastated the enemy's cultivated land and
set fire to their villages and farm buildings. Then I led the army
back and quartered it for the winter in the countries of the
Aulerci, the Lexovii, and the other tribes with whom we had
been recently at war.

✍ *BOOK FOUR: 55 B.C.* ಲ

1   GERMAN INVASION OF GAUL.
THE ROMANS CROSS THE RHINE.

In the following winter (the one in which Pompey and Marcus Crassus entered upon their consulship), two German tribes, the Usipetes and the Tencteri, crossed the Rhine in large numbers at a point not far from its mouth. Their reason for making this move was because for the last few years they had been constantly attacked by the Suebi and so prevented from cultivating their own land.

The Suebi are much the largest and most warlike of all the German nations. They are said to consist of a hundred clans, from each of which they draw every year a thousand men to be used as warriors fighting outside their frontiers. The rest, who stay at home, support both the army and themselves, and in the following year take their turn at military service, while the others stay at home. In this way their lands are cultivated without interruption and they are also continually trained and practiced in war. They have no private ownership of land, and it is their rule not to settle down and stay in any one place for more than a year. They do not use grain much for food, but live chiefly on milk and meat and spend a lot of time in hunting. Their diet, regular exercise, and the fact that they are their own masters—for from their earliest years they are without any training in discipline or duty to others and never do anything contrary to their inclination—all this makes them men of great strength and enormous size. And, though they live in an extremely cold climate, they make a practice of bathing in the rivers and of wearing nothing in the way of clothes except skins, which are so scanty that they leave a great part of the body naked.

They allow traders into their country, but this is rather because they want to find purchasers for their booty than because they are particularly anxious to import anything from abroad. It is interesting to note that while the Gauls are extremely fond of horses and will pay huge prices for them, the Germans use no imported horses at all. Instead, they stick to their own breed of the animal—small, ugly creatures— and, by giving them regular training, make them remarkably tough and efficient. In cavalry engagements they often jump from their horses and fight on foot, the horses being trained to stand still meanwhile so that the warrior can remount quickly if need be. According to their way of thought, the use of a saddle is thoroughly disgraceful and effeminate. Consequently, however few they may be, they will confidently attack any body of saddled horsemen however large. They allow no wine to be imported, because they think that wine makes men soft and effeminate and incapable of enduring hardship.

They think that the greatest glory a nation can have is to keep as broad a belt as possible of uninhabited land across their frontiers, since this, in their view, is an indication that great numbers of other states are unable to stand up to them in war. So, for example, it is said that on one side of the Suebic territory one will find nearly six hundred miles of country which is uninhabited. On another side their nearest neighbors are the Ubii, who were once, by German standards, a large and prosperous nation. The Ubii are rather more civilized than the other German tribes. They live on the Rhine, are often visited by traders, and, being so close to Gaul, have themselves been influenced by the Gallic way of life. The Suebi have made frequent attempts to drive them from their country by force of arms, but have found them too strong and too numerous to be able to do so. Nevertheless they have forced the Ubii to pay tribute and made them much weaker and less important than they were before.

The above-mentioned Usipetes and Tencteri were in the same position. They had stood up to attacks from the Suebi for many years, but in the end had been driven out of their country, had wandered about in various parts of Germany for three years, and had reached the Rhine. The point at which they reached the river was in the territory of the Menapii, who had lands, buildings, and villages on both banks. The Menapii had been alarmed at the approach of such a vast horde, had evacuated their settlements on the right bank, and had posted detachments of troops along the left to prevent the Germans from crossing. The Germans did everything they could to get across, but failed. They could not force a passage because they had no boats, and the Menapian patrols prevented them from getting across by stealth. They therefore pretended that they were going back again to their own home country, marched a three-day journey in that direction, and then turned back again toward the Rhine. Their cavalry did the whole of the return journey in a single night and caught the Menapii entirely off guard. Scouts had informed the Menapii of the German withdrawal, and they had crossed the Rhine again and returned to their own villages without any apprehension. They were now killed by the Germans, who then seized their ships and got across the Rhine before the other half of the Menapii, on the left bank, knew what was happening. The Germans seized all their buildings and lived on their supplies of food for the rest of the winter.

When I received a report of these events, I was somewhat worried at the thought of the Gauls' instability. They are always making one plan after another and in general always want to change the existing regime. In my view it was impossible to rely on them at all. For example, it is a common habit of theirs to force travelers to stop, whether they like it or not, and question them on what rumors they have heard or what facts they know about each and every subject of interest; and in the towns crowds will gather round any trader who arrives and compel him to say where he comes from and what the news is there. It is often on the basis of information of this sort that they are induced to make quite important decisions, which immediately afterward they are bound to regret, since they are the slaves of baseless rumors and most of those whom they question merely make up stories which they think likely to please them.

I was aware of these characteristics of theirs, and not wanting to have to face a still more serious campaign, I set out to join the army earlier than usual. On my arrival, I found that my suspicions had been justified. Some states had sent deputations to the Germans inviting them to leave the Rhineland and promising to supply them with everything they needed. With this encouragement, the Germans were spreading over a wider area and had now reached the country of the Eburones and the Condrusi, who are dependents of the Treveri. I summoned a meeting of the Gallic chieftains but considered it best not to tell them of what I knew. Instead, I merely spoke some reassuring words of encouragement and told them to produce cavalry contingents for the campaign which I proposed to conduct against the Germans.

After arranging for the food supply and choosing the cavalry I wanted, I began to march into the country where the Germans were reported to be. I was already within a few days'

march of them when they sent a deputation to me with the
following message:

> We Germans have no wish to begin a war with the Roman
> people, but we are perfectly prepared to fight if provoked,
> since it is an ancestral custom of ours to resist any attack that
> is made upon us and never to refuse battle. We wish, however,
> to point out that we came to Gaul not by choice but because
> we were driven out of our homes. If you Romans wish to earn
> our gratitude, you will find us good friends. Either give us
> land or allow us to keep the land which we have won by con-
> quest. We ourselves acknowledge no superiors except the Suebi,
> and not even the immortal gods are as strong as they are. But
> on earth there is no other people whom we cannot conquer.

To all this I made what seemed to me a suitable reply. I
concluded by saying that I could not retain friendly relations
with them if they stayed in Gaul; that it was unreasonable to
suppose that because they had failed to protect their own land,
they were justified in seizing land that belonged to others; that
in any case there was no land in Gaul that could be given to
them without doing an injustice to others, especially considering their enormous numbers. I told them, however, that I
should be quite willing for them to settle, if they wished to do
so, in the country of the Ubii, whose representatives were in
my camp complaining of how they had been treated by the
Suebi and asking me for help; and I promised that I would give
the necessary orders to the Ubii.

The representatives who had been sent to me said that they
would report back to their people and, after my proposals had
been discussed, would return to me in three days' time. Meanwhile they asked me not to move my camp any nearer to them.
I told them that I was unable to grant this request, either. In
fact I knew that some days previously they had sent a large
detachment of cavalry across the Meuse into the country of
the Ambivariti to bring in plunder and supplies; and I thought
that their reason for delaying matters was because they were
waiting for this cavalry force to get back.

The Meuse rises in the Vosges Mountains, in the country of
Lingones. Into it flows a tributary from the Rhine, called the
Waal, and forms the island of the Batavi. The Meuse itself
flows into the Rhine about seventy-five miles from the sea.
The Rhine rises in the country of the Lepontii, an Alpine
tribe. On its long, swift course it flows through the territories
of the Nantuates, Helvetii, Sequani, Mediomatrices, Triboci,
and Treveri. As it nears the ocean it splits into several streams,
forming a number of large islands. Many of these are in-

habited by fierce savage tribes, some of whom are believed to live simply on fish and birds' eggs. The Rhine has many mouths through which it flows into the ocean.

I was no more than twelve miles away from the enemy when their representatives returned to me, as had been agreed. They met me when we were actually on the march and earnestly begged me not to advance any further. I refused this request, and they then asked me to send word to the cavalry at the head of our column, telling them not to engage in battle. They also asked me to give them a chance of sending a deputation to the Ubii and declared that they would accept my suggestion of settling there, provided that the chiefs and council of the Ubii would give them sworn guarantees. They wanted me to allow them three days for completing these arrangements. I regarded all this as a mere pretext with the same object as before, namely to secure an interval of three days, in which time their cavalry detachment could get back again. However, I told them that on that day I would only go four miles further —as I should have to do to get water. I asked them to meet me at this point on the following day with as many of their tribesmen as possible so that I might hear exactly what their proposals were. Meanwhile I sent instructions to the officers in command of the cavalry (the whole cavalry force was in the vanguard), telling them not to attack the enemy and if attacked themselves to hold on until I arrived with the main army.

Our cavalry numbered five thousand, while the enemy had no more than eight hundred, since the force that had crossed the Meuse to get provisions had not yet returned. Nevertheless, as soon as our cavalry came into sight, the enemy attacked them. Our men, who imagined that they had nothing to fear, since the enemy deputation had only just left me and had begged a truce for that day, were quickly thrown into confusion. When they turned and tried to make a stand, the Germans, following their usual practice, jumped down and unseated a number of our men by stabbing their horses in the belly. They put the rest to flight, driving them on in such a state of panic that they did not stop until they came in sight of our army on the march. Seventy-four of our cavalry were killed in this action, including Piso, a very gallant Aquitanian. He came from a most distinguished family; his grandfather had been king of his tribe and had received from our senate the title "Friend." When his brother was surrounded by the enemy, Piso succeeded in rescuing him, but his own horse was wounded and he was thrown. He fought back most gallantly as long as he could, but he was surrounded on all sides and fell after receiving a number of wounds. His brother, who had escaped from the fighting and was some way off, saw him fall; he put spurs to his horse, rode straight at the enemy, and was killed.

After this battle I realized that I was dealing with an enemy who was capable of treacherously launching an unprovoked attack just after they had asked for peace. There seemed no good reason for receiving any more deputations from them or accepting any proposals they might make. I considered too that it would be folly to wait for their cavalry to return and their forces to be increased. Knowing, as I did, the instability of the Gallic character, I was aware that the enemy had already made a great impression on them by this one battle. I concluded that I must allow the enemy no time for making further plans and, having reached this decision, informed the senior officers of my staff that I proposed to bring the enemy to battle without wasting a single day.

We then had a great stroke of luck. Early next morning a large party of Germans, including all their chieftains and the elders of the tribes, came to visit me at our camp. They were following their usual methods of treachery and deceit, for, though they claimed to have come in order to make excuses for their action on the previous day (when they had broken the agreement they themselves had asked for by launching an attack on us), they aimed too at deceiving me so that I would grant them an extension of the truce. I was delighted to find them in my power and ordered them to be kept under arrest. I then led the whole army out of camp, with the cavalry bringing up the rear, since I thought its morale had been shaken by its recent defeat.

Marching in three parallel columns, we advanced for eight miles and covered the distance so quickly that we reached the German camp before the Germans could have any idea of what was happening. What with the speed of our advance and the absence of their own leaders, everything filled them with a sudden panic; they had no time to think or to prepare for battle and were too confused to be able to decide whether it was best to march out against us, defend the camp, or run for their lives. Their terror was quite obvious from the way in which they were running about and shouting, and our men, furious about the treachery of the previous day, burst into their camp. Here those of them who could get hold of their arms quickly stood up to us for a short time, fighting among their carts and baggage wagons. However, there remained a great crowd of women and children—since the Germans had brought everything they had with them when they crossed the Rhine. These now began to flee in all directions, and I sent the cavalry after them to hunt them down. The Germans heard the noise of shouting behind their backs and could see how their own people were being slaughtered. They threw away their arms, abandoned their standards, and came rushing out of the camp. When they reached the confluence of the Moselle and the Rhine, they saw that there was no hope of escaping further. Great numbers were killed and the rest hurled themselves into the river and perished there, overcome by panic, exhaustion, and the force of the current.

Our men returned to camp without a single fatal casualty and only a very few wounded. We were relieved from the fear of what might have been a most arduous campaign, for the enemy had numbered 430,000. As for the Germans held under arrest in our camp, I gave them permission to leave, but they were terrified of being killed or tortured by the Gauls whose land they had devastated, and said that they would prefer to stay with me. I allowed them to retain their liberty.

Now that this German war was over, I decided that it would be a good thing for many reasons to cross the Rhine. My chief reason was that I wanted the Germans—who, as I saw, were only too ready to cross over into Gaul—to begin to have some worries of their own, as they would when they realized that a Roman army had both the daring and the ability to make the crossing. I was also concerned about the cavalry detachment of the Usipetes and Tencteri which, as already mentioned, had crossed the Meuse to bring in plunder and grain and had taken no part in the battle. After the rout of their people, they had retired across the Rhine into the country of the Sugambri and had joined forces with them. I had sent messengers to the Sugambri to demand the surrender of all those who had made war against me and against Gaul. They had replied that the Rhine marked the boundary of Roman sovereignty. If, they said, I thought that the Germans had no right to cross into Gaul without my permission, then how could I claim to exercise any power or authority on the German side of the river?

Finally there was the question of the Ubii—the only tribe across the Rhine which had sent representatives to me, entered into a friendly alliance, and given hostages. The Ubii were now asking me most urgently to come to their help against the Suebi, who were exercising severe pressure on them. They said that if concerns of state made this impossible, it would be enough for me to bring my army to the other side of the Rhine. This in itself would be sufficient help to them and would give them sufficient confidence for the future. According to them the effect of the defeat of Ariovistus and of this latest victory of ours had been such that our army was known and feared even among the remotest peoples of Germany; merely to have it known that they enjoyed our friendship would be enough to keep them safe. They promised to provide large numbers of boats for transporting the army across the river.

These were the reasons which made me decide to cross the Rhine. But I came to the conclusion that to make the crossing by means of boats would involve too many risks and would be a less impressive achievement than what was demanded for my own prestige and that of the Roman people. It was true that, because of the breadth and depth of the river and the swiftness of the current, there were very great difficulties in the way of building a bridge. Nevertheless I felt that this was what I must try to do, or else not take the army across at all. We therefore began to construct our bridge on the following plan. Two piles, eighteen inches thick, slightly pointed at the lower ends and of lengths varying in accordance with the depth of the river, were fastened together two feet apart; they were then lowered into the river from rafts, fixed firmly in the riverbed, and driven home with piledrivers. Instead of being driven in vertically, as piles usually are, they were fixed obliquely, leaning in the direction of the current. Opposite these again, and forty feet downstream, another pair of piles was fixed and coupled together in the same way, though this time they slanted forward against the force of the current. The two pairs of piles were then joined by a beam, two feet wide, the ends of which fitted exactly into the spaces between the two piles of each pair. The pairs were kept apart from each other by braces which secured each pile to the end of the crossbeam. The piles were thus both held apart and, in a different sense, clamped together. The whole structure was strong and so adapted to the forces of nature that the greater the strength of the current, the more tightly locked were the timbers. A series of these trestles was pushed across the river. They were connected with each other by timbers set at right angles, on top of which were laid poles and bundles of sticks. Moreover, an extra set of piles was fixed obliquely on the downstream side of the bridge; these were connected with the main structure and acted as buttresses to take the force of the stream. Other piles were fixed vertically in the riverbed a little way upstream from the bridge so that if the natives attempted to destroy it by floating tree trunks or ships down the river, this row of barriers would lessen their force and save the bridge from being damaged.

Ten days after we had started to collect the timber, the whole work had been finished and the army led across. I left a strong guard at each end of the bridge and then marched into the country of the Sugambri. Meanwhile deputations ar-

THE FIRST INVASION OF BRITAIN

rived from several states, asking for peace and friendship. I
replied courteously to these deputations and told them to have
hostages sent to me. As to the Sugambri, they had been preparing for flight ever since the moment we started to build the
bridge. They had been advised to follow this course by the
Tencteri and Usipetes who were with them, and so had evacuated their territory and, taking all their property with them,
had disappeared into the uninhabited forests. I spent a few
days in their country, burning all their villages and buildings
and cutting down their crops.

Then we moved into the country of the Ubii. After I had
promised to help them in the event of their being attacked by
the Suebi, I received from them the following information:
As soon as the Suebi had been told by their scouts that we
were building a bridge, they had, as is their usual custom
when threatened, summoned a national council and sent messengers to all parts of their country, ordering everyone to
leave the towns and to take their women, children, and property to safe places within the forests. Meanwhile all who were
of military age were to assemble in one place—a place which
was, according to the Ubii, in about the middle of the country
occupied by the Suebi. It was here that they had decided to
fight us and here they were waiting for us to arrive.

At the time I received this information I had already ac-
complished all the objects that had made me decide to lead
the army across the Rhine: the Germans had been intimidated, the Sugambri punished, and the Ubii relieved from the
pressure exercised on them by the Suebi. Altogether we had
spent eighteen days across the Rhine and had done, I thought,
all that honor or interest required. We therefore withdrew to
Gaul, breaking up the bridge behind us.

2 THE FIRST INVASION OF BRITAIN.

Not much of the summer was now left, and winter sets in early
in these regions because all this side of Gaul faces north.
Nevertheless I went ahead with plans for an expedition to
Britain. I knew that in nearly all of our campaigns in Gaul,
help had come to the enemy from Britain. Even if we should
have too short a time this season for conducting a full campaign, it seemed to me that it would be well worth while
merely to have visited the island, to have seen what sort of
people the inhabitants were, and to have gained some knowl-

edge of the country, its harbors and facilities for landing. The
Gauls knew next to nothing of these things, since no one as a
rule goes to Britain at all except traders, and these traders
are themselves only acquainted with the seacoast and coastal
regions directly opposite Gaul. So, though I made inquiries of
all the traders I could find, I could get no information concerning the size of the island, the names and populations of
the tribes inhabiting it, their methods of warfare, their system
of government, or the harbors that could accommodate a
large fleet of big ships. I naturally wanted to be informed on
all these subjects before venturing on the expedition, and so I
sent Gaius Volusenus in advance with a warship, thinking
him the best man available for the job. He was ordered to
make all the necessary inquiries and then come back to me as
soon as he could.

I myself with the whole army started for the country of the
Morini, from which there is the shortest crossing to Britain.
Here I ordered all the ships to assemble from the neighboring
districts, together with the fleet which I had built last summer
for the Venetian campaign.

Meanwhile my plans had become known. Traders had carried the news across to the Britons, and from several British
states deputations came to me with promises to give hostages
and to submit to the authority of Rome. I heard what they
had to say, promised to give the most favorable consideration
to their requests, and urged them on their side to keep their
word. When I sent them back home, I sent Commius with
them. It was Commius whom I had myself made king of the
Atrebates after I had subdued that tribe. I had a high opinion
of his courage and of his good sense; I believed that he was
loyal to me; and it was said that he had much influence in
Britain. I told him to visit as many states as he could, to urge
them to seek Roman protection, and to inform them that I
myself would soon be among them.

Volusenus carried out as full a reconnaissance of the coast
as was possible, considering the fact that he did not venture
to disembark and put himself in the power of the natives. Five
days later he returned to me and gave me his report.

While I was in this part of the country waiting for the ships
to be got ready, deputations came to me from a large section
of the Morini in order to apologize for their policy of last
year. It was, they said, only because of their lack of civiliza-
tion and their ignorance of our ways that they had made war
on Rome, and they promised that in the future they would
carry out any orders I might give them. All this, I thought, had
happened most fortunately for me. I had no wish to leave an
enemy in my rear; yet there was not time this year to carry

out a full campaign; and in any case I thought that the expedition to Britain was much more important than the settlement of these rather trivial matters. So I ordered the Morini to produce a large number of hostages and, when these had been delivered, I accepted the submission of the tribe.

By now we had secured about eighty transports and had them concentrated at one point. This was enough, in my opinion, to carry across two legions. There were also a number of warships which I entrusted to the quaestor, the generals, and the commanders of auxiliary troops. In addition to these ships, we had eighteen transports which were prevented by contrary winds from reaching the same harbor as the rest. They were eight miles further along the coast, and I allotted them to the cavalry. I handed over the rest of the army to the generals Quintus Titurius Sabinus and Lucius Aurunculeius Cotta, with orders to march against the Menapii and against those clans of the Morini which had not sent deputations to me. Another general, Publius Sulpicius Rufus, was ordered to guard the harbor and was given a force which I considered large enough for this job.

When all these arrangements had been made, we found the weather favorable for sailing and put to sea about midnight. The cavalry had been ordered to proceed to the northern port, embark, and follow after us. However, they were rather too slow about doing this and failed to catch the tide. I myself, with the leading ships, reached Britain about nine A.M. We could see the enemy's armed forces lined up all along the cliffs. At this point there was a narrow beach with high hills behind it, so that it was possible to hurl weapons down from the higher ground onto the shore. It seemed to me an extremely bad place to effect a landing, and so we waited at anchor until about three thirty P.M. for the rest of the ships to join us. During this time I summoned the generals and high-ranking officers, informed them of what I had learned from Volusenus, and told them what I wanted done. I warned them that the tactical demands of warfare in general—and especially so on sea, where things can happen quickly and unpredictably —require that orders must be carried out instantly and on the spot. The meeting was then dismissed. We had both the wind and the tide in our favor; the signal was given to weigh anchor and, after moving on about eight miles, we ran the ships ashore on an open, evenly shelved beach.

The natives, however, had realized what we planned to do. They had sent their cavalry and their chariots (a type of weapon which they nearly always use in battle) on ahead. The rest of their troops followed behind, and they now stood ready to oppose our landing. Things were very difficult for us indeed, and for the following reasons. Our ships were too big to be run ashore except where the water was deep; the troops knew nothing of the ground on which they were to fight and not only had their hands full but were weighed down by the heavy armor which they carried; they had to jump down from the transports, get a footing in the surf, and fight the enemy all at the same time. The enemy, on the other hand, were quite unencumbered and knew the ground well. Either standing on dry land or going a little way into the water, they hurled their weapons boldly at us and spurred on their horses, which were trained for this sort of fighting. All this had a most disturbing effect on our men. They had no experience at all of this sort of warfare, and they failed to show the fire and enthusiasm which could always be expected of them in battles on land.

When I saw what the situation was I ordered the warships— which were swifter and easier to handle than the transports and at the same time were of a shape which the natives had scarcely ever seen before—to move clear of the transports, to row forward at full speed and then run ashore on the enemy's exposed flank; from this position they were to make use of slings, arrows, and artillery to drive the enemy back and clear the beach. This maneuver proved to be extremely useful to us. The natives were greatly disturbed by the shape of the ships, the moving of the oars, and the strange machines used as artillery. They came to a halt and then fell back, though only a little way. Then, as our men still hesitated, chiefly because of the depth of the water, the man who carried the eagle of the Tenth Legion, after praying to the gods that what he was going to do would bring good luck to the legion, shouted out in a loud voice: "Come on, men! Jump, unless you want to lose your eagle to the enemy. I, in any case, will do my duty to my country and to my general." He then threw himself from the ship and began to go toward the enemy, carrying the eagle with him. He was followed by all the rest, who jumped into the sea together, shouting out to each other that they must not disgrace themselves by losing their eagle. When the men from the next ships saw them, they followed their example and also began to move toward the enemy.

Now both sides fought fiercely. Among our men, however, there was considerable disorder, since it was impossible for them to keep ranks, stand firmly in position, or follow proper standards; in fact, as they came to land from the ships each man attached himself to the first standard he came across. The enemy knew all the shallows; and when they saw from the beach any party of our men disembarking one by one from a ship, they spurred their horses into the water and attacked while we were at a disadvantage and they could swarm around a few of us at a time in superior numbers; and others meanwhile hurled their weapons at the exposed flank of whole units which had formed up together. Seeing what was going on, I had troops put aboard the warships' boats and the small craft used for reconnaissance, and sent these up in support wherever I saw that our men were in difficulty. As soon as our forces had gained a firm footing on shore and their comrades had formed up behind them, they charged and put the enemy to flight. However, they could not pursue them for any distance, because the cavalry transports had been unable to hold course and reach the island. This was the one thing that prevented me from enjoying my usual good luck.

When the defeated enemy had re-formed after the rout, they lost no time in sending a deputation to me asking for peace and promising to give hostages and obey any orders I might give them. With this deputation came Commius the Atrebatian, whom, as mentioned above, I had sent on ahead to Britain. When he had disembarked from his ship and had begun to give my message to the Britons in the capacity of an official envoy, the natives had seized and chained him. Now, after the battle, they sent him back and in asking for peace laid the blame for what had been done on the common people and begged me to forgive them on the grounds of ignorance. I told them that I took a serious view of their action in launching an unprovoked attack against us after they themselves had sent envoys to the Continent to ask me for peace; nevertheless, I said, I would forgive their ignorance; and I ordered them to deliver hostages.

Some of these hostages were handed over at once; the rest, they said, would have to be fetched from a distance, and they promised to produce them in a few days' time. Meanwhile they ordered their men to get back to work on the land, and chieftains began to come in from all parts of the country in order to put themselves and their tribes under my protection. In this way peace was established.

Four days after our arrival in Britain, the eighteen ships which, as already mentioned, had taken the cavalry aboard, set sail with a gentle breeze behind them from the northern port. But as they approached the shores of Britain and could be seen from our camp, suddenly such a violent storm arose that none of them could hold course. Some were carried back to the harbor from which they had set out; others, at great peril to themselves, were swept southward toward the westerly part of the island. In spite of the danger they dropped anchor, but began to ship so much water that they were forced to put out to sea again in the darkness and make for the Continent.

That night there happened to be a full moon. Though we were unaware of the fact, it is at this period of the month that one gets the highest tides in the Atlantic. So it happened that the warships used for the crossing, which had been dragged up on the beach, became waterlogged; and the transports, which were riding at anchor, were badly knocked about by the storm. It was impossible for our men to handle them or do anything to help. A number of ships broke up; the rest, after losing cables, anchors, and rigging, were rendered useless. The whole army, naturally enough, was filled with consternation. There were no other ships in which to make the return voyage, and we had with us none of the necessary materials for refitting. It had been generally assumed, too, that we were going to spend the winter in Gaul, and so no arrangements had been made for bringing grain supplies to Britain for the winter.

The British chieftains who had assembled at my headquarters after the battle saw our predicament and began to hatch plots together. They knew that we were without cavalry, grain, and ships, and they saw how few we were in number from the small size of our camp—which was all the smaller because I had brought the legions across without their heavy equipment. They therefore decided that the best thing to do was to renew hostilities, cut us off from grain and other supplies, and prolong the campaign into the winter. They felt sure that if we were either conquered in war or cut off from returning, no one in the future would attempt another invasion of Britain. So they once again exchanged oaths of loyalty, began to slip away one by one from our camp, and secretly called up again their men who had returned to work on the land.

I had not yet learned what their plans were. All the same, from what had happened to our ships and from the fact that the natives had stopped bringing in hostages, I had a suspicion that things would turn out as, in fact, they did. I therefore tried to be ready to meet any situation that might arise. Grain was brought into camp every day from the countryside. Timber and bronze from the most seriously damaged ships were used to repair the rest, and other materials for such work were ordered to be brought from the Continent. The soldiers worked magnificently, and though twelve ships were lost we were able to make all the others tolerably seaworthy.

While this work was going on, one legion had been sent out as usual to bring in grain. On this particular day it was the Seventh Legion. Up to this time we had had no reason to suspect that the enemy would renew hostilities, since many of them were still working in the fields and others actually used to visit us quite frequently in the camp. But now the guards on duty at the camp gates reported to me that an unusually large cloud of dust could be seen in the direction in which the legion had gone. I guessed what had happened—the natives had made some surprise move against us—and ordered the cohorts on guard duty to set out with me. Two other cohorts were detailed to take their place on guard and all the rest were instructed to arm and follow us at once. When we had gone forward some way from the camp I could see that our men were up against severe enemy pressure and were only just managing to hold out; the legion was crowded close together and under fire from every side.

What had happened was this. Since the grain in this area had all been cut except for what was in one place, the enemy had assumed that this was where our men would go and had hidden in the woods during the night. Then when our men, their arms laid aside, were scattered and busy reaping, they suddenly burst out on them, killed a few, and threw the rest into confusion before they could form up in proper order, swarming around them with cavalry and chariots.

The tactics employed by these charioteers are as follows: First they drive in every direction, hurling their javelins. Very often the sheer terror inspired by the galloping horses and the noise of the wheels throws their opponents into a state of confusion. They then make their way through the squadrons of their own cavalry, leap down from the chariots, and fight on foot. Meanwhile the drivers retire a little from the battle and halt the chariots in a suitable position so that, if those who are now fighting on foot are hard pressed by the enemy, they will have an easy means of retreating to their own lines. So in their battles they combine the mobility of cavalry with the stamina of infantry. Daily training and practice have brought them to a remarkable state of efficiency. They are able, for example, to control their horses at full gallop on the steepest slopes, to pull them up and turn them in a moment, to run along the pole, stand on the yoke, and dart back again into the chariot.

Our men were quite unnerved by this kind of fighting, which was so unfamiliar to them, and I came to their rescue just in time. For the enemy halted when they saw us coming and our men recovered from their terror. However, once this result had been achieved, I decided that this was not the time for provoking battle and joining in a general engagement. I therefore stayed where I was and, after a short interval, led the legions back to camp. All this kept the whole of our army fully occupied, and during this time the remaining natives who had been working in the fields made off and disappeared.

There followed several days of continuous bad weather,

which kept our men in camp and also prevented the enemy from attacking us. But during these days the natives sent out messengers all over the country. These messengers told the people that we had only a small number of troops and pointed out that there was now an excellent opportunity not only of getting plunder but of securing their freedom for all time, if they could once drive us out of our camp. In this way they soon assembled a large force of infantry and cavalry and marched up to our fortifications.

I realized that the result was likely to be what it had been before—that, even if we defeated them, they would be able to use their speed to get away safely. However, I now had about thirty cavalrymen, brought over by Commius, the Atrebatian mentioned above, so I drew the legions up in line in front of the camp. Battle was joined. The enemy, unable to stand up to our attack for long, turned and fled. We pursued them on foot as far as we had strength to do so and killed quite a number. Then we set on fire all the buildings in the neighborhood and returned to camp.

That same day the enemy sent a deputation to ask for peace. I told them that they must deliver twice the number of hostages as before and that these must be sent to the Continent. This was because the equinox was close at hand and, with the ships damaged as they were, I did not think it right to risk sailing in wintry weather. So, with a favorable wind to help us, we set sail soon after midnight and reached the Continent safely with the whole fleet.

Two of the transports, however, were unable to make the same harbor as the rest and were carried a little farther south. About three hundred troops disembarked from these ships and began to march toward our camp. Some of the Morini (the tribe whom I had left in a state of peace when I started for Britain), thinking they saw a chance of plunder, surrounded our men, at first in not very large numbers, and told them to lay down their arms if they did not want to be killed. Our men formed into a square and defended themselves, but soon they were encircled by about six thousand natives who had been attracted by the noise of shouting. When I heard what was happening I sent all our cavalry out of camp to go to their relief. Meanwhile our men held out, fighting with the utmost bravery for more than four hours: they killed many of the enemy and themselves sustained a few wounds. As soon as our cavalry came into sight, the enemy threw away their arms and fled. We killed a great number of them.

Next day I sent Titus Labienus with the legions that had returned from Britain against the Morini who had thus re-opened hostilities against us. The marshes to which they had retreated in the previous year were now dried up, and they had nowhere to take refuge; consequently almost all surrendered to Labienus.

Quintus Titurius and Lucius Cotta had led their legions into the country of the Menapii, but found that the enemy had gone into hiding in an area of dense forests. So they returned to headquarters after having laid waste all the enemy's fields, cut down their crops, and burned their buildings.

I arranged for all the legions to camp for the winter in the country of the Belgae. Only two of the British tribes sent the hostages I had demanded; the rest failed to do so.

On receiving my dispatches with an account of these achievements, the senate decreed a public thanksgiving of twenty days.

✑ BOOK FIVE: 54 B.C. ✑

1 THE SECOND INVASION OF BRITAIN.

In the consulship of Lucius Domitius and Appius Claudius, before setting out from winter quarters to Italy as I did every year, I instructed the generals whom I had left in command of the legions to have the old fleet repaired and to arrange for the building of as many new ships as possible during the winter. I told them exactly how I wanted these new ships to be built. So that they could be loaded quickly and beached easily, I had them made with a rather lower freeboard than is usual in the Mediterranean; this seemed safe enough, since I had noticed that in the Channel, owing to the frequent ebb and flow of the tides, the waves are comparatively small. So that they could carry a large cargo, which would include numerous animals, I had the ships made rather broader than those we normally use in other waters. They were all to be fitted both with sails and with oars; and this was made all the easier because of their low freeboard. Materials for equipping the ships were to be brought from Spain.

I myself, as soon as I had finished dealing with the assizes in northern Italy, set out for Illyria, since I had heard that the Pirustae were making raids on that part of the Province which was nearest to them and were doing much damage. When I arrived I ordered the local communities to raise troops and told them where to assemble. As soon as the Pirustae heard of this, they sent a deputation to me to explain that their government had had nothing whatever to do with these raids; they were ready, they said, to make every possible kind of reparation for the damage that had been done. I accepted this statement of theirs and ordered them to give me hostages who were to be delivered on a date which I named; and I told them that, if they failed to do this, I should make war on them. The hostages were brought as ordered, on the right day, and I appointed arbitrators to assess the damage that each community had sustained and to fix the amount of reparations due.

After dealing with this matter, I held the assizes in Illyria and then returned to northern Italy. From here I set out to rejoin the army. On arriving in Gaul, I made a tour of inspection of all the winter camps. I found that, in spite of a very great shortage of materials, the men had worked magnificently. They had built about six hundred ships of the type described above and twenty-eight warships. These would all be ready for launching in a few days. I congratulated the men and the officers who had been in charge of this operation, told them what I wanted done next, and ordered the whole fleet to assemble at Boulogne. I had discovered that from this port one can make the easiest crossing to Britain—the distance being about twenty-eight miles from the Continent. I left sufficient troops for carrying out this task and set out myself for the country of the Treveri with four legions, marching light, and eight hundred cavalry. I took this action because the Treveri had failed to attend the Gallic councils, had neglected my orders, and were believed to be making overtures to the Germans across the Rhine.

The Treveri have much the most powerful cavalry in Gaul and also a large army of infantry. I have already mentioned that this country borders on the Rhine. At this time two of their chiefs—Indutiomarus and Cingetorix—were struggling for supreme power in the state. As soon as it was known that I was approaching with an army, Cingetorix came to me. He assured me that he and all his followers would loyally abide by their alliance with Rome and told me what the situation was among the Treveri. Indutiomarus, on the other hand, began to prepare for war. He assembled forces of cavalry and infantry and hid all those who were too old or too young for military service in the huge forest of the Ardennes, which stretches right across the country of the Treveri, from the Rhine to the frontier of the Remi. However, several chiefs of the tribe—partly because they were friends of Cingetorix, partly because they were overawed by the presence of our army—came to me and began to beg my support in various private interests of their own, it being impossible for them, so they said, to speak openly in the public interest.

Indutiomarus now feared that he would be deserted by everyone and sent a deputation to me himself. He claimed that the reason he had been unwilling to leave his own people and come to see me was that he could best keep the tribe loyal by staying with them; if all the nobility had left, he feared that the common people would, in their ignorance, have made some serious mistake. As it was, he said, he had everything under control, and with my permission he proposed to visit me and put both himself and his tribe under my protection.

I realized well enough the purpose of this speech and also the real reason why Indutiomarus was afraid to go on with his original plan. However, now that everything was ready for the campaign in Britain, I did not want to have to waste the summer among the Treveri. I therefore ordered Indutiomarus to bring two hundred hostages with him when he came. The hostages were duly delivered, among them his son and all his family, whom I had asked for especially. I assured Indutiomarus that they would come to no harm and urged him to remain loyal to us. At the same time, however, I had private interviews with the other chiefs of the Treveri and won them over to the side of Cingetorix. I was conscious that Cingetorix deserved to be helped by me in this way, and I also thought it very important that one who had given such remarkable evidence of his loyalty to me should be as strong as possible among his own people. Indutiomarus, however, was bitterly offended by my action. He realized that he was losing prestige in the tribe, and the resentment he felt about this made him hate us even more than he had before.

When this business had been settled, I marched with the legions to Boulogne. I was informed there that sixty ships, which had been built in the country of the Meldi, had been driven off their course by a storm and compelled to return to their starting point; but I found all the rest fully equipped and ready for sailing. Four thousand cavalry from all parts of Gaul and the chieftains of the various tribes had also assembled at Boulogne. I had decided to leave behind only a few chieftains of proved loyalty to myself and to take the rest with me by way of hostages, since I feared that otherwise there might be a rising in Gaul during my absence.

Among these chieftains was Dumnorix the Aeduan, who has already been mentioned in this narrative. He was one of those whom I was particularly anxious to have with me, since I knew that he aimed at winning power for himself by revolutionary means and also that he was a courageous man with great influence among his countrymen. I discovered from some Gauls with whom I had stayed that he told the council of the Aedui that I was going to offer him the position of king of the tribe—a statement which the Aedui very much resented, though they did not dare to send a deputation to me to protest against my alleged decision or ask me to give it up.

Now Dumnorix began to put forward every possible reason for asking to be left behind in Gaul. He was unused to sailing, he said, and was frightened of the sea; next there were religious reasons which prevented him from going. He soon saw, however, that I was determined not to let him have his own way, and when he realized that there was no hope of getting what he wanted, he began to make approaches to the other Gallic chieftains, talking with them privately and trying to persuade them to stay on the Continent. He played on their fears by suggesting that I had an object of my own in thus stripping Gaul of all her nobility; my plan was, he said, to bring across into Britain and there put to death all those whom I did not dare treat in this way in the sight of their own countrymen. He pledged his own word to the rest, and asked from them a guarantee in return, that they would all work together for what they conceived to be the interests of Gaul.

I received reports of these intrigues from several people, and when I saw what the situation was, I decided that in view of the particular consideration which I had always shown for the Aedui, I ought to do everything I possibly could to keep Dumnorix under control and prevent him from carrying out his plans; and as, in fact, I saw that he was becoming more reckless and irresponsible every day, it was clearly necessary to take precautions so as to stop him from doing any harm to me personally or to the general interests of Rome. We were delayed at Boulogne for about twenty-five days, because the northwest wind—the prevailing wind in these parts—made it impossible to sail; and during this time I did my best to see to it that Dumnorix remained loyal, though at the same time I took steps to find out what his real plans were. In the end we got the right weather for sailing and I issued orders for the embarkation of both infantry and cavalry. While everyone's attention was occupied with carrying out these orders, Dumnorix, accompanied by some Aeduan cavalrymen, slipped out of camp without my knowledge and started to go home. As soon as I was informed of this, I put off sailing and, leaving everything else aside, sent a strong force of cavalry to capture him; if he resisted or refused to obey, he was to be killed; for I did not imagine that a man who had flouted my authority to my face was likely to behave sensibly when I was not there. In fact, when he was ordered to come back, he attempted to resist and to fight off his pursuers, calling on his followers to help him and repeatedly shouting out that he was a free man and the citizen of a free country. In accordance with my instructions, he was surrounded and killed. All the Aedui who were with him returned to camp.

When this was done, I left Labienus on the Continent with three legions and two thousand cavalry. His orders were to guard the ports, to arrange for our food supplies, to keep himself informed about what was going on in Gaul, and in the event of an emergency, to take whatever measures he thought fit. I myself, with five legions and two thousand cavalry, set sail about sunset. We started with a gentle south-westerly wind, but about midnight the wind dropped; failing to keep our course, we were carried on too far by the tidal current, and at dawn we saw Britain far away behind us on our left. Once again we followed the turn of the tide and attempted to row to the part of the island that (as we had discovered the past summer) was the best place for making a landing. The soldiers worked magnificently; pulling at the oars without stopping, they managed to make the heavily loaded transports keep up with the warships. The whole fleet reached the coast of Britain about midday. Not a single enemy was in sight. In fact, as we found out afterward from prisoners, large enemy forces had assembled there, but had been terrified by the great numbers of our ships and had withdrawn from the beach and hidden themselves on the higher ground. There must indeed have been more than eight hundred ships all visible at once, what with the addition of those that had survived from last year and various extra ships that had been built by individuals for their own use.

The army was disembarked and a suitable place was chosen for our camp. Then, after we had discovered from prisoners where the enemy's forces had taken up position, I left ten cohorts and three hundred cavalry on the shore to guard the ships and started out in the direction of the enemy soon after midnight. Quintus Atrius was left in charge of the fleet, and I had no anxiety about its safety, as the ships were lying at anchor on an open shore of soft sand.

A night march of about twelve miles brought us in sight of the enemy's forces. They had moved down with their cavalry and chariots from the high ground to a river, and here they attempted to check us by joining battle. They were driven back by our cavalry, but concealed themselves in the woods, where they had an extremely good position, strong in itself and strongly fortified; no doubt it had been made ready previously for some war among themselves, for every entrance to the place was blocked by numbers of trees that had been felled. The Britons themselves came out of the woods to fight in small detachments, and tried to prevent our men from getting inside their fortifications. But the men of the Seventh Legion, locking their shields together in "tortoise" formation, threw up a ramp against the fortifications, took the position, and drove the enemy out of the woods at the cost of only a few wounded. I forbade them to press the pursuit far, both because I was ignorant of the country and because much of the day had already gone and I wanted to leave time for entrenching our camp.

Next day, early in the morning, I divided the infantry and cavalry into three divisions and sent them out as flying columns to pursue the retreating enemy. They had already gone some way, so that only the rear guards of the columns were visible, when some horsemen came from Quintus Atrius with the news that on the previous night a great storm had damaged nearly all the ships and thrown them up on shore. The anchors and cables had failed to hold, and the sailors and steersmen had not been able to do anything in face of the violence of the storm, so the ships had collided with each other and very great damage had been done.

When I heard this news I ordered the legions and cavalry to be recalled; if attacked on the road, they were to beat off the attack but continue marching. I myself returned to the fleet and saw with my own eyes that the situation was almost exactly as it had been described to me by the messengers and their dispatches. About forty ships were a total loss; but it seemed that it would be possible to repair the rest, though this would mean much hard work. I therefore picked out from the legions all soldiers who were skilled craftsmen and sent instructions for others to be brought over from the Continent, and I wrote to Labienus asking him to put his troops to work and get as many ships constructed as possible. Meanwhile I decided that, in spite of the enormous labor involved, the best thing to be done was to have all the ships beached and included within the line of the camp's fortifications. We spent about ten days in getting this done, the work going on continuously day and night.

Once the ships were beached and the camp really well fortified, I set out for the point from which I had returned, leaving behind the same forces as before to guard the ships. When I reached the position from which we had retired, I found that in the interval British forces in greater numbers had come in from all parts of the country. By general consent, the supreme command in war had been given to Cassivellaunus, a chief whose territory begins about seventy-five miles inland from the sea and is separated from the territory of the coastal tribes by a river called the Thames. Previously there had been a continual state of war between Cassivellaunus and the other tribes; but our arrival had had such an effect on the Britons that they had agreed to appoint him as commander-in-chief.

* [The interior of Britain is inhabited by people who claim, on the strength of their own tradition, to be indigenous to the island. The coastal districts are inhabited by invaders from Belgium who came originally for the sake of plunder and then, when the fighting was over, remained and began to live by agriculture. They nearly all bear the names of the states from which they came before they crossed into Britain. The population is very large indeed. Farm buildings, which are very like those of the Gauls, are to be seen everywhere, and there are great numbers of cattle. For money they use either coins of bronze or gold, or iron ingots of a fixed standard of weight. Tin is found in the midland area and iron near the coast, but there is not much of it. The bronze that they use is imported. Every sort of timber that one gets in Gaul grows in Britain, except for beech and pine. They think it wrong to eat hares, chickens, or geese, but keep these animals as pets to amuse themselves. The climate is more temperate than in Gaul and the cold seasons are less severe.

Britain is shaped like a triangle. One side faces Gaul and one corner of this side, where Kent is, points east. It is to this part of the coast that nearly all the ships from Gaul put in. The lower corner of this side points south. The length of this side is about five hundred miles. Another side faces westward, toward Spain. In this direction is Ireland, which is estimated to be about half the size of Britain and is the same distance from Britain as Britain is from Gaul. Halfway between Britain and Ireland is an island called the Isle of Man, and it is thought that there are several other smaller islands too. In these islands, according to some accounts, there is continual night for thirty days at midwinter. On this point we made a number of inquiries, but found out nothing. However, by making accurate measurements with a water clock, we did discover that the nights are shorter than on the Continent. The length of this western side of Britain is, according to the opinion of the natives themselves, seven hundred miles. The third side faces north and has no land opposite it, though the eastern corner looks out roughly toward Germany. This side is supposed to be eight hundred miles long. Thus the whole island is two thousand miles in circumference.

Much the most civilized of the Britons are those who live in Kent, a part of the country which is entirely maritime and where the people have a way of life very much like that of the Gauls. Most of the tribes in the interior do not grow grain, but live on milk and meat and are clothed in skins. All Britons dye their bodies with woad, which gives them a

* The following section seems to have been interpolated and can scarcely be considered as part of Caesar's own narrative.—R.W.

blue color and thus produces a terrifying effect when they go into battle. They wear their hair long and shave every part of the body except the head and upper lip. Wives are shared between groups of ten or twelve men, particularly between brothers or between fathers and sons; but the children born from these unions are considered to belong to the man to whom the woman was married first.]

On the march the enemy cavalry and charioteers fought a fierce engagement with our cavalry; but the result was that our men proved themselves superior in every way and drove them off into the woods or into the hills. However, we pressed the pursuit too far and, though we killed a number of them, we lost some men ourselves. Then, after an interval, when our men were off their guard and busy on the work of entrenching our camp, the enemy suddenly rushed out of the woods, charged down on the detachment that was on duty in front of the camp, and made a vigorous attack on them. In support I sent up two cohorts—the first of their respective legions—which took position quite close to each other; but our men were disconcerted by the unfamiliar tactics with which they were faced, and the enemy, showing great daring, broke through the gap between the cohorts and got away safely. That day one of our senior officers, Quintus Laberius Durus, was killed in action.

More cohorts were sent forward and the enemy were driven back. The action had been fought in front of the camp with the whole army looking on, and it was clear that in fighting of this kind our men were at a disadvantage against such an enemy because of the weight of armor which we carried; we could not pursue them when they retired and we did not dare to go far from the standards. It was clear too that things were far from easy for our cavalry, for the enemy often retreated deliberately and then, when they had drawn our cavalry away from the support of the legions, leaped down from their chariots and started fighting on foot with the odds all in their favor. Another difficulty was in the fact that they never fought in close order, but always in scattered groups with wide intervals between them; moreover, they had reserves posted at strategic points, so that one unit could cover another's retreat and strong, fresh troops could relieve those who were tired.

Next day the enemy took up a position on hills some distance away from our camp. They only appeared in small parties and, though they made some assaults on our cavalry, attacked less vigorously than on the day before. But at midday, when I had sent out three legions and all the cavalry under the general Gaius Trebonius to get forage, the enemy

suddenly swooped down from all sides on the foragers and
pressed their attack right up to the ranks of the legions, which
were in battle order. Our men charged them fiercely and
drove them back. After this the pursuit continued; our cavalry,
seeing the legions behind them and relying on their support,
drove the enemy before them in headlong flight, killing great
numbers and giving them no chance to rally and make a
stand or jump down from their chariots. The immediate
effect of this rout was that the additional enemy forces that
had come in from all over the country began to disperse;
they never afterwards put their whole army into the field
against us.

After discovering what the enemy's plans were, I led the
army inland to the river Thames on the frontier of Cassivellaunus' country. There is only one point where the river can
be forded and even here the crossing is a difficult one. I observed, when we reached this place, that large enemy forces
were drawn up ready for battle on the opposite bank. The
bank itself was fortified with sharp stakes fixed along it and,
as we were informed by prisoners and deserters, other stakes
of the same kind had been driven into the bed of the stream
and were hidden by the water. I at once ordered the cavalry
to go ahead and the legions to follow them. Our soldiers
crossed with only their heads above water, but they moved
so fast and showed such fighting spirit that the enemy were
unable to stand up to the combined attack of our cavalry
and infantry; they abandoned their positions on the bank and
fled.

As already stated, Cassivellaunus had now given up all
idea of fighting a pitched battle. He had disbanded most of his
forces but kept back about four thousand charioteers. With
these he followed closely on our line of march, keeping always a little way off our route and concealing himself in the
woods and thickets. When he had found out in what direction
we were going to go, he drove into the woods all the cattle
and human beings that were in the fields. Then, whenever
our cavalry ranged any distance over the fields to get plunder
or lay waste the country, he sent his charioteers from the
forests by every available track or path to engage them in
battle. Our cavalry were in great danger from these charioteers
and the fear of them prevented us from extending our operations very far. All I could do was to tell the cavalry to keep
in contact with the marching column of the legions, which
meant that we could only burn and ravage the countryside
over an area which could be covered by the strenuous marches
of our infantry.

In the meantime, a deputation came to me from the

Trinobantes—perhaps the strongest state in this part of the country. It was from this state that young Mandubracius had come to Gaul and put himself under my protection; he had had to fly for his life after his father, king of the Trinobantes, had been murdered by Cassivellaunus. The deputation which now arrived offered the surrender of the tribe and promised to carry out all my orders; they begged me to protect Mandubracius from Cassivellaunus and to send him back to his own country as supreme ruler. I told them to bring me forty hostages and a supply of grain for the army, and I sent Mandubracius back to them. My orders were carried out promptly, both the grain and the required number of hostages being delivered.

Now that the Trinobantes were taken under Roman protection and preserved from suffering any harm at the hands of our troops, other tribes—the Cenimagni, Segontiaci, Ancalites, Bibroci, and Cassi—also sent deputations and offered to surrender. I discovered from them that we were now quite near the main stronghold of Cassivellaunus. It was a position protected by forests and marshes, and considerable numbers of men and cattle had been brought together there. Incidentally, what the Britons describe as a stronghold is any position in a thick forest which they have fortified with a rampart and trench and which they use as a place of refuge from invading enemy forces. We now started for this stronghold and found that it was extremely well placed and extremely well fortified. Nevertheless we moved directly against it, attacking it from two sides. There was a brief resistance, but the enemy could not face the vigor of our assault and rushed out of the place on another side. We found a great quantity of cattle in the stronghold and many of the enemy were captured or killed while trying to escape.

While these operations were going on, Cassivellaunus sent messengers to Kent (the aforementioned district by the sea) ordering the four kings of that part of the country—Cingetorix, Carvilius, Taximagulus, and Segovax—to mobilize all their forces and make a surprise attack on our naval camp. The Kentish army duly appeared in front of our camp, but our men made a sortie and, after killing great numbers of them and capturing one of their leaders (a man of noble birth called Lugotorix), retired again without loss. When he received the news of this engagement, Cassivellaunus, already disturbed by his many defeats, by the devastation of his country, and particularly by the fact that the tribes were beginning to come over to us, sent a deputation to me to ask for terms of surrender, using Commius the Atrebatian as an intermediary. I had decided to winter on the Continent in view of the danger of sudden uprisings among the Gauls; not much of the summer was left and I knew that for this short time the Britons could easily avoid any decisive action. I therefore ordered hostages to be delivered, fixed the tribute to be paid annually by Britain to Rome, and gave strict orders to Cassivellaunus to avoid doing any harm to Mandubracius or to the Trinobantes.

As soon as the hostages were delivered, I led the army back to the sea, where we found the ships repaired. After they had been launched I decided, in view of the large number of prisoners we had and the fact that some ships had been lost in the storm, to make the return journey in two trips. Actually it so happened that out of the whole of these great fleets on all their voyages both in this and in the preceding year, not a single ship with troops aboard was lost; while, on the other hand, out of the ships which were sent back to me empty from the Continent (i.e., those on their way back from Gaul after disembarking the first contingent, and the second fleet which had been built under the supervision of Labienus), very few indeed reached their proper destination, nearly all of them being forced back to the point from which they started. I waited some time in vain for these ships. Then, being afraid that the weather might prevent us from sailing at all (since it was nearly the time of the equinox), I had to put more men than I would normally have done aboard the ships I had. The sea then became absolutely calm; we weighed anchor soon after nine P.M. and reached land quite safely with the whole fleet at dawn on the following day.

2 A REVOLT IN GAUL. DESTRUCTION OF A ROMAN ARMY.

After we had beached the ships, a council of the Gallic chiefs was held at Amiens. That year there had been a drought in Gaul and the harvest had been a bad one. I was therefore compelled to adopt different methods from usual in arranging winter quarters for the legions and to distribute them over a larger number of states. One legion, under Gaius Fabius, was sent to the Morini; another, under Quintus Cicero, to the Nervii; and a third, under Lucius Roscius, to the Esubii. A fourth legion, with Titus Labienus in command, was ordered to winter among the Remi on their frontier with the Treveri. Three more legions were quartered among the Belgae: they were commanded by the quaestor Marcus Crassus, and the generals Lucius Munatius Plancus and Gaius Trebonius. One other legion, which had recently been raised in the country north of the Po, together with five extra cohorts, was sent, under the command of Quintus Titurius Sabinus and Lucius Aurunculeius Cotta, into the country of the Eburones. This tribe, most of whose territory lies between the Meuse and the Rhine, was governed by the chiefs Ambiorix and Catuvolcus. By distributing the legions in this way I thought that we should most easily be able to meet the difficulties of securing our grain supply. In fact, the winter camps of all the legions, except for the one under Roscius, which had been sent into a perfectly quiet and peaceful area, were within a hundred miles of each other. For the time being, I decided to stay in Gaul myself until I was informed that all the legions had reached their destinations and had fortified their camps.

Among the Carnutes was a man of noble birth called Tasgetius, whose ancestors had been kings of the tribe. He had been most remarkably useful to me in all my campaigns, and in recognition of his great abilities and his loyalty to me, I had restored him to the position once held by his ancestors. He had already been king for more than two years, but now, with the open approval of many people among the Carnutes, his enemies assassinated him. I was informed of this crime and, since it appeared that many people were involved in it, I was afraid that they might use their influence to make the whole state revolt. I therefore instructed Lucius Plancus to leave Belgium and proceed at once to the country of the Carnutes; here he was to spend the winter and was also to arrest and send to me those whom he found guilty of the murder of Tasgetius. Meanwhile dispatches reached me from the quaestor and from all the generals in command of legions. They informed me that they had reached their quarters and that the winter camps were fortified.

About a fortnight later trouble suddenly began. The originators of the revolt were Ambiorix and Catuvolcus. After coming to meet Sabinus and Cotta on the frontiers of their territory and bringing supplies of grain to our camp, they had been incited by messages from Indutiomarus of the Treveri to revolt against us. They swept down and overwhelmed a party of our men who were collecting wood, and then came on in large numbers to attack the camp. Our troops quickly armed and mounted the rampart; a detachment of Spanish cavalry was sent out from one of the gates and fought a successful action against the enemy horsemen; and giving up all hopes of success, the enemy withdrew from the attack. Then, as they usually do in such cases, they called out loudly, asking for someone from our side to come out and discuss matters with them. They claimed to have something to say which would be beneficial to both parties and which would lead to a settlement of all matters in dispute. Two of our people were sent out to confer with the enemy—Gaius Arpineius, a Roman gentleman who was a personal friend of Sabinus, and a Spaniard called Quintus Junius, who had often previously been employed by me on various missions to Ambiorix.

In the speech which he made to these two, Ambiorix began by acknowledging that he was under a great debt of gratitude to me personally. I had relieved him from the tribute which he had always paid in the past to the neighboring tribe of the Aduatuci; and I had restored to him his son and nephew, who had been sent to the Aduatuci as hostages and then been enslaved and kept in chains. As to the attack which had just been made on our camp, he said it had been carried out against his will and against his judgment; he had been forced into it by his fellow tribesmen, over whom he exercised a control which was very strictly limited. Indeed, his people had as much power over him as he had over his people. And the reason why his state had taken up arms was that it could not resist the general movement of the Gauls which had just taken place. This fact could easily be proved: he was not a person of great importance and was hardly so ignorant of the real situation as to imagine that his army could defeat the Romans. But what had happened was this: the whole of Gaul had got together and chosen this day for making attacks on every one of the Roman camps, so that one legion could not come to the help of another. It would not have been easy, he said, for one who was a Gaul himself to have refused to act with the others, especially when the object of the whole plan was to recover the national liberty. However, so far as the claims of patriotism were concerned, he had done his duty; what he now wanted to do was to show his consideration for what he owed me in return for my kindness to him. He was bound to Sabinus by ties of hospitality and, in the name of those ties, he most earnestly begged him to think of his own safety and of the safety of the troops under his command. A great force of German mercenaries had already crossed the Rhine and were due to arrive in two days. It was for the Romans themselves to decide whether or not it would be advisable to withdraw their troops from the camp before the tribes in the neighborhood could realize what the position was and march to the camp either of Cicero, who was fifty miles away, or of Labienus, who was a little farther. One thing, said Ambiorix, he would promise and would guarantee by oath, and that was that he would give them a safe-conduct through his own country. He pointed out that in making this offer he was doing the best thing for his own state by relieving them of the burden of a Roman army, and at the same time was doing something to repay me for the kindness I had shown him.

After making this speech, Ambiorix withdrew and Arpineius and Junius reported what they had been told to the generals, who were much disturbed by the sudden turn which events had taken. It was true that the information just received came from the enemy; but they did not think that it ought to be disregarded. There was one particularly disquieting factor: it scarcely seemed credible that an obscure and insignificant tribe like the Eburones dared to take the initiative in making war on Rome. Ambiorix' message was therefore discussed at a council of war. There was a wide difference of opinion among those present. The view expressed by Cotta and by several of the officers and senior centurions was that nothing should be done in a hurry and that there was no justification for leaving their winter quarters without an order from me personally. Cotta claimed that, however many Germans might arrive, the fortifications of the camp were strong enough to keep them out; this had been proved by the fact that they had held out extremely well against the original enemy attack and had inflicted a number of casualties. He pointed out too that they were adequately supplied with grain and that before long help would reach them from the nearest camps or from some other force which I would send to their relief. Finally, it would be, he said, about the most irresponsible and disgraceful thing possible to take the advice of an enemy on matters of real importance to themselves.

Sabinus disagreed. They would be leaving things too late, he insisted, if they waited for larger enemy armies, reinforced by Germans, to concentrate, or if, in the meantime, some disaster overtook the neighboring Roman camps. They had only a short time in which to make up their minds. In his own view, I had already set out for Italy; otherwise the Carnutes would not have decided upon the murder of Tasgetius, nor, if I had been in Gaul, would the Eburones have found the self-confidence to attack our camp. It was not, he said, a question of taking advice from the enemy. He was considering the facts: the Rhine was not far away; the Germans were in an angry and resentful mood as a result of the death of Ariovistus and our victories in past campaigns; the Gauls were burning with indignation at all the insults suffered since they had been brought into subjugation to Rome and at the loss of their former prestige in war. Finally, how could anyone imagine that Ambiorix could have acted as he had done unless he had been quite sure of what he was doing? Sabinus declared that his own plan was safe either way: if in fact there was no serious danger, they would reach the nearest legion in perfect safety; if, on the other hand, the whole of Gaul was in alliance with the Germans, then the only chance of escape was in moving at once. As for Cotta and the others who disagreed, what would be the result of adopting their plan? It might be safe enough for the moment, but it most certainly involved the danger of a long siege and death by starvation.

The two opposing views were discussed. Cotta and the senior centurions still objected most strongly to the plan of Sabinus. Then Sabinus raised his voice so that many of the ordinary soldiers could hear him and shouted out: "Have your own way then, if you must. You will not find me more frightened of death than the rest of you. But these soldiers of ours will be perfectly aware of what is happening and, if things go wrong, they will hold you responsible for it. If it were not for you, by the day after tomorrow they would be with their comrades in the nearest camp, ready to fight alongside them, instead of being abandoned and isolated from the rest, to die either by famine or by the sword."

The members of the council rose from their places, gathered round the two generals, and implored them not to endanger everything by disagreeing so violently. "Things will be easy," they said, "whether we go or stay, provided that we are all agreed on what should be done; but if we go on quarreling, we might as well give up hope."

The discussion continued until midnight. Finally Cotta yielded to the pressure brought to bear on him and gave way. Sabinus' plan was adopted and orders were issued for the army to leave camp at dawn. That night no one slept. Each man was going through his kit to see what he could carry with him and how much of his winter equipment he would have to leave behind. They went over every possible argument proving that it was safe to go and dangerous to remain, and so exhausted themselves by staying awake that in fact their danger was increased. At dawn they left camp in a long straggling column with a great deal of heavy baggage. It appeared as though they were convinced that Ambiorix, who had given them the idea, was not an enemy but the very best of friends.

From the noise and general disturbance of the night the enemy had gathered that we were going to leave and had posted two ambushes in a good position in the woods, well hidden from observation, about two miles away. Here they waited for the Romans to arrive, and, when the greater part of our force had descended into a deep ravine, they suddenly appeared at both ends of the column, falling upon the rear guard and trying to prevent the men in front from climbing out of the defile. They were thus engaging us on ground where all the advantages were on their side.

At this point Sabinus, who up to now had had no idea that such a thing could happen, began to grow alarmed. He hurried around, trying to get the troops into position; but even this he did nervously, making it obvious that he had completely lost control of the situation—as usually happens when one is forced to start planning in the middle of an action. Cotta, on the other hand, had thought that something like this might happen on the march and had therefore been against leaving the camp. Now he did everything possible to save the army, leading and encouraging the men like a good general, and fighting in the line like a good soldier.

Finding that the length of the column made it impossible for them to attend to everything personally and to see what was needed at every point, the two generals passed word along the line to abandon the baggage and form up in a circle. Considering the emergency, one cannot say that this was a bad plan; nevertheless, it had unfortunate results, lowering the morale of our own troops and making the enemy all the more ready to attack, since they thought that we were acting in this way because we were in a panic and had given up hope. Then too, as was bound to happen, a number of soldiers left the ranks to find and get hold of their most cherished possessions in the baggage train, shouting and cursing their luck as they did so.

The natives, on the other hand, acted most intelligently. Their leaders passed the word around among their whole army that no one was to leave the ranks; all the plunder was theirs and everything left by the Romans was reserved for them alone; meanwhile they were told to make up their minds that everything depended on winning the battle.

The Gauls showed as much courage and as much ardor as we did; yet our men, let down, as they had been, by their commander, and with all the luck against them, still relied on their fighting qualities to save them, and whenever one of our cohorts charged forward, great numbers of the enemy fell before it. Ambiorix, seeing what was happening, instructed his men to hurl their weapons at long range and not to come too close to us. Whenever we charged, they were to give ground; their light armor and their constant training would enable them to do this without any risk. Then, when our men fell back into line, they were to counterattack. These orders were carefully carried out. Whenever a cohort left the circle and charged, the enemy fell back with the utmost rapidity. Meanwhile the attacking cohort was of course unprotected on its right flank and thus exposed to a shower of enemy missiles; and when it began to retire to its original position in the circle, it was practically surrounded both by those who had fallen back in the first place and by the nearest enemy units who had remained in their positions. If, on the other hand, our soldiers merely tried to hold their ground in the circle, they had no chance at all of showing their fighting qualities; huddled closely together, they were an easy target for the weapons hurled at them by that great mass of men. Yet in spite of all difficulties and in spite of very heavy casualties, they still stood firm.

Much of the day had gone by; they had been fighting from dawn till two P.M., and in all this time they had done nothing unworthy of themselves. In this fighting Titus Balventius, a gallant soldier most highly respected by everyone, who last year had been chief centurion of his legion, had both thighs transfixed with a javelin. Another centurion of the same rank, Quintus Lucanius, was killed in a most gallant attempt to rescue his own son, who had been surrounded. Cotta himself, while cheering on the cohorts, going from company to company, was wounded by a sling stone which struck him full in the face.

Sabinus was alarmed at the way things were going. In the distance he could see Ambiorix urging on his men, and he sent Gnaeus Pompeius, his interpreter, to him to ask for quarter for himself and his troops. In reply to this appeal Ambiorix said that Sabinus could come and speak to him if he wished. So far as the soldiers were concerned, he hoped that he would be able to persuade his men to spare their lives; in any case he would personally guarantee that Sabinus himself should come to no harm. Sabinus then went to the wounded Cotta and proposed that they should both withdraw from the fight and go together to discuss matters with Ambiorix, who he hoped might be persuaded to grant them their lives and the lives of their troops. But Cotta said that he was not going to make approaches to any enemy who still carried arms, and nothing would make him change his mind.

Sabinus ordered all officers and senior centurions who were with him at the moment to follow him. When he approached Ambiorix he was told to lay down his arms, which he did and instructed those who were with him to do also. He then joined in a conversation with Ambiorix about terms. Ambiorix deliberately prolonged the discussion, and Sabinus was gradually surrounded and then killed.

The natives at once raised their customary cry of triumph

and, yelling and screaming, charged down upon our army and broke through the ranks. Cotta fell fighting where he stood and most of the troops died with him. The remainder retired to the camp from which they had set out. One of them, Lucius Petrosidius, the standard-bearer of the legion, found himself surrounded by great crowds of the enemy. He threw the eagle inside the rampart and himself died, fighting most gallantly, outside the camp. The others just managed to keep the enemy out until nightfall; in the night, since there was no hope left, every man of them committed suicide. A few soldiers had managed to slip away while the fighting was going on. By taking roundabout routes through the forests they succeeded in reaching Labienus' camp, and told him what had happened.

3 THE ATTACK ON CICERO'S CAMP.

Flushed with this success, Ambiorix at once set out with all his cavalry and, riding day and night, came to the Aduatuci, a tribe living next to his kingdom; the infantry were ordered to follow. He explained what had been done and persuaded the Aduatuci to take up arms. Next day he went on to the country of the Nervii and urged them not to let slip this excellent opportunity of winning freedom for themselves forever and of making the Romans suffer for all the outrages they had committed. He informed them that two Roman generals had been killed and the greater part of their army annihilated. It would not be difficult, he suggested, to make a sudden attack on the winter camp of Cicero and to destroy the legion under his command also. And he offered his own assistance in carrying out this enterprise.

The Nervii were easily persuaded to cooperate. Messengers were at once sent out to the dependent tribes of the Ceutrones, the Grudii, the Levaci, the Pleumoxii, and the Geidumni. The largest possible forces were assembled, and with these they suddenly swooped down on Cicero's camp. Cicero had not yet heard of the death of Sabinus, and it happened to him too, as was inevitable, that some of his troops who had gone into the woods to get timber for the fortifications were cut off by the sudden appearance of the enemy cavalry and surrounded. After this a huge host of Eburones, Nervii, and Aduatuci, with all their allies and dependents, launched a direct attack on the camp. Our men quickly ran to arms and mounted the rampart. That day they only just managed to hold out; for all the enemy's hopes lay in speed, and they were convinced that if they won the battle here they would go on winning everywhere else.

Cicero wrote to me at once and offered large rewards to anyone who could get through the enemy lines; but all the roads were blocked and his messengers were intercepted. During the night the men worked with incredible speed. Using the timber that had been brought in for the fortifications, they ran up about one hundred twenty towers and strengthened all apparent weaknesses in the defenses. Next day the enemy appeared with much larger forces than before. They assaulted the camp and filled in the ditch, but our men put up the same resistance as on the previous day. And so it went day after day. There was no breaking off work during the nights, no chance of sleep either for the sick or the wounded. Everything needed to meet the next day's attack had to be got ready during the hours of darkness; quantities of stakes with their points hardened in the fire and huge numbers of siege pikes were made; extra stories were built on the towers, and battlements and breastworks of hurdles were fitted to them. Cicero himself was in very poor health, yet he would not take any rest even during the night, until the men themselves came crowding around him and insisted that he must look after himself.

Some of the chieftains and leaders of the Nervii had been on friendly terms with Cicero and so had some excuse for approaching him. They now declared that they wished to parley. Their request granted, at this interview they adopted exactly the same line as that followed by Ambiorix when he spoke with Sabinus. The whole of Gaul, they said, was in arms; the Germans had crossed the Rhine; all Roman winter camps, including my own, were under assault. They then informed him of the death of Sabinus and produced Ambiorix as evidence for the truth of their story.

"You are making a great mistake," they said, "if you think you are likely to get any help from the others, when the others are in desperate straits themselves. We ourselves, however, have nothing against Cicero or against Rome except that we do not like this practice of quartering your armies on us for the winter and we do not want this to become an established thing. So far as we are concerned, you are free to leave the camp in perfect safety and march in whatever direction you like without any fear at all."

To all this Cicero had only one reply to make. "Rome," he said, "does not make terms with an enemy who is still bearing arms. If you lay down your arms, I am prepared to give you facilities for sending a deputation to Caesar and, as Caesar is a just man, I trust that he will look favorably on your requests."

Disappointed in this direction, the Nervii began to surround our camp with a rampart nine feet high and a ditch fifteen feet wide. They had learned how to do this by watching us in previous years and were given further instruction by prisoners from our army whom they had with them, though we did not know this. However, they had none of the proper tools for the work and had to do their best by cutting the sod with their swords, lifting out the earth with their bare hands, and carrying it away in their cloaks. With this in mind, one can get some idea of their numbers from the fact that in less than three hours they completed a line of earthworks five miles in circumference; and in the days following, still under the direction of Roman prisoners, they set to work on the construction of towers high enough to command our rampart, together with grappling irons and mantlets.

On the seventh day of the siege there was a high wind and the enemy began slinging red-hot missiles molded from clay and hurling incendiary darts onto the huts, which were thatched with straw after the Gallic fashion. The huts quickly caught fire and the strong wind spread the flames all over the camp. At this the enemy raised a great shout as though victory were not only in their grasp but already won, and began to bring up their siege towers and mantlets and to scale the rampart with ladders. But our men showed a courage and a presence of mind that were quite remarkable. They were scorched by the fire burning all around them; they were under a constant hail of missiles; and they were aware that all their baggage and all their private possessions were ablaze. Yet not a single man left his post on the rampart and scarcely one of them even looked over his shoulder. Every man of them at this moment of crisis fought with the utmost gallantry and the utmost resolution. It was much the toughest day's fighting of all, yet in the end the result was that on this day more of the enemy were killed and wounded than on any other, for the Gauls were crowded in a dense mass right underneath our rampart and those in front had no chance of retiring because of the pressure on them from behind. In one sector, when the fire had died down a little, an enemy tower was brought forward so that it was actually touching the rampart; whereupon the centurions of the third cohort withdrew from the position they were holding, ordered their men to fall back too, and then made signs and shouted invitations to the Gauls to come in if they liked. But none of them dared to come forward; they were dislodged by volleys of stones from all sides and their tower was set on fire.

In this legion there were two absolutely first-rate soldiers, Titus Pullo and Lucius Vorenus, both centurions who were nearly qualified for the top rank of seniority. These two never stopped arguing about which of them was the better soldier, and every year when it came to the question of promotion each one would try to outdo the other. Now, when the fighting round the rampart was at its fiercest, Pullo shouted out: "What are you waiting for, Vorenus? Do you want a better chance of showing how you can fight? Today will settle the argument between us." With these words he went forward beyond the fortifications and charged into the enemy at the point where their ranks were thickest. Vorenus, of course, was not going to stay behind; he knew what people would think of him if he did, and so he went straight after Pullo. When a little way from the enemy, Pullo hurled his javelin and transfixed one of the Gauls who had run forward to meet him. The Gaul was struck down unconscious, but his comrades covered him with their shields, while from all sides weapons rained down on Pullo so that he had no chance of retiring. One javelin went right through his shield and stuck in his sword belt. This twisted his scabbard out of position so that when he tried to draw his sword he could not at first seize the hilt. While he was struggling to do so, the enemy surrounded him. But now his rival Vorenus came up and got him out of his difficulties. Thinking that Pullo had been killed by the spear, the Gauls all turned away from him and immediately set upon Vorenus, who, fighting with his sword at close quarters, killed one man and was beginning to drive the others back. But in pressing forward too eagerly, he stumbled and fell into a depression in the ground. Now it was his turn to be surrounded and the turn of Pullo to come up and rescue him.

After killing a few more of the enemy, both centurions came back together safe and sound to the shelter of the fortifications. Each of them had deserved the highest possible praise, and in this bitter rivalry of theirs fortune had produced a situation in which each of the two enemies had been the friend and savior of the other, so that it was quite impossible to decide which should be considered the better or the braver soldier.

The difficulties and dangers of the siege were becoming greater every day, particularly because so many men were suffering from their wounds that only a few were left to carry on the defense. And, as matters got worse, Cicero sent more and more messengers to me with dispatches. Some of these were captured and put to death by torture under the eyes of our troops. But there was a Nervian in the camp, a man of

good family called Vertico, who had deserted to Cicero at
the very beginning of the siege and had served him loyally
ever since. This man, by offering one of his slaves his freedom
and great rewards as well, persuaded him to carry a dispatch
to me. The slave tied the dispatch round his spear shaft and,
being a Gaul himself, passed through the Gallic lines without
arousing any suspicion. He went on until he came to me, and
it was from him I heard of the danger that threatened Cicero
and his legion.

I received the dispatch in the early evening and at once
sent a messenger to the quaestor, Marcus Crassus, who was
in camp about twenty-four miles away in the country of the
Bellovaci, ordering him to start at midnight with his legion
and join me as quickly as he could. Crassus left as soon as
he received the message. I sent another messenger to Gaius
Fabius, telling him to march with his legion into the country
of the Atrebates, through which I knew I should have to
go myself. I wrote to Labienus, asking him to come with his
legion to the Nervian frontier, if he thought that he could do
so without undue risk. The rest of the legions were too far
away, and I thought it would be wrong to wait for them; but
I collected about four hundred cavalrymen from the nearest
camps.

About nine o'clock on the following morning, I was informed by Crassus' patrols that he was approaching, and I
set out myself. We covered about twenty miles that day. I
left Crassus with his one legion in command at Amiens, where
I had left all the heavy equipment of the army, the native
hostages, all my official papers, and all the grain that had
been collected to last for the winter. Fabius, who had made
reasonable speed, joined me with his legion on the march, as
he had been instructed to do. Labienus had heard of the death
of Sabinus and the slaughter of his army, but he was now
faced with a general mobilization of the Treveri. He was
afraid that if he set out from his camp it would look as though
he were running away; and he might not be strong enough
to beat off an enemy attack, especially as the enemy were now,
he knew, in a most confident mood because of their recent
victory. He therefore wrote to me to explain the dangers that
would be involved in leading his legion out of camp; he also
gave me a full account of what had happened in the country
of the Eburones and told me that the whole army of the
Treveri, both horse and foot, had taken up a position about
three miles away from his camp.

I was now reduced to two legions instead of the three which
I had expected. But I approved of the decision which Labienus
had made. I considered that our only hope of saving the

situation was to act quickly. So we came by forced marches to the Nervian frontier, where I found out from prisoners how things were going at Cicero's camp and how extremely dangerous his position was. By offering a very large reward, I induced one of my Gallic cavalrymen to carry a letter to Cicero. I wrote the letter in Greek so that if it was intercepted the enemy would not know what our plans were. I told the messenger that if he could not get near enough to deliver the letter by hand, he was to fasten it to the thong of his spear and throw the spear inside the rampart. In the letter I wrote that I had set out with the legions and would soon be there; I told Cicero to keep his courage up and be of good heart. The Gaul was afraid to approach too near and threw the spear as he had been instructed. It happened to stick fast in the woodwork of one of the towers and there remained unnoticed for two days. On the third day one of our soldiers saw it, drew it out, and brought it to Cicero. After reading it himself Cicero had the troops drawn up on parade and read it aloud to them. They were overwhelmed with joy. Soon in the distance they could see the smoke rising from the villages which we were burning on our way, and this dispelled all doubt about the fact that the legions were coming.

When the Gauls received news of our approach through their patrols, they raised the siege and marched against me with their entire force, which amounted to about sixty thousand men. Cicero took the opportunity to write to me, again asking Vertico for the use of a Gallic slave to carry the letter. In this letter he advised me to proceed with the utmost caution and described how the enemy had left his camp and were now in full force marching in my direction.

Cicero's letter was delivered to me about midnight. I informed the troops of its contents and told them to make ready for battle and to be in good heart. We struck camp at dawn next day and, after advancing about four miles, came in sight of the great host of the enemy on the far side of a valley through which ran a stream. With the small force at my disposal, it would have been very risky indeed to fight on unfavorable ground. Moreover, I knew that Cicero was no longer besieged; there was therefore no reason for anxiety and I could afford to take my time. So we halted and began to fortify a camp, choosing the best position for it that could be found. This camp would in any case have been a small one, since I had a bare seven thousand troops with me and no baggage at all; but I had it made even smaller still by limiting the width of the camp roadways, my idea being to make the enemy regard us as a contemptible little army. Meanwhile I sent out scouts in all directions to find out the best route for crossing the valley.

That day there were a few minor cavalry engagements near the stream, but the two main armies stayed where they were. The Gauls were waiting for reinforcements which had not yet arrived, and I was hoping, by making it look as though we were afraid, to draw the Gauls on to our own ground and induce them to fight on our side of the valley in front of the camp; if I failed to do this, then in any case the routes would have been explored so that we could cross the valley and the stream with the minimum of risk.

Next day at dawn the enemy cavalry rode up to our camp and engaged our own cavalry. In accordance with the plan that I had made, I ordered our men to fall back and retire inside the camp; at the same time I had the rampart built up higher all around and the gates barricaded; my instructions were that these operations were to be carried out with a lot of running hither and thither and as good a show of panic as could be put on. All this had the desired effect of inducing the enemy to bring their forces across the stream and to draw them up on unfavorable ground. Our troops meanwhile had been withdrawn even from the rampart. The enemy came nearer still. They began to hurl missiles from all sides into our fortifications and they sent heralds all around the circuit of the camp to proclaim that anyone, whether Gaul or Roman, was free to come over to their side, if he did so before nine A.M.; after that there would be no chance. In fact they showed a quite extraordinary contempt for us. They thought that they could not break into the camp by the gates, which appeared to be barricaded, though in fact they were only screened by single rows of sod; but they started to tear down the rampart with their bare hands while others of them were busy filling in the ditch. At this point I ordered the legions to sally out from each one of the gates and at the same time instructed the cavalry to charge. In a moment the enemy were routed so thoroughly that not a man of them stood his ground to fight. We killed great numbers and those who were not killed threw away their arms. But I was afraid to press the pursuit very far since there were woods and marshes in the way, and I saw too that there was not much room for doing the enemy more harm than had been done already.

Our men had suffered no casualties at all and on this same day we went on and joined Cicero. I was amazed at the sight of the towers which the enemy had erected and the shelters and siege works generally. When the legion was paraded, I

found that less than one-tenth of the men remained un-
wounded. From all this I could very well see how great the
danger had been and how courageously it had been met. I
gave Cicero the high praise that was his due and congratulated the whole legion as well. I also spoke personally with
those officers and centurions whom I discovered from Cicero's
accounts to have shown exceptional courage and ability. From
the prisoners I received a fuller account of the fate of Sabinus
and Cotta, and next day I held an assembly of the soldiers,
explained to them what had happened, and reassured them
about the future. They ought not, I said, to take this disaster
too much to heart; it had come about simply through the
criminal incompetence of a general. Now providence and
their own courage had restored the situation. The enemy's
triumph had been short-lived; so, I suggested, should be their
own feelings of despondency.

4 FURTHER
REVOLTS.

The news of my victory was brought to Labienus by the Remi
with incredible speed. Labienus was encamped more than
fifty-five miles away from Cicero, whom I had not reached
until about two o'clock in the afternoon, and yet before
midnight there was a noise of shouting outside his gates. It
was a party of Remi who had come to announce my victory
and offer him their congratulations. The news soon reached the
Treveri, and Indutiomarus, who had decided to make an
assault on Labienus' camp next day, fled away in the night
and withdrew all his forces into his own country.

After sending Fabius and his legion back to their winter
camp, I decided to spend the winter myself with three legions
in three separate camps in the neighborhood of Amiens. In
view of the serious disturbances that had broken out in Gaul,
I came to the conclusion that I should stay with the army
myself all through the winter. For as the news spread of the
disaster in which Sabinus had been killed, practically all the
states in Gaul were beginning to think of war; they kept on
sending messengers and embassies all over the country, finding
out what the others were planning to do, inquiring who would
take the initiative in opening hostilities, and holding meetings
by night in out-of-the-way places. All through this winter
there was scarcely a moment when I was free from anxiety
and practically every day I received some report or other

about plans for a general rising. Among these was a report from Lucius Roscius, whom I had put in command of the Thirteenth Legion. He informed me that large forces of Gauls from the states called Armorican had assembled to attack him and had taken up a position within eight miles of his camp; but when they had heard the news of my victory they had gone away again, so quickly that they seemed to be running rather than retiring.

I summoned the chiefs of each state to my headquarters and, partly by frightening them with declaring that I knew what was going on, partly by using methods of persuasion, succeeded in keeping most of Gaul loyal. However, the state council of the Senones—a particularly strong and influential people—attempted to put to death their King, Cavarinus, whom I had appointed to the throne. (His brother, Moritasgus, had been king at the time I arrived in Gaul, and his ancestors had held the kingship before that.) Having information of the plot, Cavarinus escaped; but they pursued him as far as the frontier, then deprived him of the kingship and declared him an exile. They had sent a deputation to me to justify what they had done, but when I had demanded that the whole of their council should appear before me, they had failed to obey. A tremendous impression had been made on these natives by the fact that someone had been found to take the first step in opening hostilities against us; and the result was such a complete change in the general attitude that there was scarcely a tribe in Gaul that we did not suspect of planning a revolt, except the Aedui and Remi, whom I had always treated with particular distinction—the Aedui because of their long-standing record of unvarying loyalty to us, the Remi because of the help they had given recently in the Gallic campaigns. That such should have been the situation is not, I think, altogether surprising. Apart from many other reasons, one must consider the very deep resentment felt by peoples who used to be regarded as the best and most courageous warriors in the world, but now, through having to take their orders from Rome, found that this reputation was either going or gone.

All through the winter Indutiomarus and the Treveri never stopped working against us. They were constantly sending embassies across the Rhine in their efforts to gain the support of various German tribes, whom they promised money and assured that all but a small portion of our army had already been wiped out. However, they failed to persuade any German state to cross the Rhine. The Germans pointed out that they had made the experiment twice already—in the campaign under Ariovistus and when the Tencteri crossed the river—and they were not going to tempt fortune for the third time. Though disappointed in his hopes of German aid, Indutiomarus still went on with his preparations—raising and training troops, buying up horses from neighboring tribes, and attracting to himself, by means of lavish offers of pay, exiles and criminals from all over Gaul. In this way he had acquired such prestige in Gaul that deputations began to reach him from all parts of the country; both states and individuals sought for his favor and protection. So, finding that people were coming over to him of their own accord and observing that in one direction there were the Senones and Carnutes, both ready for revolt because of their guilty consciences, and in another the Nervii and Aduatuci, who were getting ready to attack the Romans, Indutiomarus came to the conclusion that he would have plenty of volunteers to join him if he advanced beyond his own frontiers. He therefore gave notice of an armed convention, the usual procedure followed by the Gauls at the beginning of a war. A law, common to all tribes alike, requires all men of military age to come to the assembly armed; the one who arrives last is put to death with every kind of torture before the assembled host. At this convention Indutiomarus declared his son-in-law Cingetorix a public enemy and confiscated his property. Cingetorix was leader of the opposition party, and as already mentioned, he had put himself under my protection and had remained loyal to me. After having settled that matter, Indutiomarus announced to the assembly that he had been summoned by the Senones, the Carnutes, and several other Gallic tribes and proposed to march to them through the country of the Remi, laying it waste; but before doing this he would attack Labienus' camp. He then gave instructions as to what measures he wished taken.

Labienus was safe in a camp which was in a strong natural position and had been thoroughly well fortified. He felt no anxiety for himself or for his men; his only concern was not to lose any chance of winning a victory. So, after he had heard from Cingetorix and his relations what Indutiomarus had said at the assembly, he sent out messengers to the neighboring states in all directions and ordered cavalry contingents to be sent to him by a certain day. Meanwhile, almost every day Indutiomarus with his entire force of cavalry would ride up close to the Roman camp, sometimes to reconnoiter the position, sometimes to attempt to parley with or intimidate the soldiers; and usually every cavalryman would hurl a weapon inside the rampart. Labienus kept his men well within the fortifications and did all he could to make the enemy more and more certain that he was afraid of them.

As the days went by, Indutiomarus showed more and more contempt for us on his excursions to the camp. But on one single night Labienus brought inside the fortifications all the cavalry which he had summoned from the neighboring tribes. By a careful disposition of guards, he prevented anyone from leaving camp so that there was no possibility of anyone giving away the news or of the Treveri finding out about it.

Indutiomarus rode up to the camp as usual and spent most of the day there. His cavalrymen hurled their weapons and used a good deal of insulting language as they challenged our men to come out and fight, but they got no reply from us. Toward evening, when they felt like it, they began to move away in scattered groups and in loose order. Suddenly Labienus opened two of the gates and sent out his whole force of cavalry. He had given them strict orders that, as soon as the enemy panicked (as he knew they would) and were in full flight, everyone was to go after Indutiomarus and Indutiomarus alone; they were not to strike a blow at anyone else until they saw him killed; if they delayed over the rest Indutiomarus might get a chance to escape. Labienus offered large rewards to whoever succeeded in killing him, and sent out some infantry cohorts to support the cavalry.

Fortune favored the plan that Labienus had made. With everyone after him, Indutiomarus was caught and killed just as he was fording the river. His head was brought back to camp. On their return the cavalry chased and killed as many of the enemy as they could. The forces of Eburones and of Nervii which had already assembled dispersed when they heard the news, and after this action I found that things in Gaul were somewhat quieter.

⊶§ *BOOK SIX:* 53 *B.C.* §⊷

1
SUPPRESSION OF FURTHER REVOLTS.

I had many reasons, however, for expecting another, more serious outbreak of violence in Gaul, and I therefore instructed three of my generals—Marcus Silanus, Gaius Antistius Reginus, and Titus Sextius—to raise fresh troops. At the same time I sent a message to Pompey, who was now proconsul, but for political reasons was staying near Rome while retaining his military command. I requested him to mobilize the recruits whom he had sworn in in northern Italy when he was consul and to send them into Gaul to join my army. In my view it was very important, for the future as well as for the present, that the Gauls should realize that in Italy we had such reserves of manpower that, if we did suffer any misadventure in war, we could in a very short time not only make good our losses but take the field with larger forces than before. Pompey, acting like a patriot and like a friend, did as I asked; the new troops were quickly raised by my own staff officers; and before the end of the winter three new legions—twice the number of cohorts lost by Sabinus—had been formed and had been brought to Gaul. The size of these reinforcements and the speed with which they had been assembled were indications of the efficiency of Roman organization and the strength of Roman resources.

After the death of Indutiomarus, the Treveri conferred the supreme command on members of his family, who continued to intrigue with the nearest German tribes, promising to pay them for their help. They failed to make any impression on their immediate neighbors and went on to approach the more remote tribes, some of whom accepted their proposals. Oaths were exchanged and hostages given as guarantees for the payment of the promised subsidies. They also invited Ambiorix to join with them in a league of friendship.

I received reports of what was going on and could see that in every direction preparations were being made for war. The Nervii, Aduatuci, and Menapii were in arms and had been joined by all the German tribes on the left bank of the Rhine; the Senones had failed to appear at my command and were engaged in intrigues with the Carnutes and other neighboring tribes; the Treveri were continually sending deputations to the Germans across the Rhine. It seemed to me, therefore, that I must make plans for opening the campaign earlier in the year than usual.

So, before the end of the winter, I concentrated the four nearest legions and marched into the country of the Nervii. We took them by surprise and, before they could either assemble or escape, we had captured great numbers of cattle and of prisoners. These were given as booty to the troops. The fields were then laid waste. The tribe was compelled to offer its surrender and to deliver hostages. With this business quickly settled, I led the legions back again to their winter camps.

At the beginning of spring I summoned the usual Gallic council. All tribes sent representatives except the Senones, the Carnutes, and the Treveri. I regarded this failure of theirs to attend as the first step in the direction of armed rebellion and, wishing to give the impression that everything else was of secondary importance, I adjourned the council and, in a proclamation made from military headquarters, required them to reassemble at Paris. The Parisii shared a frontier with the Senones and in the previous generation had been united with them in one state; but it was not thought that they had anything to do with the present intrigues. On the same day as the proclamation was made, I started out with the legions against the Senones and after a series of forced marches we crossed their frontier.

When Acco, the leader of the conspiracy, heard that we were on our way, he ordered the whole population to retire to their strongholds. This they attempted to do, but before they could carry out the operation, news came that we were actually among them. There was nothing that they could do except give up their original plan and send a deputation to me to ask for my forgiveness. They made this approach to me through the Aedui, who had long exercised a kind of protectorate over them; and, at the instance of the Aedui, I gladly pardoned them and accepted their excuses. This was because I had a war on hand and summer was the time for fighting rather than for holding judicial investigations. However, I ordered them to deliver one hundred hostages, whom I gave to the Aedui to look after. While I was still here the Carnutes also sent a deputation and delivered hostages. The deputation was sponsored by the Remi, whose dependents they were, and I gave them the same reply as I had given to the Senones. I then completed the business of the Gallic council and instructed the various states to send me contingents of cavalry.

Now that peace had been restored to this part of Gaul, I put my whole heart and soul into the war to be fought against the Treveri and Ambiorix. I told Cavarinus to accompany me with the cavalry of the Senones, as I did not want any trouble caused in his tribe by his bad temper and the unpopularity which he had incurred. Once this was settled, I began to imagine what were the courses that Ambiorix might possibly take, having already ruled out the supposition that he would venture on fighting a pitched battle. The Menapii were close neighbors of the Eburones; they were protected by a continuous line of marshes and forests; and they were the only people in Gaul who had never sent deputies to me to ask for peace. I knew that Ambiorix had formal ties of hospitality with the Menapii, and I had also been informed that, by means of the Treveri, he had formed an alliance with the Germans. It seemed to me best to deprive him of these supports before making a direct attack on him; otherwise he might in desperation be forced to go into hiding among the Menapii or else join the Germans beyond the Rhine. With this plan in mind, I sent the baggage of the whole army to Labienus in the country of the Treveri and ordered two legions to set out there too. I myself marched against the Menapii with five legions unencumbered by equipment. The enemy made no attempt to get an army together. Relying on the protection that their country afforded, they all fled into the forests and marshes, taking their property with them.

I divided our forces into three, taking one division myself and entrusting the command of the other two to the general Gaius Fabius and the quaestor Marcus Crassus. Bridges were quickly constructed and the three columns moved forward, burning the villages and farm buildings, carrying off great numbers of cattle, and taking many prisoners. The result was that the Menapii were forced to send a deputation to me to beg for peace. I accepted hostages from them but told them that I should regard them as enemies if they allowed Ambiorix or any of his agents to enter their country. When this business was settled, I left behind Commius the Atrebatian with a detachment of cavalry to keep an eye on the Menapii and set out myself against the Treveri.

While all this was going on, the Treveri had got together a very large army of infantry and cavalry and were preparing to make an attack on Labienus and the one legion which had been spending the winter in their country. They had already got within two days' march of his camp when they heard of the arrival of the two other legions which I had sent. So they pitched camp about fifteen miles away and decided to wait there for their German allies. Labienus realized what their intentions were, but hoped that they might prove reckless enough to give him a chance of fighting. So, leaving five cohorts to guard the baggage, he set out against the enemy with a force of twenty-five cohorts and a large body of cavalry. He entrenched a camp about a mile away from them.

There was a steep-banked river, very difficult to cross, between him and the enemy. Labienus had no intention of crossing it himself and did not believe that the enemy would do so either. And with each day that passed, the chances of the arrival of enemy reinforcements increased. Labienus therefore deliberately said in the presence of a number of the men that since the Germans were said to be approaching he was not going to risk the safety of himself and the army, and would strike camp at dawn on the following day. It was natural that out of the large number of Gallic horsemen with Labienus some should be on the side of the Gauls; consequently these remarks of his were quickly reported to the enemy. During the night Labienus called a council of officers and senior centurions and explained his plan. In order to make the enemy still more likely to believe that he was frightened, he gave orders that camp should be struck with much more shouting and general disturbance than is usual in a Roman army. In this way he made it look as though he was running away rather than withdrawing. All this too, since the camps were so close together, was reported to the enemy by their scouts before dawn.

The Gauls now began to excite each other to action. Why, they asked, should they let the plunder which they had hoped for slip through their hands? The Romans were already terrified and it would be a long business to wait for the Germans. Moreover, it would be a disgraceful thing, considering the size of their army, to shrink from attacking such a small enemy force, particularly as it was already in full retreat and hampered by its baggage. So, almost before our rear guard had got clear of the fortifications of the camp, the Gauls came boldly across the river to fight us on ground that was very unfavorable to themselves.

This was just what Labienus had expected. So as to draw the whole lot of them across the river, he continued to go quietly ahead, keeping up the pretense that he was marching away. Soon he sent the baggage a little forward and had it all collected on some higher ground, and then, turning to his men, he said: "Soldiers, here is the chance that you wanted. You have the enemy in your grasp, fighting in a bad position and on difficult ground. I want you to show under my command the same qualities as you have often shown under the commander-in-chief. Imagine that he is here and that he is watching you with his own eyes." With these words he ordered the army to face about and form into line of battle. Sending a few squadrons of cavalry to guard the baggage, he stationed the rest on the two flanks. Our men quickly raised a shout and discharged their javelins. The enemy, who had imagined that we were in flight, now most unexpectedly saw us bearing down on them in attack formation; they could not even stand up to the first charge, but, as soon as the ranks met, were routed and hurried to gain the shelter of the nearest woods. Labienus followed them up with his cavalry, killed a great number of them, and took many prisoners. Within a few days he received the submission of the state. For the Germans who were coming to the help of the Gauls went home again when they heard that the Treveri had been defeated, and the relatives of Indutiomarus, who had been responsible for the revolt, fled from the country and went back with the Germans. Cingetorix, who as already mentioned had been loyal to us from the beginning, was given the supreme civil and military power over his tribe.

After marching from the country of the Menapii into that of the Treveri, I decided to cross the Rhine for two reasons: first, because the Germans had sent reinforcements to the Treveri for use against us; second, because I wanted to prevent Ambiorix from escaping to Germany. Once the decision had been made, I set about having a bridge built a little above the place where we had crossed before. The principles of construction were now well known, and the men worked so well that the bridge was completed in a few days. I left a strong garrison to hold the bridgehead in the country of the Treveri in case there might be any sudden rising on their part, and led the rest of the army and the cavalry across the river. The Ubii, who had already produced hostages and offered submission, sent a deputation to me to clear themselves of any suspicions I might entertain and to assure me that they had not broken faith with me and had not sent any troops at all from their state to help the Treveri. They earnestly begged me to spare them and not, out of a general hatred of all Germans, to allow the innocent to suffer with the guilty; and they promised to give me more hostages if I wanted them. From inquiries I discovered that the troops sent had come from the Suebi; so I accepted the Ubii's explanations and began to collect information about possible lines of advance into the country where the Suebi lived.

In a few days' time, I was informed by the Ubii that the Suebi were concentrating all their forces into one area and were sending messages out to all their subject tribes telling them to send contingents of infantry and cavalry. As soon as I got this information, I made arrangements to secure our grain supply and chose a good position for a camp. I ordered the Ubii to bring in all their cattle and movable property from the fields into their strongholds, hoping that lack of provisions might induce the ignorant and half-civilized Suebi to fight on ground where conditions would be against them. I also told the Ubii to send frequent patrols into the country of the Suebi to find out what they were doing. My instructions were carried out, and after a few days the Ubii came back to report that as soon as the Suebi had received fuller accounts of the Roman army, they had all retired, with the whole of their own force and all the allied contingents, to the most remote parts of their country, where there was an enormous forest called Bacenis which stretched far into the interior and formed a natural barrier between the Suebi and the Cherusci and prevented either tribe from invading and ravaging the territory of the other. It was on the edge of this forest, so the Ubii informed me, that the Suebi had decided to await our arrival.

2   CUSTOMS AND CHARACTERISTICS OF THE GAULS AND GERMANS.

At this point it may not be out of place to give something of an account of the customs of the Gauls and Germans and of the differences between these two races. In Gaul one finds that every tribe, every clan, every subdivision of a clan—indeed, practically every individual household—is divided into rival factions. The leaders of these factions are men who enjoy a particular prestige among their followers, who are prepared to give them supreme authority in judging and deciding any question whatever which comes up for discussion. This is a time-honored custom of theirs and its object seems to have been to provide protection for every man of the common people against those who are stronger than he is. For none of these leaders will allow his own followers to be oppressed or cheated; otherwise he would lose all authority over them.

The same principle applies to Gaul as a whole; all the tribes fall into two separate groups. When I first came to Gaul, the leaders of one of these groups were the Aedui and of the other the Sequani. The Aedui had from ancient times been the most powerful state of all and had numbers of other states dependent on them. Thus the Sequani, considered as a power by themselves, were the weaker of the two. However, the Sequani had made an alliance with Ariovistus and his Germans and, by promising much and sacrificing much, had brought them in on their side. Several battles were fought in which the Aedui were defeated and their nobility wiped out. In this way the Sequani had become the predominant power; they had taken over a number of states that used to be dependent on the Aedui; they kept as hostages the children of the leading men of the Aedui and had compelled the Aeduan government to swear an oath that they would never plot against their conquerors. They had occupied with their own tribesmen part of the Aeduan land along their frontier which they had seized in war, and indeed had established their hegemony over the whole of Gaul.

It was to deal with this desperate situation that Diviciacus had made the journey to Rome to ask help from the senate. He had returned again to his tribe without having achieved anything. With my arrival in Gaul, however, the situation changed. The Aedui had their hostages given back to them and their former dependencies restored. I even helped them to acquire control over states which they had not controlled before. This was because those who joined in alliance with them found that they were better treated and better governed than they had been previously. In other ways too the Aedui were given more influence and greater prestige. The Sequani lost the supreme power which they had exercised, and their place was taken by the Remi. As it was known that the Remi were as much in my favor as the Aedui, all those states which because of old feuds could never be induced to throw in their lot with the Aedui now began to come into the sphere of influence of the Remi, who took good care of them and thus were able to retain this new and very rapidly acquired authority of theirs. At the time of which I am writing, the Aedui were acknowledged to be much the most important state in Gaul, with the Remi occupying second place.

Throughout Gaul there are only two classes of men whom we considered of any real importance. The common people, regarded virtually as slaves, never venture to act on their own initiative and are never consulted about anything. Most of them, crushed down by debt, heavy taxation, or the oppression of more powerful men, enter the service of the nobles, who exercise over them the same rights as masters have over slaves.

The two privileged classes are the Druids and the knights. The Druids are in charge of religion. They are responsible for all sacrifices, public and private, and they decide all questions of ritual. Great numbers of young men come to them for instruction, and the Druids are very greatly honored by their pupils. It is the Druids, in fact, who are the judges in nearly all disputes, whether between tribes or between individuals; in every case of crime or murder or question of a disputed legacy or boundary, they are the people who give the verdict and assess the damages to be paid or received. Any individual or community failing to abide by their verdict is banned from the sacrifices—and this is regarded as the worst punishment that one can have. Those who are excommunicated in this way are counted as criminals and evildoers; no one will come near them; people will neither meet them nor speak with them for fear of contracting some guilty infection from any kind of contact; if they ask for justice they do not get it; and they are debarred from any position of distinction. One Druid is at the head of all the rest and has supreme authority over them. On his death he is succeeded by whatever Druid is most honored among the others; if there are more than one of equal dignity the succession is determined by a vote of the Druids, though sometimes they actually go to war for the leadership. Each year on a fixed date they hold an assembly on consecrated ground in the territory of the Carnutes, whose land is supposed to be in the very center of the whole country of Gaul. Those who have disputes to settle come from all over Gaul to this assembly and accept the verdicts and rulings given to them by the Druids. It is thought that the Druidical doctrine was discovered, already in existence, in Britain and was brought from there to Gaul. Even today it is the rule for those who want to become really expert in the doctrine to go to Britain and learn it there.

The Druids are exempt from military service and do not pay taxes like the rest. These important privileges attract a great number of students, some of whom come of their own accord to be taught, while others are sent by their parents or relatives.

During their training they are said to learn a great number of verses by heart—so many, in fact, that some people spend twenty years over their course of instruction. They do not think it right to commit these doctrines of theirs to writing, though for most other purposes (public and private accounts, for example) they use the Greek alphabet. I should imagine, however, that they had two other reasons for this practice: they did not want their teaching to become available to everyone, and they did not want those who learned their doctrine to rely on the written word and so fail to train their memories; for it is usually the case that when we have the help of books, we are not so keen on learning things by heart and allow our memories to become idle.

They lay particular stress on their belief that the soul does not perish but passes after death from one body to another, and they consider that this belief is the best possible encouragement to courage, since it does away with the fear of death. They also hold long discussions about the heavenly bodies and their movements, the size of the universe and of the earth, the physical principles of nature, and the power and properties of the immortal gods; and on all these subjects they instruct the young men who are their pupils.

The second class is that of the knights. Whenever they are required for service in any war that has broken out—and intertribal wars, either aggressive or defensive, used to break out almost every year before my arrival in Gaul—they all serve on the campaign. Each one is attended by his own band of fighters and armed retainers, and the more of these that he has, the more noble and rich he is esteemed to be. Indeed this is the only criterion they have of a man's position and influence.

The Gauls as a nation are extremely superstitious. As a result people who are seriously ill or who have to face the dangers of battle will either make or promise to make human sacrifices, employing the Druids as officiating ministers at these rites. They believe that the divine majesty can only be appeased if one human life is offered in exchange for another, and they have sacrifices of this kind established as a regular state institution. Some of them make use of enormous wicker-work images, the limbs of which are filled with living men; they are set alight and the men perish in the flames. They believe that the gods prefer the execution of men who have been caught in the act of theft or armed robbery or some other crime; but if there are not enough of such criminals available, they will make up the number by sacrificing men who are perfectly innocent.

The god most worshiped by them is Mercury, and very many images of him are to be seen. They regard him as the inventor of all the arts, the guide on every road and on every journey, and the god who has most power in connection with moneymaking and commercial undertakings. After Mercury they chiefly worship Apollo, Mars, Jupiter, and Minerva, and hold roughly the same opinions about them as do other nations: that Apollo averts diseases, Minerva gives us the first principles of all sorts of craftsmanship, Jupiter holds power over the heavens, and Mars controls war. When they have decided to fight a decisive battle, they generally dedicate to Mars all the spoils which they hope to win; and after a victory they sacrifice the captured animals and bring all the rest of the captured property together in one place. In many states one can see great piles of these objects lying in consecrated ground; and it has scarcely ever been known to happen that anyone will dare to go against the injunctions of religion and either hide his booty in his own house or remove any of the things that have been consecrated. The punishment established for such a crime is death under the most severe torture.

The Gauls claim to be all descended from Father Dis and say that this is a tradition that has been handed down to them by the Druids. For this reason they measure periods of time by nights instead of by days, and in keeping birthdays or reckoning the first of the month or the beginning of the year they go on the principle that the night comes first and the day follows it.

In the ordinary customs of life, one of the chief differences between them and other people is that they do not allow their sons to approach them in public until the youths have reached the age for military service; they consider it a shocking thing if a son who is still in his boyhood stands in a public place where his father can see him.

When he marries, a man contributes from his own property a sum equivalent in value to what he has received from his wife by way of dowry. A joint account is kept of the total and the profits are set aside. Whichever of the two lives longer receives both portions together with the profits that have accumulated over the years. Husbands have the power of life and death over their wives as well as over their children. When the head of any noble family dies, his relatives meet together, and if there is anything suspicious about the way he died, they examine his wives under torture, as we do in the case of slaves; if guilt is proved, the punishment is a slow and very painful death. Considering the fairly low standard of living in Gaul, funerals are splendid affairs and cost a lot of money. They cast onto the funeral pyre everything that the dead man is supposed to have been fond of, including animals; and not long ago slaves and dependents who were known to have been particular favorites of their masters were burned with them at the end of the funeral ceremony.

Those states that have the reputation of running their affairs most efficiently have laid down a law by which anyone who hears from a neighboring state any news or rumor which concerns his own country is to report it to a magistrate without speaking of it to anyone else. This is because experience has shown that false rumors often have a disturbing effect on ignorant and unbalanced minds, driving people into criminal actions or leading them to interfere with important matters of policy. The magistrates suppress whatever news they think fit and only tell the public what they think is good for them to know. No one is allowed to discuss politics except in a public assembly.

The German way of life is quite different from that of the Gauls. They have no Druids to lead them in matters of religion and they do not take much trouble about sacrifices. The only gods they recognize are visible objects with obviously beneficial effects, such as the Sun, the Moon, and Fire. They have not even heard of any other gods. Their whole life is spent in hunting or in military pursuits, and from their earliest years they train themselves to endure toil and hardship. Those who retain their chastity longest are most highly honored among their fellows because the Germans believe that continence makes a man grow taller and stronger and increases his muscular development. It is considered absolutely disgraceful in anyone under twenty to have had intercourse with a woman. Nevertheless, there is no secrecy about the facts of sex: men and women bathe together in the rivers and they wear nothing except skins or short cloaks of reindeer hide which leave most of the body bare.

They do not go in much for agriculture but live mostly on milk, cheese, and meat. No one possesses any definite portion of land which he can call his own property; each year the magistrates and chiefs of the tribe allot a piece of land, using their own judgment as to its size and position, to clans or groups of kinsmen living together, and in the following year they make the tenants move on to another holding. They give a number of reasons for this custom of theirs, for example: to prevent people from getting so attached to a particular spot that they will lose their enthusiasm for war and take up agriculture instead; to check any desire for large estates, which would result in the strong driving the weak off their land; to discourage the building of houses specially designed to protect the inmates from heat or cold; to prevent people from becoming fond of money, a vice which tends to lead to division and party strife; and to keep the common people happy and contented by letting each man see that he himself is just as well off as the most powerful people in the tribe.

What makes a German tribe particularly proud of itself is to live in the middle of a wilderness, with as much land as possible beyond its frontiers waste and derelict. They think it is the real mark of being a great and powerful nation to be able to force their neighbors off their land so that no one dares settle near them; and at the same time they regard themselves as being more secure this way, since there will be no risk of any sudden invasion. Whenever a tribe is involved in any war, offensive or defensive, supreme commanders are chosen and are given the power of life and death over their fellow tribesmen. In peacetime there are no magistrates with general powers; the chiefs of various districts and the leaders of clans administer justice and settle disputes among their own people. There is no disgrace in committing acts of brigandage so long as these are done outside the frontiers of the tribe; indeed, this is regarded as good training for the young men and something which will prevent them from getting lazy. When one of their chiefs gets up in an assembly to say he will lead a raiding party and asks for volunteers to come with him, those who like the idea and approve of the leader rise to their feet and, amid general applause, promise him their help. If any of these fail to follow him in the end, they are regarded as traitors and deserters and will never be trusted again in anything. They think it wrong to commit any violence against a guest; anyone who comes to a house of theirs for whatever reason is safe from injury and treated as sacrosanct; he can go to any man's home he likes and will receive his share of food there.

There was a time in the past when the Gauls were a more warlike race than the Germans. They actually invaded Germany and settled colonies beyond the Rhine, because their own population was too large for the land available to them. In this way the Volcae Tectosages seized and occupied the most fertile district of Germany. This is the part near the Hercynian forest—which, I see, Eratosthenes and other Greeks had heard about and called the "Orcynian" forest. The Volcae Tectosages still maintain themselves as a nation in this area and have a very high reputation for good government and for military ability. At the present time, since their living conditions of want, poverty, and hardships are the same as those of the Germans, they eat the same kind of food and live in the German way. The Gauls, on the other hand, living near our Province and acquainted with goods that come to them from overseas, are well supplied with both necessities and luxuries; they have gradually become used to defeat, and after fighting and losing so many battles they do not even pretend to be the equals of the Germans in war.

* The Hercynian forest which has just been mentioned ex-

* The rest of this chapter is regarded by many scholars as an interpolation.—R.W.

tends so far that a man traveling light would take nine days to cross it; this is the only way they have of describing it, since the Germans have no words for the measurements of distances. The forest begins on the frontiers of the Helvetii, the Nemetes, and the Rauraci and runs right along the bank of the Danube to the country of the Daci and the Anartes. At this point it turns away from the river in a northeasterly direction. As it is of such an enormous extent, it touches the countries of a number of different peoples; indeed one cannot find anybody in the part of Germany which we know who would claim to have reached the eastern end of this forest, even after traveling for sixty days in that direction; nor has anyone learned where it begins.

It is known that there are to be found in this forest many kinds of wild animals which are not to be seen elsewhere. Some of these seem to be worth mentioning since they are remarkably different from the animals one finds in the rest of the world. There is, for example, an ox shaped like a deer, which has a single horn projecting from the middle of its forehead between its ears; this horn is straighter and sticks up higher than those of the animals we know, and at the top it spreads out in branches like the branches of a tree or like the palms of a man's hands. The male and female of this species are alike, each having horns of the same shape and size.

There are also animals which are called elks. They are like goats in shape and have the same kind of dappled skins, but they are rather bigger than goats and have horns that are only stumps. Their legs have no joints or articulations and they never lie down to rest; if they fall down by accident they are unable to get up again from the ground. They use trees as a means for getting repose; they lean against the trunks and so rest, supported in this way. Hunters who track the elks to the place where they usually go to rest undermine the roots of all trees in the neighborhood or cut the trunks nearly through so that, though they look solid, they are really on the point of falling. When the elks lean upon the trees in their usual way, they are too heavy for the weakened trunks, which collapse and take the animals down with them.

A third species is called the aurochs. This animal is rather smaller than the elephant and looks like a bull in color and shape. They are very strong and very fast on their feet, and they will attack any man or beast they catch sight of. It is a great thing among the Germans to capture these animals in pits and then kill them. This is a sport that involves hard work and provides good training for the young men. Those who have killed the largest numbers of these animals produce the horns in a public place as evidence of what they have done and win great praise for their achievements. Even when caught quite young, these animals can never be tamed or domesticated. Their horns are much bigger than those of our oxen and of a quite different shape and appearance. They are much sought after by the Germans, who put silver round their rims and use them for drinking cups at their grandest banquets.

3 PURSUIT OF AMBIORIX.

After the Ubian scouts had told me that the Suebi had retired into their forests, I decided not to advance any farther. I was afraid that we might run short of grain, since the Germans as a whole, as I have just explained, pay very little attention to agriculture. However, I did not want the natives to feel that they need have no further fear of us, nor did I want their reinforcements to get together too quickly; so, after withdrawing the army, I broke down two hundred feet of the bridge from the point where it touched the Ubian bank of the Rhine and at the other end constructed a tower four stories high with strong defense works all around it. To protect this position and the bridge, I left behind twelve cohorts under the command of young Gaius Volcatius Tullus.

As soon as the crops began to ripen, I set out myself on the campaign against Ambiorix, marching through the forest of the Ardennes, which is the largest forest in Gaul; it extends from the Rhenish frontier of the Treveri to the Nervian frontier, and is more than five hundred miles long. I sent Lucius Minucius Basilus with all the cavalry in front of the main army, hoping that by advancing quickly he might get a chance of doing something valuable. I ordered him not to allow any fires in his camp, so that the enemy could not get warning of his approach while he was still far off, and told him that I should be following him directly.

Basilus carried out these instructions and completed his march much more quickly than most people thought possible. He took the natives by surprise, captured a number of them in the fields, and acting on information received from them, made directly for Ambiorix himself in the place where he was reported to be with only a small cavalry escort. In war, as in everything else, fortune plays a very great part. Basilus was extremely lucky in catching Ambiorix completely off his guard and unprepared—indeed, he appeared on the scene before there was the slightest rumor that he was on his way. But it was by an extremely great stroke of luck that Ambiorix himself escaped with his life, after losing all the military equipment he had with him, including his carriages and his horses. Yet this was what happened. The house where he stayed was in the middle of a wood, as is usual among the Gauls, who generally build their houses near woods and streams in order to avoid the heat. Fighting in a confined space, his friends and followers managed for a short time to hold up the attack of our cavalry. While this fighting was in progress, one of Ambiorix' men mounted him on a horse and he escaped under cover of the woods. So by pure luck he was first of all brought into danger and then liberated from it.

It is difficult to be sure why it was that Ambiorix had not mobilized his army. It may have been part of his policy, taken in the belief that it would be unwise for him to fight a general engagement; or he may simply not have had time, being surprised by the sudden appearance of our cavalry and believing that the main army was not far behind. In any case, he now sent messengers in all directions through the country with orders that every man was to shift for himself. Some of them fled into the forest of the Ardennes, others into the long continuous stretches of marshland; those who lived nearest the sea hid in places that are cut off from the mainland at high tide; many emigrated from their own country, entrusting themselves and their property to the mercy of utter strangers. Catuvolcus, who was king of one half of the Eburones, and who had joined with Ambiorix in the plot against us, was now weak with age and unable to endure the hardships either of war or flight. After calling down every sort of curse on the head of Ambiorix, who had been the author of the plan, he poisoned himself by drinking the juice of a yew, a tree which is very common both in Gaul and Germany.

The Segni and Condrusi—two Germanic tribes who live between the Eburones and the Treveri—now sent a deputation to me begging me not to consider them as enemies and not to assume that all Germans on the Gallic side of the Rhine had made common cause against me. They assured me that they had never had any idea of attacking us and that they had sent no help to Ambiorix. I checked these statements of theirs by interrogating prisoners and then ordered them to send me any fugitives of the Eburones who had taken refuge in their country. I promised that if they would do this I would do no harm to their land.

I then divided the army into three divisions and took all the heavy equipment to Aduatuca, which is the name of the fortress, roughly in the middle of the country of the Eburones,

where Sabinus and Cotta had had their winter quarters. I had
several reasons for choosing this position, among which was
the fact that last year's fortifications were still intact, so that
the troops would not have so much work to do. To guard the
equipment I left the Fourteenth Legion, one of the three
recently formed legions which I had brought from Italy. I put
Quintus Tullius Cicero in command of the legion and the
camp and left him two hundred cavalry as well.

After dividing the army I ordered Labienus, with three
legions, to march toward the coast into the country on the
frontiers of the Menapii; I sent Trebonius, also with three
legions, to devastate the country on the frontiers of the
Aduatuci; and I took the remaining three legions myself, my
plan being to march to the river Scheldt, which flows into the
Meuse, and to the western fringe of the Ardennes where I
had heard that Ambiorix had gone with a small escort of
cavalry. Before leaving I promised that I would be back again
in a week, on the day that I knew the next issue of grain was
due to the men in the legion that had been left behind to
guard the baggage. I asked Labienus and Trebonius to come
back also on that date, if the military position permitted. This
would give them an opportunity for a further discussion and
examination of the enemy's tactics, after which they could
resume the campaign.

There was, as already explained, no regular enemy force to
contend with, no stronghold, and no garrison that would put
up any resistance. The whole population had scattered in every
direction, and individuals would settle wherever a remote
valley, a hideout in the woods, or a piece of difficult marshland offered any hope of defense and security. These hiding
places were known to the people living round about, and great
care was necessary to ensure the safety of our troops. Not that
the army as a whole was in any danger, for so long as our
men kept together nothing was to be feared from an enemy
who was both panic-stricken and scattered; the problem rather
was to provide for the safety of individual soldiers—though
this, of course, was also a consideration that affected to some
extent the security of the whole army. And in their desire to
get plunder, individual soldiers were very apt to get drawn
too far away from the main body; also it was impossible for
men in close order to advance along the narrow and overgrown
tracks through the forest.

I saw that if I wanted to finish the job off properly and
utterly exterminate the whole tribe of criminals, I should have
to divide the troops into a number of detachments and send
them out in different directions, operating at some distance
from each other. If, on the other hand, I preferred to keep

the companies in regular formation, according to usual Roman military practice, then the very nature of the ground served as a protection to the enemy, among whom were many individuals quite daring enough to lay ambushes for and surround any of our men who lost touch with the main body. Bearing all these difficulties in mind, I took every precaution that possibly could be taken. The troops were all on fire with the desire for revenge; yet even so I preferred to miss the chance of injuring the enemy rather than to do them harm at the expense of losing some of my own men. I sent messengers to all the neighboring states, inviting them, by holding out the prospect of plunder, to join in pillaging the Eburones. My object was to let Gauls rather than Roman legionaries risk their lives in the forests. At the same time I wanted, by bringing huge forces against the Eburones from all sides, to wipe this tribe off the face of the earth as a punishment for the crime it had committed. Great numbers of Gauls came in from all sides in answer to my appeal.

So every part of the country of the Eburones was being devastated, and by now the week was nearly up and the day approaching on which I had decided to return to the legion which was guarding the baggage. Here again there occurred a good example of how important a factor in warfare is luck and what consequences can follow from a pure accident. As already explained, the enemy were both panic-stricken and scattered; there was no body of troops that could cause us the slightest alarm. But the news spread to the Germans across the Rhine that the Eburones were being plundered and that everyone else had been invited to join in. At once a force of two thousand cavalry was raised by the Sugambri, who live close to the Rhine and who, as already mentioned, had received the fugitives from the Tencteri and Usipetes. About thirty miles below the place where our bridge had been built and where I had left a garrison, these Sugambri crossed the river by means of boats and rafts and invaded the country of the Eburones. Here they captured a number of the tribesmen who were scattered in flight and also seized large herds of cattle, booty which is very much sought after by these savages. Hoping for still more plunder, they advanced farther. Born and bred as they were for war and brigandage, they were not to be stopped by marshes or by forests. From their prisoners they inquired where I was and discovered that I had set off to some remote part of the country and that the whole army had left the district. Then one of their prisoners said, "Why go after the wretched, miserable booty that is available here when you are in the position to make yourselves really rich? In three hours you could be at Aduatuca, where the whole baggage of the Roman army is collected. The garrison is so small that it cannot even man the rampart and no one dares to take a step outside the fortifications." The Germans were delighted at the prospect. After hiding the plunder they had got already, they set out for Aduatuca, guided by the man who had given them the information.

Every day up to now Cicero had followed my instructions and had been most careful to see that all the troops were kept in camp, not even allowing a single sutler to go outside the fortifications. But by the end of the week, he began to doubt whether I would come back on the exact day that I had promised. He had heard that I had gone a considerable distance away and there was no sort of news about my return. He was also influenced by the way the soldiers were complaining; this strict procedure of his, by which no one was allowed to leave camp, was, they said, just as bad as an enemy blockade. He knew too that we had nine legions and a large force of cavalry in the field and that the enemy were scattered and practically annihilated. It did not therefore seem at all likely that anything serious could happen within three miles of his camp. So he sent out five cohorts to get grain from the nearest fields. There was just one hill between these fields and the camp. With the cohorts, but as a separate detachment, went about three hundred of the soldiers who had been left behind in camp because they were ill but who had recovered in the course of the week. A large number of sutlers were also given leave to accompany the party, taking with them many of the pack animals that were being kept in camp.

It happened that the German cavalry came upon the scene just at this very moment. Without pausing or slackening speed, they rode straight up to the camp and tried to break in by the back gate. On that side there were woods in the way, so that the Germans got quite close before they were seen; indeed the traders who were in their tents just underneath the rampart had no time to get away. The suddenness of the thing took our men completely by surprise and caused considerable confusion, so much so that the cohort on guard was very nearly overwhelmed by the first attack. The enemy then swept around the other sides of the camp, trying to find a way in. Our troops succeeded with difficulty in holding the gates; elsewhere the nature of the ground and the fortifications themselves barred the enemy's way. There was panic all through the camp; each man was asking the next what this disturbance was all about; no one knew where to fall in or where to go. Some said that the camp was already captured; others declared that these natives had arrived after winning a great victory in which our army and its commander-in-chief had been de-

stroyed; nearly everyone allowed his imagination to be affected
by superstitions arising from the place itself; they saw, as it
were, before their eyes the fate of Cotta and Sabinus, who had
fallen in this very fortress.

With everybody so much in the grip of a general panic the
natives became all the more inclined to believe what the
prisoner had told them—namely, that the camp had no garrison to defend it. They struggled hard to force their way in,
shouting out to each other not to let such a bit of luck slip
through their hands.

Among the sick men left behind with the garrison was
Publius Sextius Baculus, who had served under me as chief
centurion of his legion. I have already mentioned his conduct
in earlier actions. Baculus had now been five days without
food. Feeling very apprehensive about both his own and his
comrades' safety, he came out of his tent unarmed and soon
saw that the enemy were almost breaking in and the situation
was about as dangerous as it could be. Snatching arms from
the men nearest him, he took his stand right in the gateway
and was joined by the centurions of the cohort on guard. So,
all fighting shoulder to shoulder, they bore the brunt of the
battle for a while. Baculus was severely wounded and fainted,
but, passing him back from one man to another, they managed
to save him. This respite, however, gave the others a chance
to pull themselves together, to stand in their proper positions
on the fortifications, and at least to look as though they were
defending the place.

Meanwhile our troops who had gone to get grain and had
by now finished their work heard the noise of shouting from
the camp. The cavalry hurried ahead and discovered how
dangerous the position was. The men were terrified; unlike
the others, they had no fortifications to shelter them. Raw
recruits, quite inexperienced in warfare, they simply turned
their eyes toward their officers and centurions, waiting to be
told what to do. Everything had happened so suddenly that
even the bravest was thrown off his balance. The Germans,
seeing the standards in the distance, broke off their attack
on the camp. They thought at first that it was our legions
returning from the expedition which, according to the information of the prisoners, should have taken us further afield. But
soon they saw how few troops there were and, despising the
small number, charged down upon us from every side.

The sutlers rushed forward to the nearest bit of high ground
and were dislodged from it almost immediately. They then
ran back to where the men were forming up in their companies, thus increasing the alarm that the soldiers felt already.
Some of our troops were in favor of adopting a wedge forma-

tion with the idea of breaking through quickly to the camp, which, as they pointed out, was not far off; even if some were surrounded and killed, they felt sure the rest would be able to get through safely. Others were for taking up a defensive position on the ridge where they could all face the same chance together. The detachment of veterans who, as already stated, had gone out with the rest were against this second plan. They shouted out words of encouragement to each other and then, led by their commander Gaius Trebonius, a Roman knight, cut their way right through the middle of the enemy and got into camp without losing a single man. In the wake of their charge came the sutlers and the cavalry, who owed their safety to the good fight that had been put up by the veterans. But the others who had taken up their position on the ridge showed themselves still totally ignorant of the science of war. They could neither stick to their original plan of defending themselves on the high ground, nor imitate the speed and vigor which, as they had seen, had stood their comrades in such good stead. They did, indeed, attempt to get back to camp, but in doing so they came downhill and got themselves caught in an unfavorable position. The centurions, some of whom had been promoted for gallantry from the lower grades of other legions to the higher grades in this one, were not going to lose the glory which they had already won in war, and fought on most gallantly to the last. It was owing to their courage that the enemy were forced back a little. Some of our men, much to their own surprise, got into camp safely; the rest were surrounded and killed by the natives.

Seeing that our men were in position along the fortifications, the Germans now gave up all hope of storming the camp and retired across the Rhine, taking with them the booty which they had hidden in the woods. Even after they had gone, the panic among our men remained so great that when Gaius Volusenus, whom I had sent ahead with the cavalry, arrived in camp that night, he could not make them believe that I was near with the whole army, safe and sound. The men in the camp were so totally terror-struck that they were practically out of their wits; the whole army had been destroyed, they said, and only the cavalry had escaped from the rout. They insisted that if the army were really in existence the Germans would never have attacked the camp. The panic ended when I arrived.

Personally I was not without experience of the way things happen in war, and, when I reached the camp, the only complaint I had to make was that the cohorts had been sent out of camp and away from their posts in the garrison. In my view nothing at all should have been left to chance, and

I was able to remark how powerful a part had been played by fortune. It was purely by chance that the enemy had arrived so suddenly, and it was even more a matter of luck that they had diverted their attention elsewhere, when the rampart and gates were practically in their hands. Perhaps the strangest thing of all was that the Germans, who had crossed the Rhine determined to ravage the lands of Ambiorix, by making this descent on our camp actually did Ambiorix as great a service as he could possibly have desired.

I now set out on another expedition to devastate the country of the Eburones. Large forces had been raised from neighboring states and were sent out in all directions. Every village and every building they saw was set on fire; cattle from every part were driven in as booty; the grain, much of which had in any case been flattened by the rains, was consumed by the huge numbers of men and animals engaged in the operation, so that it seemed evident that even if some of the local inhabitants had managed to hide themselves for the time being, they would die of starvation after the troops had withdrawn. And with such a large force of cavalry scouring the country in every direction, it often happened that we took prisoners who a moment before had seen Ambiorix in flight, who would turn their heads to look after him and insist that he could not really be out of sight. With such hopes of catching up with him, his pursuers, thinking of the gratitude they would earn from me, took enormous trouble and made almost superhuman efforts. Always, however, they seemed just to have missed the final and crowning success; Ambiorix would manage to steal away to the shelter of some wooded glen and then under cover of night would make off in some different direction or toward some other country. He never had more than four horsemen with him, and these were the only men to whom he dared entrust his life.

After the whole area had been devastated as described, I withdrew the army—which had suffered the loss of two cohorts —to Durocortorum, a city of the Remi. Here I summoned a council of the Gauls and held an inquiry into the conspiracy of the Senones and Carnutes. Acco, the leader of the conspiracy, was sentenced with a particular severity, being flogged to death in the old Roman manner. Some, fearing the result of the inquiry, took to flight and were declared outlaws. I then arranged for the distribution of the legions in winter camps. Two were left on the frontier of the Treveri, two among the Lingones, and the other six at Agedincum in the country of the Senones. After making sure that their grain supply was secure, I set out as usual for northern Italy to hold the assizes.

∞§ BOOK SEVEN: 52 B.C. §∞

1 VERCINGETORIX. THE BEGINNING OF THE WAR.

On reaching Italy I heard the news of the assassination of Clodius and was told of the decree of the senate ordering the swearing in of all Italians of military age. I therefore proceeded to conscript recruits in all parts of my province. These events were quickly reported in Transalpine Gaul, where the Gauls themselves invented some additions to the story which seemed to fit in with the facts; they declared that I was being detained in northern Italy because of the troubles in Rome and that, in view of the very disturbed situation there, I was unable to rejoin the army. To those who had long been indignant at finding themselves under Roman sovereignty this seemed an opportunity to be grasped and they began more openly and with greater daring to make plans for war.

Meetings of Gallic chieftains were arranged in remote places among the forests, and at these meetings there were bitter protests about the death of Acco. They themselves, it was pointed out, might easily meet with the same fate, and they lamented the general condition of the whole country, offering all sorts of reward to any persons who would take the initiative in starting a war and risk their own lives in the cause of the freedom of Gaul. The first thing to be done, they said, was to find some way of cutting me off from my army before their secret plans could become known; and this, they thought, should not be difficult, since the legions would not venture to leave their winter camps in the absence of the commander-in-chief, and I would not be able to reach the legions unless I had a strong escort with me. And in any case, they said, it was better to die in battle than to fail to recover their ancient glory in war and the liberty which they had inherited from their ancestors.

As a result of all this agitation, the Carnutes came forward and said that they were willing to face any danger for the common cause and that they would strike the first blow in the war. Under present conditions it was not possible to give pledges of good faith by exchanging hostages; to do so would have the effect of making their plans public; so the Carnutes asked the others to bring together all their war standards—according to Gallic tradition a most solemn ceremony—and in front of them to swear an oath of honor not to desert them when once the war had begun. All present praised the Carnutes for what they had said and took the required oath. Then, after a date had been fixed for the beginning of the revolt, they left the assembly.

When the appointed day came the Carnutes, led by two thoroughly abandoned characters called Cotuatus and Conconnetodumnus, at a given signal made a sudden descent on Cenabum, where they massacred all Roman citizens who had settled there as traders and plundered their property. Among those killed was Gaius Fufius Cita, a distinguished Roman knight, whom I had put in charge of the grain supply. The news spread quickly through all the states of Gaul. In fact when anything happens in Gaul that is particularly important or remarkable, the people shout out the news from one to another across the whole extent of the country; each takes up the report in turn and passes it on to his nearest neighbor. So it happened in this case. What had taken place in Cenabum at dawn was known before eight P.M. in the country of the Arverni, about one hundred fifty miles away.

There the initiative was taken by Vercingetorix, a young Arvernian with very great influence among his people. His father, Celtillus, had once been the leading man in the whole of Gaul and had been murdered by his subjects because he wanted to go still further and make himself king. Now Vercingetorix called together his own dependents and easily aroused their enthusiasm for the cause. When his plans became known, people came in arms to join him from all sides. His uncle, Gobannitio, and the rest of the tribal chiefs, who were against taking the risks involved, tried to restrain him and in fact expelled him from the town of Gergovia. However, he did not give up but proceeded to recruit all sorts of beggars and outcasts in the country districts. With these bands to support him, he brought over to his side all the Arvernians whom he approached. Calling upon his countrymen to take up arms in the cause of the liberty of Gaul, he soon got together large forces and drove out of the state those opponents of his who had just expelled him. He was proclaimed king by his followers. Deputations were sent out in every direction urging other tribes to stand by him, and in a very short time he had acquired the support of the Senones, Parisii, Pictones, Cadurci, Turoni, Aulerci, Lemovices, Andes, and all the other tribes on the coast. By general consent he was given the supreme command.

With this power in his hands, Vercingetorix demanded hostages from all the above-mentioned states, ordered each of them to send to him at once a fixed number of troops, and assigned the quantity of arms which had to be got ready in each state before a certain time. He paid particular attention to his cavalry. He combined very great efficiency with extreme strictness of discipline, and the severity of his punishments had the effect of bringing over the waverers to his side. Serious crimes were punished by death at the stake or under all kinds of torture; in the case of slighter offenses, the criminal was sent home with his ears cut off or one eye gouged out, to serve as a lesson to the rest and to frighten them by examples of severity. By such savage means as these he soon got an army together. He sent part of his forces under Lucterius, a Cadurcan and a most intrepid commander, into the country of the Ruteni while he himself marched against the Bituriges.

On his approach the Bituriges sent representatives to the Aedui, their protectors, asking for help in resisting the invasion. Acting on the advice of the generals whom I had left with the army, the Aedui sent a force of cavalry and infantry to the aid of the Bituriges. But when they reached the river Loire, which is the frontier between the Aedui and the Bituriges, they waited about for a few days and then returned home without having ventured to cross the river. They told our generals that they had come back because they were afraid of treachery on the part of the Bituriges, who, according to their information, had planned, if they crossed the Loire, to attack them on one side while the Arverni attacked from the other. As I have no evidence for knowing whether this was the real reason for their action or whether it was a question of treachery, I cannot make a definite statement on the subject. As soon as they left, the Bituriges immediately made common cause with the Arverni.

I received news of these events when I was in Italy. By this time I knew that, thanks to the vigor shown by Pompey, the situation in Rome was becoming more satisfactory, and so I started for Transalpine Gaul. When I arrived I was faced with the very difficult problem of how I was to rejoin the army. I knew that if I were to tell the legions to come to me in the Province, they would have to fight battles on the march without their commander-in-chief. The alternative was to hurry on to the legions myself; but I knew that it would be a mistake to entrust myself to any of the tribes on the way, even the ones which, at the moment, appeared harmless.

Meanwhile Lucterius the Cadurcan, who had been sent into the country of the Ruteni, had induced that tribe to join the Arverni. He went on into the country of the Nitiobriges and the Gabali and took hostages from both. Then, with the large forces which he had got together, he swept on in the direction of Narbonne with the intention of breaking into the Province. I decided that I must leave all other considerations aside and go to Narbonne myself. When I arrived there I did what I could to encourage the faint-hearted, posting garrisons among the Ruteni inside the Province, the Volcae Arecomici, the Tolasates, and around the city of Narbonne—in fact, all along the line nearest the enemy. I ordered part of the forces in the Province and some fresh troops which I had brought from Italy to concentrate in the country of the Helvii, which is on the Arvernian frontier. These measures had the effect of checking Lucterius and forcing him to retire, since he thought it too risky to bring his troops inside the line of our garrisons. I therefore set out for the country of the Helvii. It was the hardest time of the year, and on the Cévennes Mountains, which separate the Helvii from the Arverni, the snow lay thick, blocking up all the roads. However, by shoveling away the snow to a depth of six feet, the soldiers cleared a way, and thanks to their toil and sweat, I was able to reach the country of the Arverni. I caught them entirely off their guard. They had imagined that behind the Cévennes they were as safe as if behind a wall; never before at this time of the year had even single travelers managed to get across the passes. So I ordered the cavalry to range over as much of the country as they could and spread as much terror as possible among the inhabitants. Rumors and definite reports of this soon reached Vercingetorix, and all his Arvernian followers came up to him in terror, begging him to think of their interests and not allow their property to be carried off by the enemy, especially since it appeared that the whole Roman war effort was now directed against them. Vercingetorix listened to their entreaties and moved from the country of the Bituriges toward that of the Arverni.

This was just what I had imagined he would do. So, after staying there for only two days, I went off on the pretext of collecting cavalry and reinforcements. I left young Brutus in command of the troops, instructing him to overrun the country as far as possible in all directions, and I told him that I would try not to be away for longer than three days. Once this had been settled I greatly surprised my own escort by hurrying off at full speed to Vienne. There I picked up a fresh contingent of cavalry which I had sent on some time before and, without stopping by day or night, went straight on through the country of the Aedui to that of the Lingones, where two of the legions were in their winter camps. It was possible, I thought, that the Aedui might actually have designs on my life, so I moved too fast for them.

After reaching the winter camp, I sent messengers to the other legions and had them all concentrated in one place before it was possible for the Arverni even to have heard that I had got there. When he did receive the news, Vercingetorix led his army back again into the country of the Bituriges and went on from there to attack Gorgobina, a town of the Boii, whom I had settled there under Aeduan protection after their defeat in the battle I fought with the Helvetii.

This move of Vercingetorix made it very difficult for me to decide what to do next. If I kept all the legions together for the rest of the winter, a people supposedly under Aeduan protection might be overpowered and all the rest of Gaul, thinking that I was incapable of bringing help to my friends, might join in the revolt. On the other hand, if I led the army out of winter quarters too early in the year, difficulties of transport might give us serious trouble with regard to our grain supply. However, it seemed to me better to undergo every sort of difficulty rather than to suffer a loss of prestige and consequently lose the good will of all my supporters. I therefore told the Aedui that I relied on them to bring up supplies, and I sent to the Boii to inform them that I was coming and to encourage them to remain loyal and to stand up bravely to the enemy's attack. Then, leaving two legions at Agedincum with the baggage trains of the whole army, I started for the district where the Boii were settled.

On the following day I reached a stronghold of the Senones called Vellaunodunum. I did not want my grain supply to be endangered by an enemy left in my rear, and so I decided to attack the place. In two days it was surrounded by our entrenchments, and on the third day a deputation came out of the stronghold to discuss terms of surrender. I ordered them to hand over their arms, to deliver up all their pack animals, and to produce six hundred hostages. I left one of my generals, Gaius Trebonius, to see that these orders were carried out and, since I wanted to get to Gorgobina as soon as possible, went on myself to Cenabum in the country of the Carnutes. Here the people had only just heard that Vellaunodunum was being besieged. They had imagined that this would be a long-drawn-out business and were arranging to have troops sent in to garrison Cenabum when, after an interval of two days, we appeared in front of the place.

Because it was too late to attack immediately, we pitched camp near the city and I put off the assault until the next day, telling the soldiers meanwhile to get everything ready for the operation. As there was a nearby bridge over the Loire, I ordered two legions to stand by under arms for the night, since I feared that the people might attempt to escape from the town under cover of darkness. And, in fact, just before midnight the inhabitants of Cenabum came out of the town in complete silence and began to make their way across the river. When our patrols informed me of this I had the gates set on fire and sent into the town the two legions which I had ordered to be ready for action. I captured the town and, since the bridge and the other ways out were too narrow to allow any general exodus, took as prisoners practically the entire enemy population. The place was sacked and everything it contained was distributed as booty among the soldiers. I then brought the army across the Loire and reached the country of the Bituriges.

When Vercingetorix heard that I was coming, he raised the siege of Gorgobina and set out to meet me. I had begun to invest Noviodunum, a stronghold of the Bituriges which lay on my route, and deputies from this place had come out to beg me to forgive them and to spare their lives. We had already enjoyed some rapid successes and, wishing to finish off this campaign with the same speed, I ordered arms to be surrendered, horses to be produced, and hostages to be delivered. Some of the hostages had already been handed over and the rest of my conditions were in process of being fulfilled as some centurions with a few troops had gone into the town to collect the arms and the livestock. At this moment Vercingetorix' cavalry, which was riding in advance of his marching column, came into sight in the distance. As soon as the people in the town caught sight of it and thought that there was a prospect of being relieved, they raised a shout and began to seize hold of their arms, to shut the gates, and to man the walls. The centurions inside the town saw from the way the Gauls were behaving that there had been some change in the situation; drawing their swords, they seized the gates and brought all their men safely out.

I ordered our cavalry out of camp to engage the enemy cavalry; then, when I saw that our men were in difficulties, I sent to their support about four hundred German horsemen whom I had kept with me from the beginning of the campaign. The Gauls could not stand up to the attack of these

Germans; they were put to flight and, after suffering severe
losses, fell back on their main column. Once they were routed,
the people of Noviodunum again became terrified; they arrested the people who, according to them, had been responsible for the popular rising and, after handing them over
to me, surrendered themselves. Once this business was settled,
I set out for Bourges, the largest and best fortified town of
the Bituriges, lying in a particularly fertile part of the country.
I felt sure that by capturing this town I would secure the
submission of the whole tribe.

2 THE SIEGE OF
BOURGES.

At Vellaunodunum, Cenabum, and Noviodunum, Vercingetorix had suffered a continuous series of setbacks. He now
called his followers to a council of war and proposed that
the war should be fought on entirely different lines from those
which had been followed up to now. Their chief endeavor,
he said, must be to do everything possible to cut the Romans
off from forage and supplies. This should be easy, since the
Gauls were exceedingly strong in cavalry and were also
helped by the time of the year. There was no grass to cut
and therefore the enemy would have to disperse his forces in
order to get fodder from barns and storehouses; each one of
these scattered parties could be marked down daily by the
Gallic cavalry. Then, since the safety of everyone was at
stake, individuals must give up their rights in their own property; all villages and farm buildings must be set on fire on
each side of the Roman line of march to the distance within
possible reach of their foragers. The Gauls themselves had
plenty of supplies, being able to draw on the resources of any
tribe in whose country they might be operating. The Romans, on the other hand, would either starve or be forced to
take the great risk of marching a long way from their camp;
and it was immaterial whether the Gauls killed them or merely
deprived them of their baggage, since without this they were
unable to carry on a campaign. Finally, all towns which were
not so well fortified or so well placed as to be safe from
any danger ought to be set on fire; otherwise they might be
used as refuges by Gauls wishing to escape military service
or by Romans who would plunder their supplies. And if,
Vercingetorix concluded, these measures seemed cruel and
difficult to bear, they should consider how much worse than

all this it would be to have their wives and children carried
off as slaves and to be killed themselves—which would certainly happen if they were conquered.

The council unanimously approved of this proposal and in
a single day more than twenty cities of the Bituriges were set
on fire. The same thing was done in the other states; fires
could be seen in every direction—a sad sight for all, yet they
consoled themselves with the reflection that victory was now
practically in their grasp and felt confident that they would
quickly recover everything they had lost. With regard to the
town of Bourges, there was a discussion in a general assembly
as to whether it should be burned or defended. The representatives of the Bituriges went down on their knees in front
of delegates of the other tribes and begged that they should
not be compelled to set fire with their own hands to a city that
was perhaps the most beautiful in the whole of Gaul, a city
in which they took such pride and which was so essential for
the security of their state. It was naturally so strong, they said,
that it could easily be defended, being almost entirely surrounded by the river and by marshes through which there
was only one very narrow way of approach. This request
of theirs was granted. Vercingetorix was against it at first, but
in the end gave in to the prayers of the Bituriges and the general compassion that was felt for them. Specially chosen
troops were detailed for the defense of the town.

Vercingetorix now came after us by easy stages and chose
for his camp a position well protected by marshes and woods
about sixteen miles from Bourges. His patrols were constantly
on the watch and kept him informed of what was going on at
the town throughout every moment of the day, and he issued
his orders accordingly. He was always on the watch for parties
of our men going out to get fodder or grain; and when they
went far afield, as they had to do, and scattered over the
country, he would attack them, often causing serious losses,
though we on our side took all the precautions against him
that we could think of, setting out at different times every
day and going by different routes.

My own camp was on the side of the town where there
was a gap in the line formed by the river and marshes—
the narrow entrance mentioned above. Here we began to move
up mantlets and to construct a ramp with two towers, for
the terrain made it impossible to build fortifications all around
the place. Meanwhile I kept on asking the Boii and the Aedui
to send grain. The Aedui showed no enthusiasm at all and
were not much help, while the Boii, a small and weak tribe,
had very little to spare and soon used up what they did have.
So, what with the poverty of the Boii, the slackness of the

Aedui, and the burning of all granaries, our army was in very serious difficulties with regard to the grain supply. Indeed, for several days the soldiers had no grain at all and only managed to keep themselves from starving by driving in the cattle from distant villages. Yet one would not have heard a word from any of them that was unworthy of the greatness of Rome and of the victories they had won already.

I used to go and speak to the men of each legion while they were working. I would tell them that, if they found their privations unbearable, I was quite ready to raise the siege; but one and all they would beg me not to do so. They had now, they said, served under me for many years without ever disgracing themselves or even failing to finish any task to which they had set their hands; they would count it as a disgrace if they were to abandon this siege which they had begun; and they would rather undergo any hardship than fail to avenge the Roman citizens who had been treacherously massacred by the Gauls at Cenabum. Messages to the same effect were given by the troops to their centurions and officers with the request that they should be passed on to me.

Our siege towers had already been pushed up close to the wall when I discovered from prisoners that Vercingetorix had run out of forage, had moved his camp nearer to the town, and had gone off himself with the cavalry and the light infantry which normally fought in conjunction with the cavalry, to set an ambush in a place where he thought our foragers would go next day. On receiving this information, I set out at midnight, making as little noise as possible, and reached the enemy's camp early in the morning. Their patrols had acted quickly and told them of our approach, and after hiding their wagons and baggage in the thickest parts of the woods, they had drawn up all their forces in the open on top of some rising ground. When I was informed of this, I immediately ordered our troops to pile their packs and make ready for action.

The hill which the enemy occupied sloped up gently from the base and was almost entirely surrounded by a marsh not more than fifty feet across but very difficult to pass. The Gauls had broken down the causeways over the marsh and were no doubt confident in the natural strength of their position. They were formed up by tribes and stationed so as to guard every ford and thicket which led into the marsh, and their intention was, if we attempted to force our way through, to charge down on us while we were struggling in the muddy water. Seeing how close they were, anyone might have thought that the Gauls were ready to stand up to us in fair fight; but if one took note of the inequality of the conditions, he could have recognized that this was mere show and empty bravado on their part. Our troops were furious at the enemy's daring to stand waiting for them at such close range and clamored for the signal to charge, but I explained to them that victory here would be a costly business and could only be won by the loss of many gallant lives. I told them that, after I had seen them so ready to face any danger in order to win me glory, I should myself be guilty of the worst sort of injustice if I failed to put their lives first and my own interests afterward. In this way I calmed them down and led them back to camp on the same day. Here we went on with our preparations for the siege of the town.

When Vercingetorix got back, he was accused of treachery on the grounds that he had moved his camp nearer to the Romans, that he had gone away with all the cavalry, that he had left such a large army behind him with no one in supreme command of it, and that as soon as he had gone the Romans had appeared upon the scene, thus making the quickest possible use of their opportunity. All this, it was contended, could not have happened by accident; it must have been planned; no doubt Vercingetorix wished to be granted the kingship of Gaul by Caesar rather than to have it bestowed upon him by his own people. To these accusations Vercingetorix replied that he had moved camp because they were short of fodder and that he had done so at their own request; he had gone nearer to the Romans because he had seen the advantages of the position which was naturally so strong that it needed no defense works; as for the cavalry, there should have been no need for it on marshy ground, whereas it had been useful in the district where he took it. He had deliberately refrained from appointing anyone to the supreme command when he left, because he was afraid that whoever held such a post might be forced to fall in with the wishes of the majority and fight a pitched battle—which he could see they all wanted to do merely from lack of resolution and inability to go on bearing hardships. If the enemy's arrival was due to chance, then they had chance to thank for it; if it was due to information supplied by one of themselves, they ought to be grateful to whoever it was for giving them the chance of seeing from above how weak the Roman army was and of being able to despise the cowardice of troops who went ingloriously back to camp without daring to offer battle.

"As to the supreme power," he said, "I have no need to seek that from Caesar as the reward of treachery, when I could win it for myself as the result of a victory which I and all the Gauls together have already almost won. If you think that by giving power to me you are gratifying my vanity rather than increasing your own security, then take back all the titles that you have given me. And now, so that you may believe that I am telling you the plain truth, listen to what these Roman soldiers have to say."

He then produced some slaves whom he had captured a few days previously when foraging and had since exposed to the tortures of hunger and of chains. They had already been told what to say when questioned and now stated that they were Roman legionaries who had been forced by the pangs of hunger to slip out secretly from camp to see if they could find any grain or cattle in the fields. The whole army, they said, was suffering from starvation just as they were; no one had any strength left; it was impossible to carry on with the daily work; and for this reason the commander-in-chief had decided that if they made no further progress with the siege of the town he would withdraw the army in the next three days.

"And this," said Vercingetorix, "is what you owe to me whom you are now accusing of treason. Thanks to me you see a great and victorious army worn out by hunger, and this has been achieved without the shedding of a drop of your blood. And I have also made sure that when this army has to turn tail disgracefully and try to make its way back, not a single state will allow it inside its frontiers."

The whole assembly cheered and clashed their arms together, the usual Gallic way of showing approval of what a speaker has said. Vercingetorix, they declared, was a general of the first order; his loyalty could not be questioned; his conduct of the war could not have been more intelligent. They decided to send into the town ten thousand troops picked from all the tribal contingents, the reason for this being that they did not want the Bituriges to be given sole responsibility for this national effort, since they realized that if they saved the town the Bituriges would be able to claim all the credit for the final victory.

Our men showed the most remarkable courage and energy, but were confronted by all sorts of contrivances on the part of the Gauls, who are indeed a most ingenious race, wonderful imitators, and very good at making practical use of ideas suggested to them by others. For example they lassoed our siege hooks and, when they had caught them fast, pulled them aside and hauled them into the town by means of windlasses; they also tried to undermine our ramp and did this remarkably skillfully, for they do a lot of iron mining in their country and know all about the various methods of working underground. Moreover, they had built towers all along the whole circuit of their wall and covered them with hides. They were constantly

making sorties by both day and night and either trying to set
fire to our ramp or attacking the men who were working on it.
And as our ramp rose day by day and our towers came up
higher, they correspondingly raised the level of their own
towers by building on extra stories. They also countermined
our subterranean tunnels and tried to prevent their extension
to the wall by making fences of fire-hardened stakes, by
pouring in boiling pitch, or by blocking the way with enormous
stones.

Nearly all Gallic town walls are built on the following plan.
Beams of timber are laid on the ground at intervals of two
feet all along the length of the wall and at right angles to it.
The beams are then fastened together on the inside and banked
up with a good lot of earth; the intervals between them are
fitted in with large stones facing outward. When this course
has been laid and the beams tightly fastened together, another
course is laid on top of it. This is arranged so that, while the
same interval is maintained between the beams, those of the
second course are not in contact with those of the first,
but are laid on a layer of stones two feet high. Thus each
beam has one stone between it and the one below and is kept
firmly in position. Course is added to course in the same
way until the wall reaches the required height. This is an agreeable
style of building to look at, with the variety of alternate layers
of timbers and stones, all running in straight lines at proper
intervals from each other. It is also, from a practical point of
view, a style that is very useful for the defense of cities. The
stone gives protection from fire and the wood resists battering-
rams, which can neither breach nor shake to bits a structure
that is secured on the inside by beams which generally run to
a length of forty feet.

All these expedients of the Gauls certainly held up operations. Our men were also hampered by cold weather, which
lasted all the time, and by continual showers of rain. But by
never stopping work, they overcame every difficulty; in twenty-
five days they raised a ramp 320 feet wide and nearly eighty
feet high, which almost touched the wall.

One night just before midnight when, as usual, I was staying
out with the men on duty, encouraging them not to relax their
efforts for a moment, we saw smoke rising from the ramp.
The enemy had driven a tunnel underneath it and set it on
fire. At the same moment, we heard the noise of shouting all
along the wall and the enemy came pouring out of the town
by the two gates on either side of our towers. Others, standing
on the wall, flung torches and dry wood onto the ramp or
poured down pitch and every other sort of inflammable material. It was hard to know which sector needed relief most or

where one should first meet the attack. However, I regularly had two legions stationed outside the camp and ready for action every night, while still larger numbers of soldiers worked by shifts on the siege operations, so it was quickly arranged for some of our men to beat off the attacks from the town, while others dragged back the towers and cut a gap in the ramp and everyone in the camp rushed out to extinguish the fire.

Fighting continued at all points through the rest of the night. The enemy's hopes of victory kept on rising again and again, particularly when they saw that the protective screens around the towers were burned up, so that it was not easy for our men without cover to come up in support of their comrades; meanwhile, on their side, fresh troops constantly relieved those who were exhausted, and they all believed that on these few moments of time depended the fate of Gaul. Before our eyes one incident took place which we thought most remarkable and which I ought to mention. Standing in front of the town gate was a Gaul who took lumps of tallow and pitch as they were handed to him and threw them into the fire that was burning near one of our towers. He was struck in the right side by an arrow from a catapult and fell down dead. Another man standing nearby stepped over the prostrate body and went on with the job. He too was killed in the same way by a shot from a catapult; then his place was taken by a third man, who in turn was followed by a fourth; indeed, that position was never abandoned until the fire on the terrace had been put out, the enemy pushed back everywhere, and the fighting come to an end.

The enemy had now tried everything without success. Next day they decided to follow the advice and instructions of Vercingetorix and to try to make their escape from the town. By making the attempt at dead of night, they hoped to be able to get away without serious loss, since Vercingetorix' camp was not far from the town and the continuous lines of marshes which filled all the space between would delay our pursuit. Night came and they were already getting ready to make the attempt when suddenly the wives came running out into the streets and threw themselves down in tears at the feet of their husbands, begging and praying them not to abandon them and their children to the vengeance of the enemy, simply because they were by nature not strong enough to join in the escape. When they saw that the men were not going to change their minds (for it is generally the case that in extreme danger fear drives out pity), they began to cry out all together and make signs to our troops to show that an escape was intended. The Gauls now became alarmed and gave up their plan, for they feared that our cavalry would seize the roads before they could get to them.

Next day the siege works which we had begun were completed and one of the towers was moved forward. A great storm of rain blew up and it occurred to me that this might be the right moment to make the assault, as I noticed that the guards on the wall were not so carefully posted as usual. I told our men to go about their work as though they were not taking things very seriously and explained to them what I wanted done. Under cover of screens and out of view of the enemy, the legions got ready for action. Now at last, I told them, they could enjoy the fruits of victory in reward for all that they had done. I offered prizes to those who first scaled the walls, and then I gave the signal for attack. The men suddenly dashed forward from every direction and quickly lined the wall. Confused and terrified by the unexpectedness of it all, the enemy were dislodged from the fortifications and the towers, but they stood firm in the market place and other open spaces, forming up in compact bodies with the intention of deploying into line to meet any attack that might be made on them and fighting to the finish. But when they saw that no one was coming down to meet them on level ground, but instead our troops were coming all around them, occupying the entire circuit of the walls, they began to fear that they were being cut off from all hope of escape, and throwing away their arms, they all made a combined rush to the farthest part of the town. Some of them, crowded up together in the narrow passage leading to the gates, were killed there by our troops, others got through the gates only to be cut down by our cavalry.

It did not occur to any of our men to make money by taking prisoners. They were so infuriated by the massacre at Cenabum and by all the trouble they had had over the siege that they spared no one, neither old men, women, nor small children. In the end, out of a total population of about forty thousand, scarcely eight hundred, who had taken to flight at the very first sound of the attack, got safely through to Vercingetorix, who took them in late at night and as quietly as possible. He was afraid that the whole crowd of them together in his camp would arouse such compassion that there would be a risk of a general mutiny, and so he stationed his own friends and chieftains of the states along the roads some distance away with instructions to sort out the fugitives and have them conducted to their own people in whatever part of the camp had been allotted to the various tribes at the beginning of the campaign.

Next day a council of war was called, and Vercingetorix did what he could to encourage his people, telling them not to be

too downhearted or distressed by what had happened. The
Romans, he said, owed their victory not to courage in the field
but to a kind of technical proficiency and a knowledge of siege
craft, in which the Gauls lacked experience. It was a mistake
to imagine that in warfare everything would always go one's
own way. And in this instance his hearers could bear witness to
the fact that he himself had never been in favor of trying to
defend Bourges. What had really caused the present disaster
was that the Bituriges had been unwise and that the rest had
been too easily influenced by them. He promised, however,
that he would soon bring them advantages which would more
than make up for this defeat. His efforts were now directed
toward bringing over to their side those states which so far
had not joined the Gallic alliance. He would then establish one
policy for the whole of Gaul; if Gaul were united, the whole
world could not stand against her. Moreover, these plans of
his were already on the point of being carried into practice.
Meanwhile he felt that, for the safety of everyone, he could
reasonably ask them to set to work and fortify their camp so
that they would be in a better position to meet any sudden
attack that the enemy might make.

This speech of his went down well with the Gauls, largely
because Vercingetorix himself had not lost heart after such a
great disaster and had neither hidden himself away nor avoided
contact with his army. He was considered to have shown
exceptional qualities of forethought and of intuition, because,
while things were still in the balance, he had recommended
first the burning of Bourges and, later, its evacuation. In
most cases failure diminishes the prestige of a commander;
but in this case, on the contrary, Vercingetorix found that
every day which followed his defeat brought him more honor.
At the same time the Gauls were much encouraged by his
assurances of bringing over the other states to join them. Now,
for the first time, they actually set to work on building a
fortified camp. To such an extent had they gained in resolution that, though they are by no means used to hard work,
they thought that they ought patiently to do whatever they
were told to do. And on his side, Vercingetorix did no less than
he had promised. He took every measure that he could think
of to bring in the states that still remained outside the alliance
and tried to attract their leaders by bribes and by promises.
His agents were specially selected for the job, being all men
who were either friends of the people concerned or else able
to sway opinion by their skill in argument. He provided arms
and clothing for those who had escaped from the sack of
Bourges. Also, in order to bring his weakened forces up to
full strength again, he ordered the various states to send fixed

numbers of fresh troops, telling them exactly how many each
state was to produce and on what day they were to be brought
into camp. And he ordered that all archers (of whom there
were a great many in Gaul) were to be called up and sent to
him. In these ways he quickly made up the losses that had
been sustained at Bourges. Meanwhile Teutomatus, a king of
the Nitiobriges, whose father Ollovico had been granted the
title "Friend" by our senate, brought to Vercingetorix a large
detachment of cavalry, some from his own tribe and others
whom he had hired in Aquitania.

3   DEFEAT AT GERGOVIA AND
      REVOLT OF THE AEDUI.

I stayed for several days at Bourges. The enormous quantities
of grain and other supplies which we found then made it possible for the troops to get back their health after the hardships
and lack of food from which they had suffered. Winter was
now nearly over; it was the right time of the year for beginning
military operations, and I had already decided to march against
the enemy, hoping either to entice them out of the marshes and
forests or else to be able to blockade them where they were.

At this point some leading men of the Aedui came to beg
me to intervene in what was a most critical situation in their
country. Here, they said, there existed a most dangerous state
of affairs. Their custom was and long had been to elect one
magistrate each year to hold sovereign power, but there were
now two such magistrates in office and each of them claimed
to have been legally elected. One was Convictolitavis, a wealthy
and distinguished young man, and the other Cotus, who came
from a very ancient family, was himself a person of great
influence and with important connections, and whose brother
Valetiacus had held the same office in the previous year. Now
the whole state was up in arms; the council was split and so
were the people in general, each of the two claimants having
his own following. If the quarrel went on any longer, civil war
was a certainty. It was up to me, they said, to prevent this by
looking into the matter and exercising my authority.

I thought that it would be much against our interests to
abandon the campaign and move away from the enemy. On
the other hand, I knew only too well how serious can be
the results of such political strife. The Aedui were a large
state, very closely bound to us; I had always done what I could
for them and had treated them with particular distinction. I
did not want them now to come to blows with each other and

for the side which thought itself the weaker to call in the aid of Vercingetorix; indeed, it seemed to me that I should do everything possible to prevent this from happening. According to Aeduan law the holders of the chief magistracy are not allowed to go outside their country; so, in order to avoid giving the impression that I was lacking in respect for their established constitution, I decided to go myself into their country and invited their whole council and the two parties to the dispute to meet me at Decetia. Almost all members of the council came to the meeting place and I was informed that what had happened was this: a small secret assembly had been held at the wrong time in the wrong place and at this assembly Valetiacus had declared his brother duly elected, although according to law it was forbidden for two members of one family to be elected magistrates during the lifetime of both or even to sit together as members of the council. I therefore ordered Cotus to resign from his position and told Convictolitavis, who had been elected constitutionally at a time when the office was vacant and with approval of the Druids, to continue in power.

After making this decision between the two parties, I urged the Aedui to think no more about their differences and their quarrels, and, leaving all such things aside, to devote themselves exclusively to this war which we were fighting. I told them that once I had completed the conquest of Gaul they could expect to receive from me the rewards which they deserved, and I asked them to send me at once their entire cavalry force and ten thousand infantry to be stationed in various positions to guard our convoys.

Next I divided the army in two. I gave Labienus four legions and instructed him to lead them against the Senones and the Parisii. I took the other six myself and led them along the river Allier to Gergovia in the country of the Arverni. I took some of the cavalry with me and gave some to Labienus. As soon as he heard what we were doing, Vercingetorix had all the bridges over the Allier destroyed and began to march along the bank opposite us.

Separated as they were, the two armies were in sight of each other. The Gauls usually camped just opposite us, with patrols posted along the banks to prevent us from building a bridge and getting across to their side of the river. My position was thus extremely difficult. Usually the Allier cannot be forded until autumn, and I began to fear that this river was going to hold me up for most of the summer. To prevent this, I pitched camp in a wood opposite one of the bridges which Vercingetorix had destroyed, and on the following day kept two legions hidden there while sending on the rest of the army with all the baggage, as usual. Some cohorts had been broken

up into smaller detachments so that it would look as though
all six legions were on the march. I ordered them to go
forward as far as they could and when it came to the time of
day at which I supposed them to be safe in camp, I began
to rebuild the bridge, using the original piles, the lower parts
of which were still intact. The work was soon finished; I took
the legions across, selected a good place for a camp, and then
recalled the rest of the army. When Vercingetorix heard of
this, he hurried ahead as fast as he could, not wanting to be
forced to fight against his will.

From here we reached Gergovia after five days' marching.
On the day we arrived, a slight cavalry skirmish took place
and I reconnoitered the position of the town. It was built on
a high mountain and was very difficult to approach from every
direction. I could see no hope of taking it by assault and
decided not to do anything about besieging it until I had made
sure of our grain supply. Vercingetorix on his side had made
his camp near the town; the various tribal contingents were
each in their separate quarters all around him; every height
along the ridge from which one could get a good view had
been occupied by his men, and the general appearance of
his forces was formidable enough. The chieftains of states
whom he had appointed to act as his councilors were summoned to meet him every morning at dawn to exchange information and attend to business. And he scarcely let a day pass
without sending into action some detachment of cavalry inter-
spersed with archers so as to test the spirit and fighting
qualities of each man under his command.

Opposite the town and rising from the very foot of the
mountain there was a hill which, with precipices on all sides of
it, formed a remarkably strong position. If we could get hold
of it, it seemed certain that we should be able to cut the enemy
off from their main water supply and make it hard for them
to go out foraging. However, the enemy had a garrison,
though not a very strong one, to hold the place. In spite of
this, I set out from camp at dead of night, drove out the
garrison before it could be reinforced from the town, and took
over the post. Here I stationed two legions, connecting the
larger camp with the smaller by a double trench twelve feet
wide, so that men could come and go, even one at a time,
without any fear of being suddenly attacked by the enemy.

While these operations were going on at Gergovia, the Aeduan Convictolitavis, who, as already mentioned, had been confirmed in his magistracy by my intervention, was approached
and bribed by the Arverni. He then entered into negotiations
with some young men who were led by Litaviccus and his
brothers, people of a very good family. He shared with them

the money he had received as a bribe and urged them to remember that they were born free and born to rule. It was only
the Aedui, he said, who stood in the way of what would otherwise be an absolutely certain victory for the Gauls; and it was
because of Aeduan influence that other states had been prevented from joining the alliance. But if the Aedui joined in with
the rest, the Romans would have no kind of foothold in Gaul.

"It is true," he said, "that I am under some sort of an obligation to Caesar, but all it amounts to is that I won my case,
which was a perfectly just one, with him as an adjudicator.
My real duty is owed not to him but to the liberty of us all.
Indeed, why should we Aedui call in the help of Caesar in
interpreting our own legal rights? We might just as well expect
the Romans to come and ask us to arbitrate in their affairs."

The young men were quickly won over by the speech of
the chief magistrate and by the money which he offered them.
They readily undertook to take the lead in the plot, but it was
first necessary to decide how to go about it, since they were
by no means sure that the state could be induced to go to war
without some compelling reason. It was decided that Litaviccus
should be appointed to the command of the ten thousand
troops who were being sent to me for use in the war. He was
to organize the march of this army, and meanwhile his brothers
were to go on ahead to me. They also agreed on how the
remainder of the plan was to be carried out.

So Litaviccus took over the Aeduan army and, when he
was about thirty miles from Gergovia, suddenly called a meeting of the soldiers. He spoke with tears streaming from
his eyes.

"Where are we going, soldiers?" he said. "All our cavalry,
all the nobility of our state has perished. Two of our leading
men, Eporedorix and Viridomarus, have been accused of
treachery by the Romans and have been put to death without
a trial. You shall hear the story from men who were actually
there and escaped from the massacre. As for me, my brothers
and all my family have been killed. Grief for them makes it
impossible for me to describe to you exactly what happened."

Some people were then brought forward who had already
received from Litaviccus instructions as to what he wanted
said. They told the troops the same story he had told. Great
numbers of the Aeduan cavalry, they said, had been killed
because it was alleged that they had been in contact with the
Arverni; they themselves had managed to hide among the
crowd of soldiers and so had escaped while the massacre was
still going on.

All the Aedui shouted out in anger and begged Litaviccus
to think out what could be done for them. "It is not," he

replied, "a question of thinking anything out; it is a matter of necessity. We must march straight for Gergovia and join the Arverni. Is it not certain that the Romans, after the dreadful crime they have committed, are now on their way here to kill us too? So, if we have any spirit left in us, let us avenge the shameful death of our friends by putting an end to these robbers whom we have with us."

With these words he pointed to some Roman citizens who, relying on his protection, had been traveling with his army. He now had them cruelly tortured and put to death, and plundered the large stores of grain and other supplies they had with them. He then sent messengers all over the country of Aedui to arouse opinion by repeating the same lie about the massacre of the cavalry and the nobility and to urge the people to act as he had done and to revenge themselves on their oppressors.

The two Aeduans, Eporedorix and Viridomarus, had come to serve with the cavalry of their tribe in response to a personal summons of my own. Eporedorix was a young man who came from one of the best families and had much influence in his own country; Viridomarus, equally popular, was a man of the same age, though not well born. He had been recommended to me by Diviciacus and, though his origins were humble, I had raised him to a position of great honor and responsibility. These two were rivals for power, and in the recent dispute about the supreme magistracy Eporedorix had done all he could for Convictolitavis and Viridomarus had given equal support to Cotus. Now, when Eporedorix heard of the plans of Litaviccus, he came to me about midnight and told me all he knew. He begged me not to allow the tribe to lose the friendship and regard of Rome simply because of the wicked schemes of certain young men; yet he saw well that a breach between us and the Aedui would be inevitable if all those thousands of troops joined the enemy, since their families would have to think of their safety and the tribal government would have to take the matter seriously.

As I had invariably shown most particular consideration to the nation of the Aedui, this news came as a great shock to me. Without a moment's hesitation I set out from camp with four legions in light marching order and all the cavalry. There was no time to reduce the area of the camps. The situation was critical and everything seemed to depend on speed. I left Gaius Fabius behind with two legions to guard the camps. I ordered the arrest of the brothers of Litaviccus, but found that they had just fled to the enemy. I told the troops that this was a critical moment and that they must be prepared to put up with some hard marching. Everyone showed the greatest enthusiasm, and after advancing for twenty-five miles we came in sight of the Aeduan column. I sent the cavalry forward to slow down and hamper their march but issued orders that no one was to kill any of them. I told Eporedorix and Viridomarus—whom the Aedui imagined to have been killed—to show themselves among the cavalry and to speak to their own people. They were soon recognized, and it became plain that Litaviccus had been deceiving his troops. Thereupon the Aedui began to stretch out their hands in token of surrender, to throw down their arms, and to beg for mercy. Litaviccus with his own retainers escaped to Gergovia—for, according to Gallic custom, it is a crime for a retainer to desert his lord, however desperate the situation may be.

I sent messengers to the Aeduan government to inform them that according to the laws of war I would have been perfectly justified in putting their men to death, but that I had chosen to be merciful and had spared their lives. I then gave the army three hours of the night to rest. Then we started for Gergovia. When we had done about half the distance some cavalrymen, who had been sent by Fabius, arrived and told me what a dangerous position they had been in. Their report was that the enemy had launched an attack on our camp in full force; they had sent in more and more fresh troops to relieve those who were tired, with the result that our men, who had had no respite at all, since the siege of the camp made it necessary for the same troops to be always on duty on the rampart, had become exhausted. Many of our soldiers had been wounded by the showers of arrows and every other kind of missile that had been launched against them. Our artillery, however, had been very useful indeed in repelling the enemy attacks. In the end the enemy had withdrawn and Fabius was now blocking up all the gates except two and erecting screens along the ramparts in preparation for meeting the same sort of attack next day. On receiving this news I called upon the soldiers for a supreme effort, and we reached camp before dawn.

While these actions were going on at Gergovia, the Aedui received the first messages sent to them from Litaviccus. They took no trouble to investigate the truth of these reports. Some were swayed by greed and others by anger or by that rash impetuosity which is so characteristic of all Gauls, and the result was that they accepted mere rumor as established fact. They seized the goods of Roman citizens, killed some, and dragged others off into slavery. Convictolitavis was behind the general movement and did his best to inflame the feelings of his people in the hope that, once they had involved themselves deeply in crime, they would be ashamed to come

back to their right mind. One of my senior officers, Marcus
Aristius, was on the way to join his legion and had stopped
at the town of Cabillonum. The Aedui induced him to leave
the place by promising him a safe-conduct and then compelled all Roman traders who had settled there to leave with
him. As soon as they set out, they attacked them and robbed
them of all their baggage. The Romans fought back, but
were surrounded and blockaded for a day and a night, after
which, when many people had been killed on both sides, the
Aedui brought up still greater numbers of armed men.

It was at this point that the news arrived that their whole
army was in my hands and at my mercy. Their leaders immediately hurried to see Aristius and assured him that what
had taken place had had no sanction from the government.
They ordered an inquiry into the theft of Roman property,
confiscated the goods of Litaviccus and of his brothers, and
sent a deputation to me in order to excuse themselves. Their
object in doing this was to get their own people back safe.
At the same time, they were stained with crime, they liked
the prospect of the profit to be made out of the plundered
goods—very many of them were implicated in this business—
and they were frightened that they would have to suffer
for what they had done. So they were secretly beginning
to make plans for war and were sending around deputations
to intrigue with the other tribes.

I was perfectly aware of all this, but nevertheless I treated
their deputation in the gentlest possible way, assuring them
that I was not taking a severe view of the Aeduan government simply because the Aeduan people had behaved ig-
norantly and irresponsibly and that indeed I felt just the
same good will toward the Aedui as before. In fact, I expected
that the revolution in Gaul would spread; I had no wish to
find myself isolated with every single tribe against me; and I
was beginning to think in terms of withdrawing from Gergovia
and once again concentrating the whole army. But I did not
want such a withdrawal to look as though it were a headlong
flight occasioned by fear of a general uprising.

I was still thinking along these lines when I got what
seemed to me an excellent opportunity for fighting a successful action. I had gone to the smaller camp to inspect the
defenses, and while I was there, I noticed that one of the
hills normally held by the enemy was left unguarded. Previously there had been so many troops to hold it that one
had scarcely been able to see the ground where they stood.
This was surprising, and I questioned some of the deserters
who were now coming in to me in great numbers every day.
They all confirmed the information which I had already

received from my patrols, and which was as follows: Behind
this hill was a ridge which was practically level, but wooded
and narrow at the point where it ran up close to the further
side of the town; the enemy were exceedingly anxious about
the safety of this ridge, feeling that, if they lost another
hill in addition to the one we held already, they would find
themselves almost walled in and cut off from the open country and from foraging; Vercingetorix had therefore withdrawn
every available man to work on the fortifications of this ridge.

After receiving this information, I sent out a few cavalry
squadrons about midnight and told them to ride over the
country, making rather more noise than usual. At dawn I
ordered a large number of pack horses and mules brought
out of camp and their pack saddles taken off. The drivers
were told to put on helmets and ride around over the high
ground, looking as though they were regular cavalry. I sent
a few real cavalrymen with them and instructed them to
spread out over a wide area and let themselves be seen. They
were all to converge on the same point after making a wide
detour. All this could be seen from the town, since from
Gergovia one could look right down on our camp, but the
distance was too great for the enemy to be quite certain of
what was going on. Next I sent one legion out along the
high ground in the same direction and then, after it had advanced a little way, halted it rather lower down the hill and
concealed it in a wood. The Gauls became more and more
convinced that some move was impending, and brought all
their forces up to defend what seemed to be the threatened
spot. Once I saw that their camps were empty, I told our
men to cover up the crests of their helmets and hide the
standards. I then moved them from the large camp to the
lesser one in small parties, so as not to be seen from the
town. I told every general in command of a legion what I
wanted done and in particular I warned them that they must
keep a tight hand on their troops in case they should be carried
away by enthusiasm for the fight and hope of plunder and
should advance too far. I pointed out that we were attacking
uphill and were therefore at a disadvantage which speed
alone could overcome; the object of the operation was to catch
the enemy by surprise, not to fight him in a regular battle.
After explaining these points, I gave the signal for attack and
at the same time sent the Aedui up the hill by another route
on the right.

From the point where the ascent began, the distance up
to the town wall was about a mile—or would have been, if
the path had been straight. As it was, the troops had to go on
a zigzag route in order to make the climbing easier, and

this of course added to the distance to be covered. About halfway up, the Gauls had built a six-foot wall of large stones which followed the natural contours of the ground and was intended to check any attack we might make. The area below the wall was unoccupied, but all the upper part of the hill right up to the town walls was covered with their encampments, all placed close together.

As soon as the signal was given, our troops quickly advanced to the wall, climbed over it, and captured three of the camps. This operation indeed was carried out at such speed that Teutomatus, the king of the Nitiobriges, was caught by surprise while having an afternoon sleep in his tent. The soldiers had turned to plunder, and he just managed to get away from them, naked to the waist and riding a wounded horse.

We had now attained the aims which I had set myself. I ordered the retreat to be sounded and immediately brought the Tenth Legion, which was with me, to a halt. The soldiers of the other legions, who were at the other side of a fairly deep depression, did not hear the trumpet call; nevertheless, commanding officers and others tried to hold the men back in accordance with my instructions. The troops, however, seeing the enemy in flight and remembering all their former successes, were on fire with the hope of winning a quick victory. They thought that no obstacle could exist that they could not overcome by hard fighting, and they pressed the pursuit right up to the wall of the town and the town gates. A noise of shouting arose from every quarter of the city; those who were farthest away from the scene of action were terrified at the sudden uproar and, thinking that the enemy must already be inside the gates, fled outside the fortifications. Women threw down clothing and money from the ramparts, and leaned over with bared breasts and outstretched hands, begging the soldiers to spare them and not to massacre women and children alike, as they had done at Bourges. Some were lowered down by hand from the walls and gave themselves up to the soldiers.

Lucius Fabius, a centurion of the Eighth Legion, had, as we found out later, told his men that he had his eye on the sort of reward that I had given at Bourges and he was not going to let anyone else scale the wall before he did. Now he got three men of his company to hoist him up, mounted the wall, and then in his turn pulled them up one by one to join him.

Meanwhile the Gauls, who as already pointed out had all gone off to the farther side of the town to strengthen the fortifications, first heard the shouting and then were still further alarmed by a succession of messengers who came to tell them that the town was in our hands. Sending their cavalry on in front, they all hurried after in a dense mass of men. Each man as he arrived took up his position under the ramparts and swelled the ranks of those already in action. Soon great numbers of them had got together, and the women, who a moment before had been stretching out their hands to the Romans from the wall, now began to direct their entreaties to their own men, leaning over in Gallic fashion with their hair disheveled, and bringing forward their children for the men to see. We were now at a disadvantage as regards both numbers and position; our troops were exhausted by the rapid ascent and by the long time they had been in action; it was difficult for them to stand up against opponents who were just coming, perfectly fresh, into battle.

I saw that we were fighting in a most awkward position and that the enemy's strength was increasing. Becoming alarmed about the safety of my men, I sent to Titus Sextius, whom I had left to guard the smaller camp, and ordered him to bring his cohorts quickly into the open and draw them up at the foot of the hill on the enemy's right flank, so that, if he saw that our men were being driven down from their position, he would be in the right place to prevent the enemy from pursuing as they wished. I myself with the Tenth Legion advanced a little way from the place where we had halted and waited to see how the battle would end.

The fighting was at close quarters and was raging fiercely, the enemy trusting in their superior position and numbers, our men relying on their own courage, when suddenly the Aedui, whom I had sent up by another route to create a diversion, came into view on our exposed flank. The similarity of their armor to that of the other Gauls caused terror among our men. Even though it could be seen that their right shoulders were uncovered—the usual sign to show that they were friends—the troops still thought that this was something done deliberately by the enemy to deceive them. At the same time the centurion Lucius Fabius and the others who had scaled the wall with him were surrounded and killed and their bodies hurled down from the wall. Marcus Petronius, a centurion of the same legion, had been trying to break down the gate, but was surrounded by a host of enemies and, having been wounded again and again, saw that his position was hopeless. He shouted out to the men of his company who had followed him: "I can't save both myself and you, but at least I'll see that you get away safely. It was I who led you into danger. I was too anxious to distinguish myself. Now look after yourselves. I'm giving you the chance." With these words he charged into the middle of the enemy, killed two men, and drove the rest a little way back from the gate. His comrades tried to help him, but he called out to them: "It's no use trying to save my life. I've lost too much blood and my strength is going. Get away while you have the chance and fall back on the legion." A few moments later he fell, still fighting; but he had saved his men.

Our troops were hard pressed on every side; forty-six centurions had been lost; and in the end we were driven down from our position. But the Gauls were prevented from doing us too much damage on our retreat because they were checked by the Tenth Legion, which was drawn up in support on rather more level ground. The Tenth in its turn was covered by cohorts of the Thirteenth, which had marched out of the smaller camp with Titus Sextius and had occupied a position above the level of the plain. As soon as the legions reached level ground, they turned about and faced the enemy in battle formation. But Vercingetorix withdrew his men from the foot of the hill and led them back inside the fortifications. On that day we lost nearly seven hundred men.

Next day I called a meeting of the soldiers and reprimanded them for the overeagerness and lack of restraint which they had shown in having ventured to decide for themselves where they ought to go and what they ought to do, in failing to halt when the signal for retreat was given, and in disobeying the orders of their generals and their officers. I pointed out what the effects could be of having to fight in the wrong position, and reminded them that it was this very thing which I myself had been so concerned about at Bourges, when, after I had caught the enemy without their commander and without their cavalry, I nevertheless chose to forgo a certain victory rather than incur even slight casualties by fighting on unfavorable ground. Much, I said, as I admired their magnificent spirit, which no obstacle had been able to check—not the fortifications of the camp, nor the height of the mountain, nor the actual wall of the town—I was just as much offended by their insubordination and by their presumption in imagining that they knew more than their commander-in-chief about how to win victories and how battles would turn out. "From my soldiers," I said, "I expect not only courage and gallantry in action but also discipline and self-control." After making these points I said a few words at the end of my speech to raise the soldiers' spirits, telling them that they must not be discouraged by what had happened and must not think that their losses were due to the warlike qualities of the enemy, when in fact they were caused by fighting on unfavorable ground.

I still felt as before about the advisability of withdrawing from Gergovia, but first I led the legions out of camp and drew them up in line of battle in a good position. Vercingetorix still refused to come down onto level ground, and after a minor cavalry action in which we had the better of things, I led the army back to camp. We did the same thing next day. Then, thinking that enough had been done to humble the arrogance of the Gauls and to re-establish the morale of my own men, I moved camp and marched into the country of the Aedui. Not even at this point did the enemy make any attempt to follow us. Three days later we reached the Allier, where we repaired one of the bridges and I led the army across.

Here I was greeted by the two Aedui, Viridomarus and Eporedorix. They told me that Litaviccus had set out with all the cavalry and was trying to subvert the loyalty of the tribe. It was essential, they said, for them to get there before he did so that they could encourage the government to remain in allegiance to us. I had by now plenty of evidence to show that the Aedui were disloyal, and I thought it likely that if I let these two men go, the revolt would break out all the sooner. Nevertheless, I decided not to detain them. I did not want to appear to be acting high-handedly, and I did not want it to look as though I was afraid. Before they departed, I briefly reminded them of what I had done for the Aedui and I recalled to their memory the humiliating condition their tribe had been in when I first came to Gaul—how they had been penned inside their towns, deprived of their lands, stripped of their wealth, forced both to pay a tribute and to surrender hostages under the most shameful circumstances. From this state I had raised them to power and prosperity, not only giving them back the position which they had once held, but making them more important and more powerful than they had ever been in the past. I told the two Aeduans to hand on this message and then let them go.

In the Aeduan town of Noviodunum, which is on the banks of the Loire in a good position for defense, I had collected all the hostages from the whole of Gaul, the stores of grain, the public funds, and much of my own luggage and that of the army. I had also sent there great numbers of horses which I had brought up for this campaign from Italy and Spain. When Eporedorix and Viridomarus reached this town, they heard the news of what was happening in their tribe: Litaviccus had been received by the Aedui in Bibracte, their most important town; the chief magistrate, Convictolitavis, and most of the tribal council had joined him there; and an official deputation had been sent to Vercingetorix to make a treaty of peace and alliance with him.

The opportunity now in their hands seemed to these two Aedui too good to be missed, so they massacred the garrison of Noviodunum together with all those who had settled there as traders; they divided the money and the horses between them; and they arranged to have the hostages from the various states escorted to their own magistrate at Bibracte. Since they considered that the town could not be defended, they set it on fire so that it should not be of any use to us. All the grain that could be handled quickly was loaded onto boats and taken away; the remainder was either set on fire or thrown into the river. They then began to raise troops in the neighborhood, posted garrisons and organized patrols along the Loire, and sent out cavalry to show themselves all over the countryside and intimidate all opposition. Their aim was to cut us off from our grain supply, or to reduce us to such a state of want that we should be forced to leave Gaul and retire to the Province. Their hopes of success were very greatly encouraged by the fact that the Loire was so swollen as the result of the melting snow that it appeared to be quite impossible to ford.

When I learned what had happened, I decided that I must act quickly. If we had to build bridges, we might be forced to fight, and it would be better to do so quickly before the enemy could bring still larger forces up to the river. There were some who were frightened enough to suggest that I should alter my whole plan of campaign and fall back upon the Province. I did not think so. This would not only have been a most humiliating and shameful step to take; there would also have been great difficulties in getting across the Cévennes; and most of all I was anxious about Labienus and his legions, who were separated from me. We therefore marched by day and night, making much longer distances than usual, and reached the Loire long before anyone could have expected us. With the aid of the cavalry, a ford was found which was good enough for the emergency. The men could just keep their arms and shoulders above the water, so that the weapons were kept dry. I posted cavalry at intervals in the stream to break the force of the current. The enemy were terrified at the sudden sight of us, and so the army was brought safely across. In the fields we found grain and a good supply of cattle, enough for the army's needs. I then began to march toward the country of the Senones.

4 LABIENUS ON THE SEINE. DEFEAT OF VERCINGETORIX' CAVALRY.

While all this was happening on my sector of the front, Labienus, after leaving behind at Agedincum the new draft of recruits from Italy to guard the baggage, had set out with four legions for Paris, a town that is built on an island in the Seine. When the enemy heard of his arrival, large numbers of troops assembled from the neighboring states. The supreme command was given to an Aulercan called Camulogenus, who though an extremely old man was honored with this appointment because of his great knowledge and experience of warfare. He took up a position in a place where he had observed that there was a long chain of marshes which drained into the Seine and made the whole area almost impassable. Here he stood with the intention of preventing our men from crossing.

Labienus first tried, under cover of mantlets, to lay a foundation of hurdles and earth and so build a causeway across the marsh. Finding this too difficult, he marched quietly out of camp soon after midnight and reached Metiosedum, traveling by the same route as that on which he had come. Metiosedum is a town of the Senones, built, like Paris, on an island in the Seine. Here Labienus seized about fifty boats, quickly lashed them together to form a bridge, and sent his soldiers across to the island. Most of the townspeople had been called up for the war, and the remainder were panic-stricken by the unexpectedness of the operation, so that Labienus occupied the town without meeting with any resistance. He rebuilt the bridge which the enemy had broken down a few days before, led his army across, and began to march down the Seine toward Paris. When the enemy heard the news from fugitives from Metiosedum, they ordered Paris to be set on fire and all its bridges destroyed. They then moved forward from the marsh to the banks of the Seine and took up a position facing Labienus and in front of Paris.

It was known by this time that I had withdrawn from Gergovia, and now rumors kept on arriving of the revolt of the Aedui and of the successful course of the rebellion in Gaul. Gauls who got into conversation with our own native troops assured them that I had been prevented from crossing the Loire and had been forced by famine to fall back on the Province. And the Bellovaci, who had already made up their own minds to revolt, now that they heard of the rising among the Aedui began quite openly to mobilize their forces and prepare for war. The situation had completely changed, and Labienus realized that he would have to alter all his plans accordingly. What he had to do now was to think not of further conquests or victories in the field, but of how he could get his army back intact to Agedincum. As it stood, he was threatened on one side by the Bellovaci, who were supposed to be the toughest troops in Gaul, and on the other by

Camulogenus with a well-equipped army ready to go into action immediately. Moreover, he was on the wrong side of a large river which cut his legions off from their baggage and reserves. With all these difficulties suddenly arising at once, he saw that his only hope lay in courage and in resolution.

Toward evening he called a council of war at which he impressed upon his officers the importance of carrying out his instructions carefully and efficiently. Each of the boats which he had brought down from Metiosedum was put in charge of a Roman knight, with orders to start about ten thirty P.M. and move quietly downstream to a place about four miles off, where they were to wait for him. He left to guard the camp the five cohorts which he considered would be least reliable in action, and he ordered the other five cohorts of the same legion to set out about midnight and to march upstream with all the baggage, making as much noise as they could. He also got together some small boats and sent them in the same direction, with instructions to make a lot of splashing with their oars. Soon afterward he set out himself with three legions and marched toward the place where he had ordered the other boats to put in. Enemy patrols were posted along the banks, but a great storm had got up and they were taken completely by surprise and overwhelmed by Labienus' men as soon as they arrived. The legions and the cavalry were quickly ferried across the river under the supervision of the Roman knights in charge of the operation.

Thus, soon after dawn and almost simultaneously, the enemy received the following reports: that there was much more noise than usual in the Roman camp; that a large column was marching upstream; that the noise of oars could be heard in the same direction; and that rather lower downstream troops were being ferried across the river. On receiving these reports, the enemy believed that the legions were crossing the river in three places, that they were demoralized by the revolt of the Aedui and preparing for flight. They therefore divided their own forces also into three. One detachment was left to keep a watch on our camp; a small force was sent in the direction of Metiosedum with orders to advance upstream as far as the boats had gone; the rest of their army was led out against Labienus.

By dawn all three legions had been brought across, and now the enemy's army came into sight. Labienus addressed the troops, telling them to remember their own traditions of courage and all the great successes they had won; and he asked them to imagine that I myself, under whose leadership they had so often defeated the enemy, was there in person to watch them. Then he gave the signal for the attack. The two lines came together. On the right wing, where the Seventh Legion was posted, the enemy were forced back and routed; on the left, which was held by the Twelfth Legion, the first ranks of the enemy were broken to pieces by our javelin fire, but the rest of them stood firm and fought back fiercely, not a single man looking as though he were ever going to give in. Camulogenus himself, the enemy commander-in-chief, was there in person to encourage his men. So the issue still hung in the balance. But when the officers of the Seventh Legion heard what was happening on the left wing, they brought their men around in the enemy's rear and charged. Not even then did one of them give way; they were surrounded and cut down, Camulogenus sharing the same fate as the rest. The detachment that had been left on guard opposite Labienus' camp, when they heard that battle had been joined, marched to the help of their own people and occupied a hill, but could not hold out there against the attacks of our victorious troops. They, too, joined in the flight of their comrades, and all who failed to reach shelter in the woods or mountains were cut down by our cavalry. When the operation was completed, Labienus returned to Agedincum, where the baggage of the whole army had been left. From there he marched on with all his forces and joined up again with me.

As the revolt of the Aedui became known, the war spread. They sent deputations all over the country; they did everything they could, using every advantage they possessed in influence, prestige, and money, to bring the other tribes in on their side. They had gained control of the hostages whom I had left in their keeping, and by threatening to take measures against them, they were able to intimidate those who hesitated to join them. The Aedui invited Vercingetorix to come to them and to concert plans for the conduct of the war. He agreed to do so, and they then demanded that they should be given the supreme command. This claim was contested and a general council of the whole of Gaul was summoned to meet at Bibracte. People came to this meeting in crowds from all over the country, and when the question of the command was put to a general vote, the assembly unanimously agreed that Vercingetorix should remain commander-in-chief. The Remi, Lingones, and Treveri did not attend this council—the Remi and Lingones because they remained faithful to their alliance with us; the Treveri because they were too far away and were threatened by the Germans, which indeed was why they took no part at all in the war and did not send help to either side. The Aedui were bitterly disappointed by the rejection of their claim to the leadership. They saw with sorrow that their fortunes had changed and, remembering the special privileges which I had given them, began to feel their loss. However, they had undertaken to fight and did not dare to dissociate themselves from the rest. But those two hopeful young men, Eporedorix and Viridomarus, were far from pleased at having to take their orders from Vercingetorix.

Vercingetorix himself demanded that hostages should be sent to him from the remaining tribes and named a day by which they were to be delivered. The whole cavalry force, fifteen thousand in number, was ordered to concentrate at Bibracte. He said that he did not want any more infantry than he had before because he was not going to run the risk of fighting a pitched battle. Instead, since he was so strong in cavalry, it would be perfectly easy, he thought, to prevent us from getting grain or forage—only provided that the Gauls themselves would agree to destroy their own stores and set fire to their barns, in the knowledge that by sacrificing their private property they would be winning for themselves freedom and power forever.

After making these decisions, Vercingetorix ordered the Aedui and the Segusiavi, who live on the frontiers of our Province, to supply ten thousand infantry. He strengthened this force by the addition of eight hundred cavalry, put the brother of Eporedorix in command of it, and instructed him to invade the country of the Allobroges. He opened another front by sending the Gabali and the clans of the Arverni living next to them against the Helvii, and also sending out the Ruteni and the Cadurci to devastate the country belonging to the Volcae Arecomici. In spite of the offensive he was launching against them, he also sent messengers and deputations secretly to the Allobroges, trying to win them over in the hope that they were still hostile to us and had not forgotten the last war. He attempted to bribe their leaders and promised that the Allobrogian state should take over the whole of the Roman Province.

To meet all these attacks, a holding force of twenty-two cohorts, raised from the Province itself, had been got together by Lucius Caesar, the general whom I had left in command there. These cohorts were sent out to meet the enemy at all threatened points. The Helvii on their own initiative offered battle to the enemy from over the border and were defeated. Their chief, Gaius Valerius Donnotaurus, the son of Caburus, was among those killed. After this they were forced back into their towns and fortified places. The Allobroges posted numerous detachments of troops all along the Rhone and, showing both energy and efficiency, protected their frontier from invasion.

I knew myself that the enemy was superior to me in cavalry and realized that, with all roads blocked, there was no chance of getting reinforcements either from Italy or from the Province. I therefore sent to those German states on the other side of the Rhine that I had subdued in previous years and got them to send me cavalry and the light infantry who are trained to fight in conjunction with the cavalry. When they arrived, I found that their horses were unsuitable, and therefore I mounted these Germans on horses which I requisitioned from my officers and other Roman knights and re-enlisted veterans.

Meanwhile the enemy had been concentrating into one place the cavalry force which had been raised from the whole of Gaul, and their army which had been operating in the country of the Arverni. Great numbers of cavalry had assembled already, and while we were marching along the frontier of the Lingones toward the country of the Sequani, so as to be in a better position to defend the Province, Vercingetorix established his forces in three camps about ten miles away from us. He summoned his cavalry commanders to a council of war and informed them that the hour of victory had arrived.

"The Romans," he said, "are leaving Gaul in full flight toward the Province. So far as securing our liberty for the moment is concerned, I think we have done enough already; but to be sure of peace and quiet for the future we have still done too little. As it is, they will come back again with a larger army and go on with the war. Let us therefore attack them now, while they are marching in column and are handicapped by all their baggage. If their infantry halts in an effort to protect the column as a whole, then they will be unable to continue their march; if, as is more likely to happen, they abandon the baggage and think first of how to save themselves, then they will suffer the loss not only of necessary supplies but of the reputation which they have built up. As for the Roman cavalry, you yourselves ought to feel perfectly certain that not a man of them will dare to leave the shelter of the column; and, to give you all the more confidence, I propose to have all our infantry formed up in battle order in front of the camp so as to make the enemy more frightened still."

The cavalry commanders received this speech with loud applause and shouted out that they should all swear a most solemn oath that no one of them who failed to ride twice through the enemy's column should be allowed in the future

to enter his home or to approach his children, his parents,
or his wife. This proposal was adopted and everyone swore
the oath.

Next day they divided their cavalry into three sections,
two of which appeared in battle order on our flanks, while
the third began to impede our march at the head of the
column. When I was told what was happening, I divided
my cavalry also into three sections and ordered them to go
into action against the enemy. At one and the same moment
fighting broke out all along the column. The column itself
halted and the legions formed a square with the baggage
inside. Wherever I saw our cavalry in any difficulty or distress I would order infantry detachments to move forward
and to form lines of battle. This had the effect both of checking
the enemy's pursuit and of giving our men the support and
encouragement to enable them to stand firm. Finally the
German cavalry on our right succeeded in getting to the
top of a ridge from which they dislodged some of the enemy,
who fled right down to the river where Vercingetorix had
taken up his position with the infantry. The Germans followed
after the fugitives and killed quite a number of them, and
the rest, seeing what had happened, began to fear that they
would be surrounded and took to flight. They were slaughtered
on every side. Three Aedui of the highest rank were taken
prisoner and brought to me: Cotus, their cavalry commander,
who had had the dispute with Convictolitavus at the last
election; Cavarillus, who had taken command of the Aeduan
infantry after Litaviccus had deserted us; and Eporedorix,
who, before I arrived in Gaul, had been the Aeduan commander in their war against the Sequani.

5 THE SIEGE OF ALESIA.

With all his cavalry routed, Vercingetorix withdrew his troops
from their position in front of the camps and at once began
to march to Alesia, a town of the Mandubii, ordering the
baggage to be packed at once and brought after him. I had
our own baggage taken to a hill nearby and, leaving two
legions to guard it, spent the rest of the day in pursuing the
enemy. We killed about three thousand of their rear guard.
Next day we encamped near Alesia. I made a careful examination of the position where this town was situated. The Gauls
were thoroughly upset by the defeat of their cavalry, in which
they were used to putting more faith than in anything else. I

told my troops that the hard work I demanded from them would be worth while, and began to build lines of investment around Alesia.

The actual fortress of Alesia was on the top of a very high hill and appeared to be impregnable except by blockade. Rivers flowed along the bottom of the hill on two sides. In front of the town there was a plain about three miles long. Everywhere else it was closely surrounded by hills which were about the same height as that on which the town itself stood. The whole of the eastern slope of the hill below the town wall was filled with Gallic troops, who had fortified their camp with a ditch and a six-foot wall. The lines of circumvallation which we were now starting to build had a perimeter of nearly ten miles. Eight camps were constructed at suitable points along the lines, and in the fortifications which linked them together twenty-three redoubts were built. These redoubts were manned during the daytime by patrols in order to guard against any sudden attempt at breaking out from the town; at night they were held by strong detachments of troops with sentries always on the watch.

After we had started on our siege works, a cavalry engagement took place in the three-mile stretch of plain which, as already mentioned, lay between the hills. It was a fiercely fought battle on both sides. When I saw that our men were having the worst of it, I sent up the Germans in support and drew up the legions in front of the enemy's camp, so as to forestall any sudden move that might be made by their infantry. But our men, feeling that they had the legions behind them, recovered their confidence. The enemy were put to flight, and in trying to escape, they were handicapped by their own numbers and got wedged together in the gateways, which had been made too narrow. The Germans went after them fiercely right up to their fortifications. There was a great slaughter. Some of them abandoned their horses and tried to get across the ditch on foot and climb up the wall. I then ordered the legions posted in front of their camp to move forward a little, and the result was that the Gauls inside the fortifications became just as terrified as the rest. They thought that we were on the point of launching a general assault and shouted out their call to arms. Some rushed panic-stricken into the town, and Vercingetorix ordered the gates to be shut so that the camp would not be left unguarded. Great numbers of the enemy had been killed and many horses had been captured before the Germans withdrew.

Vercingetorix now decided to send all his cavalry away by night before we could complete the circle of our fortifications. Before they left, he told them that each man was to go

back to his tribe and summon to the war every man there
who was capable of bearing arms. He reminded them of what
they owed him; it was now up to them, he said, to see that
he was saved and not, after all that he had done for the freedom of Gaul, betrayed and handed over to his enemies to be
tortured. He pointed out that, if they failed to act with resolution, eighty thousand picked men would perish with him.
He informed them that, according to his calculations, he had
enough grain to last, if it were strictly rationed, for thirty
days, and that, by using the very greatest economy, he might
even be able to hold out a little longer. After giving them
these instructions, he sent the cavalry away quietly just
before midnight through a part of our lines where the work had
not yet been begun. He then issued an order that all grain
in the town must be brought in to him; disobedience to this
order would be punished by death. To each man he distributed
his share of the cattle, great numbers of which had been
driven in by the Mandubii; but the grain was rationed out in
small quantities at a time. All the troops which had been
posted outside the town were now withdrawn inside. So,
while waiting for the relief forces from Gaul, he prepared to
carry on the war.

Prisoners and deserters informed me of what his plans
were, and I began to build further entrenchments. I dug a
trench twenty feet across; the sides were perpendicular, so
that it was just as wide at the bottom as at the top. All the
other siege works were set back about 650 yards behind
this trench. This was because our lines had necessarily to
cover a very large area and the whole circuit could scarcely
be manned by a continuous chain of troops. I therefore wanted
to guard against any sudden night attack that the enemy
might launch en masse against our fortifications, and I also
wanted to prevent them from shooting during the day at our
men when they were at work. Behind the 650-yard interval I
dug two trenches, fifteen feet broad and of the same depth, all
the way around. The one nearer the town ran across ground
that was level with or below the level of the plain and I had
it filled with water diverted from the river. Behind the trenches
a rampart with palisades twelve feet high was erected; this
was strengthened by a breastwork with battlements; below this,
at the point where it joined the rampart, large forked branches
projected outward to prevent the enemy from climbing up.
Towers were erected at intervals of about 130 yards all around
the whole circuit of fortifications.

While these great works were being built, it was constantly
necessary to send men out to get timber and provisions, and,
as they had to go some distance away from our camp, our

forces on duty were often below strength and the Gauls would sometimes try to interrupt our work by making sorties from several of their town gates at once and attacking us with the utmost vigor. I therefore decided to make further additions to our fortifications, so that our lines could be defended by a smaller number of men. Tree trunks or very stout branches were cut down and the ends were stripped of bark and sharpened; long trenches, five feet deep, were dug and into these the stakes were sunk and fastened at the bottom so that they could not be torn up, while the top part projected above the surface. There were five rows of them in each trench, fastened and interlaced together in such a way that anyone who got among them would impale himself on the sharp points. The soldiers called them "tombstones." In front of these, arranged in diagonal lines forming quincunxes, we dug pits three feet deep and tapering downward toward the bottom. Smooth stakes as thick as a man's thigh, hardened by fire and with sharp points, were fixed in these pits and set so as not to project more than about three inches from the ground. To keep them firmly in place, the earth was trodden down hard to a depth of one foot and the rest of the pit was filled with twigs and brushwood so as to conceal the trap. These traps were set in groups, each of which contained eight rows three feet apart. The men called them "lilies" from their resemblance to that flower. In front of these was another defensive device. Blocks of wood a foot long with iron hooks fixed in them were buried underneath the surface and thickly scattered all over the area. They were called "spurs" by the soldiers.

When these defenses were completed, I constructed another line of fortifications of the same kind, but this time facing the other way, against the enemy from outside. These additional fortifications had a circuit of thirteen miles and were built along the most level ground where building was possible. My aim here was to make sure that, however large a force came against us, our garrisons in the entrenchments could not be surrounded. And to avoid having to leave camp on dangerous expeditions I ordered each man to provide himself with enough grain and fodder to last for thirty days.

While all this was going on at Alesia, the tribal chiefs of the Gauls met in council. Instead of calling up, as Vercingetorix had proposed, every single man who could bear arms, they decided to demand from each state a fixed quota of men. They feared that if Vercingetorix' plan were adopted, such large numbers would be herded together that it would be difficult to preserve discipline, to keep the various contingents separate, and to arrange for adequate supplies. The numbers of troops to be produced by the various tribes were as follows: the Aedui (with their dependents, the Segusiavi, Ambivareti, Aulerci Brannovices, Blannovii), 35,000; the Arverni (with their dependents, the Eleuteti, Cadurci, Gabali, Vellavii), 35,000; the Sequani, Senones, Bituriges, Santones, Ruteni, and Carnutes, 12,000 each; the Bellovaci and Lemovices, 10,000 each; the Pictones, Turoni, Parisii, Helvetii, 8,000 each; the Suessiones, Ambiani, Mediomatrici, Petrocorii, Nervii, Morini, Nitiobriges, Aulerci Cenomani, 5,000 each; the Atrebates, 4,000; the Veliocasses, Lexovii, Aulerci Eburovices, 3,000 each; the Rauraci and Boii, 1,000 each; the Armorican tribes living on the Atlantic coast (i.e., the Curiosolites, Redones, Ambibarii, Caletes, Osismi, Veneti, Lemovices, and Venelli), 30,000 all together. Out of all these tribal contingents the Bellovaci did not send their full quota. They said that they proposed to make war on the Romans on their own account and in their own way and were not going to take orders from anyone else. However, in response to a personal request from Commius and out of regard for their friendship to him, they did send two thousand men to join the rest.

I have already mentioned how reliable and useful I had found Commius during the British campaign three years previously. In reward for what he had done for me, I had directed that his tribe should be given back its independence and be exempt from taxation; and I had put the Morini under his protection. Now, however, the whole of Gaul was absolutely unanimous in its determination to gain her freedom and win back again her former prestige in war. No Gaul was influenced now by former kindnesses or the memories of friendship; every one of them put his whole heart and strength into the war.

When eight thousand cavalry and about 250,000 infantry had been raised, the whole army was reviewed in the country of the Aedui and its numbers checked. Officers were appointed and the supreme command was entrusted to Commius the Atrebatian, the two Aeduans Viridomarus and Eporedorix, and an Arvernian, Vercassivellaunus, who was a cousin of Vercingetorix. A council of representatives from the other states was attached to these supreme commanders in order to advise them on the conduct of the campaign. They all set out for Alesia in the highest spirits and full of confidence. Every man among them thought that the mere sight of their enormous host would prove too much for us, especially as we were to be attacked from two directions at once, and would have to face a sortie from the Gauls inside Alesia just at the moment when outside the town the huge mass of cavalry and infantry of their relief force came into view.

The besieged in Alesia, however, knew nothing of what was going on in the country of the Aedui. The day had passed on which they had expected to be relieved; they had used up all their grain; and now they called a council of war to discuss what must happen to them next. Various views were expressed. Some were in favor of surrender; others were for trying to break out while they still had their strength. The speech made by Critognatus deserves, I think, to be remembered because of its extraordinary and indeed appalling cruelty. Critognatus was an Arvernian of noble birth and a man held in great esteem by his people. He spoke as follows:

"I shall say nothing at all about the views of those who recommend surrender, by which they mean slavery and disgrace. In my opinion such people should not be considered as fellow citizens and should not be sitting in this council. My concern is simply with those who are in favor of making a sortie. It appears that you all agree that this plan of theirs shows that we have not forgotten our ancient courage. But it is weakness, not courage, to be unable to endure want for a short time. It is easier to find men who will voluntarily risk death than men who will bear suffering in patience. Certainly I respect the opinions of those in favor of a sortie and I might agree with them if I considered that this was merely a question of losing our own lives. But in making our decision, we should be thinking of Gaul as a whole, and of all those whom we have summoned to our relief. Suppose eighty thousand of us are killed on the spot here: what sort of spirit will our friends and kinsmen have, if they are forced to fight things out practically over our dead bodies?

"No, they are risking their lives to save you, and you must not deprive them of the help you can give them. Do not, by your folly, recklessness, or weakness ruin all Gaul and bring her into perpetual slavery. Do you doubt their faith and their resolution, simply because they have not arrived on the appointed day? If so, what do you think the Romans are doing? Are they working day after day on those outer entrenchments just to amuse themselves? No doubt every way of approach to you is blocked and you cannot receive the assurances you would like to have from our friends outside; but what you can do is to take the Romans as witnesses to the fact that relief is coming, since it is in terror of just this thing that they are working day and night on their fortifications.

"What, then, do I advise? I advise that we should do what our ancestors did in the war against the Cimbri and Teutons, a much less important struggle than this one. When they were forced into the towns and threatened, as we are, with starvation, they did not surrender to the enemy. Instead, they kept themselves alive by eating the flesh of those who were too

old or too young to fight. And, even if we had no precedent
for doing this, I should still think that now, fighting as we
are for our liberty, it would be a most splendid thing for us
to establish such a precedent and to hand down the memory
of it to our descendants. Indeed, there is no comparison between the two wars. The Cimbri certainly devastated Gaul
and did much harm to us; but in the end they moved out and
went off to other countries, leaving us free to live on our
own lands in accordance with our own laws and customs.
The Romans, as we know, have different aims altogether. It
is envy which inspires them. They have heard of our glory
and of our power in war, and so they want to settle on our
land and in our towns and to fasten upon us forever the yoke
of servitude. The Romans have never waged wars for any
other reason. And if you do not know how they behave in
distant countries, all you have to do is to look at that part
of Gaul which is on our frontiers and which has been reduced to a province. You will observe that laws and institu-
tions have been changed and that the whole country cowers
in perpetual slavery beneath the rods and axes of Roman
officials."

After discussion it was decided that all those who were
too old or too young or too ill to fight should be expelled
from the town; that they would not adopt the proposal of
Critognatus until they had tried everything else first; but
that, if it should prove necessary and if reinforcements failed
to arrive, they would follow his plan rather than surrender
or submit to terms. The Mandubii, who had received them
into their town, were now compelled to leave with their wives
and children. When they came up to our entrenchments,
they tearfully begged the soldiers to take them as slaves and
give them something to eat. But I had guards posted all along
the rampart with orders to see that they were not allowed
inside our lines.

Meanwhile the whole Gallic relief force under Commius and
the other commanders arrived before Alesia and took up a
position on a hill outside our entrenchments and not more
than a mile away from them. Next day they brought all their
cavalry out of camp. It filled the plain, which, it will be remembered, was three miles long. Their infantry was posted
a little farther back on some rising ground. From the town
of Alesia there was a view all over the plain, and at the sight
of these reinforcements, all the people in the town, happy
and excited, crowded together, congratulating each other on
what they saw. Then they brought all their forces out and
halted with them in front of the town. They filled up the
nearest trench with hurdles and earth and got themselves

ready to face all the risks and obstacles involved in breaking through our lines.

I had all my infantry posted along both the inner and outer lines of fortifications, so that, if need arose, every man would know where he ought to be and hold on there. I ordered the cavalry to ride out of camp and engage the enemy. There was a good view down from all the camps along the surrounding ridges, and the whole army was watching the battle intently to see which way it would go. The Gauls had archers and light infantry scattered about among their cavalry. Their duty was to check the attacks of our horsemen and to help their own people if they had to fall back. These tactics took our men by surprise, and some of us were wounded and had to withdraw from the battle. The Gauls, seeing our men hard pressed by superior numbers, felt sure that their own forces were getting the better of things. There were shouts and yells coming from all sides, both from the besieged and from those who had come to relieve them, as they cheered their men on. And as the battle was being fought in full view of everyone, so that every brave deed could be seen and no act of cowardice could be hidden, the men on each side were impelled both by the desire for glory and the fear of disgrace to fight to the uttermost of their strength.

The battle raged from midday until almost sunset and still the issue was in doubt. Then the Germans massed all their squadrons together and made a charge which broke through the Gauls. Once they were broken, the archers were surrounded and killed. And from every other part of the plain our cavalry swept forward and chased the fleeing enemy right up to their camp without giving them a chance of rallying. At this the troops who had come out from Alesia went sadly back again into the town. They had now almost given up hope of winning.

There was a day's interval, and this time was used by the Gauls in preparing great quantities of hurdles, scaling ladders, and grappling hooks. Then, at midnight, the relieving force set out in silence from their camp and came up to our fortifications in the plain. Suddenly they raised a shout, so that the besieged inside the town should know that they were there, and then they began to throw their hurdles into the trenches and to drive our men off the rampart with slings, arrows, and stones. In fact, they had everything organized for a regular assault. At the same moment, as soon as the noise of shouting was heard, Vercingetorix sounded the trumpet and led his men out of the town. Our men, as on previous days, went each to his proper place along the entrenchments and kept the Gauls off with slings, large stones, bullets, and stakes which were placed ready at intervals along the rampart. It was too dark to see far, and there were a number of casualties on both sides. A number of missiles were discharged by our artillery. Then Mark Antony and Gaius Trebonius, the generals in charge of the defense of this sector, brought up men from the more distant redoubts and used them to reinforce any point at which they saw we were hard pressed.

As long as the Gauls were at a certain remove from our lines of defense, they had more of an advantage because of the vast quantity of missiles which they discharged. But when they came in closer, they were caught on the "spurs" before they knew where they were, or fell into the pits and impaled themselves, or were killed by the siege spears shot at them from the rampart and the towers. All along their line they suffered many casualties, but at no point did they break through our defenses. When it was nearly dawn, fearing that we might attack them on their exposed flank by breaking out from our camps on the heights, they fell back and retired to their original position. As to the Gauls from Alesia itself, they brought out all the equipment that had been prepared by Vercingetorix for the sortie, and they filled up the trenches that were nearest to them. But they took up too much time over these operations and before they even got near our main defenses, they heard that their fellow countrymen had retired. So they went back again into the town without having achieved anything.

The Gauls had now been twice defeated and had suffered heavy losses each time. They held a council to decide what they should do next and, by calling in men who knew the district well, learned about the position and the state of the defenses of our camps on the higher ground. On the north of Alesia there was a hill which had such a wide circumference that we had not been able to include it in the circle of our defenses. We had had to build our camp there on a slight slope on ground that could not be considered favorable to us. This camp was held by two legions under the command of the generals Gaius Antistius Reginus and Gaius Caninius Rebilus. After sending out scouts to reconnoiter this position, the enemy commanders chose out of their whole force sixty thousand men from the states that had the greatest military reputation, secretly decided upon their objectives and their plan of action, and fixed the hour of noon as the moment for launching the attack.

This force was to be led by the Arvernian Vercassivellaunus, one of their four supreme commanders, and a relative of Vercingetorix. He left camp soon after sunset and had almost completed his march before the sun rose. He concealed his troops in the shelter of the hill and told them to rest there after their night's work. When he saw that it was almost midday, he began to move toward that camp of ours which I have already described. At the same moment the Gallic cavalry advanced toward our entrenchments in the plain and the rest of their army appeared drawn up for action in front of their camp.

From the citadel of Alesia, Vercingetorix could see his countrymen going into action. He now led his own forces out of the town, bringing with him the hurdles, poles, mantlets, grappling hooks, and all the rest of the equipment that had been prepared for the sortie. Simultaneous attacks were made all along our lines and every sort of method was used by the Gauls, who were quick to concentrate at any point where the defense seemed likely to crack. Our men, strung out over such a huge area of fortification, did not find it easy to meet these attacks coming from so many different quarters. Another thing which had a most disturbing effect on them was the noise of shouting which they could hear behind them as they were fighting. This made them realize that their own safety depended on the courage that others might, or might not, show. It is, indeed, generally the case that people are much more frightened of what they cannot see than of what they can.

I found a good place from which to see what was happening all along the line, and sent up reinforcements to sectors where our men were in difficulties. Both sides realized that this was the critical moment, the moment that called for a supreme effort. The Gauls knew that for them everything was lost unless they could break through our lines. The Romans saw in front of them, if they could only stand firm, the end of all their labors. Our difficulties were greatest at the fortifications on the hill where, as already mentioned, Vercassivellaunus had been sent. Here the unfavorable downward slope was a factor which told heavily against us. Some of the enemy hurled javelins down on us, while others advanced with locked shields in "tortoise" formation, and all the time fresh troops were ready to replace those who were exhausted. The whole Gallic force heaped earth up against the fortifications, thus making it possible for them to climb the rampart, at the same time covering over all the traps which we had hidden in the ground. Our men's supply of weapons was running short and their strength too was beginning to fail them.

Seeing what the position was and how distressed they were, I sent Labienus with six cohorts to their relief. I told him that if he found it impossible to hold the position, he must regroup the cohorts and fight his way out; but he must not do this unless it was absolutely necessary. I myself went to visit other sectors of the line, urging the men to fight on and not give in, and telling them that everything they had won in former battles was now at stake and depended on this day and on this hour.

The Gauls attacking our inner lines gave up hope of being able to break through in the direction of the plain; our defense works were on too big a scale. They now attempted to storm through our lines on the higher and more broken ground and brought up all their equipment to these points. The defenders were driven from the towers by a hail of weapons. The enemy then proceeded to fill up the trenches with hurdles and earth and to tear down the rampart and breastwork with their grappling hooks. First I sent young Brutus to the threatened spot with some cohorts, then the general Gaius Fabius with some more; and finally, as the fighting grew fiercer still, I led up fresh troops myself to the relief. When the position was restored and the enemy driven back, I hurried to the sector where I had sent Labienus. I withdrew four cohorts from the nearest redoubt and ordered some of the cavalry to follow me while other detachments were instructed to ride around the outer lines and attack the enemy in the rear.

Meanwhile Labienus had found that neither rampart nor trench had been able to hold up the furious attacks of the enemy. Fortunately he had been able to collect together eleven cohorts from the nearest redoubts. He now sent messengers to me to tell me what he thought should be done. I hurried on so as to be able to take part in the action.

The enemy could see that I was coming because of the scarlet cloak which I always wore to mark me out in action. And as the lower slopes along which I came were visible from the higher ground, they could also see the squadrons of cavalry and the cohorts which I had ordered to follow me. So the enemy rushed into battle. The shout was raised on both sides and was taken up by an answering shout from the men on the ramparts and along the whole line of entrenchments. Our men dispensed with javelins and got to work with their swords. Suddenly the Gauls saw our cavalry coming in from the rear; fresh cohorts of infantry were also bearing down. The enemy turned and ran. As they ran, the cavalry were upon them. There was a great slaughter. Sedulius, the commander and chief of the Lemovices, was killed; Vercassivellaunus, the Arvernian, was taken prisoner in the rout; seventy-four Gallic war standards were brought in to me. Out of all that great army very few got safely back to camp.

From the town the Gauls saw the rout and slaughter of their countrymen and, abandoning all hope of relief, withdrew their troops from our fortifications. There was an immediate flight too from the Gallic camp as soon as the news of the battle was received. Indeed if our soldiers had not been exhausted by the hard work they had done all through the day and the constant calls that had been made on them to reinforce threatened points, the entire enemy army could have been destroyed. As it was, our cavalry, which I sent out about midnight, caught up with their rear guard and killed and captured great numbers of them. The rest fled to the various states from which they had come.

On the following day Vercingetorix called a council. He pointed out that he had undertaken this campaign not for any reasons of his own but for the sake of the liberty of them all. "And now," he said, "I must yield to fortune. I hand myself over to you to deal with as you think best. You can either win the favor of the Romans by putting me to death, or you can surrender me to them alive." A deputation was sent to me to discuss these matters. I ordered all arms to be surrendered and the chiefs of the tribes to be brought before me. I had a seat placed for me on the fortifications in front of the camp and here the chieftains were led to me, Vercingetorix was surrendered, and the arms were handed over. I kept back the Aeduan and Arvernian prisoners since I hoped to use them in order to win back the loyalty of their tribes. All the other prisoners were distributed as booty among the whole army, each man getting one Gaul.

When this business was settled, I set out for the country of the Aedui and received the submission of the state. While I was there, the Arverni sent a deputation promising to obey any orders I might give. I told them to produce a large number of hostages. Then the legions were sent into winter quarters. I had, meanwhile, restored some twenty thousand prisoners to the Aedui and the Arverni. I ordered Titus Labienus with two legions and some cavalry to set off for the country of the Sequani, and gave him Sempronius Rutilus as second in command. I stationed the generals Gaius Fabius and Lucius Minucius Basilus with two legions in the country of the Remi, to see to it that they suffered no harm from their neighbors, the Bellovaci. Gaius Antistius Reginus was sent into the country of the Ambivareti, Titus Sextius to the Bituriges, Gaius Caninius Rebilus to the Ruteni, each with one legion. I stationed Quintus Tullius Cicero and Publius Sulpicius at Cabillonum and Matisco, Aeduan towns near the Saône, to look after the grain supply. I myself decided to spend the winter at Bibracte. When my dispatches describing this year's campaign were published in Rome, a public thanksgiving of twenty days was decreed.

❧ BOOK EIGHT: 51–50 B.C. ❧

[This book was written by Aulus Hirtius, one of Caesar's officers. In his preface, he explains why and how he came to complete Caesar's own account of the wars in Gaul. His prefatory letter is addressed to Lucius Cornelius Balbus, one of Caesar's friends and perhaps his most important political agent.]

Prefatory Letter

DEAR BALBUS,

You have constantly asked me to do what I am doing now and I have as constantly refused. It must have looked as though I was backing out of the job through laziness rather than declining it because it is too hard for me. However, you now have your own way. I have taken on this most difficult assignment and have written a supplement to our great Caesar's own account of the Gallic Wars, as otherwise there is no continuity between this work and his later writings. I have also completed his later work, which he carried as far as the operations in Alexandria and then left unfinished. I have continued the story, not until the end of civil war (no end is in sight), but up to the death of Caesar. I hope that my readers will realize how very reluctantly I have taken on this job of writing. If so, I shall perhaps avoid being considered both stupid and arrogant for having intruded myself into the middle of Caesar's works.

For it is generally agreed that in Caesar's *Commentaries* there is a kind of natural elegance which surpasses the most polished and elaborate writings of others. They were published so that future historians of those great years should have the knowledge from which to write, but they have been so admired by all good judges that it looks rather as though Caesar has not so much given these future historians their opportunity to distinguish themselves as taken away from them all possibility of doing so.

You and I, however, must admire these works even more than others do. Others can appreciate the skill and precision of Caesar's writing; we know how easily and how quickly he worked. He not only wrote with the most consummate ease and in the most masterly way, but had an absolutely sure touch when it came to explaining his plans and ideas. Unfortunately I was not engaged myself in either the Alexandrian or the African campaigns. True, I know something about them through having listened to Caesar himself talking on the subject; but then I was listening in wonder and admiration to an account of events which were strange to me. It is different when one listens to events which one is going to use later in an objective history.

But I can see that, in putting together all these reasons why I should not be compared with Caesar, I am incurring the very charge of presumption which I want to avoid. For how can I imagine that anyone would compare me with Caesar anyway? Farewell.

1 SUPPRESSION OF THE BITURIGES, CARNUTES, AND BELLOVACI.

The whole of Gaul was now subdued, and since the troops had been engaged in continual war ever since the previous summer, Caesar wanted them to have a rest in their winter quarters after all that they had been through. However, it was reported that several states at once were still planning war and plotting another revolt. The reason given for this movement was probably the correct one. The Gauls, it was said, had now realized that however many troops they might concentrate in one place, they would still not be able to stand up to us; but, on the other hand, they thought that if a number of states all started wars in different parts of the country at the same time, the Roman army would not be in a position to employ sufficient strength or sufficient manpower to deal with all of them at once. Therefore, so the Gauls concluded, every state should be prepared to make any sacrifice that might be necessary, knowing that, so long as it held up the enemy, it would be helping the rest to win back their liberty.

Caesar did not want this idea of the Gauls to take root. He left the quaestor Mark Antony in command of the winter camp and on the last day of December set out for Bibracte himself, with a cavalry escort, to join the Thirteenth Legion, which was stationed in the country of the Bituriges not far from the Aeduan frontier. Caesar brought the neighboring Eleventh Legion together with the Thirteenth, left two cohorts from each to guard the baggage, and then led the rest of the force into the most fertile part of the country of the Bituriges. This tribe covered a wide area and had a number of strongholds. A single legion in winter quarters had not been enough to stop them from preparing for war and conspiring with their neighbors.

Caesar's sudden appearance among them while they were still unprepared and dispersed brought the inevitable consequence. They were cultivating their lands without any suspicion of danger and they were cut off by our cavalry before they could escape to their strongholds. They did not even get the usual warning of an invasion—the sight of smoke rising up from burning buildings. Caesar had forbidden anything to be set on fire so as to avoid alarming the enemy and to make sure that there would be plenty of grain and fodder available if he wanted to march farther. After many thousands of their people had been taken prisoner, the Bituriges became panic-stricken. Those who had managed to escape at the beginning of our invasion had fled to the neighboring tribes, relying on personal friends to help them or else trusting in the general anti-Roman feeling which all shared. But it was no good. By means of forced marches Caesar was liable to appear anywhere; he made the tribes think about how to save themselves, allowing them no time to think about what they could do for other people. By this speed of action he retained the loyalty of those who were his friends and intimidated the waverers so that they were ready to sue for peace. The Bituriges saw that Caesar was merciful, that it was still possible for them to regain his friendship, and that the tribes on their frontiers had delivered hostages and been taken back again under his protection, without suffering any punishment. With such a prospect before them, they also made their submission.

In these winter days there had been exceptionally difficult marches and almost unendurable cold, yet the troops had stuck to the job magnificently. In reward for their hard work and their patience Caesar promised each soldier a gratuity of two hundred sesterces and each centurion two thousand sesterces in lieu of booty. He then sent the legions back to their winter camps and returned to Bibracte himself forty days after he had set out. While he was there and occupied with his judicial business, a deputation arrived from the Bituriges to complain that they were being attacked by the Carnutes and to ask him for help. After receiving this news, although he had been only eighteen days at Bibracte, he summoned the Fourteenth and Sixth Legions from their quarters on the Saône where, as explained in Book VII of the *Commentaries*, they had been posted to secure the grain supply. He then set out with these two legions on a punitive expedition against the Carnutes.

When the enemy heard that our army was on its way, they remembered what had happened to the other rebels; they abandoned their villages and towns, where they were living in wretched buildings hurriedly erected to provide shelter for the winter—for in their recent defeat they had had to relinquish a number of their regular strongholds—and fled in all directions. The weather at this time of the year is at its very worst and Caesar did not wish to expose his troops to it, so he camped inside Cenabum, the capital of Carnutes. The soldiers were billeted either in houses belonging to the Gauls or in sheds built onto them and hurriedly roofed with the thatch used for tent covers. But the cavalry and auxiliary infantry were sent out in every direction which the enemy was reported to have taken. With success, too, for our men nearly always came back loaded with booty. The Carnutes suffered badly from the rigors of the winter; they were terrified for their lives; they had been driven from their homes and did not dare to stop long in any one spot; nor, in this bitter weather, could they find safety or shelter in the forests. A large part of the population perished, and the rest scattered abroad among the tribes on their frontiers.

It was the worst time of the year for military operations. Caesar believed that to prevent war breaking out it was sufficient to disperse any native troops that attempted to concentrate, and he felt reasonably sure that no war on a really large scale could be initiated until the summer campaigning season. He therefore stationed the two legions he had brought with him in a winter camp at Cenabum and left Gaius Trebonius in command. He was constantly receiving deputations from the Remi, who reported that the Bellovaci and neighboring tribes were mobilizing and bringing their forces together under the leadership of Correus of the Bellovaci and Commius the Atrebatian. The Bellovaci had a reputation in war which was more glorious than that of any other tribe in Gaul or Belgium. The plan now was, so it was said, for them and their allies to make a concerted attack on the Suessiones, a tribe who were dependents of the Remi. Caesar knew that the Remi had a splendid record of loyalty to Rome and he believed that to save them from disaster was something which concerned not only his own honor but also the general interest. So he again called on the Eleventh Legion to leave its winter camp. He also wrote to Gaius Fabius, telling him to bring his two legions into the country of the Suessiones, and sent for one of the two legions which Labienus commanded. In this way, so far as it was possible with

regard to the situation of the various winter camps and the
general strategy of the war, Caesar took the legions out in
turn and gave each its own share of work, while he himself
worked all the time.

When the troops had been concentrated, he set out against
the Bellovaci, camped inside their territory, and sent out
squadrons of cavalry in all directions with orders to bring
in prisoners from whom he could find out what the enemy's
plans were. The cavalry did as they were ordered and reported
back that only a very few people had been found in the
houses and that these had not stayed behind to cultivate
the land (for there had been a most thorough evacuation of
the whole country), but had been sent back to act as spies.
Caesar inquired from these prisoners where the Bellovaci's
main force was and what were their intentions. The information he received was that all the Bellovaci who could bear
arms, and also the Ambiani, Aulerci, Caleti, Veliocasses, and
Atrebates, had collected together in one place. For their
camp they had chosen a position on high ground in a wood
which was surrounded by a marsh; all their property had been
carried into the more remote forests. A number of chiefs,
they said, were taking an active part in the revolt, but the
one whom the people were most glad to follow was Correus,
and this was because they knew he hated Rome with a quite
peculiar violence. Caesar was also informed that a few days
previously Commius the Atrebatian had left camp to get help
from the Germans, who were not far away and whose manpower was unlimited.

The chiefs of the Bellovaci had unanimously agreed on the
following plan, which was enthusiastically supported also by
the rank and file: If Caesar came with three legions, they
would offer battle rather than be compelled later to fight
the whole Roman army under worse conditions and with less
favorable odds; but if he brought more than three legions with
him, they would stand fast in the position they had chosen and
by laying ambushes would try to prevent the Romans from
getting grain, forage (which at the time of the year could
only be found in small quantities and in a few places), and
other supplies.

More prisoners were questioned and all told the same
story. In Caesar's view the enemy's plan of campaign was a
most sensible one and showed no traces of the recklessness
which usually characterizes these native tribes. He decided that
every effort must be made to bring the enemy to battle as
soon as possible by making them think that the troops he
had with him were few enough to be treated with contempt.
In fact his force consisted of three veteran legions of abso-

lutely outstanding quality, the Seventh, Eighth, and Ninth, and also the Eleventh Legion, which was composed of younger men of the best possible type. This legion was now on its eighth campaign and Caesar regarded it as an extremely promising body of men, even though it had not yet won the same reputation for length of service and valor as the rest.

Caesar summoned a council of war, passed on to the officers all the information he had received, and saw to it that the rank and file also were in good spirits. In the hope of being able to entice the enemy to give battle by making them believe that he had only three legions with him, he arranged the order of march as follows: the Seventh, Eighth, and Ninth Legions were to march in front; then was to come the baggage train which, even when placed all together, was quite small, as is usual on these quick expeditionary campaigns; finally the Eleventh Legion was to bring up the rear. It would thus look to the enemy as though the force were no greater than the one which they had said they were prepared to engage. Marching in this way, in what amounted, in fact, to a formation in battle column, Caesar brought his army into sight of the enemy before they expected it.

The plans of the Gauls, as they had been reported to Caesar, had seemed full of confidence; but now, when they suddenly saw the legions advancing with a firm step and formed up as though for battle, they drew up their own forces in front of their camp but did not leave the high ground. This may have been because they feared the risk of an engagement, or because we had arrived so suddenly, or merely because they wanted to see what we would do next.

Caesar had been anxious to fight, but all the same he was surprised when he saw how many the enemy were. He now built a camp facing the enemy position with a deep, though not very wide, valley between him and them. He ordered the construction of a twelve-foot rampart with a proportionately high breastwork; two trenches were to be dug, fifteen feet wide, with perpendicular sides; turrets of three stories were set at frequent intervals and connected together by floored galleries protected on the front by wicker breastworks. The idea was that the camp should be guarded not only by a double ditch but also by a double line of defenders. One line, posted in the galleries, would be high enough up to feel comparatively safe and thus could both hurl their missiles with greater confidence and make them carry farther; while the second line, posted actually on the rampart and thus nearer to the enemy, would be protected by the galleries above them from missiles shot with a high trajectory. The gateways were fitted with doors and flanked with towers that

were higher than the rest. In building these fortifications
Caesar had two objects in view. He hoped that the very size
of the works would make the natives think that he was frightened and would thus make them more confident; and he saw
too that, if he had to go rather far afield to get fodder and
grain, the elaborate fortifications themselves, with only a
small garrison, would be sufficient for the protection of the
camp.

There were frequent skirmishes between small detachments
which ran forward into the marshy ground between the two
camps. Sometimes the marsh was actually crossed by our
Gallic and German auxiliaries following hard on the heels
of the enemy; or at other times the Gauls in their turn would
come over and force our men back. It happened too that in
the course of our daily foraging expeditions, some of our
foragers got isolated and surrounded in awkward positions.
This was inevitable, as the hay had to be fetched from farms
which were very few and far between. Our losses in this
way of baggage animals and slaves were quite inconsiderable,
but were enough to put foolish ideas into the heads of the natives—all the more so since Commius, who, as I mentioned
before, had gone to get reinforcements from the Germans,
now returned with some cavalry. There were only about five
hundred of them, but the mere fact that the Germans had
come at all was enough to fill the natives with confidence.

Several days passed and Caesar saw that the enemy were
still staying in camp. He realized that it was so well defended
by its naturally strong position and by the marshes around it
that it could not be taken by assault, unless one were to risk
very great casualties; and to invest it with siege works would
require a larger number of troops. He therefore wrote to
Trebonius, instructing him to summon as quickly as he could
the Thirteenth Legion, which was in winter quarters among
the Bituriges under Titus Sextius. This would give him three
legions and he was to set out with them by forced marches
to join Caesar. Meanwhile Caesar had secured the services of
large cavalry forces from the Remi, the Lingones, and other
states. He used these tribal contingents in turns to escort the
foraging parties and guard them against sudden attacks.

This was done day after day, and as usually happens when
the same action is constantly repeated, a feeling of routine led
to a lack of vigilance. The Bellovaci got to know where our
cavalry patrols were stationed each day and laid an ambush
of picked infantrymen in a wooded place. Next day they
sent along some cavalry, who were first of all to entice our
cavalry into the ambush and then join in the attack when
they were surrounded. It happened to be the Remi who

suffered on this occasion, since it was their day on duty. They suddenly caught sight of the enemy cavalry and, with a contempt based on their own superiority of numbers, pursued them too eagerly until they found themselves surrounded on every side by the infantry. They were so alarmed at this that they retreated much more quickly than is usual in a cavalry action, with the loss of their commander, Vertiscus, who was also the chief magistrate of their tribe. Vertiscus was almost too old to ride a horse at all but, with true Gallic spirit, he would not make age an excuse for refusing the command and wanted to be present personally whenever there was any fighting. The enemy were wildly pleased and excited over this success of theirs which had involved the death of the chief magistrate and general of the Remi, and our own cavalry learned from this unfortunate experience to reconnoiter more carefully before posting patrols and to show more sense when in pursuit of a retiring enemy.

Meanwhile fighting went on every day in sight of both camps at the places where there were fords or tracks across the marsh. In one of these engagements the whole of the German infantry (which Caesar had brought from across the Rhine to fight among the cavalry) went resolutely across the marsh together, cut down the few men who stood up to them, and then pressed on vigorously in pursuit of the rest. At this the Gauls fell into a panic—not only those who were engaged in actual hand-to-hand fighting or exposed to weapons at long range, but even the reserves who were, as usual, posted some distance off. The whole lot fled in the most disgraceful way; even when they got onto higher ground they failed to make a stand, and in fact never stopped running till they reached their camp—at which point some of them, who were no doubt thoroughly ashamed of themselves, ran on still farther. The narrow escape of these men had an extraordinarily disturbing effect on the whole Gallic army. Indeed one finds with these Gauls that just as they become unduly arrogant when they have some slight success, so will they be unreasonably timid after a very minor reverse.

For several days the Bellovaci stayed in their camp. But when their leaders heard that Trebonius with the other legions was close at hand, they became afraid of being invested as Vercingetorix was at Alesia, and they sent away by night all who were too old or too weak to fight, and all who did not have arms. The rest of their baggage was to be sent off at the same time. It was a frightened and confused mass of people, with all the wagons which normally accompany Gauls on the march, even when they are supposed to be traveling light; and daylight came while they were still trying to get their column into order. They therefore drew up their army in a line in front of their camp so as to prevent the Romans from pursuing their baggage train until it was well on its way.

So long as they stood on the defensive, Caesar was determined not to attack them, as this would mean advancing up a steep hill; however, he wanted to move the legions far enough forward to threaten the enemy and make it impossible for them to leave their position without fear of being attacked. The marsh between the two camps was difficult to cross and would slow down any pursuit, but beyond it was a ridge which stretched almost as far as the enemy's camp and was only separated from it by one narrow valley. Caesar therefore had causeways laid over the marsh, led the legions across, and quickly reached the level ground on top of the ridge, which was protected on two sides by steep slopes. Here he re-formed the legions, advanced to the edge of the high ground, and halted in line of battle at a distance from which the dense masses of the Gauls were in range of his artillery.

The natives felt quite confident in the natural strength of their position and were prepared to stand and fight if by any chance we were to attempt to attack them uphill. On the other hand, they could not withdraw their forces gradually and in small detachments since they feared a state of general confusion if their army once lost its cohesion. They therefore stayed where they were in line of battle. When Caesar saw that they were not going to move, he measured the ground for a camp, and then had the fortification built under a covering guard of twenty cohorts ready for action. After the work was finished, he drew up the legions in battle order below the rampart and placed patrols of cavalry, with their horses bridled, at appropriate points.

The Bellovaci saw that if they moved, the Romans were ready to come after them; they could not stay safely where they were much longer, let alone spend the night there. So they made the following plan for getting away. They had in their camp great quantities of sticks and bundles of straw. These they passed along from hand to hand and put down in front of their line. At the end of the day the word was given and the whole lot was set on fire at once. In a moment there was a continuous line of flame which hid their entire army from the Romans. Behind this barrier the natives took to flight and ran as hard as they could.

Because of the flames, Caesar could not be sure that the enemy were in fact withdrawing, but he suspected that they had adopted the plan with the idea of making their escape, so he moved the legions farther forward and sent out some squadrons of cavalry to follow up the enemy. He himself

SUPPRESSION OF BITURIGES, CARNUTES, BELLOVACI   191

advanced with caution, since he feared the possibility of an
ambush—the enemy might have the intention of standing
firm once they had enticed us onto unfavorable ground. The
cavalry, too, feared a trap. Most of them did not dare to penetrate the line of dense smoke with the fire still burning, and
those who did press daringly into it found that they could
hardly see as far as their own horses' heads. So the Bellovaci
were able to get away without any interference from us. This
withdrawal had been the result of fear, but it had been carried out with great cleverness. They suffered no losses at all
and, after retiring about ten miles, pitched camp in a very
strong position. With this place as their base, they kept on
sending out parties of infantry and cavalry and placing them
in ambushes from which they did a good deal of harm to our
foragers.

These attacks of theirs were becoming more and more
frequent. In the end, however, Caesar found out from one
of the prisoners that Correus, the commander of the Bellovaci,
had set aside from his whole army a picked force of six thousand infantry and one thousand cavalry, intending to place
them in an ambush at a place where he felt sure that the
Romans would be sending forces of their own, because of the
supplies of grain and forage that were there. On the strength
of this report, Caesar brought out of camp more legions than
usual. He sent the cavalry in front in the normal way as an
escort for the foragers and sent out, too, some light-armed
auxiliaries to fight in the ranks of the cavalry. He led the
legions himself and came with them as near the place as possible.

The enemy were already in ambush. The place they had
chosen for this business was a plain not more than a square
mile in area and enclosed either by dense woods or by a
very deep river. Their men, hidden in ambush, formed a
cordon all around. We knew what their plan was. Our men
had their arms ready for action and were fully prepared for
the struggle; with the legions coming up behind in support,
they were ready to face anything, and so they rode, squadron
by squadron, into the plain. Correus, as they appeared, believed that the moment had come for him to set about them.
He came out into the open, at first with only a small force,
and charged the nearest squadrons. Our men stood up well
to this attack and did not make the mistake of all crowding
together—as troops very often do in cavalry engagements
after some alarm, with the result that the more of them
there are, the more casualties are inflicted on them. Our
squadrons therefore took up positions at some distance from
each other and small detachments took turns in joining the

action so as to prevent their comrades from being outflanked.

But now, while Correus was still fighting, the rest of the enemy cavalry charged out from the woods. Fierce fighting broke out in all parts of the field; for some time the struggle was evenly balanced, then little by little the enemy's infantry force came out of hiding, formed up in battle order, and forced our cavalry to give way. But we were quickly supported by our own light infantry which, as already mentioned, had been sent on ahead of the legions. These infantrymen, fighting in the ranks of the cavalry, put up a stout resistance. For some time the battle went on with no advantage to either side. In the end, however, the result was what might have been theoretically anticipated. We had held the first attack from the ambush, and the very fact that at that moment we had kept our heads and suffered no losses now began to put us on top. Meanwhile the legions were drawing nearer. Messengers kept on arriving and both sides heard at the same time that the commander-in-chief, with his troops in battle order, was close at hand.

At this news our men, now sure of the support of the cohorts, fought all the more fiercely, not wanting the business to drag on so that they would have to share the glory of victory with the legions; but the enemy's morale collapsed and they began to try, one way or another, to escape. It was no good. They now found themselves in the very trap which they had designed for the Romans. Still, broken and defeated and panic-stricken by the loss of more than half their force, they fled on, some trying to escape by way of the woods and some by the river; and as they fled they were cut down by our troops who followed eagerly after them. But Correus kept a spirit unbroken by any disaster. He refused to stop fighting and seek shelter in the woods; he refused to surrender when offered quarter. He fought on with the greatest gallantry, wounding his assailants on every side, until in the end our victorious troops, in sheer anger, stood round him and shot him down with their spears.

So the battle went, and Caesar appeared on the scene just after the fighting was over. He imagined that when the Gauls received the news of this great defeat, they would abandon the position where they had their camp, which was said to be about eight miles from the battlefield. There was a river in his way, but he nevertheless brought the troops across and went forward. Meanwhile some of the fugitives, wounded and few in number, who, thanks to the woods, had managed to escape the general fate, suddenly appeared at the camp where the rest of the Bellovaci and the other tribes were, and gave the news of the disaster. The Bellovaci and their allies, realiz-

ing that everything was against them, that Correus was killed,
that their cavalry and the flower of their infantry had been
wiped out, and thinking that the Romans would soon be upon
them, hurriedly sounded the trumpet and summoned a general
assembly at which it was insistently demanded that a deputation, with hostages, should be sent to Caesar.

This plan was approved by all; but Commius the Atrebatian
fled to the Germans from whom he had borrowed help for
the campaign. The others immediately dispatched a deputation
to Caesar, begging him to be satisfied with the punishment
they had already suffered. It was a punishment, they said,
much heavier than he, in his mercy and kindness, would
ever have inflicted on them when their forces were still un-
impaired and if he had not had to fight a battle. As it was,
they pointed out, the whole strength of their tribe had been
broken in the cavalry battle, many thousands of their best
infantry had been destroyed, and only a handful had escaped
to tell the story of the slaughter. Nevertheless, they said, great
as the disaster had been, the Bellovaci had got one solid advantage out of the battle: Correus, the demagogue who had
started the war, had been killed. For so long as he was alive,
it had been the ignorant masses and not the tribal council
who exercised real authority.

In reply to this petition Caesar made the following points.
Last year the Bellovaci, together with the other tribes of Gaul,
had made war on Rome; the Bellovaci had stuck to their warlike intentions with more pertinacity than any of the rest
and, when the others had surrendered, still refused to return
to their right minds. He knew perfectly well that the easiest
thing in the world was to blame the dead for everything that
had been done wrong; but in fact no one man, with only the
feeble backing of the common people, could be strong enough
to start and to carry on a war against the will of the tribal
chiefs, in opposition to the tribal council, and against the
feelings of all patriotic citizens. Nevertheless, he would be
satisfied with the punishment they had brought upon themselves.

That night the representatives of the Bellovaci reported
Caesar's answer to their people and got together the hostages.
Deputations now came hurrying in from all the other states
which had been waiting to see how things went with the
Bellovaci. These all delivered hostages and did as they were
told to do. The only exception was Commius, who was afraid
to trust his life to anyone. This was because in the previous
year, when Caesar was away holding the assizes in northern
Italy, Labienus had discovered that Commius was busy in
intrigues with the various states and was forming a conspiracy

against Caesar, and decided that to suppress such a traitor could not constitute an act of treachery on his part. He did not imagine that Commius would appear at his headquarters if summoned to do so, and he did not want to put him still more on his guard by trying to get him to come; so he sent Gaius Volusenus Quadratus with orders to pretend that he wanted an interview and, in the course of the interview, to have Commius killed. Labienus gave Volusenus a number of specially chosen centurions to take with him. At the interview, Volusenus gave the agreed signal by seizing hold of Commius' hand; but, either because he was unused to this sort of thing or because Commius' friends quickly intervened, the centurion who was charged with killing the man failed to do so, though he gave him a severe wound in the head with the first blow of his sword. Swords were drawn by both parties, but both sides were more concerned with getting away than with fighting—our men because they thought that Commius was mortally wounded, the Gauls because they saw that they had been led into a trap and imagined that we had more men available than those whom they could see. After this, so it was said, Commius had decided that he would never again come into the presence of any Roman.

2 FINAL OPERATIONS. CAPTURE OF UXELLODUNUM.

All the most warlike tribes had now been thoroughly subdued, and Caesar could see that there was no state left that was capable of organizing war or leading resistance. He noticed, however, that quite a number of people were moving out of the towns and leaving their lands so as to avoid having to live under Roman rule. He therefore decided to distribute his army over a wide area of the country. He kept with him the quaestor Mark Antony and the Twelfth Legion, and he sent Fabius with twenty-five cohorts to an entirely different part of Gaul, since he had heard that some of the tribes there were up in arms and doubted whether the two legions with Gaius Caninius Rebilus, the general in charge of the area, were strong enough to deal with the situation. He summoned Titus Labienus to join him, but sent the Fifteenth Legion, which had been with Labienus for the winter, into northern Italy to protect the colonies of Roman citizens there from the sort of barbarian invasion which had taken place in the previous summer, when the people of Trieste had been suddenly surprised and overwhelmed by raiding parties of brigands.

Caesar himself set out to plunder and lay waste the country of Ambiorix. This king was terrified and on the run, and Caesar had given up hope of being able to get him into his power; the next best thing and the thing which his honor demanded was, he thought, to strip his country of inhabitants, buildings, and cattle so thoroughly as to make Ambiorix an object of hatred to any of his subjects who might happen to survive, so that he would never be able to come back to a state which because of him had suffered so greatly. So Caesar sent detachments of legionaries or auxiliaries all over Ambiorix' territory, killing, burning, and plundering. There was total devastation, and great numbers of the inhabitants were either killed or captured. After this Caesar sent Labienus with two legions into the country of the Treveri. Because they are so close to Germany and constantly engaged in warfare, these Treveri were not at all unlike the Germans in their way of life and their ferocity; they never did what they were told unless there was an army on the spot to make them do it.

Meanwhile Caesar's general, Gaius Caninius, had received letters and messengers from Duratius (who had always remained loyal though part of his tribe had revolted) telling him that a large enemy army had got together in the country of the Pictones. He therefore marched toward the town of Poitiers and, when he got near, received still more definite information from prisoners. He was told that Duratius was shut up in Poitiers and being attacked there by Dumnacus, chief of the Andes, who had an army many thousands strong. Caninius would not risk battle with the enemy because his legions were below strength, so he built a camp in a strong position. As soon as he heard that Caninius was near, Dumnacus turned his whole army against the legions and tried to take the camp by storm. For several days he kept up the attack; then, after having suffered heavy losses and failed to break through our defenses at any point, he went back again and resumed operations against Poitiers.

Meanwhile Gaius Fabius had been receiving the submission of various tribes and taking hostages from them as securities. While engaged in these activities, he received a dispatch from Caninius informing him of the situation in the country of the Pictones and at once set out to the relief of Duratius. When Dumnacus heard that Fabius was on the way, he gave up hope; it would be an impossible position for him, he thought, if he had at one and the same time to watch out for a Roman attack from outside and to be in fear of a counterattack from the enemy inside the town. So he suddenly retired from

Poitiers with all his forces, feeling that he would not be really safe unless he could get them across the river Loire, which was too wide to be crossed except by one of the bridges.

Fabius had not yet come in sight of the enemy or joined up with Caninius; but, from the information he received from people who knew the country, he came to the conclusion that the frightened Gauls would take precisely the route which in fact they were taking. So he pressed on with all his forces toward the same bridge as that for which Dumnacus was making. He ordered the cavalry to ride ahead of his column of legionaries, but not to go farther than the point from which they would be able to get back, without putting too much of a strain on the horses, to the place where he and the infantry were to camp. Our cavalry, following his instructions, came up with the column of Dumnacus' men, who were already retreating in panic and were hampered by all the baggage they were carrying. Our men attacked them, killed a great many of them, and got away with a lot of booty. After this most successful action they returned and joined the others in camp.

On the following night, Fabius again sent his cavalry ahead with orders to engage the enemy and slow up the whole column until he should come up with it himself. His cavalry commander, Quintus Atius Varus, an officer of outstanding courage and intelligence, told his men exactly how Fabius' instructions were to be carried out and went after the enemy column. He posted some of his squadrons in suitable positions to act as reserves and with the rest joined battle with the enemy. The whole column halted, and the native cavalry fought back much more resolutely than before, having now the assistance of their infantry, who came up to support them against our attacks. There was some very fierce fighting. Our men despised an enemy whom they had beaten only yesterday; they remembered that the legions were coming up, and being both ashamed to give way and extremely anxious to finish the battle before the legionaries appeared, they fought against the Gallic infantry with the greatest courage. The enemy, on the other hand, judging by their experience of the previous day, imagined that no more reinforcements were coming up and thought that they had an excellent opportunity to wipe out our cavalry.

As the fighting went on for a long time, with neither side giving way, Dumnacus began to draw up his infantry in regular battle order so that it would be in position to support every squadron of his cavalry as need arose. At this moment the legions, in close order, suddenly came into sight and were seen by the enemy. Their cavalry were unnerved; their in-

fantry fell into a panic; their baggage train was left in a state
of utter confusion. Shouting and yelling, they scattered in all
directions and took to flight. Our own cavalry, who a moment
before had been struggling resolutely against a firm resistance,
were now transported with the joy of victory. On every side
they raised a great shout, swept all round the retreating enemy,
and went on killing until their horses could go no farther
and their arms were too tired to strike another blow. In this
battle more than twelve thousand men were slaughtered—
some still with arms in their hands, while others had thrown
their arms away in the panic—and the entire baggage train
was captured.

After the rout it became known that Drappes, the Senonian,
had got together from the fugitives a force of not more
than two thousand and that with these he was marching on
the Province; he was being assisted in this project by Lucterius,
the Cadurcan. (Ever since the beginning of Vercingetorix'
rebellion, Drappes had been raiding our baggage trains and
intercepting our supplies. He had collected bands of criminals
from all quarters, slaves, to whom he had promised their
freedom, exiles, whom he had summoned from every state,
and brigands, to whom he had given refuge. Lucterius, as
we know from Book VII of the *Commentaries,* had, at the
beginning of the Gallic revolt, been in favor of invading the
Province.) Caninius therefore hurried after them with two
legions, wishing to prevent what would certainly be a great
disgrace if the Province were to suffer damage or be seriously
disturbed by the wicked activities of these desperadoes.

Gaius Fabius, with the rest of the army, set out against
the Carnutes and the other states whose forces, he knew,
had been involved in the defeat which he had inflicted on
Dumnacus. He was reasonably certain that after the disaster
they had just suffered, these states would prove more easy to
handle, but felt that, if too much time was given to them,
Dumnacus might get to work and persuade them to fight
again. As it happened, everything went right and Fabius
brought back these tribes remarkably quickly to their allegiance. The Carnutes, who in spite of having often suffered
from us had never even proposed to come to terms, now
gave hostages and surrendered. Their example had its effect
on the rest, and the other states, the so-called Armorican
tribes who live in the extreme west of Gaul on the Atlantic,
submitted immediately to Fabius' demands, as soon as he
and the legions appeared. Dumnacus was driven out of his
own country; alone, wandering, and hiding in place after
place, he was forced in the end to retire to the remotest parts
of the country.

We must now return to Drappes and Lucterius. When they heard that Caninius and his legions were close after them, they realized that, with an army on their heels, they would most certainly be destroyed if they invaded the Province; and, as they no longer had the chance of ranging over the country and living by brigandage, they halted in the country of the Cadurci. Lucterius had had great influence among his fellow tribesmen in these parts in the days before the defeat of Vercingetorix; he had been consistently in favor of revolutionary policies and still had a large following among these ignorant people. With his own forces and those of Drappes, he occupied the town of Uxellodunum, a place of very great natural strength which had once been a dependency of his own, and got the townspeople to join him.

Caninius quickly arrived before the town. He observed that it was protected on all sides by rocky precipices which would be difficult enough for men in armor to climb, even if there was no one to defend them. On the other hand, he saw that the Gauls had great quantities of heavy baggage and material inside the place and that, if they attempted to get it secretly out of the town, they would have to move so slowly that not only our cavalry but our legions would be able to overtake them. So, dividing his cohorts into three detachments, he built three camps at points where the ground was very high. From these camps he began to construct, as fast as he could with the men available, entrenchments which were to run round the town.

The townspeople, seeing what he was doing, became alarmed. They remembered Alesia and feared that the same terrible fate might be theirs if they were blockaded. Lucterius, who had been at Alesia himself, particularly stressed the importance of making sure of their grain supply, and the two leaders, with the agreement of all the rest, decided to leave part of their army inside the town while they themselves went out with a body of light troops to bring in grain from the neighborhood. The plan was approved and on the following night Drappes and Lucterius, leaving two thousand soldiers behind as a garrison, led the rest out of the town. After a few days spent in the country of the Cadurci, they had got together a great quantity of grain, some from tribesmen who were ready and anxious to help them and some from people who were unable to stop them from taking it. They also made a number of night attacks on our redoubts, so that Caninius decided not to go on, for the time being, with his plan of total investment; if the circuit was complete, he thought, he would either have to leave parts of it unguarded or else have to hold some sectors with an insufficient number of troops.

After collecting great quantities of grain, Drappes and Lucterius took up a position not more than ten miles away from the town. From here they intended to bring the grain inside, a little at a time. The responsibility for this operation was shared between them. While Drappes with part of the army stayed to guard the camp, Lucterius escorted the convoys of pack animals toward the town. He posted patrols on the outskirts and then, just before dawn, started to bring the grain in along narrow paths through the woods, making enough noise to be heard by the sentries on duty at our camp. Scouts were sent out and reported back what was going on.

Caninius moved quickly. Taking the troops who were under arms in the nearest redoubt, he attacked the convoy just as it was growing light. The men carrying grain were terrified at finding themselves suddenly in danger and fled back in a disorderly way toward their own troops. Our men, now confronted with armed soldiers, attacked all the more fiercely, taking no prisoners at all. Lucterius himself with a very few men managed to escape, but did not go back to camp.

After this success, Caninius found out from some prisoners that part of the enemy army, under Drappes, was in camp about twelve miles away. This information was corroborated by interrogating a number of individuals, and Caninius thought that, with one of their leaders already routed, it ought to be easy to strike panic into the rest and overwhelm them. It seemed to him a great stroke of luck that no one had managed to get back to camp after the slaughter of Lucterius' men to tell Drappes of the disaster they had suffered. Although he could see no danger involved in this operation, he sent forward toward the enemy's camp all his cavalry and also the German infantry, troops who are exceptionally fast on their feet. He distributed the men of one legion among his own three camps and took the other legion with him, armed and ready for action. When he was near the enemy position, he was informed by the patrols whom he had sent ahead that the Gauls, as they usually do, had left the higher ground and camped on the bank of a river, and that the cavalry and the Germans had suddenly swooped down on them, taking them completely by surprise. As soon as he got this information, he brought up the legion in battle formation. The signal was given and they very quickly occupied all the surrounding heights. Now the Germans and the cavalry could see the standards of the legions, and they fought more fiercely still. Almost at once from every side the cohorts charged down.

Every Gaul there was either killed or captured, and much booty fell into our hands. Drappes himself was taken prisoner in the action.

It had been a brilliant success, achieved practically without a single casualty. Caninius now resumed the blockade of the townspeople, having destroyed the enemy force outside, the presence of which had previously made him afraid to disperse his own forces and prevented him from building a continuous line of fortifications. Now he ordered siege works to be constructed along the whole circuit. Next day he was joined by Gaius Fabius and his army, and Fabius took over our sector of the works.

Meanwhile Caesar had left Mark Antony, the quaestor, with fifteen cohorts in the country of the Bellovaci to prevent the Belgae from attempting to give any more trouble. He himself visited the other states, demanding additional hostages and also, since he found everyone in a state of terror, trying to alleviate the general anxiety. On arriving among the Carnutes, where (as Caesar explains in Book VII of the *Commentaries*) the revolt had originally broken out, he found that the people, conscious as they were of their guilt, were more than ordinarily alarmed. In order to free this state from fear as soon as possible, he demanded that Gutruatus, who had been the ringleader of the rebellion and one of the organizers of the massacre at Cenabum, should be handed over for punishment. This man was in hiding and was too frightened to trust himself even to any of his own countrymen, but they all joined actively in the search and before long he was brought in to the Roman camp. The soldiers regarded him as having been responsible for all the dangers they had undergone and all the losses they had sustained in the war. They crowded round in a dense mass, and it was because of them that Caesar, whose natural inclination was always toward mercy, was compelled to deal severely with him. He was first flogged to death and then beheaded.

While still among the Carnutes, Caesar received from Caninius several letters, one after the other, informing him of what had happened to Drappes and Lucterius and of the resolute stand taken up by the inhabitants of Uxellodunum. In Caesar's view, although the numbers engaged in this revolt were insignificant, the obstinacy which they were showing called for the severest punishment. Otherwise he was afraid that the Gauls as a whole might begin to think that their failure to stand up to Rome had been due not so much to lack of strength as to lack of perseverance, and that the other states might follow the example of Uxellodunum and, making use of whatever strong positions they possessed, attempt to regain their liberty.

He realized that all the Gauls knew that there was only one more summer to go before the end of his term of office and that, if they could hold out until that time, they would have nothing to fear afterward. So he left the general Quintus Calenus with two legions to follow at the normal pace, while he himself with all the cavalry hurried as fast as possible to join Caninius.

Everyone was surprised when Caesar appeared in front of Uxellodunum. He found that the town was by now so encircled by siege works that the enemy had no chance of getting away; but he discovered from deserters that the townspeople were very well supplied with grain. He therefore tried to cut off their water supply. The hill on which the town stood, with its steep precipices, was almost entirely surrounded by a deep valley along which flowed a river. It was impossible to divert this river because of the nature of the ground; it ran at the very bottom of the mountain, so that there was no chance at all of draining off the water in any direction by digging trenches. However, the way down to the river from the town was extremely steep and difficult; and, if our men were there to stop them, the townspeople would be unable either to get down to the water or make the steep ascent again without danger to life and limb. Caesar noted this fact and posted archers and slingers in appropriate positions. He also brought up artillery which could be brought to bear on certain points where the descent was easiest. In this way he succeeded in cutting the defenders off from the water they drew from the river.

After this the besieged could get their water from only one place. This was a spot just under the town wall on that side where, for about three hundred feet, there was a gap in the circuit made by the river. Here a spring gushed out of the ground and gave an ample supply of water. Everyone wanted to cut off the townspeople from this spring, but only Caesar saw how it could be done. Directly opposite the place, he began to push mantlets up the hill and to build a ramp. This meant not only hard work but continual fighting. The townspeople would run down from the higher ground and, without running any risk themselves, would engage us at long range, inflicting a number of casualties on our men as they doggedly worked their way up. However, our soldiers were not to be stopped; they pushed the mantlets farther and farther and overcame the difficulties of the ground by hard work and ingenuity. At the same time, from the shelter of the mantlets they were driving out tunnels toward the head of the spring, and this work could be carried out perfectly safely without the enemy having any suspicion that it was being done at all.

The ramp was built up to a height of sixty feet, and a tower of ten stories was erected on top of it—not with the object of reaching the level of the walls, which were beyond the reach of any siege works, but so as to be able to command the spring. Artillery fire from the tower was now concentrated on the approaches to the spring; the townspeople could no longer get water without risking their lives, and soon not only cattle and pack animals but the great mass of the enemy themselves began to feel the pangs of thirst.

The besieged were greatly disturbed by this setback. Their next move was to fill barrels with tallow, pitch, and dry wood, set them on fire, and roll them down onto our siege works. At the same time they engaged us in fierce fighting so that our men would be kept busy in warding off danger from themselves and would thus be unable to put out the fire. A great flame rose up at once from the siege works, since everything rolled down the hill necessarily landed against the mantlets and the ramp, and each burning piece of material set fire to whatever part of the structure it happened to be up against. Our soldiers were engaged in a hazardous form of fighting and had every disadvantage of position; yet they bore up against all difficulties with a most magnificent spirit. The action was being fought on high ground in full view of our army and there was a lot of shouting from both sides. So every man, in order to display his courage before the eyes of so many witnesses, made himself as conspicuous as possible in confronting enemy weapons or burning material.

When Caesar saw that large numbers of his troops were being wounded, he ordered the cohorts to begin climbing the hill on all sides and to raise a shout as though they were actually scaling the walls. This maneuver seriously alarmed the townspeople. As they could only guess at what was going on in other parts of the town, they recalled their armed forces from the attack on our siege works and posted them on guard around the walls. Now that the fighting was over, our men quickly put out the flames or isolated the parts of the terrace that continued to burn.

However, the besieged continued to resist obstinately and did not give in even when numbers of them had died of thirst. Finally our tunnels reached the sources of the spring, which were than tapped and diverted; the spring, which had never failed before, suddenly became dry and the townspeople now lost all hope of deliverance. They thought that the drying up of the spring was due, not to human skill, but to supernatural agency. So, yielding to necessity, they surrendered.

Caesar was aware that his clemency was known to everyone and had no fear that, if he did take severe measures, anyone would think that there was any cruelty in his character. He knew too that he would never be able to carry out his plans for Gaul if revolts of this sort were allowed to break out constantly all over the country. He therefore decided to make an example of the inhabitants of Uxellodunum in order to deter the rest. All who had borne arms had their hands cut off and were then let go, so that as many as possible could see the punishment that had fallen upon evildoers. Drappes, who as mentioned above had been taken prisoner by Caninius, refused to eat and so died within a few days; either he was unable to support the degradation of being in chains, or else he was afraid of a worse punishment. At the same time Lucterius, who as already described escaped in the fighting, came into the hands of Epasnactus, an Arvernian who was enthusiastically pro-Roman. Lucterius was well aware that he had earned Caesar's hostility and, since he knew that he could not safely stay anywhere for long, had been constantly on the move and trusting himself now to one person, now to another. Epasnactus, with no hesitation at all, had him put in chains and brought to Caesar.

Meanwhile Labienus had been in the country of the Treveri, where he had won a victory in a cavalry engagement, killing large numbers both of the Treveri themselves and of the Germans, who were always ready to help anyone against Rome. He took prisoner a number of the chiefs of the Treveri and also an Aeduan chief called Surus, a man of good family, a most distinguished soldier, and the only Aeduan still in arms against us.

On receiving this news, Caesar could see that things were going well in every part of Gaul. As the result of his campaigns, extending over the last few years, he could regard the whole country as defeated and subdued. But he had never personally visited Aquitania, although he could be said to have partially conquered it in the campaign of Publius Crassus. So he now set out with two legions for that part of Gaul to spend the last part of the summer there. His work here was, as always, carried out quickly and with complete success. Every state in Aquitania sent representatives to him and delivered hostages. Once these affairs were settled, he set out for Narbonne with an escort of cavalry, leaving his generals to see to the quartering of the army for the winter. He stationed four legions in Belgium under the generals Mark Antony, Gaius Trebonius, and Publius Vatinius; two were sent into the country of the Aedui, whom he knew to be the most important tribe in Gaul; two were posted among the Turoni, on the frontiers of the Carnutes, to hold that part of the country which extended up to the Atlantic; and the remaining two were stationed among the Lemovices, not far from the Arverni. He thus saw to it that the army was present in every part of Gaul.

Caesar himself stayed for a few days in the Province, paying rapid visits to all the towns where assizes were held, settling political disputes, and distributing rewards among those who deserved them. He had an excellent opportunity of finding out what the attitude of various people and communities had been at the time of the Gallic revolt—a revolt which he had been able to suppress because of the loyal aid which had come to him from the Province. When this business was finished, he joined the legions in Belgium and spent the winter at Nemetocenna.

While there he heard of how Commius the Atrebatian had been engaged in action with the Roman cavalry. When Antony had arrived at his winter quarters the Atrebates were quiet. But Commius, ever since the occasion already mentioned when he was wounded, had kept himself always ready to join in any trouble that his fellow countrymen might start, so that, if they ever decided on war, they should not lack a leader who could inspire them. Now, when his state was in obedience to us, he went about with his own band of horsemen, supporting both them and himself by highway robbery. By ambushing the roads he had succeeded in intercepting several convoys on their way to the Roman winter camps.

Gaius Volusenus Quadratus had been attached to Antony as cavalry commander and was with him in his winter quarters. Antony accordingly sent Volusenus out to deal with these bands of enemy horsemen. This was an assignment very much to the taste of Volusenus, who was not only a man of absolutely outstanding courage and energy, but also entertained a particular hatred for Commius. He organized patrols in various parts of the country, frequently attacked Commius' men, and won the engagements which he fought with him. Finally, in the course of a particularly fierce encounter, Volusenus, in his eagerness to capture Commius himself, followed after him rather too persistently and with only a few men. Commius fled away as fast as he could, drew the Romans farther and farther on, and then, in his hatred of Volusenus, he called out to his own people to show their loyalty and not to allow the wound that he had received through Roman treachery to remain unavenged. He wheeled his horse around and, leaving the rest behind him, recklessly charged straight at Volusenus. All his men followed his example, and our small party was forced to turn about with the Gauls in pursuit.

Commius spurred his horse on until he came up level with Volusenus, then, couching his lance, drove it with all his force through his enemy's thigh. Seeing their commander wounded, our men at once pulled in their horses, faced about, and drove the enemy back. They charged so violently that some of the Gauls were knocked off their horses and wounded, others were ridden down while trying to escape, and still others were taken prisoner. Owing to the swiftness of his horse, Commius succeeded in avoiding this fate. Volusenus was carried back to camp, so seriously wounded that his life appeared to be in danger. Either because he felt that his injury had been avenged or because he had lost the majority of his followers, Commius sent to Antony and gave hostages to guarantee that he would live where he was instructed to live and would carry out all commands given to him; he only asked one thing, which was that a concession should be made to his fears and he should not be required to come into the presence of any Roman. Antony regarded his fears as perfectly justified, granted his request, and accepted the hostages.

3 CONCLUSION.

I know that Caesar himself wrote one book of *Commentaries* for each year of his campaigns, but I have not thought it necessary for me to do this, because in the following year, when Lucius Paulus and Gaius Marcellus were consuls, no large-scale operations took place in Gaul. But in order that people may know where Caesar himself was and where his army was during this period, I have decided to write a few more words to form an appendix to this *Commentary*.

During the winter which he spent in Belgium, Caesar had just one aim in view, which was to keep the tribes loyal and see to it that none of them should have any reason for making war or should imagine that they could gain anything from doing so. The last thing he wanted was to be compelled to fight a campaign just before he was going to leave the country, for he saw that if he left behind him any kind of armed resistance when the time came to withdraw the army, the whole of Gaul, with no deterrent on the spot, would be only too ready to join in such a movement. So he expressed himself with the greatest courtesy in addressing the tribal governments, gave valuable gifts to the chieftains, and imposed no further burdens on the country, which was thoroughly exhausted as the result of so many defeats. In this way, by making the terms of subjection more tolerable, he had no difficulty in preserving peace in Gaul.

As soon as the period in winter quarters was over, Caesar, contrary to his usual practice, set out for northern Italy, traveling as fast as he could, in order to canvass in the free towns and colonies on behalf of Mark Antony, whose candidature for the priesthood he was supporting. He was glad to use his influence to help Antony, who was a great friend of his and whom he had sent ahead already to start electioneering; and he was also most anxious to oppose the small but powerful faction which was trying to get Antony defeated in the election in order to weaken Caesar's own position when he retired from his province.

As it was, he was still on the way and had not yet reached Italy when he heard that Antony had been elected. However, he felt that he still had a good reason for visiting the free towns and colonies. He wanted in the first place to thank them for coming out in such large numbers to vote for Antony, and at the same time he wished to ask them to support him when he stood for the consulship in the following year. For Caesar's enemies, using the most insolent language, were now boasting that the new consuls, Lucius Lentulus and Gaius Marcellus, had been elected simply in order to deprive him of office and of honor, and that Servius Galba, in spite of having been more popular and with a greater following among the voters, had nevertheless been kept out of the consulship because he was one of Caesar's friends and had been a general on his staff.

Caesar's arrival in these free towns and colonies was greeted with extraordinary demonstrations, showing how much he was honored and loved. For this was his first appearance there since his great victory against the whole of Gaul. Wherever Caesar was going to pass, the people did everything that could possibly be thought of in the way of decorating the gates, the streets, and all public places. The whole population of a place, all bringing their children with them, would come out to greet him; there were sacrifices everywhere; in the temples and market places the statues of the gods reclined on couches in the thanksgiving ceremonial. Everything seemed to foreshadow the joy of the triumph for which he had had to wait so long. The rich spent their money on a grand scale to do him honor, and the poor did all they could in their enthusiasm to acclaim him.

After rapidly going through the whole of Cisalpine Gaul, Caesar, again traveling very fast, returned to the army at Nemetocenna. He ordered all the legions to leave their winter camps and proceed to the country of the Treveri, and going

there himself, he held a ceremonial review. He put Titus
Labienus in charge of Cisalpine Gaul, hoping in this way to
secure still greater support for himself when he stood for the
consulship. He then undertook a series of easy marches, so
as to be on the move and to keep the troops in good training.
At this time he was often told that his enemies were trying
to win Labienus over to their side and he was also informed
of how a small group was trying to get a motion passed in
the senate which would deprive him of part of his army.
However, he refused to believe the stories about Labienus and
would do nothing to prevent a move against him in the senate.
In his view, he had nothing to fear from the senate so long
as the senators were allowed to vote freely. One of the tribunes, Gaius Curio, had undertaken to speak for him in the
senate and defend his interests. And Curio had several times
given the following promise. If, he said, anyone was really
alarmed at the prospect of Caesar taking up arms (as people
in the city were certainly alarmed by the military tyranny of
Pompey), then he would propose that both Caesar and
Pompey should resign their commands and disband their
troops. In this way, he pointed out, the state would be free
and independent.

These words of Curio were perfectly sincere, and he even
tried to get the senate to vote on his proposal. But the consuls
and Pompey's friends opposed it and, by delaying tactics, succeeded in preventing a division. This attitude of the senate as
a whole was important and in keeping with its behavior previously. The year before, Marcellus, in the course of an
attack on Caesar's whole position, had brought forward a
motion with regard to Caesar's province. This motion was
premature and contravened the law passed by Pompey and
Crassus. There was a debate at the end of which Marcellus,
whose one idea of becoming distinguished was to attack
Caesar, called for a division. The senate then unanimously
rejected his proposals. However, Caesar's enemies were not
discouraged by these setbacks, which merely prompted them
to find still more powerful arguments to compel the senate to
approve measures which they had decided upon themselves.

Then a decree of the senate was passed which ordered both
Pompey and Caesar to send one legion each for service in the
Parthian war. Quite obviously, the effect of this decree was
that both legions should be taken from Caesar. For Pompey
had originally recruited the First Legion in Caesar's province
and had then sent it to Caesar. He now offered it for the
Parthian war as though it were his own. Caesar, however,
though there could be no doubt about the aims of his enemies,
sent back the First Legion to Pompey and, in accordance with

the decree of the senate, ordered on his own account the Fifteenth, which had been on duty in Cisalpine Gaul, to be handed over for service in Parthia. In its place he sent the Thirteenth Legion to Italy to undertake the garrison duties from which the Fifteenth had been withdrawn. He personally made arrangements for the winter camps. Gaius Trebonius with three legions was stationed in Belgium; the same number, under Gaius Fabius, were sent into the country of the Aedui. In this way he thought that Gaul would be most secure, with Roman armies posted among the Belgae, who are the most warlike people, and among the Aedui, who are the most influential.

Caesar himself then set out for Italy. When he arrived there he heard that, owing to the action of the consul Gaius Marcellus, the two legions which he had sent back and which, according to the decree of the senate, should have gone to serve in the Parthian war, had been handed over to Pompey and were being kept in Italy. After this there could be no doubt whatever about the plot that was being made against him; yet Caesar decided that he would submit to anything so long as there was any hope at all of being able to reach a constitutional settlement without having recourse to arms. [He wrote a letter to the senate, demanding that Pompey should lay down his command and offering to do the same himself.] *

* Only one word of this sentence appears in the manuscript, but apparently not many words have been lost. The sentence in brackets may serve as a transition from this point to the beginning of the *Civil Wars*.—R.W.

THE CIVIL WARS

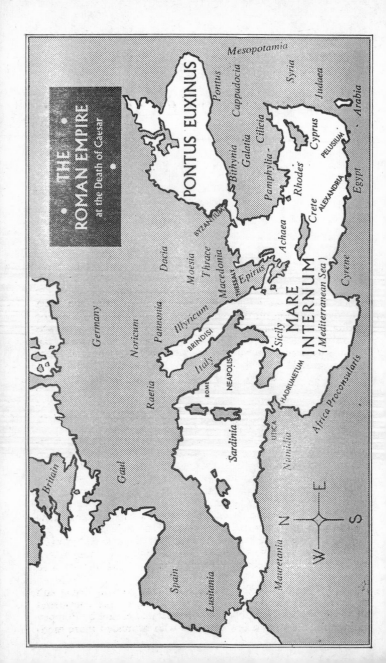

✑ *BOOK ONE: 50 B.C.* ✑

1 | THE SENATE REFUSES TO COMPROMISE.

My letter was delivered to the consuls, but it was a difficult matter to get permission for it to be read aloud in front of the senate. Indeed permission was only granted after the most vigorous agitation on the part of the people's tribunes. As for having a regular debate on the contents of the letter, it was found impossible to secure this concession at all. Instead, the consuls proceeded to bring in a motion on the political situation in general.

The consul Lucius Lentulus addressed the senate in a provocative manner. He assured them that he would play his full part in the defense of the republic, if the senators themselves would only show daring and resolution in the expression of their opinions.

"If, on the other hand," he said, "as has happened on previous occasions, you are going to let your thoughts turn toward Caesar and the prospects of making yourselves popular in that direction, then I, Lentulus, am going to make my own decisions without reference to you. I too can, if I like, make myself safe by accepting Caesar's favor and Caesar's friendship."

Scipio then made a speech to the same effect. Pompey, he said, was prepared to play his part in the defense of the republic, so long as the senate would follow his lead; if, however, the senate showed weakness and hesitation now, though they might beg for his help in the future they would beg for it in vain.

As the meeting of the senate was being held in Rome and as Pompey was near the city at the time, it was considered that this speech of Scipio's had been dictated to him by Pompey himself. There were a few senators who expressed more mod-

erate views—Marcus Marcellus, for example, who made a
speech in which he suggested that this debate should not be
held at all until recruiting had been carried out all over Italy
and until armies had been mobilized. There would then be,
he said, a force to fall back upon and it would be perfectly
safe for the senate to vote exactly as it wished to vote. Then
there was Marcus Calidius who proposed that, in order that
there should be no reason for a recourse to arms, Pompey
should leave Italy and go to his provinces. "Caesar," he said,
"has had two legions taken away from him by Pompey and is
now apprehensive because of the impression that Pompey is
holding these legions in reserve and keeping them near Rome
with the idea of using them against him." Marcus Rufus also
made a speech very much in the same terms as that of Calidius.

All these speakers were vigorously attacked by the consul
Lucius Lentulus in the most violent language. Lentulus absolutely refused to allow any discussion of the proposal
of Calidius, and Marcellus, thoroughly scared by the language
which was being used, withdrew his own proposal. So, as
a result of the consul's angry words, of the terror caused by
an army actually on the spot, and of the threats of Pompey's
friends, the senate adopted the proposal of Scipio, the majority of the senators voting under force and pressure and
against their wills. Scipio's proposal was that Caesar should
disband his army before a fixed date, and that, if he failed to
do so, he should be considered a public enemy. At this point
the people's tribunes, Mark Antony and Quintus Cassius, in-
terposed their veto. Immediately the senate was required to
discuss whether this veto should be regarded as valid or not—
a weighty and serious discussion—and the more bitter and
savage a speech was, the more it was cheered by my enemies.

The meeting of the senate ended in the evening and all
senators were then invited to visit Pompey outside the city.
Pompey offered his congratulations to those who had shown
themselves ready for action and encouraged them to preserve
the same spirit in the future; he spoke sharply to the more
lukewarm members and urged them to change their attitude.
And now numbers of reserves from the armies which had
served under Pompey in the past were called up and offered
the prospects of prize money and promotion. Also many
men from the two legions which I had handed over to him
were brought to Rome. The city (even the part of the forum
set aside for public business) was full of officers, centurions,
and reserves. Pressure was brought to bear on all who were
friends of the consuls and all who were supporters of Pom-

pey or of my old enemies to attend meetings of the senate, and so vocal a crowd had the effect of terrifying the weaker spirits and forcing their own views on those whose minds were not made up. Thus the majority were deprived of their right of coming to a free and independent decision.

The censor Lucius Piso, supported by the praetor Lucius Roscius, undertook to go and give me a personal account of the situation. They asked for six days in order to do this. Other proposals also were made for sending a deputation to me to explain what the feelings of the senate were. Every one of these speakers and every one of these proposals were attacked and opposed in speeches made by the consul, by Scipio, and by Cato. Cato was activated by his long hatred of me and by his bitter feelings at having failed in the elections. The behavior of Lentulus can be explained by the fact that he had enormous debts and was looking forward to the command of an army and of provinces and to the bribes he would acquire for bestowing regal titles on native rulers; he boasted among his friends that he was going to become another Sulla, with supreme power in his hands. Scipio too was motivated by the expectation of a province and of armies which, since he was Pompey's father-in-law, he thought he ought to share with him; other motives can be found in the fact that he was frightened of prosecution, that he had a violent, ostentatious character himself and was led on by the flattery of men of like character who at this time had great influence both in politics and in the law courts.

As to Pompey, he had been pushed into action by my enemies, and also by his own wish that no one should be placed on the same level as himself. He had entirely broken off his old friendship with me and had become friends again with those who had been enemies of us both, most of whom he personally had turned against me during the time that he was my son-in-law. He was also concerned about the discredit he had brought on himself by keeping back the two legions to serve his power and supremacy instead of allowing them to go to Asia and Syria. Therefore, Pompey was eager to have things settled by force of arms.

So everything was done hurriedly, and everything in a disorderly manner. My friends were not given the time necessary to inform me of the situation. The people's tribunes were not granted an opportunity to protest against the danger with which they were being threatened, nor were they permitted to exercise the right of veto which Lucius Sulla had left them. They had only seven days in which to think about their own safety, whereas in the past the most revolutionary

tribunes had always been able to count upon at least eight
months of office before fearing any personal danger that
might proceed from their activities. Now the government fell
back on the famous formula known as "the final decree of
the senate," a decree which previously had never been passed
except on occasions when criminal elements had got completely out of hand, when Rome itself was, one might say, on
fire and no one knew where to turn for safety. The terms
of the decree are these: "The consuls, the praetors, the
tribunes, and all who have held the office of consul and are
near the city are to take the appropriate measures for the
security of the state."

It was on January 7 that these resolutions were officially
recorded by a decree of the senate. So, leaving aside the two
days which were occupied with elections, in the first five
days of Lentulus' consulship on which meetings of the senate
could be held, decrees of the most savage and of the most
insulting kind were passed depriving me of my command and
the tribunes of their rights and dignity.

The tribunes immediately fled from Rome and joined me
at Ravenna where I was waiting to receive a reply to my
own very moderate demands and hoping that a certain sense
of fairness might be shown so that everything could end
peacefully.

On the following days the senate held its meetings outside
Rome. Pompey acted just as he had indicated that he would
when Scipio had, as it were, spoken for him. He praised
the senators for the strong and resolute line which they had
adopted. In giving an account of the forces available to him,
he stated that he had ten legions ready for action and further-
more that he knew for a certainty that I was unpopular with
my own troops; they would neither protect me nor follow
me into battle. The senate then proceeded immediately to
the discussion of further business. It was proposed that
recruiting should be organized all over Italy; that Faustus
Sulla should be sent at once to Mauretania; that money should
be granted to Pompey from the treasury. It was also proposed
that King Juba should be given the titles of "ally" and
"friend," but Marcellus refused to countenance this for the
time being. The tribune Philippus vetoed the proposal about
Faustus, but the other proposals were carried and officially
recorded. Provinces (two that should have gone to ex-consuls
and others that should have gone to ex-praetors) were given
by decree to private individuals without the proper qualifica-
tions. Scipio was to have Syria, and Lucius Domitius was
to have Gaul. The allotment was privately rigged in such a
way that Philippus and Cotta were passed over, their names

not being included among the lots which were drawn. Praetors
were sent out to the other provinces. Nor did they wait, as
had been the practice in previous years, for a bill to be brought
before the people, confirming them in their commands. Instead, they threw on their scarlet cloaks of office, carried out
the usual religious ceremonies, and left the city. And—a
thing which had never before happened in history—both
consuls also left Rome. Contrary to all tradition and precedent,
people with no official rank were to be seen in Rome and
in the Capitol itself attended by lictors. All over Italy men
were being called up and arms were being requisitioned.
Municipalities were forced to hand over sums of money;
temple treasures were seized and taken away. The rights of
men and the laws of god were disregarded. It was a state
of chaos.

2 CAESAR INVADES ITALY.

When I was informed of what was happening, I called my
soldiers together and addressed them. I gave them examples of
how my enemies had been constantly attacking me throughout my life, and I pointed out with sorrow that it was these
same enemies who had been working on the mind of Pompey
and leading him astray. They had done this by making Pompey jealous of me and anxious to detract from the glory which
I had won, although I myself had always been on Pompey's
side and had helped him to enjoy his honors and the high
position in which he was held. I went on to complain that a
new precedent was being introduced in Roman politics: the
tribunes' right of veto was now being regarded as a crime
and was being suppressed by force.

Sulla, I pointed out, had deprived the tribunes of nearly
all of their powers, but had still allowed them to retain the
right of veto. Pompey, who in the past had got the credit for
having given back to the tribunes the rights which they had
lost, had now taken away from them even the rights which
they had then. With regard to the decree of the senate "that
the government should take its own measures for the security
of the state" (a formula which amounted to putting the Roman people under martial law), I pointed out that this decree
had never been passed except in situations when dangerous
legislation was being proposed, when the tribunes had resorted
to violence, and when there had been a popular revolution
involving the seizure of temples and of strategic points in

Rome; these things, I explained, had happened in the past and
Saturninus and the Gracchi had died because of them. But at
the present moment nothing of the sort had taken place at
all or had even been contemplated. Finally, I reminded my
audience that for nine years now they had been under my
command and had served the state with the best of fortune;
they had won battle after battle and had brought order into
the whole of Gaul and Germany. Would they not now defend
their general from his enemies and safeguard for him the
fame and glory which he had won?

The men of the Thirteenth Legion—which I had called
up at the beginning of the emergency; the other legions had
not yet joined me—shouted out that they were ready to protect their general and the people's tribunes from injury and
injustice.

So, after having discovered how the soldiers felt, I set out
with this one legion for Rimini, where I met the tribunes who
had fled to me. I sent instructions to the other legions to leave
their winter quarters and march after me. At Rimini I was visited by young Lucius Caesar, whose father was on my staff.
After the usual courtesies had been exchanged, the young
man explained the real reason for his visit: he had come
to me with a personal message from Pompey. The message
was as follows: Pompey did not want me to think badly of
him for what he had done, and wished me to understand that
he was acting for the sake of the state and not with a view
to undermining and belittling me. It had always been his view
that the interests of the state should be considered as more
important than any private feelings he might have for individuals. I too, in his opinion, owed it to myself to make some
sacrifices to the public interest; I should adopt a calmer and
less angry attitude; I should not allow my hostility toward my
enemies to carry me to the point where, in the hope of doing
them harm, I was actually doing an injury to the state.

This, with a few other remarks of the same kind and with
some words spoken in excuse of Pompey, was the substance
of the message. The praetor Roscius also had an interview
with me in which he said much the same things in practically
the same language, making it clear that Pompey himself had
instructed him what to say.

Certainly there was nothing in all this which could have
the effect of putting right what had been done wrong. Nevertheless I had at least found people of the right sort to carry
back to Pompey an account of what my own wishes were. I
therefore spoke to them both and said that, since they had
brought Pompey's message to me, I hoped they would not
object to telling Pompey in reply what I myself demanded;

thus, by taking a little trouble, they might be able to settle a great dispute and free the whole of Italy from fear.

"I have always," I said, "put the good name and honor of the state first and have regarded them as more valuable than life itself. What distressed me was to find that my enemies in the most insulting manner were taking from me a privilege that had been granted to me by the Roman people; I was being deprived of six months of my command and was being dragged back to Rome, although the people had ratified the proposal that I should be allowed to stand for the consulship at the next elections without being personally present. Nevertheless, for the sake of the state I accepted this infringement of my rights and attack upon my honor with a good grace. But when I sent a letter to the senate proposing that both sides should disband their armies, I failed even to gain this point.

"Troops are being raised all over Italy; two legions, stolen from me on the pretext that they were to be used against Parthia, are still in the country; the whole state is under arms. How can all this be explained except on the assumption that there is a plan to destroy me? Yet for the sake of the state I am still prepared to make any concession and to put up with anything. I propose that Pompey should go to his provinces, that both of us should disband our armies, that everyone in Italy should return to civilian life, that the state should be freed from fear, that the holding of free elections and the general control of affairs should be handed over to the senate and the Roman people. In order that this should be done with as little trouble as possible and on fixed terms which should be ratified by oath, I propose that either Pompey should come nearer to me or else should allow me to come nearer to him. A conference between the two of us would have the effect of settling all difficulties."

Roscius undertook to deliver this message and went with Lucius Caesar to Capua, where he found the consuls and Pompey. He informed them of my demands, and after discussing the matter, they gave him their reply in the form of a written message. This was to the following effect: I was to return to Gaul, evacuate Rimini, and disband my forces; if I did so, Pompey would go to his Spanish provinces; meanwhile, until they received a guarantee that I would do as I had promised, the consuls and Pompey would continue to raise troops.

These terms were unfair. It was unfair of Pompey to demand that I should retire to Gaul while he kept both his provinces and the legions that did not belong to him; to want me to disband my troops while he himself continued to recruit new forces; to promise to go to his province, but give no definite date for when he would do so. Thus, even if he stayed in Italy until my consulship was over, he could not be considered guilty of having broken his word. Finally, what showed that there was very little real hope of peace was the fact that Pompey allowed no time for a conference and made no suggestion that he should come near me personally. I therefore sent Mark Antony from Rimini to Arezzo with five cohorts. I myself, with two cohorts, stayed at Rimini and raised troops there. I occupied Pesaro, Fano, and Ancona, sending one cohort to each place.

I was now informed that the praetor Thermus was holding Gubbio with five cohorts and was fortifying the town, but it appeared that the townspeople themselves were very much on my side. I therefore sent Curio to Gubbio with the three cohorts which he had at Pesaro and Rimini. Thermus, hearing of Curio's approach and feeling no confidence in the good will of the inhabitants of the place, withdrew his cohorts and took to flight. His troops deserted him on the march and scattered to their homes, while Curio, to the great delight of everyone, recovered Gubbio for us.

The news of these events made me feel confident that I had the good will of the people in the towns, and so I withdrew the cohorts of the Thirteenth Legion from their garrison duties and marched on Osimo. This place was held by Publius Attius Varus, who had brought his cohorts inside the town and, with the aid of senators who were being sent around the countryside, was organizing recruiting throughout Picenum.

When it was known that I was drawing near, the town council of Osimo went to Attius Varus in a body and told him that they were not free to act as they wished; in fact neither they nor their fellow townsmen could bear the thought of shutting out from their town a man like Gaius Caesar, who held an official command and who by his great exploits had so very much earned the gratitude of his country; they therefore advised Varus to think of what the future might bring and of the danger in which he stood himself. This speech had a very disturbing effect on Varus. He withdrew the garrison which he had brought into the town and took to flight. A few of my men from the leading detachments went after him and forced him to halt. In the fighting that followed, Varus was deserted by his men. Some of them scattered to their homes; the rest came over to me. Among these was Lucius Pupius, a senior centurion who had previously held the same rank in the army of Gnaeus Pompey. He was now brought to me as a prisoner. I congratulated Varus' men on their behavior and allowed Pupius to go free. I also

thanked the people of Osimo for their help and promised
to remember what they had done.

At Rome the news of these actions caused a sudden outbreak of panic. The consul Lentulus, for example, had gone
to open the treasury to take money out of it for Pompey in
accordance with a decree of the senate; but he had only got
as far as opening the inner part of the treasury when he
turned around and fled from the city. This was because it had
been incorrectly reported that I was on the point of arriving
and that my cavalry were already in sight. Lentulus' colleague
Marcellus and most of the other magistrates followed him.
Pompey had left Rome on the previous day and had gone
to join the legions which he had taken from me and put into
different winter camps in Apulia.

There was now no further calling up of men for the
army in the area of Rome; indeed, the general view was that
there was no safety anywhere north of Capua. It was at Capua
that they pulled themselves together and recovered their confidence. They began to raise troops from the colonists who
had been settled there under the Julian Law. There were
also the gladiators whom I kept at Capua in a training establishment, and Lentulus, after bringing these men into the
forum, offered them their freedom, gave them horses, and
ordered them to follow him. Later, however, on the advice
of his friends (since this action of his was generally disapproved of), he distributed these gladiators, for the sake of
security, among the households of people whom he knew in
the citizen body of Capua.

Meanwhile I had left Osimo and overrun the whole of
Picenum. Everywhere in these parts the prefectures gave
me the warmest possible welcome and did all they could to
help supply the army. A deputation actually came to me
from Cingulo, a town which had been founded and built by
Labienus at his own expense. The deputation stated that they
were most anxious to do whatever I commanded. I asked for
soldiers and they sent them.

By this time I was joined by the Twelfth Legion. So it was
with two legions that I set out for Ascoli in Picenum. This
town was held by Lentulus Spinther with ten cohorts. As
soon as he heard of my arrival, he fled from the town, attempting to take his cohorts with him, but a great number
of his men deserted. Abandoned by them on the march and
with only a few followers, he met with Vibullius Rufus, who
had been sent by Pompey into Picenum in order to keep up
the morale of the inhabitants. After receiving an account from
Spinther of how things actually were going in Picenum,
Vibullius took over the troops and let Spinther himself go on

his way. He also got together from the neighborhood all the
cohorts which he could that had been raised by Pompey's
recruiting agents. Lucilius Hirrus, in full flight from Camer-
ino with the six cohorts he had there as a garrison, was among
those who were brought in in this way. Altogether Vibullius
got together a force of thirteen cohorts. With these he went
by forced marches to join Domitius Ahenobarbus at Corfinium and reported to him that I was approaching with two
legions. Domitius had by his own efforts brought up from
Alba about twenty cohorts, having recruited the troops from
the neighboring districts of the Marsi and the Peligni.

3   CAPTURE OF CORFINIUM.

After we had taken Fermo and driven Lentulus out of Ascoli,
I ordered that the soldiers who had deserted Lentulus should
be rounded up and that a program of recruiting should begin.
I stayed there for one day, which was spent in organizing
supplies of food, and then marched on Corfinium. On my
arrival I found five cohorts, which had been sent out of the
town by Domitius, engaged in breaking down the bridge over
the river, which was about three miles from the town. Fighting broke out between these cohorts and my advanced detachments. The soldiers of Domitius were quickly defeated
and driven back into the town. I brought the legions across
the river, halted outside the town, and pitched camp close to
the wall.

When he discovered what had happened, Domitius found
some men who knew the country well and, promising them a
large reward, sent them to Pompey in Apulia. They were to
beg Pompey most urgently to come to his help and to point
out that, with two armies operating against me in a mountainous district, I could easily be cut off from supplies; if, on the
other hand, Pompey failed to come to his help, then he himself
with more than thirty cohorts and a great number of senators
and upper-class Romans would find themselves in a very dangerous position. Meanwhile Domitius encouraged his troops
to resist, placed artillery on the walls, and gave everyone his
particular duty to perform in the defense of the town. In
a speech to the soldiers he promised to give them land from
his own estates, four acres to each man, with proportionately
increased allowances for the centurions and reserves.

Meanwhile I was informed that the people of Sulmona (a town seven miles from Corfinium) were anxious to give me their support, but were being prevented from doing so by Quintus Lucretius, a senator, and by Attius the Pelignian, who were holding the town with a garrison of seven cohorts. I sent Mark Antony to Sulmona with five cohorts of the Thirteenth Legion, and as soon as the people of the place saw our standards they opened the gates and came out all together, both townsmen and soldiers, to meet Antony and to express their pleasure at his arrival. Lucretius and Attius threw themselves down from the wall. Attius was brought to Antony and asked that he might be sent to me. Antony, on the same day on which he had set out, returned bringing with him the cohorts and Attius. I incorporated these cohorts in my own army and let Attius go free.

In the course of the first days, while I was waiting for the rest of my forces to arrive, I organized the building of strong fortifications around the camp and the bringing in of supplies of grain from the towns in the neighborhood. After three days I was joined by the Eighth Legion, together with twenty-two cohorts which had recently been raised in Gaul and about three hundred cavalry sent by the king of Noricum. On their arrival I established a second camp on the other side of the town and put Curio in command of it. On the following days I began to invest the town with an earthwork and fortified posts.

At about the time that this work was nearing completion, Domitius' messengers returned from Pompey. Domitius read the message which they brought, and then, concealing the real truth, announced in a general meeting that Pompey would soon be coming to their help; he therefore urged them to keep up their spirits and do all that was necessary for the defense of the town. Privately, however, in conversations with his friends, he was planning how he could manage to run away. It was now observed that the way he looked was scarcely consistent with the speech he had made; that there was a kind of uneasy hurry and timidity in his actions which had not been noticeable on the previous days; and that, contrary to his usual habit, he was spending a lot of time in secret talk with his friends and avoiding general discussions at which large numbers were present. It became impossible for the deception and dissimulation to be kept up any longer. In fact, Pompey had written back to say that he had no intention of endangering his whole position and that it was not by his advice or with his consent that Domitius had brought his army into the town of Corfinium; finally, if at all possible, he recommended

Domitius to come to him with all his forces. This plan, however, was now becoming an impossibility because of my blockade and investment of the town.

When it became generally known what Domitius' real intentions were, the soldiers at Corfinium gathered together by themselves in the early evening and discussed matters under the guidance of officers, centurions, and reliable men of other ranks. The gist of what they said was this: "We are being besieged by Caesar; his system of fortifications is almost completed; we have remained loyal to our leader, Domitius, because we trusted him and relied upon him; but he has now abandoned all of us and is planning to run away himself; we therefore ought to think about our own safety." At first the Marsi began to object to these conclusions and seized what appeared to be the best fortified part of the town. Indeed, such was the difference between the two factions that there was a move toward fighting the matter out by force of arms. Soon, however, after messengers had been sent to and fro between the two sides, the Marsi learned what they had not known before, that Domitius was planning to run away. They were now all of the same opinion. They forced Domitius out into the open, surrounded him, and kept him under guard. They then sent some of their own men on a deputation to me to say that they were prepared to open the gates, to obey my orders, and to hand over Lucius Domitius alive.

With these facts before me, I realized clearly enough how important it was to get possession of the town and incorporate the cohorts there into my own army at the earliest possible moment; there was always a risk that they might change their minds either because of promised rewards or renewed confidence or false news, since, as I knew, it very often happens in war that decisive events proceed from some very small tipping of the scale. But I was afraid that the town might be sacked and looted in the disorder that would result from my troops entering it by night, and so, after praising the action of those who had come to me, I sent them back into the town and ordered that the gates and walls should be carefully guarded.

I personally saw to the posting of my own men along the lines of fortifications which we had been building. They were posted not, as on previous days, in a series of patrols with a fixed space of ground between each, but in a continuous line of sentries and outposts, so that each man was in touch with the man on each side of him without a gap anywhere in the whole circle of the fortifications. I sent officers around with instructions that they must not only be on their guard against a general attempt at breaking out, but

CAPTURE OF CORFINIUM 223

must also keep their eyes open for individuals who might attempt to slip through on their own. And in fact their spirit was so keen and alert that not a man among them took any rest on that night. There was a tremendous sense of something very important being about to take place; everyone was thinking or imagining what was going on in one direction or another, what was happening to the Corfinians themselves, what was happening to Domitius and to Lentulus and the others.

At about five in the morning, Lentulus Spinther, speaking from the wall, got into touch with our sentries and patrols. He said that he would like to have an interview with me, if he were allowed to do so. This permission was granted and he was escorted out of the town by some of Domitius' soldiers, who did not leave him until they had brought him actually into my presence. He then began to plead for his safety, begging and praying me to spare him. He reminded me of our old friendship and of the various kindnesses which I had done him. These, in fact, had been considerable. It was owing to me that Lentulus had been appointed to the College of Pontiffs and had received the province of Spain after his praetorship, and I had also helped him in his candidature for the consulship. Now I interrupted him in the middle of his speech.

"I did not," I said, "leave my province with the intention of doing any harm. My aim was to defend myself from the insulting behavior of my enemies; to restore the tribunes, who on this issue had been driven out of the state, to their proper position; and to free both myself and the Roman people from the oppression of a small minority party."

These words had an encouraging effect on Lentulus. He asked to be allowed to return to the town, saying that his own success in pleading for his safety would come as a great relief to the others, who were also hoping for mercy. Some of these, he said, were so terrified that they were actually contemplating suicide.

So Lentulus was allowed to go back into the town and did so. As soon as it was light, I ordered all senators and their sons, all officers, and all members of the Roman gentry outside the senate to be brought before me. There were fifty of them. Of senators there were Lucius Domitius, Publius Lentulus Spinther, Lucius Caecilius Rufus, Sextus Quintilius Varus the quaestor, and Lucius Rubrius; there was also the son of Domitius and many more young men, a large number of Roman gentlemen outside the senatorial order and town councilors whom Domitius had brought in from the municipalities. These were all brought before me, and I shielded them from the angry and violent language of the troops. In a short speech I complained that there were among them some who, in return for very great acts of kindness on my part, had shown me no gratitude at all. I then allowed them all to go free. As for the six million sesterces which had been brought by Domitius to Corfinium, placed in the public treasury, and then given back to him by the four magistrates of the town, I returned this money to Domitius. I wished it to be known that I could spare people's property just as well as I could spare their lives—although in the case of this money, there was no doubt at all that it belonged to the state and had been given to Domitius by Pompey for the payment of the troops. I ordered the soldiers of Domitius to take the military oath of loyalty to me. Then, on the same day, I moved camp and completed a full day's march. Altogether I had been seven days at Corfinium. So, going through the country of the Marrucini, the Frentani, and the Larinates, I made my way into Apulia.

4 POMPEY RETIRES FROM ITALY.

When Pompey received the news of what had happened at Corfinium, he left Luceria and went to Canossa, and from there to Brindisi. He gave orders that all the newly enrolled troops from every quarter should report to him at the latter town. He armed slaves and herdsmen and supplied them with horses, thus raising a force of about three hundred cavalry.

The praetor Lucius Manlius was in flight from Alba with six cohorts, and the praetor Rutilius Lupus from Terracina with three. On catching sight of my cavalry, under the command of Vibius Curius, they deserted their praetor and went over to Curius, bringing their standards with them. So, too, on other marches various cohorts fell in with and joined either my main army or the cavalry. Caught in this way and brought to me was Numerius Magius, of Cremona, Pompey's chief engineer. I released him and sent him to Pompey with a message. He was instructed to say that up to now no opportunity of holding a conference had been permitted; now, however, I myself was on my way to Brindisi and it was important for the state and the general welfare of everyone that I should meet Pompey personally; when we had been a long way away from each other and terms of agreement had to be carried to and fro by other people, it was much harder to come to a satisfactory understanding. Now, however, we could meet face to face and discuss all conditions that were to be considered.

After giving these instructions to Magius, I went on to Brindisi. I had with me six legions, three of which were veteran. The remainder had been recently conscripted and then brought up to their full strength on the march. I had sent the cohorts that had served under Domitius straight from Corfinium to Sicily.

I found that the consuls with a great part of the army had left for Durazzo, while Pompey with about twenty cohorts was remaining at Brindisi. It was impossible to be sure why he was doing this. In holding Brindisi he may have aimed at making it easier for him to control the whole Adriatic; he would, with bases both in the south of Italy and on the coast of Greece, be in a position to operate from both sides of the sea. On the other hand, he may simply have been short of shipping. Personally I was afraid that he might think he had an obligation not to abandon Italy; so I decided to block the harbor and make Brindisi useless as a port.

We built out walls filled with earth to form a dam from each side of the harbor entrance where it was at its narrowest. This was perfectly practicable because the water was shallow at these points. Farther out, however, in deeper water where the dam would not hold together, I had double rafts fixed at the ends of the walls. The rafts were thirty feet square and were held in position by anchors at each corner to prevent them from being shifted out of position by the waves. Once these were finished and put in the right place, we attached to them other rafts of the same size, covering them with earth and giving them a raised causeway, so that there would be no difficulty in getting men into them quickly for purposes of defense. In front and on both sides the structure was protected with hurdles and screens, and on every fourth raft we built a tower two stories high, to protect the rafts from enemy ships and attack by fire.

As a countermeasure Pompey fitted out some large merchant ships which he had captured in the harbor of Brindisi. He erected on these ships towers three stories high, and after equipping them with a number of catapults and long-range weapons of all kinds, he brought them close up to my dams, with the idea of destroying them by breaking through the line of rafts. So every day there was long-range fighting on both sides with slings, arrows, and other missile weapons.

Yet, with all these operations on hand, I still thought that no opportunity for making peace should be neglected. I was in fact extremely surprised that Magius had brought back no reply to the message which I had given him for Pompey, and I realized that these constant efforts of mine to reach an understanding were handicapping me both in action and in planning for the future. Nevertheless I thought that on all accounts I ought to go on trying for peace, and with this end in view I sent a member of my staff, Caninius Rebilus, to discuss the matter with Scribonius Libo, with whom he was on very friendly terms. Caninius was to urge Libo to use his good offices for making peace; he was to say that what I wanted most of all was to have an interview with Pompey. If this chance were given me, Caninius pointed out, I was very confident indeed that fair terms could be found for a cessation of hostilities on both sides; and much of the honor and credit for all this would go to Libo, if on his initiative and by his help both sides did lay down their arms.

After talking with Caninius, Libo went to see Pompey. In a little time he came back with the reply, which was that it was impossible to carry on any negotiations for a settlement because the consuls were not present. Having attempted so often and with such little success to come to an understanding, I now decided that the time had come to abandon these efforts and to give my attention to the war.

About half the work of blockading the harbor had been completed (nine days had been spent on it), when the ships which had transported the first part of the army to Durazzo and had been sent back from there by the consuls returned to Brindisi. As soon as they arrived, Pompey began to make his preparations for departure, either because he was alarmed by our operations or because he had intended from the beginning to leave Italy. In order to prevent my troops from attacking and breaking into the town at the very moment he was leaving it, he barricaded the gates, built roadblocks across the lanes and passages, and dug trenches across the main streets. Inside these trenches he fixed stakes of wood sharpened at the end, and concealed the trenches with a covering of light hurdles and earth. Huge pieces of timber, also sharpened at the ends, were placed in the ground at the approaches to the harbor to block up the two routes which led there. When all this was done, he ordered his soldiers to embark in silence. At intervals along the walls and in the towers, he posted light-armed troops from the reserves, archers, and slingers. He planned to withdraw these at a given signal when all the rest had embarked, and left some oar-driven ships for them in a place that would be easy to reach. The people of Brindisi, angry at the ill treatment they had received from Pompey's soldiers and at the arrogance shown to them by Pompey himself, were on my side. When they realized that Pompey was leaving, and while his men were fully occupied in hurrying to their stations, in every quarter of the town signs were made from the rooftops to show what was happening. As soon as I found this out, not wanting to let slip any opportunity for action, I ordered my men to fall in and to have scaling ladders ready.

Pompey set sail at nightfall. The men posted as guards on the wall were recalled by the signal that had been agreed upon and ran down to the ships by routes which they knew. My soldiers brought up their ladders and mounted the walls. Here they halted, as they were warned by the people of Brindisi to avoid the hidden obstacles and ditches. Then, guided by the Brindisians, they made a long detour and reached the harbor, where they found two ships with troops on board which had fallen foul of the dam. These they captured, making use of light craft of various kinds for the purpose.

In the hope of finishing the business off, I was very much inclined to get ships together, cross the sea, and go after Pompey before he could build up his strength with forces from abroad. To do this, however, would mean waiting and delaying for a long time, and I was afraid of this. Pompey had laid his hands on all the ships available and so had deprived me of any immediate opportunity of pursuing him. I could only wait for ships to arrive from the more remote parts of Gaul, from Picenum, and from the Sicilian straits; and, owing to the time of the year, this operation seemed certain to be difficult and could not be done quickly. Meanwhile there was a veteran army and the two provinces of Spain, one of which was devoted to Pompey because of great benefits received from him in the past. I had no wish that in my absence this army and these provinces should grow stronger still, that extra forces and cavalry should be raised against me and attempts made to invade Gaul and Italy.

I therefore gave up for the time being the project of going after Pompey, and decided to set out for Spain, meanwhile giving orders to the officials of all municipal towns to find ships and have them brought to Brindisi. I sent one legion, under Valerius, to Sardinia, and two others to Sicily under the command of the propraetor Curio. Curio's orders were, after recovering Sicily, to take his army immediately across to Africa. At the time, Marcus Cotta was in command of Sardinia and Marcus Cato of Sicily; Tubero, according to the allotment of provincial posts, should have been in command of Africa.

In the town of Cagliari, as soon as it was known that Valerius was on his way, even before he had left Italy, the people of their own accord ejected Cotta. Terrified because he realized that the rest of the province held the same views, Cotta fled from Sardinia to Africa.

In Sicily, Cato was repairing old warships and requisitioning new ones from the cities. He was devoting great energy to these tasks. In Lucania and Calabria, his officers were calling up Roman citizens for military service, and he was making the Sicilian cities produce a fixed quota of cavalry and infantry. These measures of his were almost complete when he heard that Curio was approaching. He then held a public meeting in which he complained that he had been abandoned and betrayed by Gnaeus Pompey, who, though totally unprepared for it, had undertaken an unnecessary war and, when questioned in the senate by himself and the others, had maintained that he had in fact got everything required for warfare ready and in order. After making these complaints in a general meeting, Cato fled from his province. So Valerius and Curio, finding no established government in either Sardinia or Sicily, occupied these places with their armies.

In Africa, Tubero found on his arrival that Attius Varus was holding the province. Varus, it will be recalled, had lost his cohorts at Osimo and had immediately fled to Africa, where he had found the province without a governor and had on his own initiative taken it over for himself. He had recruited troops and raised a force of two legions, being in a good position for doing this because he had governed Africa a few years previously after his praetorship and so was familiar with the people and the country and knew the province well. When Tubero with his ships arrived at Utica, Varus denied him access either to the harbor or to the town. He would not even allow him to land his son, who was suffering from an illness, but forced him to weigh anchor and leave the place.

5 AT ROME AND AT MARSEILLES.

After making the arrangements described above, I withdrew my troops and quartered them in the nearest towns, so as to rest them for the remainder of the season. I then set out for Rome. Here I called together the senate and informed them of how disgracefully I had been treated by my enemies. I pointed out that I had not aimed at holding any unusual or extraordinary position; instead, I had waited until I was legally qualified to stand for the consulship. I had, indeed, been content with the rights open to all citizens. In Pompey's own consulship, a law had been passed by the ten tribunes giving me the right to stand for the consulship in my absence;

my enemies had spoken against the proposal and Cato had opposed it in the most violent language and, according to his old tactics, had tried to prevent a vote by talking all day. But if Pompey had not approved of the measure, why had he allowed it to become law? If he had approved of it, why had he not allowed this act of kindness on the part of the people to become operative?

I then called attention to the patience I had shown; it was I of my own accord who had proposed that the armies should be disbanded, and in making this proposal I was showing myself ready to sacrifice my own prestige and my own rights. I pointed out how bitterly intractable my enemies had been; they had demanded for themselves just what they refused to me and preferred to bring about a state of chaos rather than to give up their armies and military power. I commented on the injustice that had been done when the two legions were taken from me, and on the insolent brutality that had been shown in depriving the tribunes of their proper powers. I recalled to their minds the terms of peace which I had offered, the opportunities for discussion which I had begged for and which had been refused.

Because of all this, I urgently recommended that the senators should take up and share with me the responsibility of government. If, however, they were frightened and shrunk from the task, I was not going to be a burden to them; I would run the state myself. What should be done, I suggested, was to send a deputation to Pompey to negotiate a settlement; and, I informed them, I was quite unmoved by that remark of Pompey's made recently in the senate to the effect that the mere sending of a deputation was a sign of fear and an acknowledgment of the superior authority of those to whom it was sent.

"That," I said, "is a weak and wretched way of looking at things. As for me, just as I did my best to attain eminence as a man of action, so I am anxious to be ahead of others in showing respect for justice and fair play."

The senate approved the plan of sending a deputation, but no one could be found to serve on it, largely because everyone was too frightened for his own safety to take on such an appointment; for Pompey, when leaving Rome, had declared in the senate that he would make no distinction between those senators who remained behind and those who were actually in my camp.

So, what with the arguing and the excuses, matters dragged on for three days. My enemies also made use of the tribune Lucius Metellus to obstruct the business of the deputation and indeed everything else that I proposed. I saw what his plan was and, after having wasted several days, decided not to lose any more time. None of the things I had meant to do had been done; so I left Rome and went to Transalpine Gaul.

Here I was informed that Vibullius Rufus (captured not long ago at Corfinium and given his liberty by me) had been sent by Pompey to Spain; and that Domitius too had set out for Marseilles with the intention of occupying it; he had with him seven rowing ships which he had requisitioned from their owners at Igilium and Cosannum and had manned with his own slaves, ex-slaves, and tenants. I heard too that he had been preceded by some young nobles of Marseilles whom Pompey, just before he left Rome, had sent home to their own country, telling them to see to it that what I had been able to do for the place recently had not been allowed to make people forget the benefits which he had conferred on Marseilles in the past.

As the result of these instructions, the people of Marseilles had closed their gates against me and had called in help from the Albici, a native tribe living in the mountains to the north which had been for a long time in their sphere of influence. They had brought in grain from the surrounding country and from all fortified areas; they had organized arms factories in the city and were busy repairing the walls and gates and putting their fleet into a seaworthy condition.

I asked fifteen of the leading citizens of Marseilles to come to see me and tried to convince them that it was no duty of theirs to start a war. Instead of giving in to the wishes of a solitary individual, they ought, I said, to follow the lead given to them by the whole of Italy, and I added all the other arguments which seemed likely to make them see sense. After reporting back what I had said, they returned to me with their government's reply, which was as follows:

"We find that the Roman people is split into two parties. This is not our business, nor have we any power of jurisdiction to decide which side is in the right. The leaders of the parties are Gnaeus Pompey and Gaius Caesar, both officially recognized as benefactors of Marseilles. Pompey gave us a grant of land in the country of the Volcae Arecomici and of the Helvii; and you, Caesar, after you had conquered the Sallyes, gave us control of them and increased our revenues. Then, since you are both equally our benefactors, we should on our side give an equal return to each of you. This can be done by remaining neutral and allowing neither side to have access to our city or to our harbors."

In the middle of all this, Domitius arrived with his ships at Marseilles. He was not only received there but was made governor of the city and commander-in-chief. On his instructions they sent out their fleet and, in a wide sweep, commandeered all the merchant ships they could find and brought them back to harbor. Those inadequately equipped were dismantled and the bolts, timber, and rigging were used for the fitting out or repairing of other vessels. All grain found aboard was confiscated and stored in the public granaries; the rest of the cargoes—merchandise or provision—were sequestered for use in case of a siege.

Realizing that I had been disgracefully treated, I brought up three legions against Marseilles. Work was begun on the towers and mantlets for an assault on the city, and I ordered twelve warships to be constructed at Arles. These were built and ready for service in thirty days from the time that the timber was first felled for them. When they reached Marseilles, I put Decimus Brutus in command of them and entrusted the task of besieging the city to Gaius Trebonius.

6

THE CAMPAIGN AT LERIDA: FIRST STAGES.

During the time that I had been occupied with these affairs, I instructed another of my generals, Gaius Fabius, to go on ahead to Spain with three legions which had been in winter camps at Narbonne or near it. He was to lose no time in seizing the passes over the Pyrenees, which were then held by units from the army of Pompey's general Lucius Afranius. I ordered the other legions, whose winter quarters were farther away, to follow Fabius and join up with him. Fabius acted as he had been instructed. Making good speed, he drove the outposts from the pass and went on by forced marches till he made contact with Afranius' main army.

It will be remembered that Pompey had sent Lucius Vibullius Rufus to Spain. When he arrived, he found the country in the control of Pompey's three generals, Afranius, Petreius, and Varro. Afranius held eastern Spain with three legions, while in western Spain Varro with two legions held the area between the Sierra de Segura and the Guadiana, and Petreius, also with two legions, held Lusitania and the country between the Guadiana and the Douro. The plan of action which they now made was as follows: Petreius with his whole army was to march out of Lusitania by way of the Vettones and join up with Afranius, while Varro, with his two legions, was to look after the whole of western Spain. Once they had agreed upon this plan, Petreius ordered all the

states of Lusitania to supply him with cavalry and auxiliary
troops, and Afranius sent out the same orders to the peoples
of Castile and the Asturias and the semicivilized tribes along
the north coast.

As soon as these troops were mobilized, Petreius marched
through the Vettones and joined Afranius. They both agreed
to base themselves on Lerida, a place with outstanding strategic advantages. Afranius, as has been already stated, had
three legions and Petreius two. They had also about eighty
cohorts of auxiliaries (those from the east armed with long
wooden shields and those from the west with light, round
ones of leather) and about five thousand cavalry from both
districts together.

I, on my side, had sent ahead of me into Spain six legions,
five thousand auxiliary infantry, and three thousand cavalry
which had served with me throughout the wars in Gaul; I had
also raised from the Gallic Province, which I had myself conquered, another three thousand cavalry by calling up individually from each state the best and bravest types of men;
those of the highest quality came from Aquitania and from
the mountain tribes on the Spanish border. I had heard that
Pompey with his legions was marching through Mauretania
on his way to Spain and would soon be arriving there. At
this juncture I borrowed money from the officers and centurions and distributed it among the soldiers. I thus killed
two birds with one stone—binding the centurions to me because I owed them money, and the soldiers because I had
given it to them.

Meanwhile Fabius was sending out letters and personal
agents in an attempt to win over to our side the tribes in the
neighborhood of Lerida. He had built two bridges, four miles
apart, over the Segre and was sending troops across the
river to bring in supplies, since in the previous days he had
used up what was available on his own side of the river.
Pompey's generals were doing the same thing for the same
reason, and there were frequent engagements between the
cavalry on each side. Fabius always sent two legions out to
protect the foragers, and on one occasion, when the legions
had already crossed by the lower bridge, with the transport
and cavalry following behind, the bridge suddenly collapsed
because of a high wind and an unusual volume of water, with
the result that most of the cavalry were left stranded on the
nearer bank. Seeing the timber and hurdles which were carried
downstream, Petreius and Afranius realized what had happened, and Afranius acted at once. Across his own bridge,
which was built to connect his camp with the city of Lerida,
he sent out four legions and the whole of his cavalry to en-

gage Fabius' two legions. These were under the command of
Lucius Plancus, who, when he found that the enemy was
approaching, took up an emergency position on higher ground
and formed his men in a double line facing in both directions,
so as to avoid being attacked in the rear by the cavalry. In
this way, though he was heavily outnumbered, he was able
to stand up to resolute attacks made on him by both Afranius' cavalry and his infantry. Fighting was still going on
between the cavalry forces when both sides saw in the distance the standards of two legions. These legions had been
sent by Fabius by way of the farther bridge to come to the
relief of our men, since he had correctly guessed that the
enemy commanders would make use of the chance that had
come their way, and would try to overwhelm them. As the
legions approached, the battle was broken off and both sides
withdrew to their camps.

Two days afterward, I arrived myself with nine hundred
cavalry which I had kept as an escort. Repairs on the bridge
that had broken down in the storm were nearly finished and
I ordered the last part of the work to be done by night. Next
day, after making myself acquainted with the lay of the land,
I left six cohorts to guard the bridge, the camp, and our
heavy equipment, and marched with the whole army in three
columns to Lerida. We halted close to Afranius' camp and
waited there for some time under arms, giving him an opportunity of fighting on level ground. Challenged in this way,
Afranius led out his troops and formed them up halfway
down the hill on which his camp was placed. When I realized
that it was his decision not to fight a pitched battle, I decided
to build a camp of my own about four hundred yards from
the foot of the hill. I did not want my men while they were
on the job to be frightened by sudden enemy attacks and
prevented from working; so I told them not to build a rampart,
which, because of its height, would obviously be visible from
a distance. Instead, they were to dig a fifteen-foot trench along
the side facing the enemy. The first and second lines stayed
in battle order as they were, and behind them, invisible to
the enemy, the third line did the digging. In this way the
whole thing was completed before Afranius could know that
we were fortifying the position at all. In the evening I withdrew the legions behind the trench and gave them a night's
rest, though they were still under arms.

Next day I kept the whole army inside the shelter of the
trench. Since it was necessary to go some way to find material for a rampart, I adopted for the moment the same
method as that of the previous day, and ordered three more
trenches of the same size as the first one to be dug so as to

enclose the whole camp. On each of these trenches one legion was occupied, while the other legions were drawn up in battle order to face the enemy. Afranius and Petreius, wishing to cause terror among our men and stop their work, led their troops down to the bottom of the hill and made some moves against us. However, I felt that I could rely on the three legions which were on guard and on the protection of the original trench; so the enemy's action caused no interruption in the work. In fact, they did not advance far from the foot of the hill and before long retired to their camp. On the third day, I had a rampart built all around the camp and ordered the cohorts which had been left in the other camp with the equipment to come and join us.

Between Lerida and the hill on which Petreius and Afranius were encamped there was a stretch of level ground of about eight hundred yards with a small hillock more or less in the middle. I believed that if I could seize and fortify this hillock, I should be able to cut the enemy off from their bridge and Lerida and from all the supplies which they had brought into the town. Hoping to do just this, I led three legions out of camp, drew them up in line in what seemed a good position, and ordered the shock troops of one legion to go forward at the double and seize the hillock. Afranius, however, saw what we were doing. He had some cohorts on guard duty in front of his camp, and he sent them by a shorter route to occupy the position we were aiming at. There was some fighting, but as Afranius' men had reached the mound first, our men were driven back and then, as more enemy reinforcements appeared, were forced to turn and retreat to the main body of the army.

These soldiers of Afranius had their own methods of fighting. They would charge forward at full speed, showing great daring in reaching their objective; they did not bother much about keeping in regular order but would fight as individuals or in small groups, and, if hard pressed, they were not ashamed to fall back again and abandon the ground they had won. This can be described as a native style of fighting, and they had got used to it in the course of their constant engagements with the Lusitanians and other native tribes. In fact, it is usually the case that when an army has had a long period of foreign service it becomes much influenced by the methods of the country where it is operating. My men, on the other hand, had had no experience of this sort of fighting and were considerably disturbed by it. They had been trained always to keep in their proper formations under their own standards and not to yield a position which they had taken up unless there was some very good reason for doing so. Now these sudden individual attacks made them think that they were being outflanked; and so, when the assault troops had been driven back, the legion on that wing abandoned its position and retreated to the nearest hill.

I found that panic was spreading along almost the whole line—a state of affairs which I had never expected and to which I was quite unused. Shouting out to the men to stand firm, I brought up the Ninth Legion in support. The enemy had shown a kind of insolent daring in their pursuit, and I put a stop to this. I forced them to turn back and retreat to Lerida, where they formed up outside the walls. But the men of the Ninth, who were full of enthusiasm and determined to make up for the setback we had received, pressed their pursuit rashly and too far. They advanced right up to the hill on which Lerida stands and here found themselves in a difficult position. They tried to withdraw, but it was now the turn of the enemy, who charged down on our men from higher ground. There were steep rocky gorges on each side of them and the space between was only wide enough for three cohorts to be drawn up in line. Thus it was impossible to give them support on their flanks or to use cavalry to help them when they were in trouble. From the town, however, the ground sloped down gently for about five hundred yards. Our men, whose enthusiasm had unwisely carried them so far, stood facing this slope, fighting in a most unfavorable position. They had no room to maneuver, and because they had halted at the very foot of the high ground, every weapon directed at them found its mark. Nevertheless they stood their ground, fighting magnificently in spite of heavy casualties. Meanwhile the enemy's strength was increasing; from their camp new cohorts were constantly being sent through the town into the fighting line so that fresh troops could relieve those who were tired. I was obliged to do the same thing and sent up other cohorts to take the places of my own exhausted men.

The fighting went on without a break for five hours, our men being in constant difficulties and heavily outnumbered. They had now used up all their ammunition and, drawing their swords, they charged up the hill against the cohorts in front of them. Some they cut to pieces, others they forced to turn and run. So, with the enemy cohorts pushed back against the wall or hurrying in terror into the town, our men could retreat without difficulty. The withdrawal was made all the easier and safer by our cavalry, who, though posted on much lower ground, very bravely managed to struggle up on both sides to the top of the ridge and then rode up and down between the two lines.

The fighting had gone first one way and then the other. In the first encounter we lost about seventy killed and had about six hundred wounded. Among the killed was Quintus Fulginius, who because of his outstanding courage had risen from the lower ranks to become a leading centurion of the Fourteenth Legion. Afranius lost more than two hundred men killed, among whom was one of his senior centurions, Titus Caecilius, and four other centurions as well.

In fact, each side thought that it had come off best in the day's fighting. Afranius' troops had been generally considered inferior to mine, yet they had stood their ground in close fighting and resisted our attacks for a long time; at the beginning of the action they had held the hillock which had been our original objective, and in the first engagement had forced us to retreat. On the other hand, our men could claim that they had fought for five hours against superior numbers and with the advantage of the ground against them too; that they had forced their way up the hill armed only with their swords; that they had made the enemy leave his higher position and driven him back into the town.

The enemy now built strong defense works around the hillock for which the fighting had taken place, and manned them with a garrison. We also suffered an unforeseen misfortune within two days from the time of the battle. There was a tremendous storm which brought with it more rainfall than had ever been known in these parts. At the same time, the snows were washed down from the mountains, so that the river overflowed its banks and in one day both of the bridges that Fabius had built were swept away. The result was that we were placed in a very difficult position.

As has already been explained, our camp was between the two rivers Segre and Cinca, which were about thirty miles apart. Neither of these rivers could be crossed, and so we were forced to remain in this confined space. The states which were on friendly terms with us were unable to send us grain; some of our own people, who had gone out for quite a distance to bring in supplies, were cut off by the floods and could not get back; and the large convoys of provisions coming from Italy and Gaul could not reach the camp. It was also the worst possible time of the year. There was no grain left in the winter stocks, and the new harvest was not quite ripe. The neighboring tribes had been drained of supplies, since Afranius had had nearly all the grain taken to Lerida before I arrived, and what little was left had been used up by us in the last few days. Meat might have been a possible substitute for the grain which we lacked, but we could not even get meat because the people of the neighborhood had driven off their cattle as soon as the war began. And those of our men who went out to look for fodder and grain were attacked by Lusitanian light infantry and Spanish targeteers, who knew the country well and had no difficulty in crossing the rivers, since they regularly carried with them on active service bladders which could be used as floats.

Afranius' men, on the other hand, had everything that they needed. There were already large stocks of grain which had been collected previously, and more was coming in from all parts of the province; there was also plenty of food for the animals. Since they held the bridge at Lerida they could bring in their supplies perfectly safely and could cross the river into country that had hitherto been untouched and from which I was entirely cut off.

The floods lasted for several days. We tried to repair the bridges, but were hindered both by the strength of the current and by enemy troops stationed along the bank, who prevented the work being done. This was easy enough for them to do. The banks were steep and the river flowed fast; moreover, their troops, strung out all along the bank, could concentrate their fire on the small cramped area where our men were working. It was a hard job to build a bridge against a great flood of water and at the same time to be trying to keep out of the way of enemy weapons.

Meanwhile Afranius was informed that large convoys on their way to us had halted at the river. There were archers from the Ruteni, cavalry from Gaul, and great numbers of wagons all heavily loaded in the usual Gallic way. There were also about six thousand civilians, people of every description, with their slaves and children. There was no fixed order on the march, and no one was in supreme command; everyone did as he liked and they all traveled without any apprehension of danger, assuming the immunity to which they had been used on previous occasions. Among them were some young men of good families from Rome, sons of senators and of gentlemen; also deputations from a number of states and officers of my own returning from various missions.

The whole lot of them were held up by the river and Afranius decided to get them into his power. He set out at night with his entire cavalry force and three legions, and launched a cavalry attack on them before they realized what was happening. Nevertheless the Gallic cavalry were soon ready for action and joined battle. Few as they were, they held their own against great numbers of the enemy so long as the fighting was confined to cavalry; but when the standards of the legions were seen to be approaching, they retired to the nearest high ground, leaving a few dead. But the fact

that the battle lasted for as long as it did had an important
bearing on the security of our people, since it gave them time
to withdraw to higher ground. Our losses on that day were
about two hundred archers, a few cavalry, a few camp
servants, and a small amount of the luggage.

As the result of all this, however, the price of grain rose
sharply, as indeed usually happens not only when there is
a real shortage but also when people think that there will be
one. Already the price of grain was about fifty denarii a peck;
lack of food was affecting the soldiers' health, and things
were getting worse with every day that passed. Within a few
days the situation had completely changed; fortune had swung
the other way, and while we were struggling with shortages
of all kinds, the enemy had everything they wanted and
appeared to be in a much stronger position. There was simply
not enough grain to be had from the Spanish tribes that had
come over to my side, so I asked them for livestock and sent
out foragers even farther afield than before, doing everything
I could to relieve the pressing needs of the moment.

In their letters to Rome, Afranius, Petreius, and their
friends gave an even fuller and more glorified account of the
situation than was justified by the facts. Rumor added to the
story, and people began to think that the war was practically
over. As the letters and messengers arrived in Rome, crowds
of people gathered outside Afranius' house by way of offering
their hearty congratulations. There were many who now left
Italy to join Pompey—some because they wanted to be the first
to tell him the good news, others to avoid giving the impression
that they had been waiting to see how the war would end
and had consequently arrived last in the queue.

As for us, we were certainly in a difficult position. Afranius'
troops and cavalry were in control of all the roads, and we
were unable to repair the bridges. What I did was to instruct
the troops to build some boats like the ones I had seen some
time ago when I was campaigning in Britain; the keels and
the basic structure were made of light wood, and the rest
was of wickerwork covered with hides. When they were
finished, each one was loaded onto a couple of wagons, and
they were then all taken down by night to the river, which
was about twenty-one miles from the camp.

I got some troops across the river in these boats and
occupied a hill near the bank without being observed. We
hurriedly fortified the position and finished the fortifications
before the enemy knew anything about it. Later I brought a
whole legion across, and we started from both banks to build
a bridge, finishing the job in two days. It was now possible
for the convoys and those of our own men who had gone far

afield for food to rejoin us safely, and I could also take measures to improve the general position with regard to supplies.

On the same day, I brought most of the cavalry across the river. Some enemy foragers, who had no apprehension of danger and had scattered in all directions, were caught off their guard and attacked by our cavalry, who took a number of prisoners and captured a lot of animals. Some cohorts of Spanish targeteers were sent out in support, but our men did the right thing by forming up in two bodies—one to guard the booty, the other to resist and drive off the oncoming cohorts. One enemy cohort which had unwisely got out of position by charging ahead of the rest was cut off, surrounded, and annihilated. Our cavalry got back safely to camp by the bridge, bringing a lot of booty with them.

7 NAVAL BATTLE AT MARSEILLES.

While these operations were going on near Lerida, the people of Marseilles, on the advice of Domitius, had got seventeen warships ready for service, eleven of which were decked. They brought into service also a quantity of smaller craft, with the idea of frightening our fleet by sheer weight of numbers. They put on board these ships a large number of archers and of those Albician troops mentioned earlier, encouraging them with high pay and promises of more to come. Domitius insisted on having some ships placed under his personal command and manned them with his own retainers and herdsmen, whom he had brought out with him. There was, in fact, nothing lacking in their preparations. They were full of confidence as they sailed out against our ships, which, under the command of Decimus Brutus, were stationed off the island that lies opposite Marseilles.

So far as ships went, Brutus was heavily outnumbered, but I had left with him to man his fleet some of the best fighting material to be found in the legions—shock troops and centurions who had volunteered for this service. They had got ready grappling irons and harpoons and had equipped themselves with large quantities of pikes, javelins, and other weapons. When they saw that the enemy was coming, they sailed out of port and joined battle. Both sides fought with the greatest courage and spirit. Indeed the Albicians, a race of tough mountaineers and well accustomed to warfare,

showed soldierly qualities that were scarcely inferior to those
of our own men. Having only just left the city, they remembered what the people of Marseilles had just promised them;
and the herdsmen of Domitius too, who had been encouraged
to fight by the prospect of gaining their freedom, were eager
to show what they could do under their master's eyes.

The Massilians could rely on fast-sailing vessels and well-
trained pilots. They avoided or parried our men's attacks and,
so long as they were allowed space in which to maneuver,
they tried to extend their line beyond ours so as to outflank
us, to bring several of their own ships against single ships
of ours, or to sweep up alongside with the aim of snapping
off our oars. But when they were forced to come to close
quarters, they relied not so much on the skill and clever
maneuvering of their pilots as on the courage of the mountaineers whom they had on board. Our own ships were
manned by less experienced crews and by less skillful pilots,
men who had just been taken into service from merchant
ships and still did not even know the technical terms in use
on warships. We were hampered too by the slowness and
heaviness of our ships, which had been hurriedly constructed
from green timber and were not as fast as they might have
been. So, whenever there was a chance of fighting at close
quarters, any one of our ships was ready enough to close with
two of the enemy. Grappling irons were thrown out, and
when the enemy were held fast, our men, fighting at both
sides of their ship, would board the enemy vessels. They killed
great numbers of the Albicians and of Domitius' herdsmen,
sank some ships, captured others with their crews, and drove
the rest back into harbor. On that day the Massilians lost
nine ships, including those that were captured.

8 THE CAMPAIGN AT LERIDA: SECOND PHASE.

I heard of the naval battle at Marseilles when I was at
Lerida. Our bridge here was now finished and things began
rapidly to go better for us. Our cavalry were very active and
the enemy became terrified of them. The enemy's liberty and
confidence in moving about was now much restricted; either
they did not venture far from their camp, so as to be able
to get back there quickly, and consequently did not cover
much ground in their foraging; or, to avoid our scouts and
cavalry detachments, they went out on long, circuitous routes;

and, if they suffered any setback at all or even caught sight of our cavalry in the distance, they would break order, drop whatever they were carrying, and run away. Finally they got into the habit of going for days on end without doing anything and adopted the unusual procedure of foraging by night.

Meanwhile the Oscenses and the Calagurritani, their dependents, sent deputations to me to say that they would obey my orders. Their example was followed by representatives from Tarragona, from the Jacetani and Ausetani, and, a few days later, from the Illurgavonenses, who live on the lower Ebro. I asked them all to send grain. This they promised to do and, getting together all the baggage animals they could find, they brought it into camp. A cohort of Illurgavonenses left their post and came over to us when they heard what their government had decided. Everything had changed, and had changed quickly. The bridge was finished; five important states had joined us; our supplies were assured; there was shown to be no truth in the rumors about Pompey marching through Africa with reinforcements for his legions; and now a number of the more remote tribes severed their relations with Afranius and came over to us.

All this had a very depressing effect on the enemy's morale. Meanwhile I took steps to avoid having always to send the cavalry around on a long detour by the bridge. After choosing a suitable place for the operation, we started to dig a number of trenches, thirty feet wide, so as to drain off into them part of the river Segre and make it fordable. By the time that we had nearly finished them Afranius and Petreius had become really frightened. They knew how strong we were in cavalry and dreaded the prospect of being entirely cut off from food and fodder. So they decided to leave their present position and to fight the next campaign in Aragon. In making this decision they were also influenced by the fact that in this area the native states had, in the previous war, either been on the side of Sertorius or had remained loyal to Rome; the former ones had been conquered by Pompey and still feared his name and power, even in his absence; the latter had been very well treated by him and were bound to him by affection, while my name, among these native tribes, was comparatively unknown. In these parts they counted on being able to raise large forces of cavalry and supporting troops, and proposed to protract the campaign into the winter on ground of their own choosing. After deciding on this plan, they ordered all ships on the Ebro to come together at Mequinenza, which was nearly thirty miles from their camp. Here they ordered a bridge of boats to be made.

They then took two legions across the Segre and built a camp
with a rampart twelve feet high.

I was informed by our scouts of what was going on, and
now our soldiers put everything they could into the work,
which went on day and night, of diverting the river. We
had got to the point where the cavalry, though it was a difficult enough proceeding, were nevertheless able to venture
across the river, though the infantry were prevented from
crossing both by the speed of the current and by the depth
of the water, which came right up to their armpits. However,
we were finding a way across the Segre, and this happened
at almost exactly the same time as I received news that the
bridge over the Ebro was nearly finished.

The enemy now came to the conclusion that it was all the
more important for them to be moving. Leaving two auxiliary
cohorts to hold Lerida, they crossed the Segre with all the
rest of their forces and rejoined the two legions which had
already crossed some days earlier. There was nothing that I
could do except to harass the enemy's marching column with
my cavalry and do it what damage I could, since, if I were
to use my own bridge for the legions, that would involve a
long, roundabout route, while the enemy would have a much
shorter distance to go to reach the Ebro. So I sent out the
cavalry. They forded the river and suddenly appeared in the
rear of Afranius' column, which had left camp soon after
midnight. Our men were in great force, and they swarmed
round the enemy flanks, holding up the march and trying
to force a halt.

At dawn the sentries posted on high ground near our
camp could see the enemy's rear guard being very roughly
handled by our cavalry; there were times when the end of
the column was forced to halt and was even cut off from the
rest. Then the enemy's cohorts would charge all together
and drive our men back, and then again our men would wheel
around and make another attack.

Now all over our camp the soldiers were gathering in
groups and complaining among themselves that the enemy
were being allowed to slip out of their grasp and consequently
the war was being dragged on unnecessarily. They approached
the centurions and senior officers, begging them to let me
know that I was not to think twice about exposing them to
any difficulty or danger; they were ready for anything, they
said; they had both the ability and the courage to cross the
river where the cavalry had crossed it. I was certainly impressed by what they said and by the spirit which they
showed; and, though I had my doubts about exposing my
army to so violent a flow of water, nevertheless I thought

that the venture was worth taking and ought to be attempted. So I ordered the soldiers who were not of the first quality— men who did not seem to have the courage or the strength for the undertaking—to be withdrawn from their companies, and left them, with a full legion, to guard the camp. I led out the other legions (each man carrying the minimum of equipment) and, after stationing large numbers of pack animals in the river above and below the ford, we started to make the crossing.

The force of the current swept a few of the soldiers off their feet, but they were picked up and helped across by some of our cavalry, and not a single man was lost. As soon as they were all safely across, I saw that they formed up in their proper units and led them forward, marching in three columns. The men showed such keenness that, although they had gone six miles farther around and had had a long delay at the ford, it was only about two thirty P.M. when they caught up with the enemy, who had started about midnight.

Afranius, who was in company with Petreius, saw us coming in the distance and was both surprised and alarmed by what he saw. He halted and formed his army up in battle order on some rising ground. I had no wish to throw my troops into battle when they were tired, and so I rested them in the fields nearby. When Afranius tried to go forward again, we followed him up and impeded his march. As a result, the enemy were forced to pitch camp earlier than they had intended. There were hills nearby, and five miles ahead the routes into the hills became narrow and difficult. What the enemy wanted was to get into the shelter of these hills so as to be safe from our cavalry, and then to leave covering detachments in the narrow passes, which would hold up our army's advance while they themselves crossed the Ebro without any danger or anxiety. They should have done everything possible to achieve this object, but they were tired after a troublesome march and a whole day's fighting, so they put off their plan until the next day. I also camped on a hill nearby.

About midnight our cavalry brought in some of the enemy who had gone rather too far from their camp to get water. I was informed by them that the enemy commanders were quietly leading their forces out of camp. As soon as I knew this, I ordered the signal to be given—the usual army order to pack up before moving—and, when the enemy heard the shouting, they canceled their departure and kept their troops inside the camp, being frightened of having to fight by night when they were loaded with their equipment or else of being held up by our cavalry in the narrow passes.

Next day Petreius went quietly out of camp with a few horsemen to reconnoiter. We did the same thing. I sent out from my camp Lucius Decidius Saxa with a small detachment to see what the country was like. Each party brought back the same report: there were about five miles of level country ahead, and after that the route became rough and mountainous; whoever managed first to occupy this narrow part of the road would have no difficulty in preventing the other side from getting through.

Petreius and Afranius held a council of war at which they discussed the question of when to depart. The majority were in favor of leaving by night, with the idea of reaching the narrow part of the road before it became known that they were on the move. Others, remembering that on the previous night the alarm had been sounded in our camp, regarded this as a proof that it would be impossible to get away without being noticed. Large numbers of our cavalry, they said, were on duty by night and would be patrolling the whole country and watching every road; then, too, battles at night ought to be avoided because, in civil wars, if the soldiers begin to lose confidence, they are apt to think more of their own fears than of the duty they owe to their generals; whereas in daytime they are ashamed to appear cowardly when their comrades are looking on, and are also affected by the presence of their officers and centurions—all known factors in preserving good order and discipline in an army. There was therefore every reason for trying to break through by day; even if they suffered some losses, it was still possible to reach their objective with their army still intact as a fighting force. It was this view that prevailed at the council of war, and it was decided to start next day at dawn.

After reconnoitering the district, as soon as the first signs of light appeared in the sky, I led out all my forces from camp. We were to go by a long, roundabout way with no clearly marked route, since the roads to Mequinenza and the Ebro were blocked by the enemy's camp. We had wide valleys to cross where the going was very difficult; often we were held up by steep cliffs, which meant passing the equipment up from hand to hand and then one man helping the next on the ascent, so that they had to go unarmed for quite long distances. But no one objected to facing all these hardships; they thought that all their labors would be over if they could only cut the enemy off from the Ebro and from his supplies.

At the beginning of our march, the soldiers of Afranius ran out of their camp in high spirits to see the sight and followed us on our way with insulting language. In their opinion, we were short of food and were therefore being compelled to retire and fall back on Lerida. And in fact our route was different from the one which we would have taken if we could. It appeared indeed to lead in the opposite direction. The enemy commanders congratulated themselves on having decided to stay in camp; and their opinion about our condition seemed to be confirmed by the fact that they could see us marching without baggage animals or heavy equipment; so they felt sure that we could not hold out much longer against hunger. But when they saw that our column was gradually wheeling to the right and then that our vanguard was already getting past the line of their camp, there was not a man among them so stupid or so lazy as not to realize that they must leave camp immediately and try to get ahead of us. The fall-in was sounded; a few cohorts were left to guard the camp, while the rest marched out and took the direct road to the Ebro.

Everything now depended on speed, the question being which side could first occupy the passes into the mountains. My own army was slowed down by the difficulties of the route, but on the other hand Afranius' men were held up by our cavalry, which hung on close to them. Afranius also had got himself into an awkward situation from which there was no way out: even if he did get first to the high ground which was his objective and so secure the safety of his army, he would still have to abandon all baggage and equipment and the cohorts which had been left behind in camp. These were now cut off by my army and could not possibly be relieved.

As it was, we reached the mountains first. After crossing over some great rocks, I found a stretch of level ground where I drew up my army facing the enemy. Afranius, with his rear guard still harassed by our cavalry and with our main force in front of him, occupied some high ground and there halted. From this position he sent out four cohorts of targeteers toward the highest mountain in sight, with orders to hurry there at the double and occupy it. He intended to follow after them with his whole army and to go on from there to Mequinenza by another route along the mountain ridges. The targeteers, cutting across country from his main army, were on their way to this mountain when they were observed and charged by our cavalry. They put up no sort of resistance and were surrounded and killed in sight of both armies.

Victory was now in my grasp. I was perfectly well aware that no army, demoralized as it had been by watching such a reverse, could hold out long, especially if it were forced to fight on level and open ground, surrounded on all sides by cavalry. And indeed I was being urged by everyone to bring on just such an action. Centurions and officers of all ranks came crowding around me, all telling me not to hesitate about joining battle. Every man in our army, they said, was ready and eager for battle, whereas Afranius' men had shown clearly enough that they were frightened. They had failed to go to the rescue of their own men; they showed no signs of coming down from the hill; they were not standing up well to attacks made on them by our cavalry; and, all crowded together with their standards in one place, they were losing formation and failing to preserve their ranks in proper order. If, so I was told, I was frightened of attacking uphill, there was sure to be a chance of engaging somewhere else, since Afranius would have to come down into the plain and could not remain where he was forever without water.

However, now that I had cut the enemy off from his supplies, I hoped to be able to finish the whole thing off without having to fight or to expose my own men to danger. Why should I lose any of my own men even in a victory? Why let them be wounded when they had served me so well? And why tempt fortune? After all, a good general should win victories by intelligence just as much as by brute force. Then, too, I felt compassion for men who were my fellow countrymen and who would certainly be killed if there were a battle. I preferred to gain my object without causing them any loss of life or limb. These views of mine, however, were not generally approved. In fact, the soldiers went about openly saying that because such a good chance of victory was being thrown away, they would refuse to fight next time I asked them to.

Nevertheless, I did not alter my point of view. I withdrew a little from my position, so as to give the enemy more confidence, and Petreius and Afranius, now they had the chance of doing so, retired to their camp. We camped as near to them as possible, after having posted detachments in the hills and blocked all roads to the Ebro.

On the following day, the enemy commanders, alarmed by the fact that they had no prospects either of reaching the Ebro or of getting supplies, debated what they should do next. There were two possible routes, one to Lerida, if they wished to retreat, the other to Tarragona, if they decided to move in that direction. While they were in the middle of their discussions, they were informed that their water carriers were being attacked by our cavalry. This news led them to station outposts of cavalry and auxiliary troops, with regular legionary cohorts in between, at frequent intervals along the way, and to set about building a rampart from their camp to the water, so that they would in future be able to bring the water inside their fortifications without anxiety and without having to use these outposts. Petreius and Afranius both took a hand in organizing this work and went personally some distance beyond the camp in order to see that it was being done properly.

Once they had gone, their soldiers had an opportunity to speak freely with mine. They came out in numbers, inquiring for friends or fellow townsmen in our camp and asking to see them. First they thanked us all together for having spared them on the previous day; they would not be alive now, they said, if it had not been for our kindness. They then inquired about me, whether I could be trusted and whether they could honorably surrender, saying that they wished they had done so in the first place instead of fighting against their own friends and relations. What they heard reassured them and they demanded that I should promise to spare the lives of Petreius and Afranius, since they did not want it to look as though they had been engaged in any underhand work or were betraying their own people. When I gave the required guarantees, they promised to come over to us at once and sent some senior centurions to me to discuss the terms of the surrender. Meanwhile my men were asking their friends on the other side to come over into our camp to be entertained, or else were being themselves invited into their camp, so that it seemed that there was only one camp where there had been two before.

Several high-ranking officers and centurions came to call on me and to establish friendly relations. So did a number of Spanish chieftains whom the enemy had called up as allies and then kept in their camp as hostages. They now tried to find friends or acquaintances in my army who would be ready to introduce them to me. Even Afranius' young son made approaches to me through Sulpicius, one of my staff officers, asking me to spare his and his father's life. Indeed it was a general scene of happiness and thanksgiving; Afranius' men were delighted at the thought of having escaped from a most dangerous position, and our men were equally delighted because it looked as though they had won a great victory without any bloodshed at all. Everyone agreed that I was reaping a handsome profit from my well-known reluctance to carry matters to extremes, and now the decision that I had previously made was generally considered to have been correct.

When the news of what was happening was brought to Afranius, he left the work on which he was engaged and returned to camp, apparently quite ready to accept quietly and with a good grace whatever situation he might find. Petreius, however, kept his original spirit and resolution. He armed his servants, and with them and his official bodyguard of Spanish targeteers and a few native cavalry, retainers of his whom he kept about his person, he suddenly rode up to the rampart. Once inside the camp, he put a stop to all fraternization, killed any of our men whom he could lay his hands on, and drove the rest out. These latter were frightened enough at finding themselves suddenly in danger; but they formed up into a body and, wrapping their left arms in their cloaks, drew their swords, and so beat off the attacks of the targeteers and cavalry. The fact that their camp was close by gave them confidence, and they got back there safely under the protection of the cohorts on guard at the gates.

After having achieved this result, Petreius, with tears in his eyes, went from company to company, appealing to the soldiers and begging them not to betray him and not to betray their general, Pompey, to the vengeance of an enemy. A crowd quickly gathered outside his headquarters. He then demanded that they should all swear an oath that they would not desert or betray the army or its commanders, and would not take any separate measures for securing their own safety apart from that of the rest. Petreius was the first to take the oath, and Afranius was compelled to take the same oath after him; then came the officers and centurions, and then the men came forward by companies and took the oath too. It was then proclaimed that anyone who was harboring any soldier of mine should bring him forward; some were brought forward and put to death publicly in front of headquarters, but most were hidden by those who had invited them and were allowed to escape across the rampart during the night. So the terrorism employed by the enemy generals, the savagery of their punishments, and the new obligations of the oath which had been sworn removed for the moment all hope of a surrender; the feelings of the soldiers reverted to what they had been, and there was hostility on both sides as before.

I ordered a careful search to be made for those enemy soldiers who had come into our camp during the period of fraternization and had them sent back to their own camp. But there were several officers and tribunes who decided that they wanted to stay with me. Later on I saw that all of these got promotion; the centurions were restored to their former rank and the officers also received the same posts as they had held previously.

Afranius' troops were now finding it difficult to get water and almost impossible to go out foraging. The men in the legions had a certain amount of grain, since they had been ordered to bring with them from Lerida rations for twenty-two days. But the Spanish targeteers and auxiliary troops had none, nor had they much chance of finding any; and physically they were quite unused to carrying heavy loads. Consequently, large numbers of them deserted and came over to us every day.

The enemy were therefore in a very awkward position. Of the two proposed plans, the simplest seemed to be to return to Lerida, where they had a small stock of grain in reserve. Once in Lerida, they felt, they would be less hampered in planning for the future. Tarragona was a long way off, and they realized that on the journey there quite a number of things might go wrong with them. So they decided on the first plan and at once left their camp. I sent forward the cavalry to attack them in the rear and slow up their march, and followed after them with the legions.

Their rear guard was given no rest and was constantly in action with our cavalry. The fighting went on in the following way. Their rear guard was composed of lightly armed cohorts, and several of these would halt and make a stand where the ground was level. If the road lay uphill, then the ground was all in their favor, as those who had gone on ahead could from their higher position give cover to their comrades on the ascent. But when they had to cross a valley or go downhill, they were always in danger; those in front were unable to be of any use to those delayed in the rear, and our cavalry from higher ground shot at them from behind. The only thing they could do in these conditions was to order the main body of their legions to halt, then charge all together against our cavalry until they had driven it back, and then, with the cavalry out of the way, to start forward immediately at the double, cross the valley, and halt again on the higher ground at the other side. As for their own cavalry, of which they had a considerable force, it had been entirely demoralized by previous engagements and was so far from being any use to them that they had to protect it themselves by keeping it in the center of their column; if any of their mounted detachments did venture to leave this protection, they were immediately rounded up by our own cavalry.

This kind of fighting means slow, gradual progress and frequent halts in order to support the rear guard. So it happened on this occasion, and, after marching rather less than four miles, all the time under heavy attack from our cavalry, they occupied a high hill and dug themselves in. Their entrenchment was only on the side facing us, and they did not unload their baggage animals. When they saw that we had halted to camp, had put up our tents, and had sent out horsemen on foraging duty, they suddenly left their position at about noon on the same day and resumed their march, hoping that we would be delayed by the absence of our cavalry. I saw what was happening and, after giving the legions a short rest, set out in pursuit, leaving a few cohorts to guard the baggage. I ordered the foraging party to follow on at four P.M. and the cavalry to be recalled at once. Before long our cavalry was again operating as it had done day after day on the march. The fighting at the enemy's rear guard was very fierce, so much so that they were almost routed and a number of their men, including some centurions, were killed. Meanwhile our main body was pressing on and threatening their whole army.

They were thus given no chance of looking for a suitable place to encamp and, finding it impossible to advance farther, were forced to halt and pitch camp in a bad position with no water nearby. However, for the reasons already mentioned, I refrained from engaging them in battle. On this day I gave orders that the tents should not be pitched, so that we should all be able to follow without delay, whether the enemy tried to escape by day or by night. As it was, after discovering what a bad position they were in, they spent the whole night in building out additional fortifications, amounting to the construction of an entirely new camp. They went on with the work next morning, starting at dawn and continuing the whole day. But the more they worked and the farther they extended their camp, the farther they got from their water supply; by trying to make things better for themselves, they were in fact making things worse. At night no one left camp to get water. Next day, leaving a small garrison to guard the camp, they led out their whole force to bring in water, but sent out no foraging parties. Personally, I preferred them to suffer in this way and so be compelled to surrender, rather than to fight a pitched battle with them. However, I tried to blockade them completely by building a rampart and a trench around them, which, I hoped, would have the effect of checking any sudden attempts of theirs to break out. They would be forced, I imagined, to make attempts of this kind. And so, partly because they were without fodder and partly because, when they did make a sortie, they wanted to be as little encumbered as possible, they had all their baggage animals destroyed.

Two days were spent in planning and conducting these operations, and by the third day the lines which we had been building were almost finished. In order to prevent us from completing what was left to be done, the enemy gave the signal for action, led out their legions, and formed up in line of battle just outside their camp. I recalled my own legions from their work, ordered all the cavalry to their stations, and formed a line facing them. My apparent reluctance to fight (which was not what my own men or the world in general expected of me) was in fact doing me considerable harm. However, I was still, for the reasons already mentioned, against joining battle, and particularly so now because the space available for fighting was so narrow that even if the enemy were routed, this would not contribute much toward final victory. The two camps were less than six hundred yards apart from each other; two-thirds of this space was filled by the two opposing armies, leaving only one-third in which there was room to advance and attack. In the event of a battle the defeated side would be able to turn and reach safety quickly inside its camp. I therefore decided that, although I would resist them if they attacked, I would not be the first to move into battle.

Afranius had drawn up his five legions in two lines, and formed a third line of reserves from the cohorts of his auxiliary troops. My army was drawn up in three lines; the first line was made up of four cohorts from each legion, and for the two other lines each legion supplied three cohorts. I kept the slingers and archers in the center and placed the cavalry on the flanks. So, with both armies drawn up and ready, it appeared that each side was keeping to its original purpose: I was not going to join battle unless forced to do so, and Afranius simply aimed at stopping our works. Things remained in this condition until sunset, when both sides withdrew to camp. Next day we got ready to complete the fortifications on which we were occupied, and the enemy turned their attention to the ford over the Segre, to see whether they could get across. When I saw what they were doing, I sent across the river some German light infantry and some of the cavalry, and had patrols posted at frequent intervals along the banks.

The end had now come. They were shut in on every side; their animals had been kept unfed for four days; they had

no water, wood, or grain. So they begged for a conference—
if possible a private one, out of hearing of the troops. This I
refused, but agreed to confer with them in public, if they
wished to do so. They gave me Afranius' son as a hostage
and met me in a place chosen by myself. Afranius then spoke,
with both armies listening to his words.

"You must not," he said, "be angry with us or with our
troops for wanting to keep faith with our general, Gnaeus
Pompey. We feel, however, that we have now done our duty
and that we have suffered enough punishment in the severe
privation that we are enduring. We are now shut in like wild
beasts, cut off from water, cut off from movement; both our
physical sufferings and the shame we feel in our minds are
unendurable. We admit that we are beaten men. But we beg
and pray that, if there is any room left for mercy, you will
not think it necessary to inflict on us the supreme penalty."

He spoke in as humble, indeed in as abject a way as it is
possible to imagine. I replied as follows:

"Your complaints and your appeals for sympathy come
worse from you than they could from anyone else. Everyone
except you and your fellow commanders has acted well. I
acted well when, with the best possible conditions of time and
place on my side, I refused to fight a pitched battle, simply
because I wanted the way to be absolutely clear for making
peace. My troops acted well when they protected and preserved men of yours whom they had in their power, although
you had treated them disgracefully and had killed their comrades; lastly, even the men of your own army behaved well.
They tried to make peace of their own accord, thinking it
right to avoid bloodshed among their own people. So men
of all ranks have stood out for compassion. It was only the
generals, you and Petreius, who shrank from the idea of
peace; you showed no respect for conferences, you disregarded the rights of a truce, you savagely put to death innocent men who were deceived into thinking that they were
safe when peace talks were going on. And what has happened
is what usually does happen when people show too much
arrogance and obstinacy—you are changing your tune and
begging most earnestly for the very thing which just now
you were too proud to accept.

"However, it is not my intention to make use of your
humiliation and my own strong position in order to increase
my own fighting forces; all I ask is that those armies which
you have maintained for so many years to be used against me
should now be disbanded. It was certainly against me that
they were directed. Nothing else would account for the sending of six legions to Spain, the raising of a seventh one on

the spot, the fitting out of powerful fleets, and the choice of commanders of proved experience. None of these measures had anything to do with establishing order in Spain or with any need felt by the Spanish provinces, which have enjoyed peace for such a long time that they require no help of this kind.

"No, it was against me that these forces were long ago mobilized and kept in readiness; it was against me that a new form of constitution was adopted, under which one man could govern Rome from outside the gates and at the same time could retain control for year after year of two warlike provinces without ever visiting them himself; it was against me that the laws concerning provincial governorships were changed, so that the men sent out to govern provinces were not, as they always had been, ex-praetors or ex-consuls, but simply people who had been chosen and approved by a political clique. It was in order to injure me that veterans were not allowed to plead their age as an excuse, and have been called up to command armies after having completed their years of military service. In my case, and in mine alone, the time-honored tradition was disregarded by which all generals who had conducted successful wars were allowed to return to Rome and then disband their armies, with honor or with some distinction, or at least without dishonor.

"All these affronts I have borne patiently and I shall continue to do so. Nor do I want now to take your army away from you and use it for myself, though I could easily do this; all I want is that you should not keep it for use against me. So, as I have said, what you must do is this: leave the province and disband your army. This is all I ask and these are the only terms on which you can have peace."

These words of mine caused much joy and relief among the soldiers of Afranius, as was evident from the way in which they behaved. They had expected and they deserved to suffer something; yet they now found themselves being rewarded with a free discharge. When various points were raised about the time and place where they should be disbanded, they all shouted and gesticulated from the rampart where they stood, indicating that they wanted to be discharged at once, and that, whatever guarantees were given, they would not feel really safe if there were any further delays. And so, after a short discussion of the arguments on either side, it was decided that all those who were domiciled or had property in Spain should be discharged at once, and that the rest should receive their discharge at the river Var.

I guaranteed that they should receive no ill treatment on the way there and that no one should be compelled to take

the oath of loyalty to me, unless he wanted to do so. I also
promised to supply them with grain until they reached the
river Var, and in addition provided that any property of
theirs which in the course of the war had come into the
hands of my soldiers should be given back to them. I paid over
the correct sums of money, after having had a fair valuation
made. After this, whenever there were any disputes between
the soldiers of the two armies, they would of their own accord
refer them to me for decision. A mutiny almost took place
when the enemy legions demanded their pay and Petreius and
Afranius claimed that it was not yet due. There was a general
demand that I look into the matter myself, and both parties
were satisfied with my ruling. About a third of their army
was disbanded in two days. I arranged that on the march two
of my own legions should go ahead and the rest should follow
in the rear, so that the camps should be quite close to each
other. One of my staff officers, Quintus Fufius Calenus, was
given the job of superintending the withdrawal. He followed
out my instructions, and after making the journey from
Spain to the river Var, the rest of Afranius' army was
disbanded.

✧ BOOK TWO: 49 B.C. ✧

1 THE SIEGE OF MARSEILLES.

During the Spanish campaign, my deputy commander, Gaius Trebonius, had been left behind to conduct the siege of Marseilles. He began by building earthworks, with sheds and siege towers, on two sides of the town—one near the harbor and the docks, and the other near the gate leading to Gaul and Spain, close to the point where the Rhone flows into the sea. Marseilles is practically surrounded by sea on three sides and only the fourth side is accessible by land. And even on this side the part below the citadel is naturally easy to defend, as it is cut off by a deep valley. Siege operations therefore must be long and difficult. For carrying them out Trebonius ordered large quantities of hurdles and of timber to be brought in to him and engaged great numbers of men and baggage animals from all over the Province. He used the material and the labor to build up an earthwork eighty feet high.

However, there had long been in Marseilles enormous stocks of armaments, and in particular such powerful artillery that no sheds made of hurdles could possibly stand up to it. Great catapults fired twelve-foot-long poles, pointed with iron, which went through four layers of hurdles before burying themselves in the ground. So the roofs of our sheds were constructed of beams a foot thick and clamped together, and under this covering the building material was passed along from hand to hand. In front went a movable shed sixty feet long, for the leveling of the ground; it was built also of very stout timber and covered with every sort of material that could be used to protect it from firebrands and stones hurled by the enemy. However, the great scale of our works, the height of their wall and the towers, together with the great number of their catapults, made our progress slow. There were also a number of sorties made by the Albici with the aim of setting fire to our siege works and towers. These were all easily repelled by our troops, who indeed inflicted very heavy casualties on the attackers before driving them back into the town.

Meanwhile Lucius Nasidius had been sent out by Pompey with a fleet of sixteen ships, some of which had bronze beaks, to reinforce Lucius Domitius at Marseilles. He sailed through the Sicilian straits without Curio having the least idea of his presence, and put in to Messina. Here his sudden arrival caused a panic, and, after the town council and leading citizens had taken to flight, he removed a ship from the dockyards and, adding this vessel to his own force, sailed on to Marseilles. He sent one of his smaller ships on ahead to inform Domitius and the Massilians of his arrival and to urge them strongly, now that they were reinforced, to join battle again with Brutus' fleet.

Since their last defeat at sea, the Massilians had brought out of their dockyards and repaired the same number of old ships as those which they had lost. They took a lot of trouble in equipping these ships, and had already a good supply of oarsmen and pilots to serve on them. They also made ready for service a number of fishing boats, which they decked so as to protect the oarsmen from enemy missiles, and then put archers and catapults aboard. And so, when the fleet was ready, the men embarked with their spirits roused to action by the tears and supplications of the old men, the mothers, and the young girls, who begged them to save the state in this moment of extreme peril.

Thus they went out with the same spirit and the same confidence as on the occasion of the previous battle; for indeed it is one of the defects of human nature itself that in conditions which are unknown or unfamiliar, we tend to be either too sure or too unsure of ourselves. So it happened then. The mere fact of the arrival of Nasidius had filled the people of Marseilles with the most extreme hopes and the most extreme enthusiasm. The wind was right for them, and they sailed out of harbor and joined him at Taurois, one of their fortified posts, where they got their ships ready for action, once more encouraged each other in view of the battle that was to come, and discussed the tactics to be pursued. The Massilians were to be on the right wing and Nasidius on the left.

Brutus also made for Taurois. His fleet had been increased. In addition to the ships which I had had built for him at Arles, he had six ships captured from the Massilians which

in the last few days had been repaired and refitted. So he
sailed out against the enemy in good heart and full of confidence. He encouraged his men by telling them that they
could afford to consider their opponents as beaten men, since
in fact they had already been defeated when they were at
full strength.

From Trebonius' camp and all the high ground around
it was easy to look down into the city and see how all the
young men who had stayed behind and all the elder men with
their wives and children were standing on the walls or watch-
towers with their hands outstretched to heaven, or were
thronging into the temples of the immortal gods and falling
down before the statues as they prayed for victory. Every
single one of them was convinced that on the event of this
one day hung the whole future of his life and fortune. Youths
of the best families and important citizens of every age
had gone aboard the ships. They had been called individually
for the service and had answered the summons, making it
clear that if they were to fail, they had put their last supreme
effort into the attempt, and if they were victorious, they could
be confident about their city's future and rely on their own
internal strength as well as upon foreign help.

So the two fleets went into action. The Massilians showed
no lack of courage. They remembered what they had just
been told by their friends and their relations; and they fought
as though this were really their last chance to show what they
could do, as though in facing the dangers of battle they were
standing for a moment in front of the rest of their fellow
citizens, who would have to suffer the same fortune of war
if their city were taken.

Our ships got gradually farther apart from one another,
thus giving the enemy an opportunity to exploit their superior
speed and the skill of their pilots. Whenever our men got the
chance of holding an enemy vessel with their grappling irons,
others came up from all directions to help the one that was
in difficulty. The Albicians who were fighting on the enemy
side showed no reluctance to engage our men at close quarters
and fell little short of them in soldierly qualities. And at
the same time, missiles were constantly being discharged from
the smaller vessels, causing a number of casualties among our
men, who had enough on their hands already when suddenly
exposed to this unexpected form of attack.

Brutus' flagship was easily recognizable by its ensign, and
seeing it, two enemy triremes bore down on him from opposite directions. Brutus, however, realized the danger and,
making full use of all the speed he had, managed to slip

between them just in time. Driving on at full speed, the triremes collided. Both were badly damaged, and one of them, with its beak broken off, was put out of action altogether. This was observed by those ships of Brutus' fleet which were nearby, and they set on the disabled ships at once and soon sank both of them.

Nasidius' ships put up no sort of a fight and quickly withdrew from the battle. Their crews were not fighting in sight of their own country and were impelled by no entreaties of their own dear ones to put their lives into jeopardy. So from this squadron not a single vessel was lost. Of the Massilian craft, five were sunk, four captured, and one joined the fleet of Nasidius, which made off for the east coast of Spain. Of the rest, one was sent ahead to Marseilles to bring the news. As it drew near, the whole population poured out to hear the result of the battle and, when they heard it, were so utterly prostrated with grief that one might have imagined that the city had fallen then and there. Nevertheless, they showed just as much resolution as before in preparing everything possible for its defense.

The soldiers who were working on the right of our lines came to the conclusion that it would be a great help to them against constant enemy attacks if they were to build a brickwork shelter or stronghold close under the wall. So they constructed one which was at first quite small, with low walls, to be used simply against sudden sorties. Here they used to retire, and from here fight back if outnumbered; from here too they would charge out to push back or to pursue the enemy. The fortification was a square, each side of which was twenty-nine feet long; the walls were five feet thick.

Later (we learn everything from experience), they began to use their ingenuity and to see that this building would be much more useful if it were raised to the height of a tower. They proceeded to do so in the following way. When they had built the walls up to the level of the first story, they laid the floor in such a way that the ends of the joists were hidden by the outer surface of the walls, so that there should be nothing projecting and vulnerable to the enemy's fire missiles. On top of this wooden structure they built walls of small bricks up to the height at which the workers were still protected by the sheds and screens. Across these brick walls they laid a pair of joists not quite long enough to reach the outer walls. These were intended to be supports for the wooden framework which in the end would be the roof of the tower. On top of these joists and at right angles to them other joists were laid and fastened with tie-beams. These joists were longer than the others and projected beyond the outside walls, so that screens could be hung from them to protect men building the outer walls up from below. The top of the platform, resting on the joists, was covered with a layer of bricks and mortar to preserve it from fire; above this they spread out mattresses to prevent javelins or artillery missiles from piercing the woodwork or crashing through the brick. Matting made out of ships' cables, four feet high and covering the three sides of the tower exposed to the enemy, was hung from the joists that projected from the walls. Past experience had taught them that this was the only kind of protection absolutely to be relied upon against artillery.

When the finished part of the tower was thoroughly shielded and protected from every kind of enemy missile, the sheds were removed for use somewhere else and the roof of the tower was hoisted up by leverage from the first floor to a height at which the hanging mats would give cover to the men who were building the walls up to the second story. They then laid another floor and hoisted the roof up again in the same way. When the time came for another story, they built in the joists, hidden in the exterior walls as before, and again used this flooring to raise the roof platform with its screen of mats. Without any casualties, they built six stories in perfect safety, leaving loopholes for artillery fire at what seemed to be the right intervals in the construction.

Once they were sure that from this tower they could protect any work going on in its vicinity, they set about constructing a mining gallery, sixty feet long and made of timbers two feet square, which was to run from the brick tower to a tower in the city wall. The plan of construction was as follows: first two beams of equal length were laid on the ground four feet apart, and into these beams were fixed posts five feet high. Rafters were laid across from post to post to form the framework of a slightly sloping roof. Two-foot beams fastened with iron plates and bolts were fixed on top of the rafters. On the ends of the beams and the edge of the roofing three-inch-square studs were fitted to support the layers of tiles that were to cover the roof. When the structure of the roof was finished, it was covered over with tiles and mortar to serve as a protection against fire thrown from the walls. Hides were stretched over the tiles so as to prevent them from being dislodged by streams of water that might be directed at them through pipes from above; and the hides themselves were protected by mattresses, so that they too should be kept safe from fire or stones. The whole of this work was completed under cover of screens quite near our tower.

Then, quite suddenly, when the enemy were off guard, rollers were put under it (as is done by the navy to move ships) and the whole structure was moved forward right up against the outer facing of the enemy's tower.

This was a sudden blow and the townspeople were dismayed by it. First they brought up with cranes the heaviest stones that they could find and rolled them down from the wall onto the gallery. But the timbers were strong enough to stand up to the force of impact, and because the roof was sloped, everything that fell on to it slid off again. Observing this, they adopted another plan. They set fire to barrels of resin and tar and rolled them down onto the gallery from the wall. These too slipped off the roof and, once they had fallen down from the tiles, were removed from the building by means of poles and long forks. Meanwhile the soldiers inside the gallery were levering out the lowest row of stones in the enemy's tower, the stones by which the foundations were held together. The gallery itself was protected by our men's covering fire from the brick fort. The enemy were pushed back from their walls and strong points. A number of the foundation stones of their tower were pried out, and part of the tower itself suddenly collapsed in ruin. The remaining part was already tilting forward and ready to fall.

At this point the enemy, terrified at the thought of their town being sacked, came rushing out of one of the gates in a body, unarmed, with fillets round their heads, and, with their hands outstretched like suppliants, appealed for mercy to the officers and men of our forces. This strange sight brought military operations to a standstill; our soldiers gave up all thought of fighting and hurried forward to find out and hear what was going on. The enemy, on reaching our lines, all fell down together at the feet of our army and its commanders. They begged them not to take any further action till I had arrived; their city, they said, was obviously practically in our hands now that our siege works were finished and their tower on the point of collapse; nothing could prevent the whole place from being pillaged on my arrival if they failed to obey my commands to the letter. They pointed out that if the tower were to collapse completely the city might be utterly destroyed, since the soldiers would expect plunder and it would be impossible to prevent them from breaking in. All these arguments and others that might be expected from intelligent spokesmen were accompanied by much weeping and general appeals to pity, which proved very effective. Our officers withdrew the men from the work and abandoned the

siege operations, merely leaving sentries in guard of the
various structures. Simply out of compassion a sort of truce
was arranged to operate until I should arrive. Not a shot
was fired either from the walls or from our lines and, as it was
assumed that everything was over, people generally relaxed
and took things easily.

In fact, I had written to Trebonius, making it perfectly
clear that I did not want him to allow the town to be taken
by storm. I was afraid that the soldiers, who were in a very
ugly mood because of the revolt itself, the contemptuous attitude shown to them by the Massilians, and the continuous
hard work that they had been doing, might slaughter everyone
in the city of military age. This was what they were threatening to do, and on this occasion it was difficult to prevent
them from breaking into the town. They were furious with
Trebonius for what appeared to be his refusal to let them
occupy the place.

The enemy, however, were without a sense of honor. They
were merely waiting for a suitable opportunity to show
treachery and deceit. They let a few days pass and then
suddenly burst out of their gates at midday when our men
were tired out or at their ease, some of them having left
their posts and others, after their long days of work, having
fallen asleep among the fortifications. All arms had been
stacked and were not available. So the enemy set fire to
the siege works, helped in this by a strong wind which spread
the conflagration so far that in a matter of moments the
mound, the sheds, the "tortoise," a siege tower, and some
artillery all caught fire and were destroyed before anyone
realized how it had happened. This sudden disaster roused our
men to action. They snatched up whatever weapons they
could find; others came hurrying from the camp, and an
attack was made on the enemy, who took to flight. But we
were prevented from following them up by the fire of arrows
and catapults from the wall. Thus the enemy, safe in the
shelter of their wall, were able, without any interference on
our part, to set fire to the gallery and to the brick tower. So
the labor of several months was destroyed in a mere moment
by enemy treachery and by a high wind.

Next day the Massilians tried to repeat their success. They
had the advantage of the same wind and sallied out against
the other tower and mound, fighting with greater confidence
than before and doing all they could to set the works on fire.
But our men had learned from what had happened on the
previous day. They had fallen back from their original state
of perfect alertness, but after that they had done everything

they could to meet another attack. So the enemy achieved nothing. Many of them were killed and the rest driven back into the town.

Trebonius now set himself to repair the losses, and the men worked more enthusiastically than ever before. They had seen all their labor and all their skill go for nothing. A truce had been wickedly violated, and they were furious at the thought of the Massilians laughing at their courage and sacrifice. There was no longer any material left for the construction of siege works on the former plan, since every tree in the whole area had already been felled and brought in for use. They therefore started to build a barrier of a kind unheard of before. It was formed of two parallel brick walls, each about six feet thick, and roofed over with wood, so that the width was about the same as that of the former structure of earth and timber. When the space between the walls seemed too great for the strength of the timber, piles were put in and crossbeams laid to give additional support. All the roofing was covered with hurdles, and the hurdles were covered with mortar. With this roof overhead, with the walls on their left and right, and with screens in front, the soldiers were able to bring up their building materials in perfect safety. They pushed on fast with the work, and by their skill and energy soon made good all that long labor of theirs that had been wasted. Gates were left in the walls at appropriate places, so that the troops could make sorties if required.

The enemy had expected that what they had destroyed would take a long time to repair. They now saw that a few days' hard work had brought things back again into such a state that they could employ neither treachery nor force of arms against us. There was no possibility of harming the troops by artillery or of setting fire to the siege works. They realized that in just the same way the whole city on the landward side would be completely shut off by towers and fortifications; that they themselves could not properly man their own defenses, since our investing walls looked almost as though they were extensions of their walls, being so close that weapons could be thrown across by hand; and that, because of this narrow space between the lines, their artillery, in which they had had such faith, was of no use to them at all, while, if they did get a chance of fighting on equal terms with our men from the walls and towers, they would be no match for them in courage and toughness. They therefore reverted to their original proposals for surrender.

2

SETTLEMENT OF WESTERN SPAIN. SURRENDER OF MARSEILLES.

Marcus Varro had been in western Spain from the beginning. When the first news arrived of events in Italy, he had felt doubtful about Pompey's prospects and was in the habit of referring to me in a most friendly way. His first duty was, he admitted, to Pompey, whose commission he held; nevertheless his close friendship with me was, he considered, an equally important tie. He was quite aware of his duties as one appointed by Pompey to a position of trust; he knew too what his own strength was and what was the general feeling in the province with regard to me. This was the way he used to speak on all occasions, and meanwhile he aligned himself definitely with neither side. Later, however, he heard that I was being held up at Marseilles; that Petreius and Afranius had joined forces and their armies had been increased by large numbers of native troops, more of which had been promised and were expected to arrive; and that the whole of eastern Spain was united against me. He heard too of what had happened later, of our difficulties with regard to supplies at Lerida. All of this was described to him in somewhat exaggerated terms in a letter from Afranius. And so Varro also began to follow the movements of fortune.

He called up men for military service throughout his province. Two legions were raised and to these he added about thirty cohorts of auxiliaries. He got together large stocks of grain, partly for Marseilles and partly for Afranius and Petreius. The people of Cadiz were ordered to build ten war-ships, while others were laid down at Seville. All the money and treasure in the temple of Hercules were moved from the temple into the town of Cadiz, and the town itself was garrisoned by six cohorts from the province, sent there by Varro, who put the place in charge of Gaius Gallonius, a Roman gentleman and a close friend of Domitius, who had sent him there to recover some property left to him in a will.

Varro himself attacked me in a number of public speeches. He made various official announcements to the effect that I had lost battles and that great numbers of my soldiers had deserted me and gone over to Afranius. He claimed that he had absolutely reliable authority for making these statements. In this way he made the Roman citizens of western Spain thoroughly frightened, and got them to promise to contribute for his expenses in administration about 18,000,000 sesterces, 15,000 pounds of silver, and 120,000 bushels of wheat. Even heavier burdens were imposed on communities which he thought were on my side. He moved troops into their territories, took proceedings against anyone who had spoken in public or in private against the existing state of affairs, and confiscated their property. He also compelled the whole province to take an oath of allegiance to himself and to Pompey. When he heard of what had happened in eastern Spain, he made ready for war. His plan was to retire to Cadiz with two legions and to keep with him there all his ships and all his supplies of food. He had discovered that the whole province was on my side, and thought that, with food and shipping at his disposal, he could easily prolong the war from the island of Cadiz.

I had a number of urgent reasons for going back to Italy. Nevertheless, since I knew that Pompey had much influence and many people bound to him by ties of gratitude in the eastern province, I decided not to leave behind me in Spain any vestiges of resistance. I sent two legions under the command of the tribune Quintus Cassius to the west of the country, and myself went on ahead, traveling as fast as possible, with six hundred cavalry. I had a proclamation published in advance, naming the day on which I wished the magistrates and chief men of every community to be at Cordova to meet me. The proclamation reached every part of the province, and every single community sent some of its council to Cordova, nor was there any Roman citizen of importance who failed to put in an appearance on the day that I had named. At the same time, the Roman citizens in Cordova closed the gates of the city against Varro, put sentries on the walls and detachments of troops into the towers, and kept in the town to serve as a garrison two cohorts of colonial troops who happened to be passing through. At about the same time, Carmona, which is much the strongest state in the whole province, ejected the three cohorts which had been put into the citadel by Varro to serve as a garrison, and closed its gates against them.

All this made Varro all the more anxious to get to Cadiz with his legions quickly, in case he might be intercepted on the march or prevented from making the crossing. It had been amply demonstrated to him that the whole province was very much on my side. But before he had gone far he received a dispatch from Cadiz informing him that as soon as my proclamation had been published there the leading citizens of the place together with the officers of the garrison had made a plan for driving Gallonius out and securing both the town and the island for me: they had next advised Gallonius to leave the city while he could still do so in safety, and told him that if he failed, they would take matters into their own hands. Gallonius had thereupon left.

When this news got about, one of Varro's two legions—called the Native Legion, since it was raised among the provincials—formed up around its standards and marched out of camp, while Varro himself simply stood there and watched. They went to Seville and took up their quarters in the town square and adjoining porticoes, doing no damage. The Roman citizens in the town were so pleased at this that they vied with each other in offering hospitality to the troops, inviting them to their own houses. All this had a most disturbing effect on Varro. He changed the direction of his march and sent on word that he was going to Italica; but he was then told by his friends that Italica had shut its gates against him. He had now nowhere to turn, and sent to me to say that he was prepared to surrender his legion to any officer I might select. I sent Sextus Caesar and ordered that it should be surrendered to him. After this, Varro came to me at Cordova with a full and accurate statement of public accounts, handed over the funds in his possession, and told me where his stocks of grain were situated and of the number and whereabouts of his ships.

In Cordova, I held a public meeting at which I expressed my thanks to every section of the population. I thanked the Roman citizens for the resolution they had shown in keeping control of the city, and I thanked the Spaniards for having driven out Varro's garrisons. I thanked the people of Cadiz for having brought the enemy's plans to nothing and for having made sure of their own freedom, and I thanked the officers and centurions of the garrison for having so courageously supported the resolution of the townspeople. I canceled the requisitions made by Varro on Roman citizens, and gave back their property to those who had been fined for showing too great freedom of speech. I made certain awards to individuals and to communities, and promised to do still more in the future.

After spending two days in Cordova, I set out for Cadiz, where I ordered that the money and treasure that had been taken from the temple of Hercules to a private house should be restored to the temple. Here too I appointed Cassius governor of western Spain, leaving him with four legions. I myself made use of the fleet built by Varro or by the people of Cadiz on Varro's instructions. On these ships I sailed for Tarragona and arrived there in a few days' time. I found waiting for me delegations from most of the states of eastern

Spain, and then, as at Cordova, I rewarded various cities and individuals. I then set out by land for Narbonne and for Marseilles. Here I heard that a law had been passed for the appointment of a dictator and that I had been nominated for this post by the praetor Marcus Lepidus.

The Massilians were now completely exhausted by their sufferings. Their supplies of grain had nearly run out; they had been twice defeated at sea and constantly routed on land whenever they attempted to break out; they were suffering from sickness in a very severe form, the result of the long siege and the consequent change in their diet (for they were now all reduced to eating stale millet and rotten barley, which had long ago been stored in the public warehouses for such an emergency as this). One of their towers and a considerable section of their wall had collapsed, and they had no hope of relief or reinforcements from other armies or from other provinces, since these, they discovered, had now come under my control. So they decided to surrender unconditionally.

A few days earlier, Domitius got news of what they intended to do. He secured three ships, two of which he gave to his friends and personal followers, and went aboard the third one himself. They set sail when the weather was stormy, but were observed by some of Brutus' ships which were, as they were ordered to do daily, watching the exits of the harbor. They weighed anchor and gave chase. The ship which was carrying Domitius himself held on its course and, with the help of a strong wind, sailed away out of sight; the other two, alarmed by the intervention of our ships, took shelter in the harbor.

In accordance with my orders, the Massilians brought out from the town all their arms and artillery, handed over their ships from the harbor and the dockyards, and gave up all the money in their treasury. When this was done, I spared the town itself, not because the inhabitants had deserved such treatment from me, but because of the antiquity of the place and its past glories. I left two legions in the city as a garrison and sent the rest to Italy. I myself set out for Rome.

3   CURIO'S CAMPAIGN IN AFRICA.

During the same period as that of the above events, Curio had set out from Sicily to Africa. From the very beginning, he thought very little of the troops under Publius Attius Varus and took with him only two of the four legions which I had left him and five hundred cavalry. He spent two days and three nights on the voyage and then landed at a place called Anquillaria, which is about twenty miles from Kalibia. It has headlands on both sides and provides fairly good anchorage in summer. At Kalibia, young Lucius Caesar was waiting to oppose him with a fleet of ten ships which had been laid up at Utica ever since the pirate war and had been refitted for the present war on the orders of Publius Attius. Lucius was terrified at the size of Curio's fleet and immediately made for the land. He ran his own decked trireme ashore at the nearest beach and, abandoning her there, fled overland to Hadrumetum, which was held by Gaius Considius Longus with one legion. The rest of his ships also came to Hadrumetum after the flight of their commander. He had been pursued by Curio's officer, Marcius Rufus, with twelve ships that had been brought from Sicily to escort the transports, and after seeing the trireme abandoned on the shore, Rufus had towed it away before rejoining Curio with his fleet. Curio then instructed him to sail on ahead to Utica, while he himself marched there with the army.

After a march of two days, Curio reached the river Bagrada. Here he left Caninius Rebilus in command of the legions and, taking the cavalry with him, went forward to reconnoiter Castra Cornelia, as this was supposed to be an excellent position for a camp. It is a straight ridge projecting into the sea, steep and rugged on both sides, but with a rather gentler slope on the side that faces Utica. It is about three miles away from Utica by the direct route, but this way there is a lot of marshy ground, because a stream rises near the road and the sea flows inland along its bed for some distance. To avoid the marsh one has to make a detour of six miles to reach the town.

In the course of this reconnaissance, Curio was able to get a view of Varus' camp, the fortifications of which were connected with the town wall near the so-called gate of Baal. It was in an extremely strong position, protected on one side by the town itself and on the other by the theater outside the town walls. There was a lot of building above and below ground near this theater which made the approaches to the camp narrow and difficult. Curio noticed at the same time that all the roads were crowded with convoys of property and livestock being brought into the town from the country owing to the fear of a sudden outbreak of violence. So he sent out his cavalry to bring in what they could get as plunder, and at the same time, in order to protect all this property, Varus sent out of the town six hundred Numidian horsemen and four hundred infantry. These reinforcements had been sent to Varus at Utica a few days previously by King Juba, whose father had been a friend of Pompey's and who had personal reasons for disliking Curio. As tribune, Curio had proposed that a law should be passed for annexing Juba's territory to that of Rome.

The cavalry on both sides engaged, and the Numidians failed to stand up to the first charge. After about one hundred twenty of them had been killed, the rest fell back toward the town and their camp. Meanwhile, his warships having appeared, Curio had a proclamation made to the two hundred or so merchant vessels lying in Utica harbor that he would treat as enemies all who did not transfer their ships to Castra Cornelia. The proclamation had an immediate effect. They all weighed anchor, left Utica, and sailed where they were told to go. As a result, our army got ample supplies of everything.

After these successes, Curio returned to his camp at the Bagrada, where the whole army saluted him as Imperator. Next day he led them to Utica and camped not far from the town. Before the construction of the camp was finished, cavalry outposts rode in with the news that large reinforcements of infantry and cavalry, sent by King Juba, were approaching Utica. At the same time, a great cloud of dust appeared in the distance and very soon the vanguard came into sight.

Curio was alarmed by this new turn of affairs and sent out his cavalry to bear the brunt of the first enemy attack and hold it off. Meanwhile he quickly recalled the legions from their work and drew them up in battle order. The cavalry went into action and, before the legions could take up position, routed the entire Numidian army, who were soon thrown into confusion, handicapped as they were by their baggage and marching in no sort of order and under no apprehension of being attacked. Nearly all their cavalry escaped, since they managed to get quickly into the town along the coast, but their infantry suffered heavy losses.

On the next night, two Marsian centurions, with twenty-two of their men, deserted and went over to Attius Varus. They told him that the whole of Curio's army was disaffected and advised him most strongly to come forward and show himself so as to provide an opportunity for reaching a settlement. Whether they genuinely held this opinion or merely wished to tell Varus what he would like to hear is uncertain. Certainly we are prone to believing what we want to, and rather hope that others feel what we feel ourselves. In any case, Varus was influenced by their views. Early next day he led his legions out of camp. Curio did the same thing, and the two forces were drawn up opposite each other with only a small valley between them.

In Varus' army was Sextus Quintilius Varus, who as was mentioned earlier had been at Corfinium. After I had given him his freedom, he had crossed over to Africa. Curio now had brought across the legions whose surrender I had accepted earlier at Corfinium. Some centurions had been changed, but otherwise the officers and men were the same. Quintilius therefore was in a good position for making an appeal to Curio's troops, and he began to go up and down the line, begging them to remember how in the old days they had sworn an oath of loyalty to Domitius and to him too, as Domitius' quaestor. He besought them not to be at war with their own comrades, who had had the same experiences and known the same sufferings as they had at the siege of Corfinium, and not to fight for people who looked down on them and called them deserters. He went on to suggest that they could expect an appropriate reward and would find that he was ready to provide them with it, if they came over to his side and joined forces with Varus. This speech of his provoked no reaction in Curio's army, and each commander led his troops back to camp.

In Curio's camp, however, everyone was becoming exceedingly anxious, and the more people discussed the situation among themselves, the more the anxiety grew. Everyone had his own version of things and made his own contribution to the general disquiet. Soon a fabrication of one man, through being repeated from one to another, appeared to be a fact known to many. . . .* In view of this state of alarm, Curio called a council of war to discuss the whole position. Some were of the opinion that action was absolutely necessary and that an attack should be made on Varus' camp. With the soldiers in their present mood, the greatest danger, they considered, was inaction; and, in any case, it was better bravely to try the fortune of war in battle than to suffer the final penalty after being deserted and betrayed by their own men. Others were in favor of leaving their present position at midnight and retiring to Castra Cornelia. In this way, it was suggested, time would be gained in which the men might come to their senses, and also, if matters got worse, it would be easier, with all the ships available there, to withdraw quite safely to Sicily.

Curio was against both plans—against the first as being too rash and against the second as being too cowardly. One proposal, he considered, was for running away in dishonor, and the other was for fighting even when the conditions were unfavorable.

* The text of the next few sentences is too imperfect to be translated with any assurance.—R.W.

"How can we possibly feel confident," he said, "that we can storm a camp that is so well placed and has been so well fortified? And what shall we have gained if, after suffering heavy losses, we give up the attempt? As though it were not perfectly well known that what gives a general the good will of his troops is success, and what arouses their hatred is failure.

"On the other hand, to change the position of our camp would look like a shameful avoidance of action; it would imply that we despaired of the whole situation and would cost us the confidence of the men. Good soldiers ought not to suspect that they are not being trusted, and bad soldiers ought not to know that they are causing anxiety; if they do, the good will become disheartened and the bad will be even less amenable to discipline than before. I myself am perfectly sure that these reports about disaffection in the army are either entirely false or greatly exaggerated; but even if we were convinced that they were true, it would be much better for us to pretend that we knew nothing about them than to corroborate them by our own behavior. Surely we ought to disguise the defects there may be in our army, just as we bandage up our wounds, so as not to give encouragement to the enemy.

"And as for the additional proposal that we should set out at midnight, this, so far as I can see, would merely give greater opportunities for indiscipline to those who want to profit from them. The chief safeguards of good discipline are a sense of honor and fear, neither of which operate well by night. For these reasons, I myself am neither bold enough to propose attacking their camp when we have no chance of success, nor am I cowardly enough to give up hope altogether. Before doing this we should, I think, try every possible course open to us, and I feel fairly certain that you and I together will be able to reach a decision on this point."

After the council of war, Curio addressed a general meeting of the troops. He reminded them of how they had felt toward me at Corfinium and of how it was owing to their good will and their example that I had been able to win over so much of Italy.

"You were the leaders," he told them, "and it was your example that was followed by town after town. Caesar naturally felt particularly warm toward you, just as his enemies particularly disapproved of you; for it was your action which set the standard for others and which resulted in Pompey's being forced to leave Italy, though he was still undefeated in battle. And it was to you that Caesar entrusted me, his dearest friend, together with the province of Sicily and Africa, the

two areas which he must hold if he is to hold Rome and
Italy. Yet there are some people who are capable of trying
to make you desert us. Indeed, what more could they want
than, at one and the same time, to ruin us and to make you
into criminals? We admit that we owe everything to you;
they believe that it is because of you that they have lost everything. How could they better satisfy their hatred of you than
by persuading you to betray us and then put yourselves into
their hands?

"Have you not heard of what Caesar has done in Spain?
Two armies defeated, two generals crushed, two provinces
won back—and all this within forty days of his appearance
in front of the enemy. They certainly could not stand up to
him when they were at full strength; will they do any better
now that they are practically finished? And you, you followed
Caesar when victory was still uncertain. Now the issue has
been decided, and are you now going to go over to the losing
side just when the time has come for you to receive the rewards of your loyalty? They claim that they have been
deserted and betrayed by you, and they talk about the oath
which you once swore. But was it you who deserted Domitius
or Domitius who deserted you? Was it not the fact that while
you were ready to do your duty to the end, he abandoned
you? Did he not try to run away to safety without your
knowledge? Is it not true that after he had deserted you,
Caesar came to your help and saved you? How can Domitius
think that you are bound to him by an oath, when he himself
gave up the emblems of authority, laid down his command,
and with no higher status than an ordinary civilian, came
as a prisoner into Caesar's power? An odd sort of a sense
of honor this is, to break the oath by which you are now
bound and go back to those obligations which you used to
have before they were canceled by the surrender of your
general and the loss of his authority.

"It may be, of course, that while you are willing to support
Caesar, you feel doubtful about me. Well, I am not going
to make a speech about what I have done for you; so far it
is less than I should like, and perhaps less than you expected.
However, soldiers always wait for their rewards until the
campaign is over, and even you must be sure of what the
final result of this campaign will be. I can claim, I think, to
have shown efficiency and to have enjoyed good luck up to
the present time. You will not object to the facts that I
brought the army across the sea without losing a single
ship, that as soon as I arrived I attacked and dispersed the
enemy's fleet, that I defeated their cavalry twice in two days,
and that I brought over to us two hundred fully loaded ships

right out of the enemy's harbor, thus making it impossible for them to get supplies either by sea or by land. Are you going to turn your backs on this leadership and this good luck? Do you prefer the idea of the disgrace at Corfinium, the overrunning of Italy, the surrender of the two Spanish provinces—all of which indicate how the war in Africa will turn out? As for me, I merely wanted to be known as one of Caesar's soldiers: you honored me with the title 'imperator.' If you regret having done so, you are free to take your gift back again. Give me the name I used to bear, so that it will not look as though you honored me only to insult me."

The soldiers were much moved by this speech. They kept on interrupting Curio while he was speaking and made it clear that they were greatly upset at having their loyalty questioned. And when he left the meeting they came thronging round him, telling him to have no doubts at all and urging him not to hesitate about proving how loyal and how brave they would show themselves in battle. It was a complete change in the general attitude and feeling of the men, and Curio, with the consent of all his officers, decided to give battle as soon as he had a chance of doing so. Next day he led his troops out and drew them up in order of battle in the same position as before. Varus took up the challenge and led his own troops out, wishing to take whatever chance was given him, either to tamper with the loyalty of Curio's men or to fight them in a favorable position.

As already explained, there was a valley between the two lines. It was not particularly large, but had steep sides that were difficult to climb. Each commander was waiting to see whether his opponent would attempt to cross the valley and so give him the advantage of position. On the left, however, the whole of Varus' cavalry with a number of light troops were seen going down into the valley. Curio sent out against them his own cavalry and two cohorts of Marrucini. The enemy cavalry failed to stand up to the first charge and galloped back to their own lines, leaving behind them the light troops who had accompanied them and who were now surrounded and cut to pieces by our men. This took place in full view of Varus' army, who could see their own people running away and being cut down.

With Curio was Rebilus, a senior officer of mine whom Curio had brought with him from Sicily, knowing what an experienced soldier he was. Rebilus now said: "You can see the state the enemy are in, Curio. Now is your chance. Take it." And Curio, merely shouting out to the soldiers that they must now remember their promises of yesterday, charged forward ahead of them, telling them to follow. The valley was so steep that the first men to get across could only climb up with the help of those behind them; but Varus' troops were aware of nothing but the panic and flight and slaughter of their own men; they imagined that they were already being surrounded by cavalry and never even thought of putting up a resistance. So, before the first weapon was thrown or our men could get at all close to them, the whole of Varus' line turned about and fled to their camp. Ahead of Curio's men in the pursuit of the defeated enemy was an ordinary private soldier, a Pelignian, Fabius by name. He kept on shouting out: "Varus! Varus!" so that he gave the impression of being one of Varus' own men who wished to give him some information or convey some warning. Varus himself, hearing his name called out so often, stopped, looked around, and asked the man who he was and what he wanted; whereupon Fabius struck out with his sword at his unprotected shoulder and very nearly killed him; Varus just raised his shield in time to ward off the blow. Fabius was then surrounded by the nearest soldiers and killed.

Now the confused mass of fugitives poured into the gates and got so jammed that they were scarcely able to move. More of them died here in the press than had died in battle or during the pursuit. They were very nearly driven out of their camp altogether, and some of them in fact ran on without stopping until they got to the town. But Curio's advance was held up by the natural strength of the position and by the fortifications. Also his troops had come out equipped for battle, not for making an assault on a camp. So Curio led his troops back to his own camp. Apart from Fabius he had suffered no casualties, while on the enemy side about six hundred were killed and one thousand wounded. All these wounded and a great many others who pretended to be injured made their way in terror from the camp to the town as soon as Curio had withdrawn. When Varus became aware of this and realized in what a state of panic his army was, he left in his camp a trumpeter and a few tents for appearance' sake and, shortly after midnight, quietly withdrew the rest of his army into Utica.

Next day Curio began to blockade the place by building an earthwork all around it. The people in the town had long enjoyed peace and were quite unused to war; the native inhabitants were very much on my side because of various kindnesses I had done to them; the Roman community consisted of people of all classes; and, as the result of previous battles, there was a general state of panic. They were all talking quite openly of surrender and Varus was being urged not to ruin everyone by insisting on holding out. But just at this moment messengers from King Juba arrived to say that he himself with large forces was approaching the city and to urge them to guard and defend it until he came. This news dispelled their fear and put fresh heart into them.

Curio received the same report, but for some time he refused to believe it, so confident was he that everything was going his own way. By now messengers and dispatches had come to Africa with news of my successes in Spain. With all this to encourage him, Curio felt sure that the king would not venture to attack him. But, on receiving definite information that Juba's army was about twenty-four miles from Utica, he abandoned his blockade and retired to Castra Cornelia. Here he began to bring in stocks of grain and timber and to build a fortified camp. At the same time, he sent to Sicily for the two other legions and the rest of his cavalry. His position at Castra Cornelia was an extremely good one for fighting a long campaign; the situation itself was strong and it was well fortified; it was near the sea; it had a good water supply; and there was also a good store of salt there which had been collected from the salt works nearby. There were forests in the neighborhood and also large tracts of cultivated land, so that there could be no shortage either of timber or of grain. Curio therefore, with the unanimous agreement of his staff, decided to hold out here, while waiting for his reinforcements.

But after these arrangements had been made and approved of, more news came in from some deserters from Utica. According to them some quarrel leading to hostilities had broken out between King Juba and the people of Leptis; Juba had therefore gone back and had stayed behind in his kingdom, while an officer of his, Saburra by name, with only quite small forces, had been sent on and was now approaching Utica. Curio unwisely believed this information to be true, altered his whole plan, and decided on fighting a pitched battle. He was a young man; he had a great spirit; things had gone well so far and he felt confident of the future—all this spurred him on to action and affected the decision which he took.

As soon as it was dark, he sent his whole cavalry force against the enemy's camp on the river Bagrada. Saburra, of whom he had already been informed, was in command of this camp, but King Juba was following behind in full force and had halted about six miles away from Saburra's position. Curio's cavalry reached the enemy under cover of night and attacked them when they were completely off their guard. In fact the Numidians, following some native custom of their own, were scattered about in all directions and in no sort of order. Finding them dispersed in this way and overcome with sleep, Curio's men rode down on them and killed a great number, while the rest fled in terror. After the action the cavalry returned to Curio, bringing some prisoners with them.

Curio himself had started marching at about three in the morning, leaving five cohorts behind to guard the camp. After going about six miles, he met the cavalry and was told of their successful action. He asked the prisoners who commanded the camp at the Bagrada, and they replied "Saburra." Curio, in his eagerness to press forward, made no more inquiries. He turned to the soldiers standing by the nearest standard and said: "There you are. The prisoners confirm what the deserters told us. The king is not here. He has only sent a small force which has proved too weak even for a few of our cavalry. Let us go ahead, then. Plunder and glory are in front of us. Now is the time for us to start thinking of our gratitude to you and of how we can repay it."

The cavalry had in fact done very well, particularly when one considers their small numbers in comparison with the great force of Numidians. Nevertheless the men had somewhat exaggerated their own achievements—not unnaturally, since people enjoy dwelling on their own merits. There was also a lot of plunder to show; captured men and horses were brought forward, so that the general impression was that any delay that might take place was merely postponing a certain victory. Thus Curio's confidence was matched by the enthusiasm of his troops. Ordering the cavalry to follow, he marched on as fast as possible so as to attack the enemy while they were still suffering from the effects of their recent defeat. The men, however, were tired out after a night's marching and could not keep up with him; various detachments were constantly falling out to rest. Even this had no effect on Curio's self-confidence.

Juba was informed by Saburra of the night battle and sent to his relief two thousand Spanish and Gallic cavalry (troops which he kept as a rule for his personal bodyguard) and the best regiments of his infantry. He himself followed slowly after with the rest of his forces and with sixty elephants. Saburra had guessed that Curio himself was approaching under cover of the cavalry which he had sent ahead. He drew up his whole army, infantry and cavalry, and instructed them to fall back gradually as though they were retreating in fear; he himself, when the right moment came, would give them the signal for joining battle and any other instructions that might be required by the situation. Curio had been confident enough already; what was happening now seemed to

justify him in his view, and under the impression that the
enemy were in flight, he led down his troops from the higher
ground into the plain.

So he marched on and on. After covering a distance of
eleven miles, he halted to rest his tired army. Saburra now
gave the signal to his men, drew up his line, and went around
the ranks encouraging the troops. He kept his infantry back,
using it only for show. It was the cavalry that went into action
against the Roman line.

Curio behaved well in the emergency. He called on his
men to fight and told them that everything depended on the
courage they showed. Nor was there any lack of courage
or willingness to fight shown either by the infantry, in spite
of their fatigue, or by the cavalry, in spite of the fact that they
were few in number and already tired out. There were only
about two hundred of them, the rest having dropped out on
the march, and wherever they charged, they forced the enemy
to fall back; but they could not pursue for any distance and
could not drive their horses too hard. The enemy cavalry
were able to get around both our flanks and to ride into the
men from the rear. Whenever any of our cohorts charged
out from the main body, the Numidians were fast and fresh
enough to avoid the attack and then, after regrouping, came
back again to surround our men and cut them off from the
line. It seemed equally dangerous to preserve proper formation in the ranks or to charge out and engage the enemy.
Meanwhile, the enemy forces were constantly increasing as
more and more men were sent up by Juba: our men's strength
began to fail as they grew more tired, and the wounded could
neither leave the line nor be carried into safety since the whole
army was entirely surrounded by the enemy cavalry. They
gave up all hope and, as men do when their last moments
have come, wept at the prospect of their own death or com-
mended their parents to the care of any who might be lucky
enough to escape. There were terror and grief on every side.

Curio saw that terror had spread throughout his army and
realized that no words of encouragement, no prayers of his
would find a hearing. In so desperate a situation he saw only
one hope left, and ordered the standards to be moved in the
direction of the nearest hills and for the whole army to
follow and occupy the position. Saburra, however, had anticipated him and sent his cavalry ahead to forestall him. Our
men were now in complete despair, and some were cut down
by the enemy cavalry as they tried to run away; others just
fell to the ground and lay there. Gnaeus Domitius, who was
in command of our cavalry, rode up to Curio with a few horsemen and urged him to run for it and try to get back to

camp, promising to stay with him all the way there. But Curio replied: "I have lost the army which Caesar entrusted to me. I can never look him in the face again." So he died fighting.

Very few of his cavalry survived the battle. Those who, as already mentioned, had halted at the rear of the column to rest their horses saw from a distance the rout of the whole army and themselves got back safely to camp. The soldiers in the legions were killed to a man.

The quaestor Marcius Rufus had been left in charge of the camp by Curio. When he heard the news of the disaster, he did what he could to keep up his men's spirits, but they begged and implored him to be sent back by sea to Sicily. He promised to do this and ordered all captains of ships to have their boats brought close inshore in the early evening. However, a state of complete panic prevailed. Some said that Juba's army was approaching, others that Varus and his legions were marching out and that they could already see the dust raised by his advancing column (though nothing of the kind had taken place at all); and others imagined that they would shortly be attacked by the enemy fleet. In the general confusion, each man thought only of himself. Those who were aboard the warships wanted to get away at once, and their eagerness to be gone made the captains of the transports want to sail too. A very few small boats obeyed instructions and appeared as ordered. But on the crowded beaches men struggled over who should embark first, and some of these small craft sank from the weight of those who were trying to get aboard, with the result that the other boats hesitated to come in close for fear of suffering the same fate.

So it happened that only a few soldiers and family men who could arouse compassion or use influence, or were able to swim out to the ships, were taken aboard and reached Sicily in safety. The rest of the army sent a delegation of centurions to Varus in the night and surrendered. Next day Juba saw the men of these cohorts outside the town and claimed them as his own booty. He ordered some to be killed and picked out a few others to be sent back to his kingdom. Varus objected, saying that his own word of honor was being broken, but he did not dare to take any action. Juba himself rode into Utica escorted by several senators, among whom were Servius Sulpicius and Licinius Damasippus. After giving brief instructions as to what he wanted to be done in the city, he withdrew in a few days to his own kingdom with all his forces.

ᶔ§ *BOOK THREE: 49–48 B.C.* §ᶔ

1 PREPARATIONS FOR THE ILLYRIAN CAMPAIGN.

As dictator I presided over the elections in Rome. The consuls elected were Publius Servilius and myself; it was in this year that I was legally eligible for the office.

I found that throughout Italy credit was becoming restricted and debts were not being paid, and so I decided to appoint assessors to make a valuation of real and personal property on a prewar basis, so that creditors should be paid accordingly. This seemed to be the most appropriate means for removing or diminishing the fear of a general cancellation of debts—a fear which is very often felt in periods of war and civil disturbances—and also for maintaining credit.

Next, by encouraging praetors and tribunes to bring bills before the people's assembly, I restored their rights to a number of people who under Pompey's law had been condemned for bribery at elections. These convictions had been secured at the time that Pompey had garrisoned his legions in Rome, and the trials had never taken up more than one day, with one panel of judges hearing the evidence and another passing sentence. The victims of these sentences had from the beginning of the civil war offered me their services if I wished to make use of them and, since they had put themselves at my disposal in this way, I regarded them just as I would have if they had actually performed these services. I had decided that they should have their rights restored to them by a vote of the people's assembly rather than by what would look like an act of grace on my part; for I did not want to seem ungrateful when it came to paying back a kindness, nor did I want to appear arrogant in anticipating the right of the people's assembly to confer favors.

I gave eleven days to the carrying out of these measures, to the celebration of the Latin Festival and the holding of elections. I then resigned the dictatorship, left Rome, and went to Brindisi, where twelve legions and all the cavalry had been ordered to assemble. However, I found that the ships available would allow, at the utmost, only the transport of fifteen thousand legionaries and five hundred cavalry. This lack of shipping was the one thing that prevented me from finishing the war quickly. And even the forces which did embark were below strength. Many men were missing after all the campaigns in Gaul; the long march from Spain had diminished numbers considerably; and the whole army had suffered in fitness as a result of the unhealthy autumn weather in Apulia and around Brindisi after the bracing climates of Gaul and Spain.

Pompey had had a year in which to build up his strength. During this time he had had no fighting to do and no enemy had approached him. Thus he had got together a large fleet from Asia and the Cyclades, Corfu, Athens, Pontus, Bithynia, Syria, Cilicia, Phoenicia, and Egypt; he had ordered still more ships to be built wherever this could be done; he had raised large sums of money from Asia and Syria, from all the kings, dynasts, and tetrarchs, and from the free states of Achaea; and in all the provinces under his control he had forced the representatives of Roman financial companies to make large contributions to his funds. He had formed nine legions of Roman citizens. Five of these he had brought over with him from Italy; one, a veteran legion, was from Cilicia and was known as the Twin, since it was made up of two legions; one was formed from veterans who had been discharged by their former commanders and had settled in Crete and Macedonia; and two came from Asia where they had been recruited by the consul Lentulus. Included in these legions were a number of supplementary troops from Thessaly, Boeotia, Achaea, and Epirus, and also some who had previously served with Gaius Antonius.

In addition to these nine legions, he was expecting two more to be brought from Syria by Scipio. From Crete, Sparta, Pontus, Syria, and the other states he had raised three thousand archers; two cohorts of slingers, each of six hundred men; and seven thousand cavalry. The cavalry consisted of six hundred men from Gaul brought by Deiotarus and five hundred from Cappadocia by Ariobarzanes; from Thrace, Cotys had sent the same number with his son Sadala; two hundred had come from Macedonia under the command of Rhascypolis, a most able and distinguished soldier; from Alexandria, Pompey's son had brought aboard his fleet five

hundred Gauls and Germans whom Aulus Gabinius had
left there as a bodyguard for King Ptolemy; eight hundred
had been raised from Pompey's own slaves and herdsmen;
Tarcondarius Castor and Domnilaus had provided three hundred from Gallograecia; one of these came personally with
his men and the other sent his son; two hundred, among
whom were many mounted archers, had been sent from Syria
by Antiochus of Commagene, who was lavishly rewarded by
Pompey; and the number, as mentioned above, was made up
with Dardani and Bessi—some serving as mercenaries, some
secured by Pompey's name or authority—Macedonians, Thes-
salians, and others.

He had collected enormous quantities of grain from Thessaly, Asia, Egypt, Crete, Cyrene, and other areas.

He had decided to spend the winter at Durazzo, Apollonia,
and other towns on the sea in order to prevent me from
crossing. With the same end in view, he had stationed units of
his fleet all along the coast. Young Pompey was in command
of the Egyptian ships; Decimus Laelius and Gaius Triarius of
the Asiatic contingent; the Syrians were commanded by Gaius
Cassius; the Rhodians by Gaius Marcellus acting together
with Gaius Coponius; the Liburnian and Achaean fleet was
under Scribonius Libo and Marcus Octavius. But the supreme
commander by sea, who had final authority over all naval
dispositions, was Marcus Bibulus.

2   THE LANDING IN ILLYRIUM
    AND FIRST MOVES.

As soon as I reached Brindisi, I addressed the troops. I told
them that, since we were now nearing the end of our difficulties and dangers, they must not mind leaving their slaves and
heavy baggage behind and going aboard themselves as lightly
equipped as possible, so that we could embark all the more
men; as for the future, once we had won, they could rely on
my generosity. The men all broke into cheering and told me
to give them whatever orders I liked; they would gladly do
whatever they were asked.

So we put to sea on January 4. Seven legions, as already
explained, were on board. Next day we reached land and
found a quiet anchorage between the Ceraunian rocks and
other dangerous parts of the coast. I avoided all regular harbors, assuming them to be occupied by the enemy, and disem-

barked at a place called Palaeste without a single ship's being damaged.

Lucretius Vespillo and Minucius Rufus were at Palaeokastro with eighteen of the Asiatic ships. They had been given this force by Laelius. Bibulus was at Corfu with one hundred ten ships. But Vespillo and Rufus were so unsure of themselves that they did not venture out of the harbor, even though we had only twelve warships in all (including four decked ships) to protect the convoy. And Bibulus was too late on the scene; his ships were not ready for action and his rowers were not on the spot, because our fleet was actually sighted off the mainland before any rumor of our arrival reached that area.

When the troops had landed, I sent the ships back to Brindisi on the same night, so that the other legions and the cavalry could be brought across. One of my officers, Fufius Calenus, was put in charge of this operation, with orders to carry it out as quickly as possible. But the ships were late in getting out to sea, missed the night breeze, and ran into serious trouble on this return voyage. Bibulus had got news at Corfu that I was arriving and still hoped that he might intercept some of the transports while they were loaded. As it was, he intercepted some of them after they had already landed the troops and got about thirty of them into his power. On these ships he vented the anger and shame which he felt at the thought of his own inefficiency. He burned all of them, captains and crews together with the vessels, hoping that this savage punishment would have the effect of discouraging the rest. Next he occupied with his fleet every harbor and anchorage the whole way along the coast from Saseno to Veglia. Patrols were carefully organized, and he himself spent the nights aboard, though the weather was bad, showing himself ready to undertake any task or difficulty, with or without help, so long as he could get to grips with me.*

After the Liburnian fleet had left Illyrium, Marcus Octavius came to Salonae with the ships under his command. There he carried on agitation among the Dalmatians and other native tribes and induced the town of Vis to go over from my side to that of Pompey. At Salonae neither his promises nor his threats had any effect on the town council, so he decided to attack the place. The town was well protected by its position on a hill and the Roman citizens there rapidly built wooden towers to reinforce the defense. Resistance was difficult, however, because of their small numbers, and after many of them had been wounded, they resorted to extreme

* The text of the foregoing passage is too imperfect to be translated with assurance.—R.W.

measures: they freed all their slaves of military age and cut
off the hair of all the women, using it for the making of
catapult ropes. Seeing how determined they were, Octavius
built five camps all around the town, bringing pressure to bear
on the inhabitants both by siege works and by assaults. The
defenders were ready to endure anything, but were in great
difficulties over their grain supply. They sent a deputation to
me to ask for my help in this respect, being prepared to put
up with all the other hardships by themselves. And, after
a long time had passed and the very length of the siege had
made Octavius' men somewhat careless, the defenders, taking
their chance at midday when the enemy had withdrawn, first
stationed the boys and women on the walls so that everything
should look as usual, and then all together in one body, both
the citizens and the recently freed slaves, burst into the nearest
of Octavius' camps and took it by storm. They went straight
on to the second, third, fourth, and finally the fifth, drove
the men out of each camp, killed many of them, and forced
Octavius with the survivors to fly to their ships. So ended the
attempted siege. By now winter was approaching, and Octavius, after the great losses he had suffered, despaired of taking
Salonae and retired to join Pompey at Durazzo.

It has already been mentioned that Pompey's chief engineer,
Lucius Vibullius Rufus, had twice fallen into my hands and
had twice been set free, once at Corfinium and again in Spain.
In view of the fact that I had treated him so well, I thought
he would be the right person to send with a letter to Pompey,
with whom I knew also that he had considerable influence.
The following is a summary of what I wrote:

> We should, both of us, adopt a less obstinate attitude. Could
> we not both lay down our arms and tempt fortune no further?
> We have both suffered heavily already, and these losses should
> be enough to serve as a lesson to us and make us wish to avoid
> more misfortune in future. You have been driven from Italy
> and lost Sicily, Sardinia, the two Spanish provinces, and one
> hundred thirty cohorts of Roman citizens in Italy and Spain. I
> on my side have had Curio killed, a great army in Africa anni-
> hilated, and other troops forced to surrender at Veglia. Thus we
> have had enough experience to teach us how great is the element
> of chance in war. Should we not try to preserve both ourselves
> and our country? And now is the one time when we can talk
> about peace, when each of us is confident in himself and both of
> us appear evenly matched.
>
> If we wait until chance gives one of us some slight advantage,
> then the one who thinks he is on top will not consider terms
> of compromise; he will refuse a fair share once he believes
> that he is going to get everything. Now, since we have failed

to come to any agreement previously, the terms of peace should be referred to the senate and people in Rome. Meanwhile we should have acted in accordance with our own interests and those of the state if we were both publicly to swear an oath to disband our armies within the next three days. If we laid down our arms and gave up the forces on which we now relied, we should each necessarily have to be contented with the decision of the senate and Roman people.

So that Pompey might be induced to agree with these proposals, I promised to disband all my land forces. . . .*

This was the message which Vibullius received from me. He decided that before Pompey should begin discussing it, it was just as important that he should be informed of my sudden arrival, so that he could take steps to deal with that; and so he traveled night and day without stop, changing horses at every town, so as to get to Pompey as fast as possible and tell him of my approach. Pompey was at that time at Candavia, on his way from Macedonia to winter quarters at Apollonia and Durazzo. He was much alarmed at the news and pushed on by forced marches to Apollonia in order to prevent us from occupying the towns along the coast.

As it happened, as soon as the troops were landed, I set out on the same day for Palaeokastro. Lucius Torquatus, with a garrison of Parthini, had been put in command of this place, and when he arrived he had the gates shut and attempted to defend the town. But when he ordered the Greek troops to take up arms and man the walls, they refused to fight against one who held an official command from the Roman people. The townsmen also took their own measures to admit me. Since there was no hope of help from elsewhere, Torquatus opened the gates and surrendered. I saw that he was kept safe and uninjured.

As soon as we had occupied Palaeokastro, we made straight for Apollonia. Here Lucius Staberius was in command. When he heard of our approach, he began to fortify the citadel, to fill up the water supply there, and to collect hostages from the citizens. The citizens, however, refused to give hostages; they said they would not shut their gates against one who was a consul or take up a line that was different from that adopted by the whole of Italy and by the Roman people. Finding that this was the way they felt, Staberius fled secretly from Apollonia. The citizens then sent a deputation to me and admitted me into this town. Their example was followed by Byllis, Amantia, the other places in the neighborhood, and all Epirus; deputations kept on arriving to promise obedience to my orders.

* The text of this sentence is imperfect.—R.W.

When Pompey heard what had happened at Palaeokastro and Apollonia, he feared for the safety of Durazzo and made all haste to get there, marching by night and day. Just then a rumor got about that my troops were approaching. Pompey in his hurry had been turning night into day, and there was now such a panic in his army that all the men from Epirus and the districts near Epirus deserted, many of them throwing away their arms, and the march became more like a rout. Finally Pompey halted near Durazzo and ordered the ground to be measured out for his camp. Even now the army was still terrified, but Labienus took the initiative in coming forward and swearing an oath that he would not desert Pompey and would accept the same lot as fortune gave him, whatever it might be. The other senior officers took the same oath; they were followed by the rest of the officers, the centurions, and every man in the army.

Finding that Pompey had got ahead of me on the way to Durazzo, I made no further attempt to press on. I pitched a camp on the river Seman, not far from Apollonia, in order to protect the states that had come over so loyally to my side. I decided to wait here for the arrival of the other legions from Italy and to spend the winter in our tents. Pompey did likewise and pitched his camp on the other side of the Seman, bringing into it all his forces and auxiliaries.

Meanwhile Calenus had followed out my instructions. He had embarked at Brindisi all the legionaries and cavalry for whom he had shipping and had put out to sea. But after going a little way out of the harbor, he received a dispatch from me informing him that all ports and the entire coastline were patrolled by enemy fleets. On hearing this, he returned to harbor and recalled all his ships. One of these, because it had no troops on board and was sailing under private enterprise, disregarded Calenus' signal and continued on her course toward Palaeokastro. She was captured by Bibulus, who massacred every single person on board: slaves, freedmen, even young boys. So the fate of the whole army was determined in a few seconds and hung on one critical moment.

Bibulus, as already mentioned, was at sea off Palaeokastro with his fleet. He was certainly succeeding in cutting me off from the sea and from the harbor, but he was himself cut off from landing anywhere in those parts. I had patrols posted all along the shores, and he had no chance of getting wood or water from the land or of mooring his ships close inshore. He was therefore in an extremely difficult position, suffering from the lack of all necessities, and was compelled to bring not only all normal supplies but also wood and water from Corfu by merchant ship. There was even one occasion when, in very bad weather, they were forced to catch the night's dew in the skins with which the ships were covered. However, they bore all these hardships bravely and patiently enough and were determined not to raise their blockade of the shores and the harbors.

While they were experiencing all these difficulties, Libo joined Bibulus. One day both of them from shipboard got in touch with two officers of mine, Marcus Acilius and Statius Murcus, one of whom was in command of the fortifications of Palaeokastro and the other of the detachments on shore. Libo and Bibulus declared that they wished, if the opportunity were given them, to confer with me on matters of the greatest importance, and they added a few words to strengthen the impression they had made that what they wanted was to talk about peace terms. Meanwhile they asked for a truce and this was granted. Acilius and Murcus considered that they really had something important to say; they knew that I was particularly anxious for peace and it looked as though something had been gained by the message I had given to Vibullius.

At this time I was at a town called Buthrotum, opposite Corfu. I had gone there with one legion to bring over to my side some of the more distant tribes and to make arrangements for the supply of grain, which was becoming scarce. When I was informed in a letter from Acilius and Murcus about the request of Libo and Bibulus, I left the legion there and went back myself to Palaeokastro. On arriving there, I invited Libo and Bibulus to a conference. Libo came and made excuses for the nonappearance of Bibulus, who was, he said, known for his extremely violent temper and who had also a particular dislike for me, a feeling that dated back to the day that we had been aediles and praetors together; he had therefore absented himself from the conference so that there should be no risk of his bad temper's interfering with a discussion on matters which promised so much good for the future.

Libo then stated that he personally most earnestly desired and always had desired that a settlement should be reached and that both sides should disband their armies, but he had no power in the matter at all, since by the decision of their council the whole conduct of the war was in the hands of Pompey. But, if I would tell him what I wanted, he would pass on the information to Pompey, who would deal with the rest of the negotiations himself after listening to what Libo and Bibulus had to say. Until the messengers should return from Pompey, he proposed that the truce should remain in force and that neither side should take action against the other. He concluded with a few words about the general issues involved and about the forces at his disposal. I did not regard these remarks as being worth a reply at the time and cannot now see any reason why they should be recorded.

I asked to be allowed to send people of my own choice to deal with Pompey, and that Libo and Bibulus should either guarantee them a safe journey or else should provide an escort. With regard to the question of the truce, I pointed out that each side at present had its own military advantage: they with their fleet were holding up my ships and my reinforcements; I was preventing them from landing and getting water. If they wanted concessions from me, then they must relax their naval blockade; if they maintained that, then I would maintain my position too. Nevertheless, I said, it was still possible to negotiate even if none of these concessions were made; the absence of agreement here need not be an obstacle to a discussion of peace terms.

Libo would neither escort my messengers nor guarantee them a safe-conduct. He wanted to refer all this to Pompey; his one aim was to get a truce, and on this point he spoke with much eagerness. I realized that all this talk had been started merely because of their present difficulties and as a means toward easing their situation with regard to supplies; no real prospect or proposal for peace was being offered at all. I therefore turned my attention again to military operations.

Bibulus had been kept from land for many days and, as a result of the cold and of overwork, had fallen seriously ill. No medical attention was available, and since he refused to give up the task which he had undertaken, he lost strength and succumbed to his illness. After his death there was no longer any supreme naval commander-in-chief; each admiral acted separately and used his own fleet as he thought best.

Now Vibullius had waited until the commotion occasioned by my sudden landing had quieted down. Then, as soon as the moment seemed propitious, he opened the question of the proposals which I had delivered to him. He had with him Libo and Lucius Lucceius and Theophanes, all people with whom Pompey was in the habit of discussing matters of importance. But as soon as he began to speak, Pompey interrupted him and told him to say no more.

"Neither life," he said, "nor my rights as a citizen would be of any value to me at all if it were thought that I owed them to the kindness of Caesar. And no one could help thinking this if it were believed that I had been fetched back to Italy, which I left of my own accord, now that Caesar has finished his campaign."

I heard this from people who were present at the conversation. Nevertheless, I still tried by other means to arrange for a peace conference.

There was only the river Seman between my camp and Pompey's. The soldiers on each side often had talks together, and by mutual agreement no hostilities took place while these talks were going on. I sent one of my officers, Publius Vatinius, right down to the riverbank to bring forward for discussion some of the most important points as regards peace. I instructed him to keep on shouting out: "Cannot citizens send representatives to their own fellow citizens to discuss peace? Even fugitives in the forests of the Pyrenees have been allowed to do this, and so have pirates. Why not citizens, whose object is to put an end to fighting among citizens?" So he spoke at some length, adopting a humble manner as befitted one pleading for his own safety and that of everyone else. The troops on both sides listened to him in silence.

Then it was announced from the other side that Aulus Varro had agreed to come on the following day and join in discussions as to arranging safe-conduct for a deputation and a proper opportunity for them to express their views. A definite time was fixed for this meeting. So on the next day great numbers of troops came together from both sides; there was a general feeling that something important was happening and everyone's thoughts seemed turned toward peace. Then out of the middle of the crowd Titus Labienus stepped forward. Instead of making any reference to peace, he began talking to Vatinius in the most abusive manner. This conversation was suddenly interrupted by a shower of spears and arrows coming from all quarters. Vatinius, protected by our soldiers' shields, got away safe, but a number of people were wounded, including Cornelius Balbus, Marcus Plotius, Lucius Tiburtius, and some centurions and soldiers. Labienus then shouted out: "This will show you that you can give up talking of peace. There can be no peace with us until Caesar's head is brought in."

3   THE CONSPIRACY OF CAELIUS.

In Rome at about this time the praetor Marcus Caelius Rufus took up the cause of the debtors. From the beginning of his period of office, he set up his tribunal next to that of the city praetor Gaius Trebonius and announced that he was prepared to give assistance to anyone who appealed against the valuations and orders to pay fixed by the method of arbitration that I had devised when I was last in Rome. The method itself, however, was a fair one and Trebonius applied it with great humanity, being of the opinion that in these difficult times the law should be administered with mercy and moderation. Thus no one could be found to come forward and appeal against it. For it is no doubt a normal enough thing to make the excuse of poverty, to complain of one's own hardships or the misfortunes of the times, or to point out how hard it is to get a good price for auctioned property; but it is downright effrontery to hold onto everything one possesses and still admit that one is in debt. Consequently, no one could be found to make the application which Caelius wanted, and Caelius showed himself harsher in his manner than those whose personal interests were concerned in recovering their debts. Wishing to avoid giving the impression that he had not only taken on a bad cause but failed to do anything with it, Caelius went on to propose a law providing that the payment of debts should be postponed for six years and that during this period no interest was to be charged. The consul Servilius and the other magistrates opposed this proposal and Caelius found himself less effective than he had expected. In order to excite opinion on his side, he withdrew his first proposal and put forward two new ones—one for abolishing all rents on houses and apartments for a year, and one for the cancellation of all debts. Riots took place in which many people were wounded, and Trebonius was driven from his tribunal.

The consul Servilius reported the affair to the senate, and the senate voted that Caelius should be removed from office. In accordance with this decision, the consul refused to allow him to take his seat in the senate, and when he tried to make a speech in public, had him removed from the platform. Caelius was deeply wounded by this humiliation and in public gave out that he was going to report personally to me. Secretly, however, he sent agents to recall Milo, who had been in exile since being condemned for the murder of Clodius, and who, after the many gladiatorial shows which he had given, still had with him the remains of a whole training establishment for gladiators. Milo then joined Caelius, who sent him ahead to stir up trouble among the shepherds in the neighborhood of Thurii. Caelius himself got as far as Casilinum when, on the same day, Milo's standards and arms were seized at Capua and the band of gladiators, whose job it was to betray the city, was seen at Naples. The plot was discovered and Caelius was now shut out of Capua, where the Roman citizens of the place took up arms and denounced him as a public enemy. Seeing the danger he was in, Caelius gave up his plan and took another road.

Meanwhile Milo had written to the town councils claiming that what he was doing was by the orders and under the authority of Pompey, who had sent Vibullius to him with instructions. He attempted to win the support of all those whom he thought to be suffering from their debts, but had no success at all in this agitation. Then, after freeing a number of slaves from their barracks, he began to attack the town of Cosa near Thurii, which was held by the praetor Quintus Pedius with one legion. Milo was killed by a stone thrown at him from the wall.

As for Caelius, he got as far as Thurii, after having professed to be going to join me. Here he tried to intrigue with various townspeople and offered bribes to some of my own Spanish and Gallic cavalry who had been sent there to garrison the place. They killed him. So ended, quickly and easily, a dangerous revolutionary movement which was affecting the whole of Italy and imposing a serious amount of labor on the government.

4 REINFORCEMENTS ARRIVE FROM ITALY.

Libo, meanwhile, with his fleet of fifty ships, had sailed from Palaeokastro to Brindisi and occupied an island lying off the harbor, his idea being that it was better to occupy one single position directly in the line that would have to be taken by our reinforcements than to keep up a blockade on all the harbors and the entire coastline. Since he arrived suddenly and unexpectedly, he intercepted some merchant ships, which he burned, except for one ship loaded with grain, which he towed away. This caused a good deal of panic among our men, and at night Libo landed some soldiers and archers and forced a cavalry outpost of ours to abandon its position. In fact, he made such good use of his opportunity that he wrote to Pompey to say that, if he liked, he could have his other ships drawn up on land for refitting; he himself, he said, with his own fleet, was quite capable of preventing any reinforcements from reaching me.

At this time Mark Antony was at Brindisi. He could count on the fighting quality of his troops, and so he put picked men aboard about sixty ships' rowing boats which he had strengthened with screens of wickerwork, and stationed the boats separately at various points along the shore. He then ordered the two triremes which he had had built for him at Brindisi to row out to the harbor mouth ostensibly by way of exercising the crews. Libo, seeing them coming out so boldly, sent four quadriremes against them in the hope of intercepting them.

When the enemy ships drew near, our veteran crews began to retire inside the harbor, and the enemy, elated by the pursuit, rashly followed them. Then in a moment the signal was given and from every direction Antony's boats bore down upon the enemy. They immediately captured one of the quadriremes, complete with its rowers and fighting troops, and forced the rest to take to flight in the most disgraceful manner. To add to the enemy's discomfiture, Antony posted cavalry all along the shore to prevent them from getting water. So, what with his difficulties of supply and his bitter feelings occasioned by his ignominious defeat, Libo gave up the idea of blockading our men and left Brindisi.

Months passed and winter was drawing to a close, but still no ships bringing the legions came to me from Brindisi. It seemed to me that a number of opportunities for sailing had been missed. There had often been a steady wind blowing, and on these occasions they ought unquestionably to have set out. As time went on the enemy naval commanders became more and more efficient in guarding the coasts and still more confident in their ability to stop reinforcements from arriving. Pompey had frequently written blaming them for not having prevented my landing in the first place, and telling them that at least they must prevent the arrival of the rest of the army. Also, since by now the winds were beginning to slacken, they assumed that it would be more difficult still to make the crossing.

All this was very disturbing to me, and I wrote sharply to my officers at Brindisi, telling them that they must sail on the first occasion when the wind was suitable, either in the direction of Apollonia or of Scutari, at both of which it was possible to run the ships ashore. These places were not so much under enemy observation as others, since their fleets did not venture too far from their harbors.

At Brindisi they now acted with daring and resolution. Mark Antony and Fufius Calenus were in charge of operations, and the soldiers backed them up enthusiastically, showing that they were willing to take any risk when my safety was at stake. They left Brindisi on a south wind, and next day were carried past Apollonia. Sighting them from the mainland, Coponius, the commander of the Rhodian fleet at Durazzo, sailed out of the harbor and, as the wind began to slacken, drew nearer and nearer our ships. The same south wind began to blow strongly again and came to our rescue. Nevertheless, Coponius would not give up. He hoped that if his rowers stuck to it and gave their best, they could overcome the force of the gale, and though we were driven before the wind right past Durazzo, he kept at his pursuit.

Our men had certainly enjoyed good luck, but were still afraid of being overtaken by him if the wind dropped. So when they came to a harbor called Nymphaeum, about three miles beyond Lissus, they ran their ships in there, believing the threat of the storm was less than that of the enemy fleet. For this harbor, while protected from the southwest, was exposed to the south wind. As soon as they got inside, by an incredible stroke of luck, the south wind which had been blowing for two days veered round to the southwest.

It was a remarkable example of how fortune can change in a moment. Our men who a moment ago were fearing for their safety were now perfectly secure in harbor; and the enemy who just now were threatening to destroy us found that they had cause to fear for themselves. So, as circumstances changed, the weather protected us and at the same time caused such havoc among the Rhodian vessels that every one of them, sixteen decked ships, was driven ashore and wrecked. Of the great numbers of rowers and regular troops on board, some were thrown up on the rocks and killed, and others were rescued by our men. I saw to it that these came to no harm and were allowed to return home.

Two of our ships, which had got behind the rest, at night-fall, not knowing where the others had gone, dropped anchor off Lissus. Otacilius Crassus, in command at Lissus, took steps to seize them by sending out numbers of rowing boats and other small craft. At the same time he tried to get the men on board to surrender, promising that they would come to no harm if they did so. Of these two ships one had on board two hundred twenty men from a legion recently recruited, and the other rather less than two hundred veterans. The sequel will show what a help it is to have a resolute and determined spirit. The recruits were terrified at the number of craft coming up and were also in a bad state because of the rough sea and their seasickness. After receiving a guarantee that the enemy would do them no harm, they surrendered to Otacilius, who had them all brought before him and then, in violation of the solemn pledge that he had given, had them cruelly killed in front of his eyes. The soldiers of the veteran legion, on the other hand, who had suffered just as much as the others from the storm and the filthy bilge water, remembered their long record of valor and determined to live up to it.

They spun out the first part of the night in discussing terms of
a possible surrender, then made the pilot run the ship ashore,
found a good position, and passed the rest of the night there.
At dawn Otacilius sent out against them about four hundred
cavalry who were guarding that part of the coast and some
armed detachments from the town garrison. But the veterans
beat off the attack and, after killing a number of the enemy,
retired without loss and joined up with our main body of
troops.

After this the Roman community at Lissus (it was a community that I had established there myself and fortified some
years previously) opened the gates of the town to Antony and
gave him every possible assistance. Otacilius, fearing for
his life, fled and went to Pompey. Antony disembarked his
complete force, which consisted of three veteran legions,
one of recruits, and eight hundred cavalry. He sent most of
the ships back to Italy to transport the rest of the infantry
and cavalry, but kept at Lissus the boats he had, which were
of the Gallic type called pontoons. This was so that I should
have some means of pursuit if, as many people thought likely,
Pompey considered Italy to be unguarded and took his own
army there. Antony immediately informed me by messenger
of where he had landed and in what strength.

Both Pompey and I heard of Antony's arrival at about the
same time. The ships had been seen passing Apollonia and
Durazzo, but for a day or two no one knew how far they
had been carried up the coast. When we did know what had
happened, we both acted with different aims in view: my aim
being to join forces with Antony as soon as possible, and
Pompey's to intercept him on the route and, if possible, to
catch him in an ambush. We left our winter camps on the
Seman within twelve hours of each other. Pompey led his
army away quietly by night; I went openly by day. But I had
the longer route, since I had to make a detour and go upstream to find a ford. Pompey had no river to cross and so
could travel more quickly. He hurried by forced marches
toward Antony until he received information that Antony was
quite close. Then he chose a good place for his purpose, kept
all his troops in camp, and forbade them to light any fires
in the hope that his presence would not be detected. But all
this was immediately reported to Antony by the Greeks of
the neighborhood. Antony sent word to me of what the
position was and kept his men in camp for one day. Next day
I joined him. When Pompey heard that I had arrived, he
withdrew in order to avoid being caught between two armies
and marched in full strength to Asparagium near Durazzo,
where he chose a good position and pitched camp.

5

SCIPIO IN ASIA AND MACEDONIA.

During this time Scipio had been in the east. After suffering considerable losses near Mount Amanus, he had adopted the title of Imperator. He went on to demand great sums of money from the various states and local rulers, and also exacted from the Roman taxation officers not only the amount of tax owing for the last two years, but also a loan of the money that would become due next year. He also ordered cavalry to be recruited throughout the province. When this had been done, he moved with his entire infantry and cavalry force out of Syria, leaving behind him on the frontier those enemy forces of Parthians who had recently killed our general Marcus Crassus and had besieged Bibulus. This action of his caused great anxiety among the Syrians, who feared an attack from Parthia, and Scipio's own soldiers were heard saying that they would follow him if they were led against the enemy, but would not fight against one who was a fellow citizen and a consul. Scipio then led his troops into winter quarters in Pergamum and the richest cities of Asia, made lavish gifts to the soldiers, and, in order to secure their loyalty, gave them a free hand to plunder the provincial communities.

Meanwhile the money that had been so ruthlessly demanded was being brought in from all parts of the province. Many entirely new means of extortion were discovered to minister to his avarice. A poll tax was imposed on all slaves and children; taxes were also levied on pillars, doors, grain, soldiers, arms, rowers, pieces of artillery, carriages; in fact, anything for which a name could be found was regarded as a source of tax. Officials with military power behind them were to be found everywhere, not only in charge of cities but in practically every village or isolated post, and among these officials those who excelled the rest in cruelty and hardheartedness were regarded as "real men" and "true patriots."

The whole province was overrun with officials and commissioners, crammed with organizers and collectors, all of whom were interested not only in raising the sums required by the government but also in making a good thing of it for themselves. They gave out that they were in the position of exiles from home and fatherland, consequently in need even of the necessities of life, and so found a plausible pretext for their thoroughly disgraceful behavior. In addition to all this there were very high rates of interest, as usually happens in war when money is levied from the whole population; and to postpone the date of payment was called "a free gift." So in these two years the indebtedness of the province was more than doubled. Nevertheless, the Roman citizens in the province still had to pay various taxes which were levied on them, not as individuals, but as corporations or communities; these exactions were described as "loans" and were said to be made in accordance with a decree of the senate. And, as had been done in Syria, the tax collectors were required to produce the tax not only for the current year but also for the year following.

At Ephesus, Scipio ordered the removal from the temple of Diana of the money which from very ancient times had been deposited there. A day was fixed for this operation, and those who were to remove the treasure, accompanied by several people of senatorial rank invited by Scipio, had arrived at the shrine when Scipio was handed a dispatch from Pompey, informing him that I had crossed the Adriatic with my legions and instructing him to postpone all other business and to hurry back to join him. As soon as he had read the dispatch, Scipio dismissed those who had come to the temple and began to make preparations for marching into Macedonia. Within a few days he was on his way, and the temple treasure at Ephesus was saved.

After I had joined forces with Antony, I recalled from Palaeokastro the legion that I had left there to guard the coast and proceeded to march inland with the purpose of winning the provinces over to my side. Deputations reached me from Thessaly and from Aetolia, and I was promised that the states in those areas would join me if I sent troops to protect them. I sent to Thessaly Lucius Cassius Longinus with the Twenty-seventh Legion (made up of recruits) and two hundred cavalry; and to Aetolia I sent Gaius Calvisius Sabinus with five cohorts and a small cavalry force. As these districts were quite close, I gave them special instructions to arrange for the grain supply.

I ordered Gnaeus Domitius Calvinus to march into Macedonia with two legions, the Eleventh and Twelfth, and five hundred cavalry. From the part of Macedonia called "Free" came Menedemus, the leading man in that area, and assured him that his people were all enthusiastically on our side.

These officers fared as follows: Calvisius was welcomed by the whole population of Aetolia as soon as he arrived. He drove the enemy garrisons out of Calydon and Lepanto and gained control of the whole area.

Cassius, on reaching Thessaly with his legion, found that the country was split up into two parties and so met with a reception that varied from place to place. The parties were led by Hegesaretus and Petraeus. Hegesaretus had been for a long time a person of importance in Thessaly and was on Pompey's side. Petraeus, a young man from one of the best families, supported me with all the resources that he had.

Domitius at the same time reached Macedonia. Numerous deputations from the various states had begun to come to him when it was suddenly reported that Scipio with his legions was close at hand. There were all sorts of stories and rumors, as normally happens in an unexpected situation when everything is exaggerated before the facts are known. Scipio, as it happened, wasted no time anywhere in Macedonia. He marched rapidly toward Domitius and then suddenly, when he was about twenty miles away, turned aside toward Cassius Longinus in Thessaly. He moved so quickly that the news of his arrival came at the same time as the news of his approach. To insure speed on the march, he had left Marcus Favonius with eight cohorts to guard the baggage of the legions at a point on the river Aliacmon (the boundary between Macedonia and Thessaly) and had ordered him to build a fort there. At the same time, the cavalry of King Cotys, which was normally stationed along the Thessalian frontier, came riding up in force to Cassius' camp. Cassius, terrified by the arrival of Scipio, which had been reported, and by the sight of this cavalry, which he assumed to be Scipio's, marched into the mountains that surround Thessaly and began to make his way toward Ambracia. Scipio hurried after him in pursuit but was overtaken by messengers from Favonius who told him that Domitius was approaching with his legions and that, without the help of Scipio, Favonius could not hold the position where he had been posted. On reading this news, Scipio changed his plan and altered the direction of his march. He gave up the pursuit of Cassius and hurried to relieve Favonius. Marching both by day and by night, he arrived in the nick of time, for the dust cloud raised by Domitius' army and his own advance guards became visible to Favonius at the same moment. So Cassius was saved by the energy of Domitius and Favonius by the quick response of Scipio.

Scipio halted for two days in his camp on the river Aliacmon, which flowed between him and Domitius' camp. At dawn on the third day, he brought his army across the river by the ford, built a camp, and early on the next day drew up his forces in front of it. Domitius then considered that the time had come for him to lead out his own forces and to show

that he had no hesitation about offering battle. There was a
plain stretching for about two miles between the two camps
and Domitius brought his men across the plain and close to
the enemy camp; but Scipio would not move far from his own
rampart. Domitius had some difficulty in holding his men back;
nevertheless, it so happened that no battle took place, largely
because below Scipio's camp there was a stream with steep
banks which prevented our men from advancing farther.

Scipio, however, had observed the spirit of our men and how
eager they were to fight. He thought it likely that on the following day he would either be forced to give battle against his
will or else keep his troops in camp—a very inglorious thing
to do after all the high hopes which his appearance had
aroused. Indeed his rash advance now ended in a discreditable
withdrawal. He crossed the river under cover of night without
even giving the signal for striking camp and went back again
to the place from which he had started. There he built a camp
on high ground near the river. A few days later, he set an
ambush of cavalry by night in the area where for the last few
days our men had been in the habit of foraging. When Quintus
Varus, Domitius' cavalry commander, came with his men as
usual, Scipio's cavalry rushed out on them from their ambush;
but our men stood up well to the attack; they quickly formed
up in their proper order and then, in a compact body, took the
offensive themselves. They killed about eighty of the enemy,
put the rest to flight, and returned to camp with the loss of
only two men.

After this, Domitius, hoping to be able to entice Scipio into
a position where he would have to fight, pretended that he was
being forced to withdraw because of shortage of supplies. The
usual signal for striking camp was given; then, after marching
for three miles, he halted in a good position with all his infantry and cavalry out of sight of the enemy. Scipio prepared
to follow him, but first sent out most of his cavalry to explore
the route and find out where Domitius was. As they went
forward, their first squadrons rode right into the ambush, but
they became suspicious when they heard the neighing of horses
and started to withdraw again. Those behind, seeing how fast
they were retiring, halted. Our men realized that the ambush
was discovered and that there was no point in waiting for the
main body to enter it. But they succeeded in cutting off two of
the enemy squadrons, among whom was Marcus Opimius,
Scipio's cavalry commander. Opimius managed to escape, but
the rest were either killed or brought to Domitius as prisoners.

6 THE MAIN FRONT AT DURAZZO.

After withdrawing the legion from its work in coastal defense, as explained above, I left three cohorts at Palaeokastro to defend the town and to guard the warships which I had brought over from Italy. I made one of my officers, Acilius Caninus, responsible for both the town and the ships. He brought the ships into the inner harbor behind the town, moored them to the shore, and blocked the mouth of the harbor by sinking a merchant ship there. He put another ship alongside this merchant ship and anchored it in the middle of the channel. A tower was built on it and it was manned by a detachment of troops ready to defend it in any emergency.

Pompey's son Gnaeus, who was in command of the Egyptian fleet, heard of what was being done and sailed to Palaeokastro. With the aid of a winch and numerous ropes, he managed to hoist up to the surface the ship that had been sunk and then attacked the guard ship with a number of ships of his own which had been equipped with high turrets. He was thus able to fire down on our men from above and he could always replace his own men when they got tired by sending in fresh units. At the same time he kept our forces divided by making attacks in other directions, assaulting the town walls both from the sea with his fleet and from the land by troops with scaling ladders. So by continuous effort on the part of the enemy and an unceasing rain of missiles, our men were overwhelmed and driven out of the guard ship, which was captured, though all the defenders got away safely in small boats.

At the same time, Gnaeus seized the natural breakwater at the other side of the harbor, which forms the peninsula on which the town stands. From here he got four triremes across into the inner harbor by placing rollers underneath them and pushing them forward by levers. So our warships, empty and moored to the shore, were attacked from two sides; four were dragged off and the rest burned. After the action was over, Decius Laelius, an officer from the Asiatic fleet, was left behind and stopped any supplies from reaching Palaeokastro from Byllis and Amantia. Gnaeus Pompey himself then went on to Lissus, where he attacked and burned thirty merchant ships that had been left behind in the harbor by Antony. He attempted to storm Lissus itself, but the town was defended by the citizens of the Roman community there and by the troops whom I had left as garrison. He stayed for three days and, after losing a few men in his attacks on the town, sailed away without having achieved his object.

I myself marched toward Asparagium as soon as I found out that that was where Pompey was. On the way we took by storm a town of the Parthini in which Pompey had placed a garrison. Two days later, I reached Pompey's position and camped near him. Next day I brought the whole army out in battle order and gave him the opportunity to fight. When I saw that he was staying where he was, I led my men back to camp, realizing that I should have to form some other plan.

On the following day, I set out in full force for Durazzo, making a long detour by difficult and narrow roads. I hoped that Pompey would either be forced to make for Durazzo also or else might be cut off from the place which was his main base for supplies and military equipment. And this, in fact, was what happened. At first he did not realize what my plan was because he saw us marching off in the opposite direction and imagined that we had been compelled to withdraw because of shortage of food. Later, however, his scouts informed him of our actual position and on the next day he also struck camp, hoping to be able to get ahead of us by a shorter route. This was what I expected would happen, and I addressed the soldiers, asking them to bear cheerfully the exertion which I was demanding from them. So, after only a few hours' rest that night, we reached Durazzo early in the morning and pitched camp there, just at the time that the vanguard of Pompey's army came into sight in the distance.

Pompey, cut off from Durazzo, had failed to achieve his original purpose. He now adopted another plan and fortified a camp at a place called Petra, which stands on high ground, below which is a reasonably good harbor, sheltered from certain winds. He ordered some of his warships to sail in here and grain and other supplies to be brought in from Asia and all other areas under his control.

It now seemed to me likely that the campaign was going to be a long one. I had no hope of getting supplies from Italy because the whole coast was closely blockaded by Pompey's fleet, and my own fleets which were being built in Sicily, Gaul, and Italy were still not ready. So I sent two of my officers, Quintus Tillius and Lucius Canuleius, into Epirus to requisition food. As Epirus was a considerable distance away, I established granaries at various points and ordered the local communities to furnish carts for the transport of grain to these places. I also ordered a collection of all the grain that could be found at Lissus, among the Parthini, and in all fortified settlements. Only a very little was found, partly because of the nature of the country, which is wild and mountainous so that as a rule the people live on grain imported from elsewhere; partly because Pompey had forestalled me. Some days earlier his cavalry had plundered the whole district of the Parthini, had broken into and dug up the floors of their houses, and then carried off to Petra all the grain that had been discovered.

So, after I had found out how matters stood, I adopted a plan that was based on the nature of the ground in front of me. All around Pompey's camp were a number of steep hills rising to considerable heights. First I occupied these hills with garrisons and built forts on them. Then, proceeding in each case according to the lay of the land, we built earthworks connecting the forts together and so began to enclose Pompey behind lines of circumvallation. In making this plan I was actuated by the following considerations: As we were short of food and Pompey was particularly strong in cavalry, I wanted to be able to minimize the risk of bringing in grain and stores for my army from all directions. Secondly, I aimed at preventing Pompey from foraging and so at making his cavalry useless for active operations. And thirdly, I wanted to strike a blow at Pompey's prestige, which was what he seemed chiefly to rely upon in his relations with foreign powers. This would be diminished when it became known throughout the world that he was being blockaded by me and did not dare to risk fighting a pitched battle.

Pompey was unwilling to move away from Durazzo and the sea. All his war matériel—weapons, armor, artillery—was stored at Durazzo, and the grain supply for the army was coming in by sea. He could only stop the building of my lines by fighting a battle, and he had decided that this was not the moment for fighting. There was therefore only one course left to him, and that was to push the strategy initiated by me to its extreme—to occupy himself as many hills as possible, to hold as much ground as possible with his own garrisons, and so to make me extend my forces over the widest possible area. This, in fact, was what he did. On a circuit of fourteen miles he built twenty-four forts, and inside this space could forage safely. It also contained a large area of crops which could be used for feeding the animals when no foraging expedition was being made. Thus, just as our men were building lines of fortifications to prevent Pompey's soldiers from breaking through and attacking them in the rear, so Pompey's men were making their own inner ring of fortifications to stop us from breaking into it at any point and taking them in the rear. But they were the first to finish the operation, because they had more men working on it and because, being on the inside, they had a smaller circuit to complete.

Although Pompey had decided not to bring his whole force into action against us and not to fight a pitched battle, nevertheless whenever we had to occupy a position, he always sent up slingers and archers, of whom he had a great number, to attack us from positions of his own choice. Many of our men were wounded, and there was a general terror of the arrows. To protect themselves against these and other missiles, most of the soldiers equipped themselves with tunics or paddings of felt, quilting, or hides.

Each side did its utmost in the struggle for seizing these positions for defense. My aim was to pen Pompey in as small an area as possible, while he wanted to seize as many heights as he could and so widen the circuit of his defense works. There was consequently a good deal of fighting. On one occasion a legion of mine, the Ninth, had occupied a position and was beginning to fortify it when Pompey seized another hill close by and straight in front of us. From here he proceeded to harass our men while they were working. From one side our position could be approached on practically level ground, and here Pompey first threw out a screen of archers and slingers, then sent up a great number of light-armed troops and brought forward his artillery. He was thus able to stop our men from working, since it was not easy for them to build fortifications and defend themselves at the same time. I saw our men being shot at and wounded from all sides and ordered them to leave the position and retire. Their way back was downhill, and the enemy now pressed on all the more eagerly, hindering our retreat, since they imagined that we were being driven from the position in a panic. It was at this point that Pompey is said to have boasted to his friends: "If Caesar's legions get out of this without heavy losses, you can tell me that I know nothing about generalship. It was foolhardy of them to have put themselves into such a position."

I had some apprehensions about the men's retreat and ordered hurdles to be carried up to the farthest point on the slope and to be fixed facing the enemy; under cover of these the soldiers were to dig a trench of moderate width and to put as many obstacles as possible in the enemy's way. I then posted slingers in a suitable position for covering our men's retreat and, when all these preparations were completed, gave orders for the legion to be withdrawn. At this the enemy showed all the more contempt for us and pressed on all the more confidently. They tore down the hurdles that had been fixed across their path and went on to cross the trenches. On observing this, I feared that we might suffer worse losses if it appeared that we were being driven from our position instead of making a voluntary withdrawal. The legion was now about halfway down the slope, and I instructed Antony, who was in command, to have the trumpet sounded and give the order to charge. The soldiers of the Ninth immediately pulled themselves together, hurled their javelins, and starting from lower ground, broke into the double, charged uphill, and drove the Pompeians before them in a headlong flight. The enemy's retreat was considerably hindered by the overturned hurdles, the uprights sticking in the ground and the lines of trenches. Our men, however, were satisfied with being able to retire without serious losses. A number of the enemy had been killed, and their own losses were only five men all told. So they withdrew at their leisure and, after occupying some other hills rather nearer our lines, brought them into the system of our fortifications.

This was an altogether new type of warfare. The great numbers of forts, the extent of ground covered, the size of the fortifications, and the whole system of blockade were unprecedented, and there were all sorts of other unusual conditions as well. Normally when one army blockades another, it is attacking an enemy who is weakened or demoralized, who has been conquered in battle or is suffering from the effects of some failure or other; the blockading army is numerically superior in infantry and cavalry; and the whole idea of the blockade is to prevent the enemy from getting supplies. But now I was in the inferior position numerically and was blockading an army that was undefeated and had not yet even been engaged. Moreover, they had plenty of everything; every day great numbers of ships arrived to bring them supplies; in fact, from whatever direction the wind blew, it would be favorable for some of these ships. We, on the other hand, had used up all the grain from all areas available to us and were now in considerable difficulties. Nevertheless, the men endured these hardships with remarkable patience. They remembered that last year they had suffered the same hardships in Spain and, because of their endurance and hard work, had been totally victorious in a great war. They could remember too how short they had been of supplies at Alesia and the even more serious famine at Bourges; yet in these cases the campaigns had ended in the defeat of the most powerful nations in Gaul. So now, when they were issued barley or vegetables, they made no complaints; and they were actually extremely pleased to get meat, with which they could be supplied plentifully from Epirus. Some of the men when off duty had discovered a kind of root called *chara*, which, when mixed with milk, was a useful supplement to their rations. There was plenty of it and they made a sort of bread out of it. When Pompey's soldiers mocked our men for being half starved, they retaliated by

throwing some of these loaves over into the enemy lines to
show them that there was no reason for them to feel so confident.

By now too the grain was beginning to ripen. The men
were confident that they would soon have plenty, and hopes
for the future made the present shortage easier to bear. One
often heard the soldiers, whether on guard or talking among
themselves, say that they would rather live on the bark of
trees than let Pompey slip through their hands. They were
cheered too by hearing from deserters that, though the
enemy's cavalry horses were being kept alive, all their baggage
animals had died, and that the troops themselves were in a
bad state of health, as a result of cramped quarters, the
stench of vast numbers of corpses, and the continual hard
work to which they were unused. They were also extremely
short of water. All the rivers and streams flowing into the sea
had either been diverted by us or else dammed up by engineering works on a large scale. It is rough, mountainous country, and we blocked up the narrow river valleys by sinking
piles into the ground, which made a framework for the
banked-up earth that was to dam the water. So the enemy
were forced to keep to the low-lying marshy ground and to dig
wells there, which gave them still more work to do. Moreover,
these springs were sometimes at a considerable distance from
the forts and were apt to dry up quickly in the hot weather.
My army, on the other hand, enjoyed excellent health; we had
plenty of water and indeed of everything else except grain,
and, as the troops saw the grain steadily growing ripe, they
could tell that here too prospects were daily improving.

In this new type of warfare, new tactics were evolved by
both sides. The enemy, for example, had observed from the
watch fires that our men were sleeping out at night by the entrenchments. So they would creep up silently in a body, shoot
their arrows into the general mass, and quickly retire to their
own lines. Taught by experience, our men found ways of dealing with this form of attack. Lighting fires in one place . . . *

When I left I had put Publius Sulla in charge of the camp.
He was informed of the situation and came to the cohort's
relief with two legions. As soon as he arrived, Pompey's troops
were easily driven back. The sight of our men was enough for
them, and they made no resistance to our attack. Once the first
of them had given way, the rest turned and fled from the posi-

* Here there is a considerable break in the manuscripts. From Appian,
2, 60, it may be inferred that the missing passage described an unsuc-
cessful attack on Durazzo by Caesar and an attack on Caesar's lines
made by Pompey. The text begins again with an account of how this
attack of Pompey's was beaten off.—R.W.

tion they had occupied. Our men pursued them, but Sulla recalled them in case they should go too far. Many people think that if he had followed them up with more energy, the war could have been won on that day; but personally I do not think he can be blamed for the decision he made. The duties of a deputy commander and of a commander-in-chief are quite different: one should act entirely in accordance with his instructions, whereas the other is free to make important decisions on his own when the situation demands them. Sulla had been left in charge of the camp by me; he had rescued some of his men from a difficult position and was content with that; not wishing to assume the functions of a commander-in-chief, he did not choose to fight a pitched battle which could conceivably have gone against him.

Pompey's men were now in a position from which it was not easy for them to withdraw. They had advanced from low ground to the top of a hill and, in retiring down the slope, they were afraid of the attacks launched by our men from above. Also, there was not much daylight left. In their confidence of winning a complete success, they had prolonged the action almost until nightfall. Pompey was therefore forced to adapt his actions to the circumstances. He occupied a hill which was far enough from our fort to be out of range of our artillery and fortified this position after bringing all his forces to it.

There was also fighting going on at two other points during this time. Pompey had attacked several of our forts simultaneously with the idea of keeping our forces equally divided, so that one garrison should not be able to come and give help to the next. In one place Volcacius Tullus with three cohorts stood up to an attack launched by a whole legion; in another our Germans sallied out from the lines and returned again without loss after killing considerable numbers of the enemy.

So six battles were fought on one day, three at Durazzo and three at various points along our fortifications. On reckoning everything up, we found that Pompey had lost about two thousand men, including a number of veterans and centurions. Among these was Valerius Flaccus, son of the Lucius Flaccus who had governed Asia as praetor. Six of their standards were captured. On our side there were not more than twenty missing after all these engagements. But in the fighting at the fort every single one of our men was wounded and four centurions out of one cohort lost their eyes. Wanting to give me some proof of the trouble and danger that they had been in, they showed me, properly counted, about thirty thousand arrows that had been shot into the fort, and they brought me a shield belonging to the centurion Scaeva which had one hundred

twenty weapon holes in it. It was clear that it was largely
owing to Scaeva that the fort had been saved, and for his
services to me and to the state I granted him two hundred
thousand sesterces, publicly congratulated him, and promoted
him from the eighth cohort to the position of first centurion
of the first cohort. Later I gave full recognition to the cohort
as a whole, presenting the men with double pay, decorations,
and free issues of grain and clothing.

During the night Pompey built new and stronger defense
works and in the next few days erected towers, raised the
height of his fortifications to fifteen feet, and placed screens
along the top. Five days later he took advantage of a cloudy
night, barricaded all the gates, fixed stakes in the ground to
hold up any pursuit, and soon after midnight led his forces
quietly out of camp and retired to the fortifications which they
had held previously.

Every day after this, I drew up my army on level ground
and gave Pompey an opportunity to fight. I brought the legions
up quite close to his camp; in fact, my front line was only
just out of range of artillery planted on his rampart. Pompey
also, in order to safeguard his name and reputation, drew his
army up in battle order in front of his camp, but so close to it
that his third line was practically touching the rampart and the
whole army was sheltered by his artillery.

7 FURTHER OPERATIONS.
A POMPEIAN SUCCESS.

As already explained, Aetolia, Acarnania, and Amphilochia
had been occupied for us by Calvisius Sabinus and Cassius
Longinus. I now thought that we should push on a little farther
and attempt to occupy Achaea. I therefore sent Fufius
Calenus into that area and instructed Sabinus and Cassius to
join him with their cohorts. Rutilius Lupus was Pompey's
commander in Achaea, and when he heard of the approach of
my forces, he prepared to defend the Isthmus so as to keep
Calenus out of his province. Calenus meanwhile received the
voluntary submission of Delphi, Thebes, and Orchomenus;
he took other cities by storm and sent envoys to the rest in
an attempt to win them over to our side. He was thus fully
occupied with these and other matters.

While these operations were continuing in Achaea and at
Durazzo, the news arrived that Scipio had appeared in Macedonia. I had not forgotten my original determination to come

to a peaceful understanding, and so I sent to Scipio our mutual friend Aulus Clodius. Clodius had originally been introduced to me by means of a recommendation from Scipio, and I counted him among my intimate friends. I now gave him a letter and verbal messages to take to Scipio. They may be summarized as follows: "I have done everything possible to reach a settlement, but with no success. I attribute this failure to the fault of those whom I have used as intermediaries; they were afraid to bring my proposals to Pompey's notice at what they considered the wrong moment. You, on the other hand, can speak with your own authority. You can not only say freely what you think right, but can even to some extent force your own opinions on Pompey and exercise some restraint on him if he is in the wrong. In fact, since you command your army in your own right and not as a subordinate of his, you have physical force as well as moral authority on your side. Now if you could use your influence as I suggest, you and you alone would be gratefully acknowledged by all to have saved Italy from disruption."

Clodius gave Scipio this message, and for a few days it looked as though the proposals were being well received. But later he was given no further opportunity of speaking to Scipio and returned to me without having effected anything. After the war was over, we discovered that Favonius had bitterly opposed Scipio and that this had been the reason for the change in his attitude.

At Durazzo, in order to pen in Pompey's cavalry and keep them from foraging, I had constructed strong defense works across the two approaches, which as already stated were very narrow, and had built forts at both points. After a few days, when Pompey realized that his cavalry were no better off than before, he brought them back again by sea to the main position behind his entrenchments. There was extreme shortage of fodder; so much so that they fed their horses on leaves stripped from the trees and on the pounded-up roots of young reeds. They had already used up all the crops planted inside their lines and had to import fodder from Corfu and Acarnania, which meant a long sea voyage. Even so, they still had not enough and had to supplement their rations with barley. In these ways they managed to keep their horses alive. But finally there was no more barley or any other kind of fodder left; all the grass had been cut, all the trees stripped of their leaves. The half-starved horses were weakening and Pompey decided that somehow or other he must try to break out.

Among my cavalry officers were two Allobrogian brothers, Raucillus and Egus, sons of Adbucillus, who had been chief of the tribe for many years. They were excellent soldiers and had

done outstandingly good work for me in all my campaigns in
Gaul. In return I had given them important official positions
in their own country; had arranged for them to be members
of the council of their tribe before they were, strictly speaking,
eligible for this honor; had given them land in Gaul confiscated
from the enemy, together with large sums of money; and had,
in fact, raised them up from poverty to wealth. Because of
their fine soldierly qualities they were not only highly thought
of by me but were generally popular throughout the army.
However, my friendship and a kind of native arrogance of
their own went to their heads. They began to look down on
their own countrymen, embezzled the men's pay, and sent all
the booty, which should have been distributed, back to their
own homes. The men were enraged by this and came to see
me in a body to complain openly of how they had been treated.
In addition to other charges made against the brothers, they
accused them of sending in false returns of the numbers of
the cavalry and appropriating the extra pay for themselves.

In my view, this was not the time for taking severe measures. I was prepared to overlook much in consideration of
their past services, and so I postponed any inquiry into the
charges. Privately, however, I reprimanded them for having
tried to make money out of their own men; I told them that
they could rely on my friendship for everything and asked
them to judge their future prospects by thinking of what I had
done for them in the past. Nevertheless, the whole affair made
them generally disliked and despised, and they were made
aware of this not only by complaints heard everywhere but also
by the attitude of their own people and by the effects of their
own guilty consciences. This feeling of guilt and perhaps also
a suspicion that they had not been acquitted but only reserved
for punishment at a later date made them decide to desert me
and try their luck at making new friends elsewhere. They discussed their plans with those few of their personal retainers to
whom they dared to admit the crime that they proposed to
perpetrate, and first of all (as was discovered after the war
was over) plotted to kill Gaius Volusenus, our cavalry commander, so that they should be able to give the impression of
having done something for Pompey before deserting to him.
But as they got no opportunity to commit this murder, they
decided that it was too difficult, and, after borrowing all the
money they could lay their hands on, ostensibly in order to
pay back to their own men the sums of which they had been
defrauded, they bought up a number of horses and, with those
who were their accomplices, went over to Pompey.

They were men from good families and they were splendidly
equipped in every way; they had a large company with them

and numerous horses; they had a fine reputation as soldiers and had held a high place in my estimation; moreover, the desertion itself was something quite new and unprecedented. For all these reasons Pompey escorted them all around his defense works, from post to post, and showed them to his men. For up to this time not a single man, whether from the infantry or the cavalry, had left me and gone over to Pompey, though nearly every day deserters from Pompey came over to me, and indeed there were mass desertions of the troops that had been raised by Pompey in Epirus and Aetolia and other districts occupied by me.

But Raucillus and Egus were well informed about everything. They knew what parts of our defenses were still unfinished and what sectors were considered by military experts to be the weakest ones. They knew the times at which guards were changed and the distances between one post and another, and, being able to judge from the character or efficiency of the various officers in charge of each sector, they could tell what parts of the line would be best guarded. All this information they passed on to Pompey.

As has been pointed out above, Pompey had already decided on trying to break out, and now, with this new intelligence in his hands, he ordered his men to make wickerwork coverings for their helmets and to collect material for filling in trenches. When this was done, he embarked by night a great number of light troops and archers and all the material that had been collected on small boats and merchant ships, and about midnight led sixty cohorts drawn from his largest camp and the forts in its proximity down to our lines of fortifications at the point where they were nearest the sea and farthest from our main camp. He sent to the same sector the ships which, as already mentioned, were carrying the material and light troops, and also the warships that he had at Durazzo. All his commanders had been given full instructions as to what to do.

I had placed in command of this sector my quaestor, Lentulus Marcellinus, with the Ninth Legion, and, as his health was bad, had sent Fulvius Postumus to assist him. The position was defended from direct enemy attack by a ditch fifteen feet wide and a rampart ten feet high and ten feet across the top. About two hundred yards behind this line and facing in the opposite direction was another rampart not quite so high as the first one. I had had this double line of defenses made here because for some time I had been apprehensive about our being outflanked from the sea, and I wanted us to have means of defense if we were attacked from two directions at once. But our works were on such a scale (we had a circuit of sixteen miles to fortify) and there was so much to be done every day that we had not had time to complete the defenses here. The cross rampart facing the sea and connecting the two other ramparts had not yet been finished. Pompey had been informed of this by the Allobrogian deserters. Their information did us much harm.

We had two cohorts on sentry duty by the sea, and it was here that Pompey's troops suddenly appeared at dawn. The soldiers were carried around on their ships and began to hurl their weapons at the southern rampart and to fill up the ditch with the material they had brought. At the same time, Pompey's legionaries from the land were assaulting the northern fortification. Ladders were brought up, and artillery and missiles of all kinds were used to terrify the defenders. Archers seemed to be pouring in arrows from every side. The only weapons available to our men were stones, and the enemy were well protected against these by the wickerwork coverings on their helmets. Then, just when we were hard pressed all around and only standing our ground with difficulty, the enemy observed the weak point in our defenses that has already been mentioned; they disembarked troops in the gap between the two ramparts where the fortifications had not been finished, attacked our men from the rear on both ramparts, drove them down, and forced them to take to flight.

Informed of this sudden attack, Marcellinus sent out from his camp several cohorts to help our men in their difficulties. But they found them already in flight; their appearance had no effect in steadying them, and they were not able to stand up to the enemy's attack themselves. Additional reinforcements also were infected by the panic of those already in flight and merely added to the confusion, making the situation more dangerous still, since the very numbers of men involved made a retreat more difficult. In this battle one of our standard-bearers, seriously wounded and his strength failing him, caught sight of some of our cavalry and cried out to them: "I have guarded this eagle faithfully for many years of my life and in the same faithfulness I give it back to Caesar now that I am dying. Take it and carry it to him safely. Do not, I beg you, let it be lost. That would be a disgrace that none of Caesar's armies has ever suffered." So the eagle was saved; but every centurion of the first cohort was killed except the senior centurion of the second squad.

Now, after a great slaughter of our men, Pompey's troops were approaching the camp of Marcellinus, where the remaining cohorts awaited them in a state of considerable terror. But news of the battle had reached Mark Antony, who was in command of the nearest fort, and at this point he could be seen, with twelve cohorts, marching down from the higher ground. His arrival checked Pompey's men and put fresh heart into ours, so that they recovered from their panic. Soon afterward I arrived myself with some cohorts that I had withdrawn from various outposts. I had received the news by means of the old method of sending smoke signals from one fort to another. I was informed of our losses and discovered that Pompey had broken through our lines and was building a fortified camp near the sea; this would allow him to forage as he liked and also to keep a point to which his ships could sail freely. My own plans had miscarried; I therefore changed my strategy and ordered our men to fortify a camp close to that of Pompey.

The entrenchment had been finished when my scouts observed that behind the wood there were some cohorts, apparently in the strength of a legion, being led into the old camp. By "the old camp" I mean the one that had been made some days previously at the time that the Ninth Legion, as already described, had engaged Pompey's troops and then attempted to blockade them. The camp bordered on a wood and was about three hundred yards from the sea. Afterward, various reasons had induced me to alter my plans; I had moved camp a little way from this original position and, a few days later, Pompey had occupied the old camp. Since he intended to bring several legions into it, he built larger lines of fortifications all around, leaving the original fortifications intact, like a citadel or strong point inside a bigger fortress. He had also dug from the left corner of his camp a line of entrenchments about four hundred yards long, running down to the river, so that his men could get water easily and safely. However, he also, for reasons which need not be mentioned here, had changed his plans and moved from this position. So for some days the camp had remained unoccupied though the fortifications were still in a good state of repair.

Now my scouts informed me that the standards of one legion had been carried into this camp. This had also been observed from some of our forts on the higher ground. The position was about five hundred yards from the new camp that Pompey had just made.

I was anxious to make up for the losses we had suffered that day, and I saw here a chance of being able to surprise and destroy Pompey's legion. I left behind two cohorts to give the impression that we were still working on our fortifications, and then marched out myself with as much secrecy as possible by a route which appeared to lead away from our objective. I had with me the remaining cohorts, thirty-three in all, which included the Ninth Legion, though this unit was below strength and had lost many of its centurions. Marching in two lines abreast, we made for Pompey's legion in the old camp. My original idea proved to be a sound one. We arrived before Pompey could know of it and, though the defenses of the camp covered a wide area, on the left wing, which I commanded myself, our rapid attack drove the defenders down from the rampart. At the gates, which were barricaded with studded beams, the fighting lasted for a little time as our men tried to break in and the enemy fought back to save their camp. In this engagement Titus Pulio (the man who, as already mentioned, had been responsible for the betrayal of Gaius Antonius' army) fought magnificently. However, our men's courage was irresistible; they broke through the barricade and first forced their way into the larger camp; next they broke into the smaller fortification within the larger camp, to which the defeated legion had retreated. Here they met with some resistance and inflicted a number of casualties.

But fortune, powerful enough everywhere, plays a particularly important part in war; the slightest tilting of the scale can lead to a complete reversal of a situation, as happened on this occasion. It has already been mentioned that there was a line of entrenchments extending from the camp to the river. Now the cohorts of my right wing, not knowing the layout of the place, mistook these entrenchments for the fortifications of the camp and went along them looking for a gate. When they found that these lines merely connected the camp with the river, they pulled down a section of them and, meeting with no resistance, crossed over. All our cavalry followed them.

These operations had taken some time, and by now Pompey had been informed of what was happening. He withdrew five legions from their work on his defenses and led them to the rescue. At the same moment, his cavalry drew near ours and his line of infantry, formed up in order of battle, became visible to those of our men who had occupied the camp. The whole situation was transformed. Pompey's legion inside the camp took heart again at the prospect of being speedily relieved, stood firm at the western gate, and even counterattacked. My cavalry, which was climbing up by a narrow track over the earthworks, feared that they would be cut off from retreat and set the example of running away. My right wing, cut off as it was from the left, saw the panic of the cavalry and, fearing that they might be caught inside the defenses, began to retreat through the gap in the rampart which they had made. Some of them, afraid of being crushed in the narrow opening, jumped down from the ten-foot rampart into the trench beneath and were trampled to death by others who tried to make their way to safety over their bodies. And the men on the left wing, seeing from the rampart Pompey approaching and their own comrades running away, were frightened of being cut off in an enclosed space with the enemy both inside and outside the fortifications; they therefore tried to look after themselves by retreating along the same way as they had come. It was a state of utter confusion, panic, and terror, so much so that * . . . when I seized hold of the standards carried by the fugitives and ordered them to stand firm, some rushed straight on at a gallop, others just dropped the standards in terror; not a single man halted.

The position was so desperate that the whole army might well have been destroyed. What helped us and saved us was that Pompey for some little time did not venture to bring his troops up to the rampart. I imagine that this was because he was afraid of an ambush, since everything had happened so unexpectedly and only a short time before he had seen his men in full flight from their camp. And at the same time, his cavalry were slowed because the way into the entrenchment was narrow and was also occupied by our troops. So, small things often have great consequences, consequences that can turn, as it were, in both directions. For instance, these entrenchments from the camp to the river first of all caused me to miss a victory which, once Pompey's camp had been stormed, was virtually in my hands, and then, by slowing the speed of Pompey's pursuit, saved us from annihilation.

In these two battles fought on the same day, I lost nine hundred sixty men from the legions; two hundred cavalry, including Tuticanus, a Gaul whose father belonged to the governing body of his tribe, Gaius Fleginas of Piacenza, Aulus Granius of Puteoli, and Marcus Sacrativir of Capua; many senior officers and thirty-two centurions. The majority of these were not killed in the fighting but perished in the trenches and at the defense works and by the banks of the river, trampled to death in the panic-stricken flight of their own comrades. Thirty-two standards were lost.

After the battle Pompey was acclaimed as Imperator. He kept the title and afterward allowed himself to be addressed by it; but he did not as a rule use it in signing his letters, and he did not have laurel twined around his fasces.

Labienus had asked Pompey to be allowed to deal with the prisoners and had his request granted. He was a traitor him-

* There must here be a gap in the manuscripts. It appears that Caesar is now outside the camp and is attempting to rally his cavalry on the right wing.—R.W.

self and no doubt wished to give an example of how traitors
can be trusted. After having the men brought forward and
paraded and after addressing them as "comrades-in-arms," he
went on to cover them with insults, asking whether it was
usual for veterans to run away, and then had them killed with
all his own troops looking on.

These successes had such an effect on the spirit and confidence of Pompey's army that they gave up thinking about
strategy in the belief that they had won the war already. It
did not occur to them to reflect on the real causes of our
defeat, which were as follows: We had been at a disadvantage
both as regards numbers and position; space for maneuver
was restricted by their having occupied the camp ahead of us;
we had suffered from two outbreaks of panic, both inside and
outside the fortifications; and our army had been split into two
parts so that one could not come to the help of the other.

They also failed to notice that no pitched battle had been
fought with the two sides meeting in regular encounter, and
that the losses which we had suffered were the result not so
much of enemy action as of our own numbers and the confined space. Finally, they chose to forget the part that can
always be played in warfare by chance, and how frequently
it has happened that great disasters have resulted from
trifling causes—a suspicion that proves ill founded, a sudden
attack of fear, a religious scruple—and how often an army
has come to grief because of the incompetence of its general
or a mere mistake made by one of its officers. Instead, they
behaved as though they had been victorious because of their
own fighting qualities and as though their fortune could never
change. They sent out reports and dispatches all over the
world proclaiming the victory they won on this day.

Finding that my original plan had ended in failure, I
realized that I must adopt an entirely new strategy. I withdrew
all garrisons from the forts simultaneously, gave up the idea
of the siege, and bringing the army together in one place,
addressed the troops as follows:

"I do not want you to be too much depressed by what has
happened or to be frightened of the future. Think of the many
victories you have won and set them against this one not very
important defeat. You have plenty of reasons for giving thanks
to fortune. Think, for instance, of your bloodless conquest of
Italy, of how you subdued the two provinces of Spain though
you were opposed by people well known for their fighting
qualities and by first-rate generals. Think of how you gained
control of the two main areas from which we get our grain.
And finally you should remember how fortune helped you

when you all were brought across the sea safely through the middle of the enemy's fleets and with enemy forces occupying not only the harbors but the whole coastline. Now, if everything has not turned out successfully, it is up to you to do your own part and help fortune to help you.

"As for the defeat which you have just suffered, you can blame it on anyone you like, but not on me. I led you into a good position for fighting, and together we captured the enemy's camp, drove them out of it, and beat them in fighting. Victory was ours already. What prevented us from grasping it may have been a lack of resolution on your part, a mistake made by someone, or simply some stroke of fortune. Whatever it may have been, you must now do all you can to wipe out this loss by your own courage and gallantry. Do this and you will find the same thing happening as happened at Gergovia. Defeat will turn to victory, and the cowards of yesterday will be the heroes of tomorrow."

After this speech had been delivered to the troops I had a number of standard-bearers publicly disgraced by being deprived of their rank. But in the army as a whole there was such a feeling of distress because of the defeat and such a determination to wipe out the disgrace, that everyone, by way of punishing himself, went out of his way to look for more work to do without waiting for orders from officers or centurions; they were all burning with the desire to fight, and indeed there were a number of senior officers who were so impressed that they thought we ought to stay where we were and risk everything on a pitched battle. I, on the other hand, had not sufficient confidence in troops who had recently been in a state of panic. I thought it better to give them time in which to recover their morale; and I was also extremely anxious about the grain supply now that we had abandoned our lines.

So I waited no longer than was necessary for looking after the sick and wounded and then, with as little disturbance as possible, at nightfall sent all the baggage ahead to Apollonia with orders not to stop to rest until the journey had been completed. I sent one legion to guard the baggage. Once this operation was over, I kept two legions in camp and sent the rest, by different gates, out along the same road at about three A.M. Then, after a short interval, since I wanted the news of our departure to reach the enemy as late as possible but at the same time wished to keep to the normal military procedure, I ordered the signal to be sounded for breaking camp and immediately set out after the rear guard. Before long we were out of sight.

Once Pompey discovered our plan, he wasted no time in coming after us. His aim was to catch up with our army on the march while it was still in a state of terror and confusion, and so he led his legions out of camp and sent his cavalry on ahead to slow down our rear guard. However, he was unable to overtake us; we were marching light and had got too far ahead. His cavalry only caught up with the rear guard when we had reached the Genusus, a river with steep, difficult banks. Here they engaged us. I sent my own cavalry to oppose them, together with four hundred light-armed shock troops who fought alongside the cavalry. They did so well that, after joining battle with Pompey's horsemen, they entirely routed them, killed quite a number, and rejoined the rest of the column without suffering any losses.

The crossing of the Genusus completed the march for the day. We established ourselves in our old camp at Asparagium, and I kept all troops inside the rampart. I sent out detachments of cavalry to get fodder, but ordered them to return without delay by the far gate. Pompey too at the end of his day's march occupied his old camp at Asparagium. His soldiers had no work to do because the fortifications were still intact. Some went off to a considerable distance to fetch wood and fodder; others, since their last camp was not far away, stacked their arms in the tents, left the rampart, and went back to fetch articles of equipment and personal luggage, much of which had been left behind when it was suddenly decided to depart. They were thus in no condition for continuing the pursuit. I had imagined that this would happen, and about midday I gave the order to march and led the army out of camp. We went about eight miles, twice the distance covered on the first day. As his men had gone away, Pompey was unable to follow our example.

Next day I followed the same plan as at first, sending the baggage ahead at nightfall and following with the legions at about three A.M. I did this so that if I were forced to fight, I could meet the emergency with an army already prepared for action. I adopted the same procedure on the following days, and in this way it happened that, in spite of the deep rivers we had to cross and the difficulties of the routes, we sustained no damage at all. Pompey was handicapped by the delay on the first day; and though on the following days, in his desire to overtake us, he made his men press on by forced marches, all this labor was in vain. By the fourth day he gave up the pursuit and realized that he would have to adopt some other plan.

8 THE MOVE INTO THESSALY.

A number of reasons made it necessary for me to go to Apollonia. Arrangements had to be made for the wounded; the troops had to be paid; our allies needed encouragement; and garrisons had to be left in some of the cities. But I dealt with these matters as quickly as possible, since I was in a hurry. I was anxious about Domitius and feared that Pompey might be upon him before he realized what was happening. So I was extremely eager to join him and marched toward him with all the speed possible. I was basing my whole plan of campaign on the following considerations: (1) If Pompey followed us, he would be drawn away from the sea and cut off from the supplies which he had at Durazzo and so would be forced to fight us on equal terms. (2) If Pompey crossed to Italy, I would combine forces with Domitius and march by way of Illyrium to Italy's relief. (3) If Pompey tried to take Apollonia and Palaeokastro so as to cut us off entirely from the coast, then I would move against Scipio and Pompey would be forced to come to the aid of one of his own armies. So I sent messengers on ahead to Domitius with letters informing him of what I wanted done. Then, after leaving garrisons of four cohorts at Apollonia, one at Lissus, and three at Palaeokastro, and having seen that the wounded were billeted in various places, I began to march through Epirus and Athamania. Pompey guessed what my plan was and decided to move also in the direction of Scipio. If I marched against Scipio, then he would go to his assistance; and if I, while waiting for legions and cavalry from Italy, preferred to stay near the coast in the neighborhood of Palaeokastro, then he would attack Domitius in full force.

Each of us realized how important it was to move quickly; each had another army of his own to help; and each wanted to be in a position to deliver a crushing blow, should the opportunity present itself. But I had had to leave the direct route in order to go to Apollonia, while Pompey had an easy journey into Macedonia by way of Candavia. Another unfortunate thing had happened too, quite unexpectedly. For some days Domitius had been camping close to Scipio, but now, in order to get supplies, he had moved away from him and gone to Monastir. Fate itself seemed to have thrown him directly in Pompey's path. At the time, however, I did not know this. After the battle at Durazzo, Pompey had sent dispatches into all the provinces and to all the native states giving a much more highly colored picture of his success than was justified by the facts. The report had spread that I was in flight after having been defeated with the loss of almost my entire army, and because of this rumor the roads were unsafe and a number of states were changing from my side to Pompey's. As a result, messengers sent by me to Domitius and by Domitius to me, though traveling by a number of different routes, always failed to get through. However, some Allobroges, friends of Raucillus and Egus who, as already mentioned, had deserted to Pompey, happened to meet some of Domitius' scouts on the road. Perhaps they found it natural to get into conversation, since they had been in many campaigns together in Gaul, or perhaps they were carried away by the thought of their successes. In any case, they gave a full account of what had happened and told Domitius' men that I was on my way and that Pompey was very nearly there. Domitius, when he received this information, had less than four hours in which to get away. But thanks to the kindness of the enemy, he succeeded in doing so and joined forces with me as I was on the way to the town of Aeginium on the Thessalian frontier.

Now that our armies were united, I went on to Gomphi, which is the first town in Thessaly that one reaches on the road from Epirus. A few months previously, the people of this place had sent a deputation to me of their own accord, offering to put themselves at my disposal and asking me to send a garrison. But the greatly exaggerated rumors about the battle of Durazzo, which I have already mentioned, had reached the town before me. Androsthenes, the governor of Thessaly, preferred to share in Pompey's victory than to join me in defeat; and so he ordered in from the country the whole population, slaves and freemen, shut the gates and sent messengers to Scipio and to Pompey asking them to come to his assistance. So long as help came quickly, he said, he could rely on the fortifications; but he would not be able to stand out against a long siege. Scipio, after learning that the armies had left Durazzo, had marched to Larissa; Pompey had not yet reached Thessaly.

As soon as I had fortified a camp, I ordered scaling ladders, sheds, and hurdles to be got ready for an immediate assault. When these orders had been carried out, I spoke to the troops, pointing out to them that to gain possession of a rich and well-stocked town was just what we needed to relieve our difficulties of supply, that at the same time the example of this town would strike terror into the rest, and that the operation must be carried out quickly before reinforcements could arrive. The soldiers showed a wonderful spirit, and I made full use of it. We began the attack at about four P.M. on the day of our arrival, and in spite of the high walls, we took the town by storm before sunset. I gave it over to the soldiers to plunder, then moved camp immediately and marched on Metropolis, where we arrived before any news or any rumor had been heard of the storming of Gomphi.

The people of Metropolis had also heard the rumors about Durazzo, and at first they followed the same policy as the others, shutting the gates and manning the walls with armed men. However, I had prisoners brought out in front of the wall, and when they learned from them what had happened at Gomphi they opened their gates. I took care to see that the townspeople came to no harm. People contrasted what had happened here with the fate of Gomphi, and every state in Thessaly except for Larissa, which was occupied by Scipio with large forces, submitted to me and carried out my instructions. In the country the crops were now nearly ripe, and finding a good position there, I decided that this was where I would fight the campaign and here I would await the arrival of Pompey.

9 THE BATTLE OF PHARSALUS.

After a few days Pompey arrived in Thessaly. In an address delivered to the whole army, he thanked his own men for what they had done and invited Scipio's soldiers to share with them the plunder and the rewards of a victory which was already as good as in their hands. Both armies were brought into one camp, and Pompey shared with Scipio the honors of the command, giving him a special trumpeter and ordering a second tent to be set aside for him as his personal headquarters.

Pompey's soldiers had been confident enough before, and now that their strength had been increased by the addition of another great army, they became more confident still. They were surer than ever of the coming victory and thought that to delay action was merely to postpone their return to Italy. Whenever Pompey took time over his dispositions or acted with caution, they would declare that the whole business could be over and done with in a day and that the only obstacle to this was Pompey's love of power and the pleasure

he took in treating men of consular and praetorian rank as
though they were his servants. Among themselves there were
open squabbles about how they should be rewarded and who
should get various priesthoods and official posts; they decided too about who should hold the consulship for years
ahead. Others were putting in claims for the houses and property of those who were in my camp. And there was a particularly violent discussion in their council as to whether Lucilius
Hirrus, who had been sent by Pompey to the Parthians, should
be allowed to stand for the praetorship at the next elections
without being personally present in Rome. His friends begged
Pompey to keep the promise that he made to him on his
departure, so that it should not look as though Hirrus had
relied on his authority in vain; while the others objected that
one man should not get the advantage over the rest when
the hardships and dangers had been the same for all.

There were daily quarrels about who should succeed to the
priesthood held by me. The competitors were Domitius, Scipio,
and Lentulus Spinther. In the course of their discussions they
could not restrain themselves from using publicly the most
insulting language about each other. Lentulus made much
of the respect due to his age; Domitius boasted of his popularity and high position in Rome; Scipio relied on his rela-
tionship to Pompey. Then Acutius Rufus accused Afranius
before Pompey of having betrayed the army during the
Spanish campaign. And in a meeting of the council Domitius
proposed that when the war was over, those among them of
senatorial rank who had taken part in the campaign should
be given three voting tablets each for deciding on the fate of
those who had remained behind in Rome or had been in
towns occupied by Pompey and had not offered their services
in the army. One tablet, it was proposed, would indicate a
complete acquittal, one the loss of all civil rights, and one the
imposition of a fine. Indeed, they were all occupying their
time and thoughts on the honors and rewards they were
going to receive and on how they would revenge themselves
on their personal enemies. They gave no consideration to the
problems of how they were to achieve victory in the first place
or of how they were to use it afterward.

Our grain supply was now assured and the soldiers had re-
gained their strength. Since the battles at Durazzo enough
time had passed for me to be able to feel confident that the
morale of the troops was high. I considered that the moment
had come to find out whether Pompey intended or was willing
to fight a pitched battle. So I led the army out of camp and
drew it up in battle formation, first of all in a position favorable to us and at some distance from Pompey's camp, but on

the following days moving farther away from our camp and close up to the hills held by Pompey. This had the effect of making my army become more confident with every day that passed. As to the cavalry, I retained a system of organization which I have already described. In actual cavalry we were very heavily outnumbered, so I selected a body of young men from among the shock troops, who were chosen with a special view to their speed in action and were lightly armed, and made them go into battle fighting side by side with the cavalry. They were given daily practice in this mode of fighting so as to become thoroughly familiar with it. As a result, one thousand of our cavalry, having gained this experience, were quite prepared to stand up to seven thousand of the enemy even on open ground without being seriously disturbed by the disparity in numbers. Even during these days of practice, in fact, we fought one successful cavalry engagement in which we killed, among others, one of the two Allobroges who, as already described, had deserted to Pompey.

Pompey invariably drew up his line at the bottom of the hill on which his camp was situated, no doubt hoping that I would expose my troops on unfavorable ground. It looked as though there was no chance of enticing him out to fight a battle, and I came to the conclusion that my best policy was to move camp and to be constantly on the march. By always moving from one place to another it would be easier to secure our supplies, and at the same time I hoped that we might get an opportunity to engage Pompey on the road and that by these daily marches we would wear out his troops, who were not accustomed to hard work. After reaching this decision, I gave the signal for moving. The tents had already been struck when it was observed that Pompey's line had advanced rather farther from his rampart than usual, so that it looked as though we could give battle with him on ground that was not unfavorable to us.

The head of our marching column was just at the gates of the camp when I called out to the men: "We must put off our journey for the moment and think of fighting, as we have been wanting to do all this time. Now you can fix your thoughts on battle. We shall not easily get another opportunity like this." I then immediately led the army out in fighting order.

As we found out afterward, Pompey had been urged to fight by all his friends and had decided to do so. Indeed, he had stated in a council of war a few days previously that we would be forced to run away even before the two lines met. And, as many of those present were surprised at such a statement, he had said: "I realize that it looks as though

I am promising you something almost incredible. But listen to the plan I have in mind and you will go into battle all the more confidently. I have discussed this plan with our cavalry commanders and they have undertaken to carry it out. What they will do is this. When the two armies draw close together, they will attack Caesar's right wing on its open flank, ride around, and encircle his line from the rear, thus throwing his army into confusion and routing the whole force before our troops have even thrown their javelins. In this way we shall finish the war without exposing our legions to any risk and probably without any casualties at all. Considering our great superiority in cavalry, there is no difficulty in carrying out this plan." He then told them to be ready for battle next day and urged them, now that they had got the opportunity for fighting which they had constantly demanded, not to disappoint the high hopes which he and the rest of the senatorial party had of them.

Labienus followed him, speaking with contempt of my forces and in the most laudatory terms of Pompey's strategy. "Do not imagine, Pompey," he said, "that this is the army that conquered Gaul and Germany. This is a subject on which I am well qualified to speak, since I took part personally in all the battles. Only a very small part of that army has survived. A great many, as was bound to happen in so much fighting, have perished; many others fell victim to the plague last autumn in Italy; many have gone back to their homes; and many have not crossed over into Greece. You must have heard that whole cohorts have been formed at Brindisi out of men who stayed behind because of ill health. The forces which you see before you have been raised during the last two years' recruiting in Cisalpine Gaul, most of them from colonial cities north of the Po. And the flower even of this army has already been destroyed in the two battles at Durazzo."

After making this speech, he swore an oath not to return to camp unless as a conqueror and he urged all the others to follow his example. Pompey praised Labienus for what he had said and took the same oath himself—and so indeed did everyone else without any hesitation at all. After these transactions, the meeting of the council broke up in a general feeling of confidence and joy. Their thoughts were already dwelling on what they believed a certain victory, for it seemed to them incredible that on such an important matter so experienced a general could raise their hopes without good reason.

I went out toward Pompey's camp and observed that his line was drawn up in the following way. On his left wing were the two legions (now known as the First and the Third) which, in accordance with a decree of the senate, I had handed over to him before the beginning of the civil war. Pompey himself was with these legions. The center of the line was held by Scipio with the legions from Syria. The Cilician legion together with some Spanish cohorts which, as has been mentioned, were brought over by Afranius, occupied the right wing. These were the troops which Pompey regarded as the most reliable of all. The rest were posted between the center and the two wings. Altogether he had made up the number of one hundred ten cohorts, amounting to forty-five thousand men, including about two thousand discharged veterans who had earned special rewards from him in his past campaigns and had now rejoined his service; they were distributed at points along the whole line. Seven other cohorts had been left to guard the camp and various strong points in the neighborhood. His right wing was protected by a stream with steep banks, and he had therefore concentrated all his cavalry, archers, and slingers to cover his left.

I followed my usual practice by stationing the Tenth Legion on the right wing and the Ninth on the left. The Ninth had been considerably weakened in the battles of Durazzo, and so I put the Eighth next to it, practically forming one legion out of two and giving each orders to support the other. Altogether I had eighty cohorts drawn up in the line, a total of twenty-two thousand men. I had left seven cohorts to guard the camp. I had put Mark Antony in command of the left wing, Publius Sulla of the right, and Gnaeus Domitius of the center. I myself took up my position opposite Pompey. As already mentioned, I had observed the enemy dispositions and I was afraid that my right wing might be outflanked by the great numbers of their cavalry. I therefore hurriedly withdrew individual cohorts from the third line and formed out of them a fourth line to oppose the enemy's cavalry. I told them what I wanted done and warned them that it was on them and their courage that the day's victory would depend. I also instructed the third line not to charge until they received the order, and said that I would signal by flag when I wanted them to go into action.

In accordance with the custom of war, I addressed some words of encouragement to the army before battle. I reminded them of how I had always and invariably thought of the interests of my men. In particular I asked them to remember that they had seen with their own eyes how anxious I had been to make peace: there were the conversations initiated through Vatinius, the attempt to deal with Scipio through Aulus Clodius, and the efforts which I had made at Palaeokastro to get Libo's permission to send representatives to Pompey. Finally I told them that I had always wished, whenever possible, to avoid shedding the blood of my soldiers and that even now I wanted Rome to retain the services of both armies, Pompey's and my own.

After these words had been spoken, the men shouted out for battle, burning with eagerness for the fight. It was at this moment that the trumpet gave the signal for action.

In my army there was a veteran soldier who had rejoined me, Gaius Crastinus by name, a man of quite outstanding courage. A year previously he had been the senior centurion of the Tenth Legion. Now, as the signal for battle was given, he shouted out: "Follow me, old comrades, and give your general the good service you have always given. There is only this one battle to be fought. When we have won it, we shall regain our liberty and Caesar his proper place in the state." Then, looking back at me, he said: "My Imperator, I shall make you want to thank me today, whether I am alive or dead at the end of it." With these words he ran forward into battle in front of the rest of the right wing, and about one hundred twenty volunteers, all picked men, of the same cohort followed behind him.

Between the two lines there was just enough space to allow each army to move into the attack on the double. But Pompey had ordered his men to stand firm and wait for our charge, in this way meeting us when we had lost our original close order. He was said to have adopted this plan on the advice of Gaius Triarius. The idea was that the force of the impact of our initial charge would be diminished and our line would lose its cohesion; thus Pompey's soldiers, standing in their correct formations, would be able to move against us when we were in disorder. It was also hoped that our javelins, hurled against men who remained stationary, would have less effect than if these same men were to move forward and hurl their javelins too. At the same time it was thought that our men, with double the distance to run which they had expected, would be tired and out of breath by the time they came into action.

My own view is that this plan of Pompey's had nothing whatever to recommend it. The fact is that there is a kind of quickening of the spirit, a sort of extra zest which is born and implanted in men by nature and which receives its great stimulus from the ardor with which they go into battle. The duty of a general is to encourage and not to repress this quality, and our ancestors were perfectly sensible when they established the custom of having trumpets blown all along the line and of encouraging the whole army to shout out together; they realized that these sounds have a double effect —they frighten the enemy and they give added confidence to one's own side.

As it was, our men, as soon as the signal was given, charged forward with their javelins at the ready, but they noticed that the enemy were not moving forward to meet them. They then showed what they had learned from their training and from the experience gained in previous battles. They checked their speed of their own accord and halted about halfway between the two lines, so as not to use up their energy before they reached their objective. After a short pause they went on again at the double, hurled their javelins, and immediately, as they had been instructed to do, drew their swords.

Pompey's men stood up to the attack well. They met the javelins with their shields, took the shock of the charge without breaking ranks, hurled their own javelins, and then began to use their swords. At the same moment, the cavalry on Pompey's left wing all charged together, as they had been told, and the whole mass of archers and slingers came surging around us. Our cavalry could not hold this attack and were gradually forced back and out of the way. This made Pompey's cavalry press on all the more fiercely. They now began to deploy by squadrons and to sweep around our exposed flank. Observing this, I gave the signal to the six cohorts which constituted my fourth line. They went forward immediately to the attack and fell upon Pompey's cavalry with such violence that not one of the enemy stood up to the charge; the whole lot wheeled around; it was not so much a retreat as a complete rout in which they galloped off to find safety among the highest hills in the neighborhood. Once the cavalry was out of the way, the archers and slingers, unsupported, abandoned and defenseless, were slaughtered to a man. In the main line of battle, Pompey's men were still fighting and standing firm, but my cohorts, carrying on their advance, swept around their flank and began to attack them from the rear.

It was at this moment that I ordered my third line to charge. Up to this time they had stayed in position and had not been in action. Pompey's men now found themselves attacked by an entirely fresh body of troops, who brought relief to their exhausted comrades; at the same time others were attacking them from the rear. They were unable to resist; the entire army turned and fled.

After seeing the rout of his cavalry and the total demoralization of that part of his forces in which he placed the greatest confidence, Pompey despaired also of the rest, left the battle line, and rode straight to his camp. Here he spoke to the centurions on guard at the praetorian gate, raising his voice so that the men could hear. "See to the defense of the camp," he said, "and be ready to fight for it, in case things go badly with us. I am going around to the other gates to say what I can to the guards there." With these words he withdrew to his tent, with little hope as to the final issue, yet still waiting on the event.

Now that the enemy had been driven in flight inside their fortifications, I thought that in their present state of terror they should not be allowed a moment's respite. So I called upon my men to make full use of the fortune we had had and to go on to storm the camp. Though exhausted by the extreme heat (the battle had lasted until midday), they nevertheless showed a spirit that was ready for anything and willingly obeyed the order. The camp was well defended by the cohorts who had been left on guard, and some Thracian and other foreign auxiliaries fought back even better still. The soldiers who had fled there from the battlefield were both tired out and demoralized; many of them had thrown away their arms and lost their standards; and their thoughts were more on escape than on defense of the camp. And, in fact, those who did man the rampart were not able to stand up for very long to the shower of missiles. Worn out and wounded, they left their posts; and then all of them, led by their centurions and officers, fled for safety to the high ground above the camp.

Inside Pompey's camp were a number of especially constructed arbors and much silver plate all set out ready for a banquet; the floors of the tents were laid with freshly cut turf, and the tents of Lucius Lentulus and some others were shaded with ivy. There were other signs too of excessive luxury and of a complete confidence in victory. In fact it was easy to see that men who so went out of their way to indulge their appetites unnecessarily could have had no doubt at all about the issue of the day's fighting. Yet these were the men who used to criticize my long-suffering and patient army for living a too easy life, while in fact we were never adequately supplied even with necessities.

When our men were already inside the rampart, Pompey, after removing his marks of rank as Imperator, mounted a horse, hurriedly rode out of camp by the rear gate, and, without drawing rein, galloped on to Larissa. He did not stop there. After picking up some of his fleeing men, he hurried on as fast as ever, without breaking off his journey by night. He reached the sea with an escort of about thirty cavalry and boarded a grain ship. They say that he constantly complained of how completely he had been deceived, saying that when he considered how the very men whom he had counted upon to give him victory had been the first to run away, it almost looked as though he had been betrayed.

After occupying his camp, I urged my men not to spend their time on plunder and so let slip the opportunity of finishing off the whole campaign. They were ready to do as I asked, and so I began to surround with lines of earthworks the hill to which the enemy had fled. The hill had no water supply, and Pompey's men, seeing that it was a hopeless position, abandoned the summit and began to retire in one body along the ridges in the direction of Larissa. When I saw what they were doing, I split up my forces. I ordered part of them to remain in Pompey's camp, and sent back some to our own camp. Then, with the remaining four legions, I marched out, taking a short cut, to intercept the retreating Pompeians. After a march of four miles we formed up in order of battle. The enemy, seeing us there, halted on some high ground. The river flowed through the plain beneath them. It was now almost night, and my men were worn out by all that they had done from break of day. But I appealed to them once again, and by building a line of fortifications between the river and the mountain, we were able to prevent the enemy from coming down to get water by night. Once this had been done the enemy sent a deputation to discuss terms of surrender. A few men of senatorial rank who had been with them went off individually during the night.

At dawn I ordered all the troops on the mountain to come down into the plain and throw down their arms. This they did without raising any objections, and then, with arms outstretched and weeping, they flung themselves to the ground and begged me to spare their lives. I told them to stand up and, in order to reassure them and to calm their fears, spoke a few words in which I pointed out that it was my nature to be merciful. I spared them all and asked my own troops not to harm any of them and to see that their property was not confiscated. After making these arrangements, I ordered the legions from the camp to replace those who had marched out with me, and sent back the latter to have their turn of rest. On the same day I arrived at Larissa.

In this battle no more than two hundred men from the ranks were missing on our side, but we lost about thirty centurions, all very fine soldiers. Crastinus, who has been mentioned above, was one of them. He died fighting gallantly, killed by a sword thrust in the face. The words which he had spoken as he went into battle proved true indeed. For this was my opinion of him: in that battle Crastinus had fought with absolutely outstanding courage, and I considered that

I owed him a great debt of gratitude for his loyal service. Out of Pompey's army it was reckoned that about fifteen thousand were killed; but more than twenty-four thousand surrendered, including the cohorts which had been on garrison duty, who gave themselves up to Sulla. Many besides fled to the various states and cities in the neighborhood. There were brought to me after the battle one hundred eighty captured military standards and nine eagles. Lucius Domitius, exhausted by fatigue, was killed by our cavalry as he was attempting to escape from the camp to the higher ground.

10 DEATH OF POMPEY. OPERATIONS IN EGYPT.

At about the time of the battle, Decius Laelius sailed up to Brindisi with his fleet. He seized an island opposite the harbor (as, it will be recalled, Libo had done previously). And Vatinius, who was in command of Brindisi, acted just as Antony had done before. He had some light craft decked and equipped for his purpose, enticed some of Laelius' ships into the harbor and in the narrows captured one quinquereme and two smaller vessels that had advanced too far. He also stationed cavalry along the shore to prevent the enemy crews from getting water. But Laelius had the advantage of a better season of the year for naval operations. He brought over supplies of water for his men from Corfu and Durazzo in merchant ships and kept up his blockade in spite of all difficulties. Neither the disgrace of losing his ships nor the shortage of necessary supplies was enough to make him abandon the island and leave the harbor alone. In fact, he did not do so until the news arrived of the battle that had been fought in Thessaly.

At about this time too, Gaius Cassius came to Sicily with the Syrian, Phoenician, and Cilician fleets. My own naval forces in these waters had been divided into two squadrons, one at Bivona under the praetor Publius Sulpicius, the other at Messina under Pomponius. Cassius sailed into Messina before Pomponius had even heard that he was coming. He found him in a state of complete disorganization, with no guards posted and no one knowing what to do or where to be. So, taking advantage of a high wind, he loaded a number of merchant ships with pine wood, pitch, tow, and other combustible materials, set them on fire, and let them drift down upon Pomponius' fleet. The result was that he burned all thirty-five ships, twenty of which were decked. This action caused such dismay in Messina that, though the place was garrisoned by a whole legion, it was held only with difficulty. Indeed, the general opinion was that it would have been lost if it had not been for the fact that just at this moment news of my victory at Pharsalus, carried by relays of horsemen, was brought to the town. This news arrived just at the right time and so Messina was defended.

Cassius sailed away next against the fleet of Sulpicius at Bivona. He found our ships moored to the shore and, using exactly the same methods as at Messina, he sent fire-ships against them, again with the help of a favorable wind. Fire broke out at both ends of our line and five ships were burned out. A strong wind was blowing and the fire began to spread. Some soldiers from the veteran legions, who had been left behind because of illness and were responsible for guarding the ships, could not endure the disgrace of seeing them lost and, without waiting for orders, went on board, put out from shore, and bore down upon the fleet of Cassius. They captured two of his quinqueremes and sank two triremes. Cassius himself was on board one of the two quinqueremes, but he got into a boat and escaped. Soon afterward the news arrived of the battle in Thessaly, and this time even the enemy believed it. Previously they had considered it to be a false report spread by friends and agents of my own. Now that the facts were known, Cassius sailed away.

After the battle it seemed to me that I ought, leaving everything else aside, to go after Pompey, wherever he fled, so that he should not have another chance of raising fresh troops and renewing the war. I therefore pushed on as far as possible every day with my cavalry and ordered one legion to follow by shorter marches. At Amphipolis a decree had been published in Pompey's name ordering all the young men of the province, whether of Greek or Roman citizenship, to report for military service. It was impossible, however, to say whether this measure of his was designed to allay anxiety and to disguise the fact that he was planning a further flight, or whether he really aimed at holding Macedonia, if he were left alone to do so. In fact, his ship anchored for one night at Amphipolis. He summoned to him various members of his party from the town, borrowed money for his immediate expenses, and then, hearing that I was on my way, sailed from there and after a few days put in at Mytilene. Here he was detained for two days by stormy weather, during which time he was joined by a number of other small ships. He then sailed for Cilicia and after that to Cyprus, where he received news that by general agreement of the people of Antioch and the Roman citizens who were there as businessmen and merchants it had been decided to exclude him, if necessary by force, from the city. They had also sent messengers to other members of his party who were said to have fled for refuge to various states in the neighborhood and had warned them that, if they came to Antioch, they would do so at peril of their lives. The same thing had happened at Rhodes to Lucius Lentulus, last year's consul, to Publius Lentulus, also an ex-consul, and to others who were following the flight of Pompey and had arrived at the island. They had been refused permission to enter the harbor or the town, had been officially asked to leave Rhodian waters, and had thus been forced to sail on, though they had intended to put in there. News that I was on my way was already reaching the states and cities in this area.

After hearing the reports from Antioch, Pompey gave up the idea of going to Syria. He requisitioned money from the taxation officers and borrowed also from various individuals; he put aboard his ships a large quantity of copper coinage to be used for paying troops, and armed two thousand slaves, some of whom were conscripted from the establishments of the local businessmen and others specially selected by their owners as good material. He then set sail and came to Pelusium.

It happened that the boy-king Ptolemy was at Pelusium with a large army. He was at war with his sister Cleopatra, whom he had driven from the throne a few months earlier by the help of his relatives and friends. Cleopatra's camp was not far distant from that of Ptolemy. Pompey sent to Ptolemy asking him, in view of the close bonds of friendship and hospitality that there had been between himself and his father, to receive him into Alexandria and to use his power to protect him in his misfortune. After making this formal request, Pompey's messengers began to speak more freely with the Egyptian king's soldiers, urging them to do their duty to Pompey and not to regard his cause as lost. Among them were a number of Pompey's old soldiers whom Gabinius had taken over from his army in Syria and, at the end of his campaign, had left with Ptolemy Auletes, the father of the young king.

The whole matter was referred to the king's friends, who, because of his youth, were in actual control of the kingdom. It may be, as they asserted afterward, that they were really afraid that Pompey might tamper with the loyalty of the royal army and occupy Alexandria and Egypt; or it may be that they regarded his prospects as hopeless and acted according to the common rule by which a man's friends become his enemies in adversity. In any case, they gave what appeared to be a friendly and generous reply to Pompey's messengers and invited him to come and visit the king. Meanwhile they had their own secret plan; they sent Achillas, the commander of the king's bodyguard, an utterly unscrupulous character, and Lucius Septimius, a Roman officer, to assassinate Pompey. They greeted him in a friendly and respectful manner, and he was all the more inclined to trust them because he had known Septimius before, having served under him as centurion in the pirate war. So, with a few attendants, he was induced to go into a small boat and there he was murdered by Achillas and Septimius. Lucius Lentulus was also arrested by the king's orders and put to death in prison.

Before this I had arrived in Asia, where I was informed that Titus Ampius had attempted to remove the treasure from the temple of Diana at Ephesus. He had summoned all the senators in the province to act as witnesses of the amount taken, but had been interrupted by the news of my arrival and had taken to flight. There were thus two occasions on which I was able to preserve the treasure at Ephesus.

It was also established by a careful investigation of the dates that in the temple of Minerva at Elis on the day of my victory at Pharsalus, a statue of Victory that had stood facing the statue of Minerva turned around of its own accord so as to face the threshold and main entrance to the temple.

On that day too at Antioch in Syria there was twice heard the sound of an army's battle cry and the sound of trumpets. It was so loud that the whole population took up arms and ran to positions on the city walls. The same thing happened at Acre. At Pergamum the sound of drums was heard from the innermost and most secret parts of the temple, where only the priests are allowed to go and which are called in Greek the *adyta*. Also at Tralles in the temple of Victory, where the people had dedicated a statue of myself, there was exhibited a palm tree which, at this very time, had shot up through the joints of the paving stones.

After staying for a few days in Asia, I heard that Pompey had been seen in Cyprus. Because of his friendly relations with the Egyptian kingdom and other advantages which the place had to offer him, I guessed that he was on his way to Egypt. I therefore set out for Alexandria and arrived there with the one legion that I had ordered to follow me from Thessaly, another which I had recalled from Quintus Fufius, my commander in Achaea, eight hundred cavalry, ten warships from Rhodes and a few from Asia. These two legions together only amounted to three thousand two hundred men; the rest, either because of wounds received in battle or the hardships of so long a march, had been unable to keep up with the main body. However, I relied on the prestige of our achievements and had no hesitation in setting out with such a weak force; we should be, I imagined, safe wherever we went.

At Alexandria I received the news of Pompey's death. As soon as I landed I was greeted by the angry shouting of the soldiers whom the king had left to garrison the city, and I saw a great mob rushing toward me. This was because the fasces were being carried in front of me, and the whole crowd considered this to be an infringement of the royal authority. The disturbance was put down, but for several days on end rioting broke out as a result of mass demonstrations and many of my soldiers were killed in all parts of the city.

Seeing how things were, I ordered from Asia other legions which had been formed out of Pompey's army. I myself was unable to move because of the prevailing northwest winds which at this time make it impossible to get out of Alexandria. Meanwhile I came to the conclusion that the quarrel between the two rulers of Egypt affected the Roman people and consequently myself, as consul. Indeed I was myself particularly closely concerned with Egypt since it was during my previous consulship that the alliance had been made between Rome and the elder Ptolemy—an alliance ratified both by law and by a decree of the senate. I therefore made it known that I wished King Ptolemy and his sister Cleopatra to disband their armies, to appear before me, and to settle their dispute in a legal way rather than by force of arms.

Because of the king's youth, his tutor, a eunuch called Pothinus, was in real control of the kingdom. He began by expressing among his own party his grief and indignation at the idea of the king's being called upon to come and plead his cause. Then, finding accomplices among the king's friends, he secretly withdrew the army from Pelusium and brought it to Alexandria, where he gave supreme command of all forces to the Achillas whom we have already mentioned. Achillas was promised rewards in the name both of Pothinus and the king, and was told by messenger or by letter what Pothinus wanted him to do.

Now in the will of the late King Ptolemy, the heirs were the elder of the two sons and the elder of the two daughters. In the same will Ptolemy called upon the Roman people, in the name of all the gods and in conformance with the treaty he had made at Rome, to see that his last wishes were carried out. One copy of the will had been taken by his ambassadors to Rome to be placed in the treasury, but political disturbances had prevented its being officially deposited there and so it had been left in the keeping of Pompey. A duplicate copy was left under seal at Alexandria.

Just when I was engaged in a consideration of all this, being particularly anxious to act as a friend to both parties in the dispute about the throne and to settle the question justly by arbitration, I was suddenly faced with the news that the king's army and his whole cavalry force were marching on Alexandria. My own forces were certainly not large enough for me to be able to count on success if we were forced to fight a battle outside the city. All we could do, therefore, was to stay where we were and wait to see what Achillas intended to do. Nevertheless, I ordered all my troops to stand by ready for action, and I asked Ptolemy to send to Achillas some of his most influential friends and to tell him how he wished him to act.

The king sent Dioscorides and Serapion, both of whom had been ambassadors at Rome and most trusted counselors of his father. When they reached Achillas and were brought into his presence, he ordered them to be arrested and put to death without even troubling to listen to them or find out why they had been sent. One of them, after being struck down, was carried away hurriedly by his own people as if he were dead; the other was killed on the spot. After this I took steps to see that I had the king under my own control. In my view the very name "king" carried great weight with his subjects; and if hostilities broke out I wished it to appear that they were not caused by any wish of the king but were entirely the work of a small gang of criminals.

Achillas had an army which in numbers, quality, and military experience was very far from being contemptible. There were twenty thousand men under arms, most of whom had once served under Gabinius, but had now grown accustomed to Alexandrian life with all its license; had forgotten what was meant by discipline and by the name of Rome; and had married native wives, by whom many of them had children. Their numbers were augmented by men gathered together from the bands of pirates and robbers from Syria, the province of Cilicia, and neighboring parts. They had also been joined by a number of convicts and exiles. Moreover, Alexandria offered a perfectly safe way of escape to our own slaves: all they had to do was to give in their names and join the Egyptian army. If any of them was afterward seized upon by his rightful owner, his fellow soldiers would all come together to rescue him. Being all involved in the same sort of guilt, they regarded any violence directed against one of them as a threat to all. It had become a kind of ancient tration in the Alexandrian army that these troops had the right to demand the execution of the king's favorites, to rob rich men of their property, to make and unmake kings. There were also two thousand cavalry. And all these troops had had long experience in many wars at Alexandria. They had restored the elder Ptolemy to the throne; they had killed Bibulus' two sons; they had fought in many campaigns against the Egyptians. So much for their record and experience in war.

Confident in these troops of his and contemptuous of the small numbers of my own army, Achillas seized Alexandria, except for that part of the town which we already held. In his first attack he tried to break into the palace where I was in residence, but was beaten off by the cohorts which I had posted in the streets. At the same time, fighting broke out in the harbor area. Here the struggle was the hardest of all. Street fighting was going on between scattered bodies of troops in different streets, and simultaneously large numbers of the enemy were trying to get possession of our warships. These included fifty ships which had been sent out as reinforcements to Pompey and then, after his defeat in Thessaly, had returned to Alexandria. They were all quadriremes or quinqueremes, well equipped and ready for action. In addition to these, there were twenty-two ships, all decked, which constituted the fleet normally on duty for the defense of the harbor. The enemy realized that if they could gain possession of these ships, I should be left without a fleet, and they, with the harbor and the whole sea in their control, would be able to cut me off from both reinforcements and supplies. Consequently the fighting was of a most bitter character, as it was bound to be, for the enemy saw in this action the chance of a quick victory while we knew that our very existence depended on the result.

In the end success was ours. We burned all the ships already mentioned and others that were in the dockyards, because it was impossible to guard so wide an area with the small forces at my disposal. I then immediately embarked some troops and landed them on Pharos.

The island of Pharos gives its name to the lighthouse there, an extremely high tower and a wonderful piece of engineering. This island lies opposite the city of Alexandria and so helps to form the harbor. Previous kings had connected it with the city by a narrow causeway about three-quarters of a mile long and built like a bridge resting on piles. On the island there are houses where Egyptians live; in fact, there is a village almost big enough to be called a town. Any ships which go a little off their course either because of bad weather or careless navigation are liable to be plundered by the inhabitants, who behave exactly like pirates. Moreover, the entrance to the harbor is so narrow that those who control Pharos can stop any ship from sailing in. It was because I was afraid of such a contingency that, while the enemy were fully engaged in fighting, I landed troops on Pharos, seized the place, and installed a garrison there. In this way I made sure of being able to receive supplies and reinforcements by sea. I had already sent out to all the neighboring provinces asking for reinforcements.

In the other parts of the city each side lost a few men, but the fighting was broken off without either side's having secured a definite advantage, or having been driven from its positions: this was natural considering the narrow space in which the fighting took place. During the night, I took into my defenses and strengthened with barricades that area of the town which seemed to me the one that was vitally important to hold. It included a small part of the royal palace where I had originally been given quarters and an adjoining theater which took the place of a citadel and commanded the approaches to the harbor and the docks. In the following days, I increased the strength of these defenses, so as to leave, as it were, a wall between myself and the enemy and not to be forced to fight unless I chose.

Meanwhile the younger daughter of the late king, hoping that the throne would soon be vacant and that she would occupy it, made her way out of the palace, went over to Achillas, and began to act with him as joint commander. But they very soon began to quarrel about who was actually in control. This led to a great increase in the pay offered to the soldiers, as each party tried to win over the army to its side by greater and greater bounties. While the enemy were occupied in these disputes, Pothinus kept on sending instructions to Achillas, urging him to persevere with his attack and not to lose heart. His messengers were informed against and arrested, and I had Pothinus put to death. This was the beginning of the Alexandrian war.

In this translation of the *War Commentaries of Caesar*, certain geographical names appear in their modern forms, so as to be readily recognizable to the reader. The following list gives their ancient equivalents.

Aisne River, *Axona*

Allier River, *Elaver*

Amiens, *Samarobriva*

Ardennes forest, *Arduennam*

Arles, *Arelate*

Besançon, *Vesontio*

Bivona, *Vibo*

Boulogne, *Itius portus*

Bourges, *Avaricum*

Brindisi, *Brundisium*

Cadiz, *Gades*

Cagliari, *Caralis*

Calabria district, *Bruttium*

Canosa, *Canusium*

Corfu island, *Corcyra*

Doubs River, *Dubis*

Durazzo, *Dyrrachium*

Ebro River, *Hiberus*

Garonne River, *Garumna*

Geneva, *Genava*

Geneva, Lake, *Lemannus lacus*

Guadiana River, *Anas*

Ireland, *Hibernia*

Kalibia, *Clupea*

Kent district, *Cantium*

Lepanto, *Naupactus*

Lerida, *Ilerda*

Loire River, *Liger*

Marne River, *Matrona*

Marseilles, *Massilia*

Mequinenza, *Octogesa*

Meuse River, *Mosa*

Monastir, *Heraclia*

Moselle River, *Mosella*

Narbonne, *Narbo*

Palaeokastro, *Oricum*

Paris, *Lutetia*

Po River, *Padus*

Poitiers, *Lemonum*

Rhine River, *Rhenus*

Rhone River, *Rhodanus*

Sambre River, *Sabis*

Saône River, *Arar*

Scheldt River, *Scaldis*

APPENDIX

Segre River, *Sicoris*

Seine River, *Sequana*

Seman River, *Apsus*

Seville, *Hispalis*

Spain, *Hispania*

Thames River, *Tamesis*

Toulouse, *Tolosa*

Var River, *Varus*

Veglia island, *Curicta*

Other MENTOR Books of Interest

The Greek Philosophers *edited by Rex Warner*. Basic writing of philosophers from Thales to Plotinus revealing the roots of Western philosophy in ancient Greece.

(#MP442—60¢)

The March Up Country: Anabasis *by Xenophon. W. H. D. Rouse, translator*. The famed account of the bloody march of 10,000 Greeks back to their homeland, by the great military commander and historian. (#MD278—50¢)

The Greek Experience *by C. M. Bowra*. An extraordinary study of Greek culture, its achievements and philosophy. 48 pages of photos. (#MP349—60¢)

On Love, the Family, and the Good Life, *Selected Essays of Plutarch. Translated with introduction by Moses Hadas.* Seven of the most famous of Plutarch's *Moral Essays* are here newly translated by the distinguished scholar, Moses Hadas. A wonderfully warm and humane book by one of the greatest writers of ancient times. (#MD202—50¢)

Three Great Plays of Euripides, *translated by Rex Warner.* The tragedies of "Medea," "Hippolytus," and "Helen," in a new translation by Rex Warner, classical scholar and author of "The Young Caesar." (#MT241—75¢)

Mythology *by Edith Hamilton.* A brilliant re-telling of the classic Greek, Roman and Norse legends of love and adventure, by the author of *The Greek Way.* (#MP520—60¢)
